Dynamics of International Advertising

PETER LANG
New York • Washington, D.C./Baltimore • Bern
Frankfurt am Main • Berlin • Brussels • Vienna • Oxford

Barbara Mueller

Dynamics of International Advertising

Theoretical and Practical Perspectives

PETER LANG
New York • Washington, D.C./Baltimore • Bern
Frankfurt am Main • Berlin • Brussels • Vienna • Oxford

Library of Congress Cataloging-in-Publication Data

Mueller, Barbara.
Dynamics of international advertising: theoretical
and practical perspectives / Barbara Mueller.
p. cm.
Includes bibliographical references and index.
1. Advertising. I. Title.
HF5823.M829   659.1—dc22   2003027817
ISBN 0-8204-6360-4

Bibliographic information published by **Die Deutsche Bibliothek**.
Die Deutsche Bibliothek lists this publication in the "Deutsche
Nationalbibliografie"; detailed bibliographic data is available
on the Internet at http://dnb.ddb.de/.

Cover design by Lisa Barfield

The paper in this book meets the guidelines for permanence and durability
of the Committee on Production Guidelines for Book Longevity
of the Council of Library Resources.

FOR SOPHIE

Contents

Preface

An ever-increasing number of universities—both in the United States and abroad—are attempting to internationalize their curricula by offering courses in international communication, intercultural communication, international business, and international advertising. *Dynamics of International Advertising: Theoretical and Practical Perspectives* is a response to the demand for texts dealing with global issues and globalization. First and foremost, it is the ideal textbook for upper-division undergraduate and graduate students in specialized courses dealing with international advertising or marketing. It is also an effective supplemental text for introductory advertising, marketing, or mass communications courses seeking to expand coverage of the international dimension. The text should also prove useful to practitioners of international advertising, whether on the client side or within the advertising agency. Finally, researchers of international advertising and marketing will find it a valuable resource.

This book introduces the student, practitioner, and researcher to the challenges and difficulties in developing and implementing communications programs for foreign markets. While advertising is the major focus, the author recognizes that an integrated marketing communications approach is critical to competing successfully in the international setting. In order to communicate effectively with audiences around the globe, marketers must coordinate not only advertising, direct marketing, sales promotions, personal selling, and public relations efforts, but also the other aspects of the marketing mix as well. Therefore, the basics of international marketing are briefly reviewed in the first several chapters of this text. The remainder of the book explores international advertising.

Every attempt has been made to provide a balance of theoretical and practical perspectives. For example, the issues of centralization versus decentralization and standardization versus localization or specialization are addressed as they apply to the organization of international advertising programs, development and execution of creative strategy, media planning and buying, and advertising research. Readers will find that these are not black-and-white issues. Instead, they can be viewed as a continuum. Some marketing and advertising decisions can be centralized while

others may be decentralized. Similarly, depending on the product to be advertised and the audience to be targeted, some elements of the marketing and advertising mix may be standardized while others will be specialized.

This text is not intended to provide a country-by-country analysis of the global marketplace (a futile effort, given how quickly our world changes). Instead, using current examples and case studies, *Dynamics of International Advertising* addresses the key issues that advertisers must keep in mind to create effective communications programs for foreign markets. The text comprises a total of ten chapters. In Chapter 1, factors influencing the growth of international advertising are examined. Chapter 2 highlights the role that product, price, distribution, and promotion play in selling abroad. Domestic advertising and international advertising differ not so much in concept as in environment; the international marketing and advertising environment is outlined in Chapter 3. Chapter 4 is devoted to developing a sensitivity to the various cultural factors that impact international marketing efforts. Chapter 5 addresses the coordination and control of international advertising. Chapter 6 deals with creative strategies and executions for foreign audiences. Chapters 7–9 explore media decisions in the global marketplace, international advertising research and methods for obtaining the information necessary for making international advertising decisions, and, finally, regulatory considerations. Finally, Chapter 10 focuses on the social responsibility of international advertising agencies and multinational corporations in foreign markets.

I am indebted to a great many individuals for the successful completion of this text. I am very grateful to the folks at Peter Lang Publishing for supporting the idea of a textbook on international advertising. In particular, my appreciation goes to my editor, Chris Myers. I wish that every author could have the kind of experience I had with Chris. He has the fine knack of making just about everything related to writing a textbook as painless and easy as it possibly can be. A number of colleagues provided detailed reviews of this manuscript. In particular, the author wishes to thank Dr. Steve Jones at the University of Illinois at Chicago for his invaluable comments and ideas. Thanks also go to Paul Schlotthauer, who did a wonderful job editing the manuscript, and to Lisa Dillon, who saw me through the production process and is responsible for the attractive cover. On a personal note, this book would not have been possible without the unconditional love and support of my husband, Juergen, and my daughter, Sophie. Both stood by me—without complaint—through the many months that I labored on this project.

Barbara Mueller

CHAPTER ONE

Growth of International Business and Advertising

The keystone of our global economy is the multinational corporation. A growing number of corporations around the world have transversed geographical boundaries and become truly multinational in nature. As a result, consumers around the world smoke Marlboro cigarettes and write with Bic pens, watch Sony television sets and drive Toyota autos. Shoppers can stop in for a McDonald's burger in Paris or Beijing, and German and Japanese citizens alike increasingly make their purchases with the American Express Card. And, for most other domestic firms, the question is no longer, Should we go international? Rather, the questions relate to when, how, and where the companies should enter the international marketplace. The growth and expansion of firms operating internationally have led to the growth in international advertising. U.S. agencies are increasingly looking abroad for clients. At the same time, foreign agencies are rapidly expanding around the globe, even taking control of some of the most prestigious U.S. agencies. The United States continues to both produce and consume the bulk of the world's advertising. However, advertising's global presence is evidenced by the location of major advertising markets. In rank order, the top global advertising markets are the United States, Japan, Germany, the United Kingdom, France, Italy, Brazil, Spain, and Canada. And today, 7 of the top 10 world advertising organizations are headquartered outside the United States (Advertising Age 2002). This chapter outlines the growth of international business and advertising.

▐▐▐ Historical Overview

There have been three waves of globalization since 1870. The first wave, between 1870 and 1914, was led by improvements in transport technology (from sailing ships to steam ships) and by lower tariff barriers. Further driving this first wave of modern globalization were rising production scale economies due to advancements in technology that outpaced the growth of the world economy. Product needs also became more homogenized in different countries as

knowledge and industrialization diffused. Communication became easier with the telegraph and, later, the telephone. By the early 1900s, firms such as Ford Motor, Singer, Gillette, National Cash Register, Otis, and Western Electric already had commanding world market shares. Exports during this first wave nearly doubled to about 8 percent of world income (World Bank 2002, 326).

The trend to globalization slowed between 1914 and the late 1940s. These decades were marked by a world economic crisis as well as two world wars, which resulted in a period of strong nationalism. Countries attempted to salvage and strengthen their own economies by imposing high tariffs and quotas so as to keep out foreign goods and protect domestic employment. It was not until after the Second World War that the number of U.S. firms operating internationally again began to grow significantly.

The second wave of globalization was from 1945 to 1980. International tensions—whether in the form of cold war or open conflict—tend to discourage international marketing. However, during this period, the world was, for the most part, relatively peaceful. This, paired with the creation of the International Monetary Fund (IMF) and the General Agreement on Tariffs and Trade (GATT) at the close of World War II, facilitated the growth of international trade and investment. Indeed, during this period, tariffs among the industrialized nations fell from about 40 percent in 1947 to roughly 5 percent in 1980. In 1950 U.S. foreign direct investment stood at $12 billion. By 1965 it had risen to $50 billion, and by the late 1970s to approximately $150 billion (U.S. Bureau of the Census 1995, 870).

The third wave of globalization has been from approximately 1980 to the present. Spurring this third wave has been further progress in transport (containerization and air freight) and communication technology (falling telecommunication costs associated with satellites, fiber-optic cable, cell telephones, and the Internet). Along with declining tariffs on manufactured goods (currently under four percent), many countries lowered barriers to foreign investment and improved their investment climates. After the September 11 attacks in the United States, some economists worried that the year 2001 could mark a reversal of the current era of globalization. Recession, U.S. security concerns, and resentment abroad seemed aligned against the forces that drove companies abroad in the 1990s in search of new markets. But it appears that the same forces that drove globalization in the past might in fact be intensifying. Indeed, according to a PriceWaterhouseCoopers survey of 171 business executives at large U.S. multinationals, commitment to international expansion has actually risen since September 11. Of those surveyed, 27 percent planned some sort of geographic expansion during the coming year, up from 19 percent prior to the attacks (Hilsenrath 2002). A 2003 *Fortune* magazine survey reports that the top 500 multinational companies alone generated almost $14 trillion in sales in 2002. The United States led all countries, with 192 companies on the list; Japan ranked second (88 companies), and Germany third (35). As outlined in Table 1.1, U.S. firms are ranked first in 14 of the top 25 industries (*Fortune* 2002).

In addition to these large corporations, thousands of smaller firms are engaging in international marketing. In the United States, smaller firms account for an amazing 97 percent of the companies involved in direct merchandise exporting. Yet these same companies generate only about 30 percent of the dollar value of U.S. export sales. Smaller firms thus represent the largest pool

TABLE 1.1 World's 25 Biggest Companies by Industry, 2001 (in U.S. million $)

	Industry	Company	Country	Revenues
1.	Aerospace	Boeing	U.S.	$ 58,198
2.	Beverages	PepsiCo	U.S.	26,935
3.	Building Materials	Saint-Gobain	France	27,214
4.	Chemicals	BASF	Germany	29,103
5.	Computers	IBM	U.S.	88,866
6.	Electronics	Siemens	Germany	77,358
7.	Entertainment	Vivendi-Universal	France	51,365
8.	Food/Consumer	Nestlé	Switzerland	50,192
9.	Food & Drug Stores	Carrefour	France	62,224
10.	Food Services	McDonald's	U.S.	14,870
11.	Forest/Paper Goods	International Paper	U.S.	26,363
12.	General Merchandise	WalMart	U.S.	219,812
13.	Health Care	Aetna	U.S.	25,190
14.	Household/Personal	Procter & Gamble	U.S.	39,244
15.	Industrial/Farm Equip.	Thyssen Krupp	Germany	33,796
16.	Metals	Alcoa	U.S.	22,859
17.	Mining/Crude Oil Prod.	Pemex	Mexico	39,400
18.	Motor Vehicles	General Motors	U.S.	177,260
19.	Petroleum Refining	Exxon Mobil	U.S.	191,581
20.	Pharmaceuticals	Merck	U.S.	47,715
21.	Publishing/Printing	Bertelsmann	Germany	17,886
22.	Scientific/Photo Equip.	Fuji Photo	Japan	19,203
23.	Specialty Retailers	Home Depot	U.S.	53,553
24.	Telecomm	Nippon T & T	Japan	94,424
25.	Tobacco	Philip Morris	U.S.	72,944

Source: Fortune (2002) F1–F10.

for potential growth in export sales. Microbreweries provide an excellent example. With production normally limited to less than 15,000 barrels a year, microbreweries would seem more local than global players. But the microbrewery industry is going through a transition in which exports make sense. With more than 33 regional specialty breweries and 424 microbreweries in the United States, the field has become too competitive. As a result, several of the most successful "craft" brewers are among a growing number of smaller U.S. companies looking to foreign markets to expand sales. Brewers have had the greatest successes in Sweden, Italy, and, to a lesser extent, Great Britain.

Corporations look abroad for the very same reasons they seek to expand their markets at home. Where economies of scale are feasible, a large market is essential. However, if a single market is not large enough to absorb the entire output, a firm may look to other markets. If production equipment is not fully utilized in meeting the demands of one market, additional markets may be tapped. Seasonal fluctuations in demand in a particular market may also be evened out by sales in another. During economic downturns in one market, corporations may turn to new

markets to absorb excess output. Firms may also find that a product's life cycle can be extended if the product is introduced in different markets—products already considered obsolete by one group may well be sold successfully to another. In addition to the reasons noted, significant changes in the United States and around the globe have helped fuel this phenomenal growth in international business.

Saturated Domestic Markets

As many markets reach saturation, firms look to foreign countries for new customers. Take the case of Starbucks. Starbucks began with 17 coffee shops in Seattle 15 years ago. Today there are 4,247 stores scattered across the United States and Canada, though there are still eight states in the United States with no Starbucks stores. Frappuccino-free cities include Butte, Montana, and Fargo, North Dakota, but big cities, affluent suburbs, and shopping malls are full to the brim. In Manhattan's 24 square miles, Starbucks has 124 cafes, which translates into 1 for every 12,000 New Yorkers. In coffee-crazed Seattle, there is a Starbucks outlet for every 9,400 people, and the company considers that the upper limit of coffee-shop saturation. Indeed, the crowding of so many stores so close together has become a national joke, eliciting quips such as the headline in *The Onion*, a satirical publication: "A new Starbucks Opens in Restroom of Existing Starbucks" (Holmes 2002, 101). To keep up the growth, Starbucks realized it had no choice but to export its concept aggressively. Some analysts give Starbucks only two years at most before it completely saturates the U.S. market. By 1999, Starbucks had 281 stores abroad. Today it has about 1,200 outlets in 28 countries—and it is still in the early stages of a plan of globalization. About 400 of its planned 1,200 new stores will be built overseas, representing a 35 percent increase in its foreign base. Starbucks expects to double the number of its stores worldwide, to 10,000 in three years. During the past 12 months alone, the chain has opened stores in Vienna, Zurich, Madrid, Berlin, and even Jakarta. The Starbucks name and image connect with millions of consumers around the globe. It was ranked as one of the fastest-growing brands in a *Business Week* survey of the top 100 global brands (Khermouch 2002, 99).

Higher Profit Margins in Foreign Markets

According to *Business Week*, "American manufacturers with factories or sales subsidiaries overseas outperform their domestic counterparts. A study of more than 1,500 companies reported that U.S. multinationals posted faster growth than domestics in 19 out of 20 major industry groups, and higher earnings in 17" (*Business Week* 1991, 20).

The typical U.S. industrial company today rings up 25 percent of its sales overseas, compared with only 15 percent in 1980 (*Hoover's Handbook of World Business* 1993, 104). Currently, General Electric's percent of sales coming from outside the home market is 30.1, and McDonald's is 61.5 (Edmondson et al. 2000). This trend of higher profit margins in foreign markets is clearly not limited to U.S. firms. Nokia sells over 97 percent of its products outside the home market. In 2001, Toyota sold more vehicles in the United States (1.74 million) than in Japan (1.71 million). Analysts figure that almost two-thirds of the company's operating profits come from the United States. With its 10 percent U.S. market share, Toyota is within striking distance of DaimlerChrysler's 14.5 percent. Some auto executives think it's only a matter of time before Toyota steals DaimlerChrysler's place in the "Big Three" (Dawson 2002, 53).

Increased Foreign Competition in Domestic Markets

Over the past few decades, foreign products have played an increasingly significant role in the United States. Classic examples are the phonograph, color TV, video- and audiotape recorder, telephone, and integrated circuit. Although all were invented in the United States, domestic producers account for only a small percentage of the U.S. market for most of these products today—and an even smaller share of the world market. For example, in 1970 U.S. producers' share of the domestic market for color TVs stood at nearly 90 percent. By 1990 it had dropped to little more than 10 percent. The decline in sales of U.S.-produced stereo components is even more serious—from 90 percent of domestic sales to little more than 1 percent during the same time span (Business Week 1989, 14). Brand names such as Sony and Panasonic have become household words for most American consumers.

Foreign companies continue to play a prominent part in the daily lives of Americans today. When a U.S. consumer buys new tires, shops for the latest best-seller, or purchases a jar of mayonnaise, chances are increasingly good that the supplier will be a local subsidiary of a company based in Japan, Europe, or elsewhere outside the United States. For example, both Firestone Rubber and CBS Records were acquired by Japanese firms; and Macmillan Publishing and Pillsbury are now owned by British firms (Shaughnessy and Lindquist 1993). Most recently, Switzerland's Nestlé and the Anglo-Dutch giant Unilever have moved into the U.S. market to grow their businesses. Unilever set the pace, paying $20.3 billion for Bestfoods, whose brands include Hellmann's Mayonnaise and Skippy Peanut Butter, as well as acquiring Slim-Fast, a diet-supplement firm, and Ben & Jerry's Ice Cream. Meanwhile, Nestlé acquired pet food manufacturer Ralston Purina, best known for its Purina Dog Chow brand. It was a logical move, as the pet food market is growing faster than Nestlé's traditional, matured businesses—particularly in the United States, where animal owners are buying higher margin products that promise both dietary and health benefits for their pets (Bernard 2001). This "selling of America" has caused a good deal of concern among the business community as well as the general public. Table 1.2 outlines the 25 largest foreign investors in the United States.

Increased foreign competition on domestic soil is not unique to the United States, but rather is occurring both in other developed countries and in emerging economies. Worldwide, foreign direct investment (FDI) fell in 2001 to $735 billion, half the amount seen in 2000, and the first decline in a decade. That happened as a slowing economy and stock market declines around the world dampened investor's appetites to pour money abroad, including into the

TABLE 1.2 The 25 Largest Foreign Investors in the United States

Rank	Company	Country	U.S. Investment	Percent Owned	Revenue ($ mil.)
1.	DaimlerChrysler AG	Germany	DaimlerChrysler Corp.	100	
			Freightliner	100	90,157
			Mercedes Benz US Intl.	100	
	Mitsubishi Motors	Japan	Mitsubishi Motor Mfg.	100	
2.	BP Plc	U.K.	BP America	100	72,884
3.	Royal Ahold	Netherlands	Ahold USA	100	27,973
4.	Royal Dutch/Shell Group	Netherlands	Shell Oil	100	26,671
5.	Tyco International	Bermuda	Tyco International US	100	24,618
			CIT Group	100	
6.	ING Group	Netherlands	ING N. American Ins.	100	
			ING Aetna	100	22,512
			ING Barings US	100	
7.	Petroleos de Venezuela	Venezuela	Citgo Petroleum	100	22,151
8.	Toyota Motor	Japan	Toyota Motor Mfg.	100	
			New United Motor Mfg.	50	21,306
	Denso		Denso International	100	
9.	Nortel Networks	Canada	Nortel Networks US	100	20,044
10.	Nestle SA	Switzerland	Nestlé USA	100	
			Alcon Laboratories	100	18,704
	L'Oreal		L'Oreal US	100	
11.	ABN-Amro Holding NV	Netherlands	ABN Arro N. America	100	18,486
			European American Bank	100	
12.	UBS AG	Switzerland	UBS PaineWebber	100	18,217
			UBS Americas	100	
13.	Sony	Japan	Sony Music Entertainment	100	17,439
			Sony Pictures Entertainment	100	
14.	Deutsche Bank AG	Germany	Deutsche Bank	100	16,000
15.	AEGON NV	Netherlands	Aegon USA	100	15,734
16.	Siemens	Germany	Siemens USA	100	15,599
17.	GlaxoSmithKline Plc	U.K.	GlaxoSmithKline	100	14,282
			Block Drug	100	
18.	Vodafone Group Plc	U.K.	Verizon Wireless	45	14,236
19.	Honda Motor	Japan	Honda of America Mfg.	100	14,000
20.	Credit Suisse Group	Switzerland	Credit Suisse First Boston	100	13,644
			Winterhur US Holdings	100	
21.	Delhaize "Le Lion" SA	Belgium	Delhaize America	100	12,984
			Super Discount Markets	60	
22.	Vivendi Universal SA	France	Vivendi Universal US	100	12,899
23.	Skandia Insurance	Sweden	American Skandia	100	12,191
24.	Prudential Corp Plc	U.K.	Jackson National Life	100	11,567
			Jackson National Life NY	100	
25.	Zurich Financial Group	Switzerland	Zurich US	100	11,547
			Nurick Reinsurance Centre	100	

Source: Hoover's Handbook of World Business (2002).

TABLE 1.3 Foreign Direct Investment Inflows, 2001 (in U.S. billion $)

Developed Markets	Amount	Developing Markets	Amount
Belgium/Luxembourg	15,868	Mexico	$ 11,568
Canada	24,268	South Korea	8,798
France	37,416	Czech Republic	4,877
Germany	52,503	Hungary	1,944
United Kingdom	82,176	Turkey	783
United States	282,507	Greece	529

Source: Statistical Abstract of the United States (2002), 867.

United States. The slump was concentrated in the world's richest countries, where the frantic pace of cross-border mergers and acquisitions flagged after years of growth. FDI flows to the European Union shrank by 60 percent, while North America's inflows slowed by 59 percent. FDI into Africa almost doubled, although from a modest base, rising from $9 billion in 2000 to over $17 billion in 2001. But most of this investment was concentrated in a few large projects in South Africa and Morocco. In the emerging markets, Argentina, Brazil, and Hong Kong suffered a combined $57 billion decline in inbound FDI. In 2001, America continued to attract more FDI than any other country; it also invested the most abroad of any country (*Economist* 2002). Analysts predict that 2004 will again show acceleration (Hagenbaugh 2002).

The Trade Deficit

Exports have accounted for an ever-increasing proportion of the U.S. gross domestic product—more than 11 percent in recent years. In 2000 the United States exported an estimated $781 billion of goods and services. However, imports during that same year totaled well over $1 trillion (*Statistical Abstract of the United States* 2001, 799). For 2002, the balance-of-trade deficit was more than $436 billion (Leonhardt 2003). Exports are considered a central contributor to economic growth and well-being for a country. For example, every $1 billion earned in U.S. export dollars generates about 20,000 jobs in that country. The current trade deficit has made it a matter of vital national interest to increase exports.

The Emergence of New Markets

European Union

The emergence of new markets has stimulated interest in international business. On December 31, 1992, many physical, fiscal, and technical barriers to trade among the 12-nation European Union (EU) began to disappear, giving birth to something akin to the United States of Europe. The original "European 12" (Belgium, Denmark, France, Germany, Greece, Ireland,

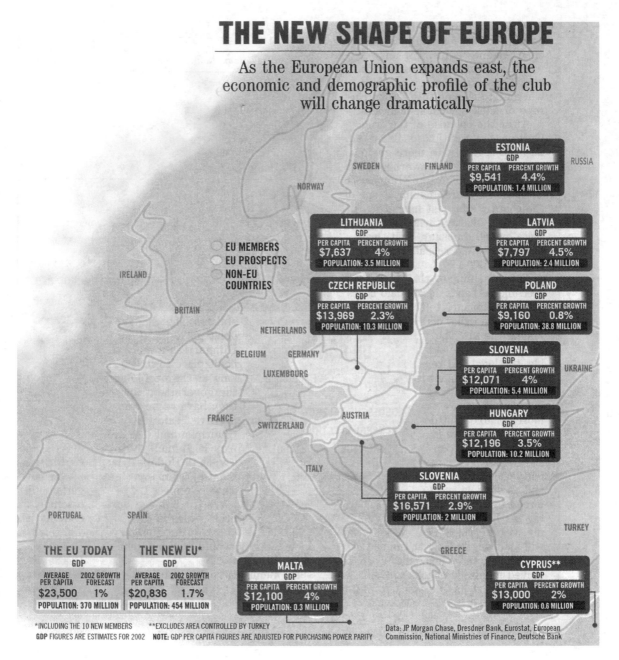

THE NEW SHAPE OF EUROPE

As the European Union expands east, the economic and demographic profile of the club will change dramatically

EU MEMBERS
EU PROSPECTS
NON-EU COUNTRIES

ESTONIA
GDP
PER CAPITA $9,541 PERCENT GROWTH 4.4%
POPULATION: 1.4 MILLION

LITHUANIA
GDP
PER CAPITA $7,637 PERCENT GROWTH 4%
POPULATION: 3.5 MILLION

LATVIA
GDP
PER CAPITA $7,797 PERCENT GROWTH 4.5%
POPULATION: 2.4 MILLION

CZECH REPUBLIC
GDP
PER CAPITA $13,969 PERCENT GROWTH 2.3%
POPULATION: 10.3 MILLION

POLAND
GDP
PER CAPITA $9,160 PERCENT GROWTH 0.8%
POPULATION: 38.8 MILLION

SLOVENIA
GDP
PER CAPITA $12,071 PERCENT GROWTH 4%
POPULATION: 5.4 MILLION

HUNGARY
GDP
PER CAPITA $12,196 PERCENT GROWTH 3.5%
POPULATION: 10.2 MILLION

SLOVENIA
GDP
PER CAPITA $16,571 PERCENT GROWTH 2.9%
POPULATION: 2 MILLION

THE EU TODAY
GDP
AVERAGE PER CAPITA $23,500 2002 GROWTH FORECAST 1%
POPULATION: 370 MILLION

THE NEW EU*
GDP
AVERAGE PER CAPITA $20,836 2002 GROWTH FORECAST 1.7%
POPULATION: 454 MILLION

MALTA
GDP
PER CAPITA $12,100 PERCENT GROWTH 4%
POPULATION: 0.3 MILLION

CYPRUS**
GDP
PER CAPITA $13,000 PERCENT GROWTH 2%
POPULATION: 0.6 MILLION

*INCLUDING THE 10 NEW MEMBERS **EXCLUDES AREA CONTROLLED BY TURKEY
GDP FIGURES ARE ESTIMATES FOR 2002 **NOTE:** GDP PER CAPITA FIGURES ARE ADJUSTED FOR PURCHASING POWER PARITY

Data: JP Morgan Chase, Dresdner Bank, Eurostat, European Commission, National Ministries of Finance, Deutsche Bank

Figure 1.1 The new shape of Europe. Source: *Business Week,* 25 November 2002, 63.

Italy, Luxembourg, the Netherlands, Portugal, Spain, and the United Kingdom) were joined by Sweden, Norway, and Austria, bringing the total population to 375 million with an average per capita gross domestic product of $23,500. And by 2005, 10 additional countries will join the union, making a new "Mega-Europe" of 25 states and more than 450 million consumers. The newcomers are Poland, Hungary, the Czech Republic, Slovakia, Slovenia, Lithuania, Latvia, Estonia, Cyprus, and Malta (see Figure 1.1). At a time when the European Union is

flirting with recession, most of its formerly communist neighbors to the east have respectable growth rates of between 3.5 percent (Hungary) and 4.5 percent (Latvia). Only Poland, which may grow by less than 1 percent in the coming year, is lagging. Mega-Europe's economy of $9.3 trillion will approach that of the United States. Many companies have already approached Europe as a single market—rather than as a group of distinct countries—by realigning their product lines and developing strategies that can be employed throughout the EU. For example, Canon, the camera-to-copier giant, has released a pan-European campaign designed to forge closer emotional ties with its consumers. The campaign, which will employ the tagline "You Can," will run in all 15 of its European markets. The ads were shot at landmark locations in major European cities, and will show individuals posing a series of questions about whether they can achieve certain aims with Canon products, to which the answer is "You Can." This campaign follows the radical streamlining of Canon's European advertising lineup in 2001, which saw the appointment of the Dentsu Network—which trades under the CDP name in the United Kingdom—to its consumer account and the TBWA network to its business account. Canon previously had used more than 50 agencies across different products and territories, and anticipates the move will save them at least 10 percent on their ad spending (Chandiramani 2002).

Commonwealth of Independent States

With the failed coup of August 1991, the subsequent resignation of President Mikhail Gorbachev, and the relegation of the former Soviet Union to official oblivion, trade and investment opportunities in the newly formed Commonwealth of Independent States (CIS) increased dramatically. Corporations around the globe eyed the CIS, with its population of over 275 million, as the next marketing frontier. The CIS consists of former Soviet constituent republics. Members in 2002 included 12 of the 15 (Armenia, Azerbaijan, Belarus, Georgia, Kazakhstan, the Kyrgyz Republic, Moldova, the Russian Federation, Tajikistan, Turkmenistan, Ukraine, and Uzbekistan). The population is a heterogeneous one, and while the official language is Russian, there are more than two hundred languages and dialects (at least 18 with more than 1 million speakers). Table 1.4 presents basic demographic information for the CIS. Note that Russia, with its 146 million consumers, is by far the largest of the republics. As one advertising executive noted, "If I were a Western company, I'd get on a plane and come here right now" (*Advertising Age* 1991, 1). Indeed, a multitude of Western companies did just that. Procter & Gamble signed a joint venture agreement in August 1991 with Leningrad State University to begin marketing and distributing consumer products, such as Wash & Go shampoo (the European name for Pert Plus) throughout the Ukraine and Baltics. Philip Morris signed agreements with the Soviet government and the Russian republic to supply more than 20 billion cigarettes—the largest order in the company's history, but still only 5 percent of the market for cigarettes in the CIS. And, in late 1991, Visa became the first credit card available to the general public in the CIS.

However, by late 1998, an overriding feeling of uncertainty replaced the rosy glow of optimism regarding marketing opportunities in the Commonwealth. Political and economic chaos

in the region brought many marketing activities to a slowdown if not an actual halt. Ruble values plummeted, inflation jumped, per capita income dropped, and the gap in income levels between the rich and poor increased. To make matters worse, crime and corruption flourished. According to a survey for the American Chamber of Commerce, nine out of ten companies at the time significantly reduced their advertising budgets. Nearly all shifted their emphasis to less expensive product lines to compete with domestic goods, and a few companies even suspended sales of products. For example, General Motors suspended sales of its Chevy Blazer, despite having just kicked off a new ad campaign for the vehicle. Fortunately the Commonwealth's economy is now on the rebound. For example, Russia's GDP between 1997 and 2000 reportedly rose almost 38 percent to $623.1 billion. The U.S. Department of Commerce reports that the GDP for the United States, by comparison, was nearly $10 trillion in 2000, up about 20 percent from its level in 1997. Inflation in Russia is also dropping, from 36.5 percent in 1999 to 20 percent in 2000, and down to about 14 percent in 2001 (Bertagnoli 2001, 1). Russia's middle class now numbers anywhere from 12 to 30 million people, or about 8 to 20 percent of that country's population. The list of Western companies making new investments in Russia recently is a veritable Who's Who of multinational business. Ikea, the Swedish furniture manufacturer, had a vision of placing the firm's simple shelves, kitchens, bathrooms, and bedrooms in millions of Russian apartments that had not been remodelled since Soviet days. On the day that Ikea opened their first store in Moscow in 2000, the wait to get in took an hour. Highway traffic backed up for miles and more than 40,000 customers crammed into the store and picked the shelves clean. Based on this phenomenal success, Ikea opened a second store in Moscow and, at the close of 2002, unveiled a "megamall" with two kilometers of shop fronts and 150,000 square meters of retail and restaurant space. The center is expected to attract between 25–40 million customers per year. The mall was built

TABLE 1.4 Demographic Profile of the Commonwealth of Independent States, 2001

Republic	Population (millions)	Gross National Income (U.S. billion $)	Gross National Income	
			Per Capita	Global Rank
Armenia	4	2.0	$ 520	155
Azerbaijan	8	4.9	600	148
Belarus	10	28.7	2,870	94
Georgia	5	3.2	630	146
Kazakhstan	15	18.8	1,260	125
Kyrgyz Republic	5	1.3	270	184
Moldavia	4	14	400	162
Russia	146	241.	1,660	114
Tajikistan	6	1.1	180	197
Turkmenistan	5	3.9	750	143
Ukraine	50	34.6	700	144
Uzbekistan	25	8.8	360	171

Source: World Bank (2002).

Dynamics of International Advertising

around a 31,000-square-meter Ikea store and a 24,000-square-meter hypermarket run by the French retailing group Auchan. The hypermarket sells over 40,000 items and requires more than 100 truck deliveries a day to keep its shelves stocked. A further 250 shops include international brand names such as Tommy Hilfiger, Reebok, Wolford and Levi's, together with restaurants, a skating rink and Russia's biggest multiplex cinema (FT.com 2002). Given the success of Ikea, and in particular Auchan, French rivals Carrefour and Casino, as well as the U.S. giant Wal-Mart are now also studying the market.

 China

As recently as 1977, the total volume of two-way trade between the People's Republic of China and the United States was under $400 million. Less than two years later, China began to experiment with open markets and continued to liberalize trade laws. In 1979 Coca-Cola became the first American product available in China when the company was awarded the sole privilege of selling soft drinks to the Chinese market. That same year, for the first time, Chinese authorities permitted domestic product advertising in newspapers. By 1988 two-way trade between the United States and China had jumped to almost $17 billion. Despite the events in Tiananmen Square in June 1989, U.S. businesses continued to knock on China's door. In 1992, in a joint venture with a Chinese state-owned company, McDonald's opened a restaurant in Beijing, with 700 seats and 29 cash registers—the biggest McDonald's in the world, slightly bigger than the one that opened in Moscow in early 1990. At the close of the first day of business, the restaurant had registered 13,214 transactions—representing approximately 40,000 customers—setting a new one-day sales record for any McDonald's in the world.

With over 1.3 billion consumers, China is the world's largest single-country market. More than 22 million new consumers are added each year. Including Taiwan, the country consists of 30 provinces, municipalities, and autonomous regions. China is a land of youth—almost 50 percent of the population is under age 24. The average family size ranges from 3.7 individuals in the Beijing municipality to 5.2 in the Yunnan and Qinghai provinces. While China is a unified country, it is composed of many different nationalities. Bolstering the economy is a burgeoning middle class, which is wealthy enough to afford Western goods and services. Such statistics have foreign companies climbing over one another to get a piece of the market. Indeed, many perceive China as the new gold rush. For example, Yum! Brands, owner of Kentucky Fried Chicken and Pizza Hut, posted higher 2003 earnings because of aggressive expansion in China. Yum! says China is its fastest growing and most profitable country outside the United States, and KFC has been rated the No. 1 brand in China. "We are extremely bullish on China," chief executive Dave Novak told analysts recently. "It's an absolute gold mine for us" (Gu 2003). Yum!'s 761 restaurants in China, most of which are company operated, now generate almost one-third of its international profits, and Yum! is opening more than 200 restaurants in the coming year.

But China's potential is not limited to chicken wings and pizza. China is already the world's largest mobile phone market, and is signing up about 4 million wireless users every month—or about the population of Kentucky—to its 200 million cell-phone user base.

Mobile handsets maker Motorola Inc. now sells 13 percent of its products in China. China also recently displaced Japan to become the No. 2 market for computers and Internet use, helping computer makers as well as chip makers. General Motors Corp. expects China to be the world's second largest vehicle market by 2010, and to take the No. 1 car sales spot by 2025. For an increasing number of firms, China is their best-performing market and top cash generator.

China's economic policies over the past few years have borne remarkable fruit. In 2001, China gained admission into the World Trade Organization (WTO). China has long held "most favored nation" trading status with the United States, which grants it the same tariff rates that many other foreign countries receive. China's admission into the WTO will now force places like the European Union, Mexico, and Taiwan to lower trade barriers against a host of Chinese products. At a time when growth has stalled in most other parts of the world, China appears set to continue its 8 percent growth of 2002. Foreign direct investment in China was up 15 percent during the same year, to a new high of just under $52 billion. Although it accounts for just 3.8 percent of the world's gross domestic product, the country contributes more than 15 percent of global growth. In fact, economists predict that sometime in the next 10 to 15 years, China may well surpass the economic might of Europe. China's advantages are numerous. Its wage rates are one-third of Mexico's and Hungary's, and 5 percent of those in the United States or Japan. China's investments in education and training are attracting research facilities from companies such as IBM, Motorola, and Microsoft. The critical mass of factories, subcontractors, and specialized vendors has created a manufacturing environment in which few can complete. But China is not simply an export platform. Its large and ever-expanding domestic market is another attraction. Mushrooming investment reflects the obsession of many global CEOs to lower production costs by outsourcing whatever they can to large-scale specialists. Indeed, estimates suggest that 50 percent of all manufacturing could be outsourced to China by 2010 (Garten 2002). Today, China mainly manufactures goods that are labor-intensive. It makes 60 percent of the world's bicycles, including 85 percent of those sold in the United States, and is also dominant in the production of shoes, toys, clothing, and furniture. It is only a matter of time before China is also a big factor in capital-intensive industries, such as high tech. High tech manufacturing will become centered in Asia and China by the 2006–2010 period (Bauder 2003). The dark cloud on the horizon is that the world economy may be growing increasingly reliant on these factories.

Canada/Mexico

Negotiations between President Bill Clinton, Mexican President Carlos Salinas de Gortari, and Canadian Prime Minister Brian Mulroney resulted in the signing of a North American Free Trade Agreement (NAFTA) on December 17, 1992. This pact created a market of 360 million consumers with a gross national product of over $6 trillion, representing a formidable competitor to the 15-nation EU. More than 10 years later, NAFTA remains a contentious issue in all three countries. Mexican farmers are staging protests near and around Mexico City, calling for government protection when tariffs on most agricultural livestock products fall to zero

in 2003, as stipulated in NAFTA. Mexican farmers are also complaining of unfair competition from subsidized U.S. farmers. In the United States, labor and environmental groups and many Americans are raising havoc about Mexican trucks being allowed on highways throughout the United States, another policy stipulated by NAFTA. And in Canada, a poll indicated that 47 percent of Canadians believe NAFTA has been a loser (the same poll shows that 37 percent of Americans and 52 percent of Mexicans share a similar view) (Corchado 2002).

Despite these criticisms, the benefits of NAFTA have been many. Canada and Mexico have become the United States's largest trade partners. NAFTA has benefited Mexico in numerous ways: 20 percent of Mexico's current gross domestic product is now attributable to NAFTA reforms, according to figures from the U.S. embassy. Agricultural exports to the United States have doubled to $6.7 billion since 1993, and bilateral trade grew by 115 percent according to the Mexican Ministry of Economy.

U.S. trade with Mexico (more than $270 billion per year) exceeds U.S. trade with Japan, even though Mexico's economy is less than one-eighth the size of Japan. And, thanks to NAFTA, Canada's exports to the United States and Mexico increased 95 percent. Trade between Canada and the United States alone now accounts for almost $500 billion per year. The lesson of NAFTA is that good trade agreements, whether they are bilateral or multilateral, provide the foundation for regional and global trade liberalization, which spurs economic competitiveness and almost universal benefits for consumers around the world (Brock 2002). Indeed, many would like to see the entire hemisphere totally free trade. And the next step is apparently a Free Trade Agreement of the Americas—34 countries stretching from Canada to Chile, with 800 million people and a GDP of $12.5 trillion. That agreement is slated to be signed in 2005.

World Trade

In the past 20 years alone, world trade has expanded from $200 billion to over $6 trillion. The International Monetary Fund estimates growth in global trade slowed from 12 percent in 2000 to just 1 percent in 2001—due in great part to September 11—the slowest growth rate since 1982. For 2002 the IMF projected 2.1 percent growth in global trade. But the belief is that as soon as the world economy turns around in 2003, world trade will again go back to high growth rates of about 6 percent annually. The United States was once considered the "hub" of world trade. While it remains a major player, U.S. participation in world trade, measured as a portion of world market share, has declined drastically. Whereas in 1950 the United States accounted for nearly 25 percent of the world trade flow, its current share is less than 10 percent. It is not that U.S. exports have actually dropped during this period; rather, these figures reflect the entrance of other trading partners into the picture. In 1980, 23 American companies made *Fortune*'s top 50, compared with only 5 Japanese firms. Today, the number of Japanese companies has increased to 12. Competition for world markets comes not only from other industrialized countries but from newly industrialized countries as well. Among the top

100 companies are three Chinese firms (State Power—no. 60, China National Petroleum—no. 81, and Sinopec—No. 86), a Venezuelan firm (PDUSA—no. 66) and a Mexican company (Pemex—No. 92). American corporations have come to realize that the United States is no longer an isolated, self-sufficient national economy but, rather, simply another player in the global marketplace.

IIIII Growth in Advertising Expenditures Worldwide

Patterns in the growth of international advertising mirror those of international business. At the end of World War II, the bulk of advertising activity was domestic, and 75 percent of recorded advertising expenditures worldwide was concentrated in the United States. Since then, the growth in advertising expenditure worldwide has been phenomenal. In 1950 estimated advertising expenditure totaled $7.4 billion worldwide, including $5.7 billion in the United States alone. By the late 1970s the advertising expenditure had swelled to nearly $72 billion worldwide, including $38 billion in the United States. Table 1.5 presents global advertising spending worldwide over the past five years (Coen 2001). Global figures in 2002 exceeded $699 billion. McCann-Erickson typically multiplies this figure by 1.5 to add an estimate for unmeasured media and to obtain what it calls a "global disposable" for all advertising—which for 2002 would be $1.165 trillion. Zenith Optimedia, in its most optimistic forecast of the past few years, predicts that the global advertising recession will end and that global advertising spending (adspend) will grow 2.9 percent in 2003. While U.S. ad spending is only forecast to grow by 1.9 percent, spending in Europe is expected to increase by 2.5 percent, 4.1 percent in Asia, and 4.5 percent in Latin America (Wentz 2002).

The role of advertising varies significantly from country to country, as the figures in Table 1.6 suggest. Table 1.6 lists countries with over $1 billion in advertising expenditures in 2000. Countries spending the most on advertising are primarily the rich industrialized nations, such as the United States, which spent more on advertising than the next nine countries combined. The United States has traditionally been the world leader in total advertising expenditure, contributing 50 percent or more of the total figure year after year.

TABLE 1.5 Global Advertising Spending Worldwide

Year	U.S. Spending (U.S. billion $)	Percent	Non-U.S. Spending (U.S. billion $)	Percent	Worldwide Total (U.S. billion $)
1998	$ 201.6	50	$ 205.4	50	$ 407.0
1999	215.3	50	213.8	50	429.1
2000	243.7	53	220.2	47	463.9
2001	233.7	51	222.4	49	456.1
2002	239.3	51	226.8	49	466.1

Source: Coen, Robert J. (2001) Forecast of Global Ad Expenditures. McCann-Erickson. Presented at the annual UBS Media Week Conference in New York City, Dec.

TABLE 1.6 Total Advertising Expenditures by Country (in U.S. millions $ at constant 2002 prices)

2000 Rank	Expenditure	2003 Rank	Expenditure
1. U.S.	$ 147,110	1. U.S.	$ 145,609
2. Japan	42,003	2. Japan	45,048
3. Germany	17,913	3. Germany	19,149
4. U.K.	15,896	4. U.K.	15,949
5. France	9,323	5. France	9,835
6. Italy	7,259	6. Italy	8,206
7. South Korea	6,721	7. South Korea	7,879
8. Canada	5,813	8. China	6,998
9. Spain	5,162	9. Spain	5,770
10. China	4,773	10. Canada	5,671

Source: Zenith Media, 2001, Advertising Expenditure Forecasts, *Zenith Media* 2001, 1–10.

For the most part, the developing countries tend to be light advertisers. However, economic development is not the sole predictor of advertising expenditure. Some relatively rich countries, such as Austria, are not even on this list, while countries such as South Korea are. This suggests that other variables, such as culture, must be considered in attempting to understand the role of advertising in a particular country. Nor do the figures in the table reflect the relative costs of media time/space in each of the countries. It should be noted that media costs in many developing countries tend to be rather low, and this factor should be taken into consideration when making comparisons.

The leading 50 advertisers, based on total worldwide media spending, are listed in Table 1.7. Procter & Gamble Co. heads the list with worldwide media spending at $3.82 billion, followed by General Mills Corp. and Unilever. The three are the only marketers to spend more than $3 billion each on advertising worldwide in 2001, according to *Advertising Age*'s 16th annual Top Global Marketers Ranking. *Advertising Age* ranks marketers by total worldwide media spending in 77 countries. A company must advertise in at least three of four regions (United States, Europe, Asia, and Latin America) to qualify as a global marketer. Overall, the top 100 spent $70.95 billion on media advertising in 2001—almost half of it, or $34.17 billion, in the United States. Europe was the next biggest region, with $24.09 billion, followed by Asia ($9.19 billion) and Latin America ($1.79 billion). "Half of the top 100 global marketers and six of the top 10 are U.S. companies. None are from Latin America, 19 are Asian and 32 are based in Europe. But their spending patterns are very different. Thirteen of the U.S. marketers still spend more than 80 percent of their media dollars in the United States, including Wal-Mart Stores, Anheuser-Busch Cos., Hershey Foods Corp., and most pharmaceutical and media companies. But that may change in the near future. Wal-Mart, for instance, is the biggest retailer in Mexico and is building huge new stores in China. Even non-U.S. pharmaceutical marketers devote most of their budgets to the U.S. market, where consumers buy more and costlier drugs, and ads for prescription medication are allowed. At the other extreme, some of the U.S. brands most often seen around the world are running more commercials and print ads in Europe

TABLE 1.7 Top 50 Global Marketers, 2001 (U.S. million $)

Rank	Marketer	Headquarters	Measured Worldwide Ad Spending	U.S. Measured Media
1.	Procter & Gamble	Cincinnati	$ 3,820.1	$ 1,702.2
2.	General Motors	Detroit	3,028.9	2,206.9
3.	Unilever	London/Rotterdam	3,005.5	571.2
4.	Ford Motor Co.	Dearborn, Mich.	2,309.0	1,269.8
5.	Toyota Motor Corp.	Toyota City, Japan	2,213.3	769.5
6.	AOL Time Warner	New York	2,099.8	1,564.8
7.	Philip Morris Cos.	New York	1,934.6	1,325.5
8.	DaimlerChrysler	Stuttgart	1,835.3	1,399.6
9.	Nestlé	Vevey, Switzerland	1,798.5	495.4
10.	Volkswagen	Wolfsburg, Germany	1,574.1	458.7
11.	Honda Motor Co.	Tokyo	1,426.0	678.3
12.	McDonald's Corp.	Oak Brook, Ill.	1,405.3	666.1
13.	Coca-Cola Co.	Atlanta	1,402.4	411.1
14.	L'Oreal	Paris	1,348.8	499.6
15.	Walt Disney Co.	Burbank, Calif.	1,260.4	1,054.4
16.	Johnson&Johnson	New Brunswick, N.J.	1,227.3	881.8
17.	Nissan Motor Co.	Tokyo	1,224.0	546.2
18.	Sony Corp.	Tokyo	1,218.9	635.4
19.	GlaxoSmithKline	Greenford, U.K.	1,130.1	766.6
20.	PepsiCo	Purchase, N.Y.	1,025.8	674.2
21.	Peugeot Citroen	Paris	1,006.2	—
22.	Pfizer	New York	992.5	804.6
23.	Mars Inc.	McLean, Va.	953.2	279.7
24.	Fiat	Turin, Italy	890.8	0.9
25.	Vivendi Universal	Paris	881.2	383.8
26.	Renault	Boulogne-Billancourt, France	799.1	—
27.	Diageo	London	797.4	472.3
28.	Viacom	New York	796.9	715.6
29.	Yum Brands	Louisville, Ky.	786.7	566.2
30.	Reckitt Benckiser	Windsor, U.K.	743.5	210.2
31.	Mitsubishi Motors	Tokyo	710.8	229.2
32.	Henkel	Duesseldorf	706.7	8.9
33.	News Corp.	Sydney	706.6	502.8
34.	Danone Group	Paris	682.9	65.3
35.	Matsushita Electric	Osaka, Japan	681.5	35.5
36.	General Mills	Minneapolis	669.4	636.1
37.	Microsoft Corp.	Seattle, Wash.	656.0	524.2
38.	Ferrero	Perugia, Italy	628.9	35.9
39.	Hewlett-Packard	Palo Alto, Calif.	618.4	287.6
40.	Beiersdoft	Hamburg	597.1	101.9
41.	Vodafone	Newbury, U.K.	576.3	2.1
42.	Colgate-Palmolive	New York	548.1	106.6
43.	IBM Corp.	Armonk, N.Y.	527.3	333.6
44.	France Telecom	Paris	503.8	2.4
45.	Bristol-Myers	New York	485.4	457.7
46.	Mazda Motor Corp.	Hiroshima, Japan	464.8	179.6
47.	Kellogg Co.	Battle Creek, Mich.	459.2	255.0
48.	Anheuser-Busch	St. Louis	439.9	367.2
49.	Hyundai Motor Co.	Seoul	439.3	172.5
50.	S.C. Johnson	Racine, Wis.	430.1	287.3

Source: "Top 100 Global Marketers," *Advertising Age,* 11 November 2002, 28–30.

than in the United States. Coca-Cola Co. and Mars each devote 29 percent of their media budgets to the United States, but spend much more in Europe. And Colgate-Palmolive Co. spends just 19.4 percent of its global total in the United States, 49 percent in Europe, 17.9 percent in Asia, and 11 percent in Latin America" (Wentz 2002, 28).

Trend Toward International Agencies

Around the turn of the century, in order to better service clients who were beginning to market their products internationally, advertising agencies also moved abroad. The first U.S. agency to establish itself overseas was J. Walter Thompson, which opened an office in London in 1899 to meet the needs of its client General Motors. By the early 1920s both J. Walter Thompson and McCann-Erickson had large overseas networks with offices in Europe, India, and Latin America. Overall, however, agency movement to foreign soil was rather slow prior to 1960.

A study of 15 large American multinational agencies revealed that in the 45 years between 1915 and 1959, these agencies had opened or acquired only 50 overseas branch offices. Yet in the subsequent 12-year period, 210 overseas branch offices were opened or acquired—a fourfold increase (Weinstein 1974, 29).

When firms began to expand to foreign markets, their advertising agencies were faced with the following options: (1) allow a local agency abroad to handle the account, (2) allow a U.S. agency with an established international network to service their client, or (3) open or acquire an overseas branch. Initially, when multinational clients were the exception rather than the rule, the second alternative was the most common practice. However, allowing another agency to handle a client's international business became rather risky. For example, when D'Arcy, the agency handling advertising for Coca-Cola, was unable to provide service to Coca-Cola's overseas branches, the client turned to McCann-Erickson to handle its international account. Shortly thereafter, Coca-Cola dropped D'Arcy altogether, giving McCann-Erickson both its international and domestic accounts (Tyler 1967, 366).

The 1960s were characterized by rampant expansion abroad by U.S. advertising agencies. Agencies began to see many advantages to joining their clients in foreign markets. By moving abroad, these agencies could not only service their domestic clients but also compete for the foreign accounts of other U.S.-based multinational firms and for the accounts of local foreign firms. Thus, as domestic advertising volume began to taper off, foreign markets looked increasingly appealing. In addition, there was the attraction of potentially higher profits. Overseas salaries of advertising staff members in the 1960s were as much as 70 percent lower than in the United States, while average agency profits were often twice that of what they were in the United States (*Business Week* 1970, 48). Setting up offices overseas had the additional benefit of freeing U.S. agencies from a total dependency on the performance of the U.S. economy as a whole. For example, during the 1970 recession, domestic advertising agency billings declined 1 percent while the foreign billings of multinational agencies increased 13 percent (*International Advertiser*, 1971).

In contrast to the 1960s, the 1970s was a period of consolidation and retrenchment for many U.S. advertising agencies. While the combined annual billings of multinational agencies continued to increase, many smaller multinational agencies with a limited presence overseas were forced to withdraw from foreign markets. Many realized that in order to compete successfully, they had to maintain offices in almost all of the important countries of Europe, Latin America, and the Far East—a commitment that only the largest multinational agencies were prepared to make. In 1970 *Advertising Age* listed 58 agencies that had international billings; by 1977 that number had dropped to just 36.

In the late 1980s, the profile of the industry changed substantially. In 1986, a small London-based agency, Saatchi & Saatchi, systematically grew over a two-year period to become a mega-agency network with capitalized billings of over $13 billion. As part of its growth, Saatchi & Saatchi purchased three U.S. agencies in 1986—Dancer, Fitzgerald, Sample; Backer & Spielvogel; and Ted Bates—and for a short time became the world's largest advertising organization. In 1989 the British WWP Group brought two of U.S. advertising's most glamorous names—J. Walter Thompson

TABLE 1.8 Top 25 World Advertising Organizations, 2002

Rank	Ad Organization	Headquarters	Gross Income (U.S. million $)
1.	Omnicom Group	New York	$ 7,536.3
2.	Interpublic Group of Cos.	New York	6,203.6
3.	WWP Group	London	5,781.5
4.	Publicis Group	Paris	2,711.09
5.	Dentsu	Tokyo	2,060.9
6.	Havas	Suresnes, France	1,841.6
7.	Grey Global Group	New York	1,199.7
8.	Hakuhodo	Tokyo	860.8
9.	Cordiant Communication Group	London	788.5
10.	Asatsu-DK	Tokyo	339.5
11.	TMP Worldwide	New York	335.3
12.	Carlson Marketing Group	Minneapolis	328.5
13.	Incepta Group	London	240.9
14.	Protocol Marketing Group	Deerfield, Ill.	225.0
15.	Digitas	Boston	203.9
16.	Daiko Advertising	Tokyo	203.0
17.	Tokyu	Tokyo	180.4
18.	Maxxcom	Toronto	169.5
19.	Cheil Communications	Seoul	165.0
20.	George P. Johnson Co.	Auburn Hills, Mich.	149.3
21.	Aspen Marketing Group	West Chigaco, Ill.	125.0
22.	Doner	Southfield, Mich.	121.5
23.	Select Communications	Koblenz, Germany	110.0
24.	ChoicePoint Precision Marketing	Alpharetta, Ga.	105.8
25.	Alloy	New York	101.2

Source: Advertising Age, Agency Report, April 2003, S-4.

and the Ogilvy Group—into its "family" via hostile takeovers. Madison Avenue, it was said, was being invaded by an army speaking the Queen's English (Rothenberg 1989, 14). French agencies, too, looked to U.S. soil. In 1988, Publicis Group formed the first big Franco-American alliance with Chicago-based Foote, Cone & Belding Communications. In 1989, Della Femina became a subsidiary of Eurocom, France's top agency. In 1990, Paris-based Boulet Dru Dupuy Petit bought 40 percent of Wells, Rich, Green. Then, in 1994, Publicis Group acquired Bloom FCA, with offices in New York and Dallas (Toy and Lindler 1990, 74). Two Japanese agencies, Dentsu (Japan's largest agency) and Hakuhodo, also opened offices in the United States. As part of Dentsu's plan to establish majority-owned advertising and sales promotion networks in the world's major markets, the agency opened Nova Promotion Group in New York (Kilburn 1991, 3).

Over the past decade, the United States has lost its long-unchallenged grip on huckster-ism—not only at home but abroad as well. European, Japanese, Australian, and Brazilian agencies have expanded or merged operations with agencies in other countries in order to meet the needs of their clients. Today, many of the largest multinational agencies have regrouped, and regrouped again, into multimillion- and multibillion-dollar multiservice transnational mega-advertising organizations, which own the bulk of the advertising agencies throughout the world. Table 1.8 lists the world's top 25 advertising organizations. *Advertising Age* notes that an advertising organization may be either an agency or agency holding company and qualifies for the ranking if it owns 50 percent or more of itself. This table ranks advertising organizations by worldwide revenues. Twelve of the top twenty-five agencies have their headquarters in the United States, and the top agency is American. Five agencies are headquartered in Japan, and three more are based in London. Beyond their sheer size, such mega-advertising organizations offer a number of benefits to their clients. They can clearly present clients with a significant-ly larger pool of talent, and the potential for service synergies exists as well. In addition, cli-ents have the ability to shift portions of accounts from one agency to another without going through the time consuming process of an agency review. Coca-Cola is just one marketer who has switched assignments for its brands among several of Interpublic Group of Cos. agencies and given new product assignments to others. On the downside, clients must content with potential conflicts with competing accounts.

Summary

The growth of international business has paralleled the growth of international advertis-ing. Before turning our attention to the development of effective advertising programs for foreign markets, it is essential to understand the role that advertising plays in the internation-al marketing mix and the challenges posed by the international marketing environment. These topics are the subject of Chapters 2 and 3.

References

Advertising Age. 1991. New marketing era for U.S.S.R. 21 August, 1.

Advertising Age. 2002. Agency report. <www.adageglobal.com/cigi-bin/gages.pl?link+513>

Advertising Age. 2002. Top 100 Global Marketers. 11 November, 28–30.

Advertising Age. 2002. Top 100 Global Marketers. 11 November, 28–30.

Advertising Age. 2003. Agency Report. April, S-4.

Bauder, Don. 2003. China factor involves hefty helping of angst. *San Diego Union-Tribune,* 19 February, C-1.

Bernard, Bruce. 2001. Food firms fight for world market. *Europe,* June, 16.

Bertagnoli, Lisa, 2001. To Russia with . . . reservations. *Marketing News,* 9 April, 1,11.

Brock, William. 2002. Happy 10th NAFTA, but don't celebrate just yet, there's more to do. *Washington Times,* 12 December, A-23.

Business Week. 1970. Madison Avenue Goes multinational. 12 September, 48–51.

——. 1991. For manufacturers, the grass is far greener overseas. 23 December, 20.

Business Week 2002. The new shape of Europe. 25 November, 63.

Coen, Robert. (2001). Presented at 29th annual UBS Warbung Media Week Conference, 12 December, New York. Robert Coen is Senior Vice President and Forecasting Director at Universal McCann.

Chandiramani, Ravi. 2002. Canon shifts strategy in brand ad debut. *Marketing,* 21 February, 7.

Corchado, Alfredo. 2002. Three former leaders push expansion of NAFTA. *Pittsburgh Gazette,* 10 December, A-8.

Dawson, Chester. 2002. The Americanization of Toyota. *Business Week,* 15 April, 52–54.

Economist. 2002. Emerging market indicators. 21 September, 98.

Edmondson, Gail, Kerry Capell, Pamela Moore, and Peter Burrows. 2000. See the world, erase its borders. *Business Week,* 21 August, 113. Fortune. 2002. Fortune global 500. <22 JulyF1-F10.>

Fortune. Fortune Global 500. 21 July, 97–122.

FT.com. 2002. Ikea is building a shopping center on a scale Russia has not seen before. 26 April. Financial Times, London <http://80-proquest.umi.com.webgate.sdsu.edu:88/pgdweb?Did=0000001161046768fmt=3.>

Garten, Jeffrey. 2002. When everything is made in China. *Business Week,* 17 June, 20.

Gu, Wei. 2003. U.S. Companies in China find the silk road. *San Diego Union-Tribune,* 23 February, H-3.

Hagenbaugh, Barbara. 2002. Foreign investment in USA, worldwide showing decline. *USA Today,* 18 September, B05.

Hilsenrath, Jon E. 2002. Globalization efforts will see revival—search for new consumers, low cost suppliers, power expansion abroad. *Asian Wall Street Journal,* 2 January, 1.

Holmes, Stanley. 2002. To keep up the growth it must go global quickly. *Business Week,* 9 September, 100–10.

Hoover's Handbook of World Business. 1993. 25 companies with the largest non-U.S. sales, 109.

———. 2002. The 25 largest foreign investors in the U.S., 51.

International Advertiser. 1971. International agencies. 12(3): 44.

Khermouch, Gerry. 2002. The best global brands. *Business Week,* 5 August, 92–99.

Kilburn, David. 1991. Dentsu opening U.S. promo shop. *Advertising Age,* 8 July, 3, 34.

Leonhardt, David. 2003. U.S. trade deficit hit new high in December. *San Diego Union-Tribune,* 21 February, C-1.

Port, Otis. 1989. Back to Basics. *Business Week,* 16 June, 14–18.

Rhoads, Christopher. 2003. The Davos debate: China is a bright spot in the global economy. *Wall Street Journal Europe,* 24 January, A3.

Rothenberg, Randall. 1989. Brits buying up the ad business. *New York Times Magazine,* 2 July, 14–38.

Shaughnessy, Rick, and Diane Lindquist. 1993. Foreign investment in the United States drops 47 percent. *San Diego Union-Tribune,* 9 June, C2.

Statistical Abstract of the United States. 2001.

Statistical Abstract of the United States. 2002.

Toy, Steward, and Mark Lindler. 1990. And now, rue de Madison. *Business Week,* 21 May, 74–75.

Tyler, Ralph. 1967. Agencies abroad: New horizons for U.S. advertising. In *World Marketing,* ed. John K. Ryans and J. C. Baker. New York: Wiley, 366–380.

U.S. Bureau of the Census. 1995. *Statistical History of the United States.* New York: Basic Books.

Weinstein, Arnold K. 1974. The international expansion of U.S. multinational advertising agencies. *MSU Business Topics* 22 (3): 29–35.

Wentz, Laurel. 2002. P&G and GM lead global ad spending. *Advertising Age,* 11 November, 28.

World Bank. 2002. *World Development Indicators.*

Zenith Media. 2001. *Advertising Expenditure Forecasts.* 1–10.

CHAPTER TWO

The International Marketing Mix

The primary focus of this text is international advertising. However, because an advertising campaign is part of an overall marketing strategy and must be coordinated with other marketing activities, the role of the other marketing mix elements will be reviewed. Companies operating in one or more foreign markets must decide whether to adapt their marketing mix to local conditions; and if so, to what degree. The concept of a marketing mix, popularized by Jerome McCarthy, includes the following four P's:

1. Product: includes a product's design and development, as well as branding and packaging;
2. Place (or distribution): includes the channels used in moving the product from manufacturer to consumer;
3. Price: includes the price at which the product or service is offered for sale and establishes the level of profitability;
4. Promotion: includes advertising, personal selling, sales promotions, direct marketing, and publicity. Broadly defined, it also includes sponsorships, product integration and even trade fairs. (McCarthy 1960)

 Standardization versus Specialization of the Marketing Mix

Experts disagree over the degree to which firms should standardize their marketing programs across markets. At one extreme are companies that support the use of a fully standardized approach. Marshall McLuhan coined the term "global village" to describe an emerging world tightly linked through telecommunications. Many marketers believe that these advances in telecommunications, along with cheaper air transportation and the resulting increase in international travel, have created increasingly international consumers, making the world ripe for global marketing—at least for selected products.

This concept is not new. Debates regarding the viability of global marketing surfaced as far back as the late 1960s (Buzzell 1968). However, the concept was popularized by Harvard marketing professor Theodore Levitt, who suggested that people everywhere want goods of the best quality and reliability at the lowest price; and that differences in cultural preferences, tastes, and standards are vestiges of the past, because the world is becoming increasingly homogenized (Levitt 1983, 92). With a global approach to the marketing mix, a firm utilizes a common marketing plan for all the countries in which it operates—essentially selling the same product in the same way everywhere in the world. Major benefits associated with such standardization include lower production, distribution, management, and promotion costs. Yet the number of firms with the potential to standardize the majority of their marketing mix elements are indeed few.

Samsung is one such advertiser:

> Just a few years ago, Samsung was the brand you bought if you couldn't afford Sony or Toshiba. Suddenly, it's the name that consumers all over the world—especially young ones—seek out for the most fun and stylish models of everything from cell phones to flat-panel plasma TVs. One of the driving forces behind this transformation is Eric Kim, head of global marketing for Samsung. When Kim arrived in 1999, Samsung was already turning out some cool products. But nobody noticed. Its brand image was fuzzy and inconsistent from market to market. One reason was that it employed a gaggle of 55 advertising agencies. Kim consolidated that work in a single shop, assigning Foote, Cone & Belding Worldwide to coordinate Samsung's global marketing. The result was a daring $400 million worldwide advertising campaign. "I convinced the company we had to have a single message," said Kim. (MacIntyre 2002)

Ads focus on the company's promise to provide a "DigitAll Experience." The approach clearly has paid off. The company earned $2.5 billion in net profits in 2001, was listed as the 42nd most valuable brand last year by the consultancy Interbrand, rising faster through the ranks than any company except Starbucks, and became the No. 3 producer of cell phones, with a premium-priced line that includes handsets with color screens. See Figure 2.1 for a sample of this global campaign.

At the other extreme are companies committed to specialization. They argue that because consumers and marketing environments in different countries vary so greatly, it is necessary to tailor the marketing mix elements to each foreign market. Although such a customized approach typically results in higher costs, marketers hope that these costs will be offset by greater returns and a larger market share.

Wal-Mart serves as an excellent example of the specialized approach:

> Long before it was fashionable, Wal-Mart pushed responsibility and information to the lowest ranks. Managers of departments such as sporting goods or women's apparel get detailed reports of sales and profits in their areas and they have a say in which products get stocked. Store managers can buy locally and ask headquarters to adjust inventory of company brands that it has asked them to stock.

Figure 2.1 Global print campaign for Samsung Color Phone.

Wal-Mart does not stray from its locals-know-best model. Thus, their Shenzher store, just north of Hong Kong, is crowded with tanks of crabs, fish, frogs and shrimp, which can be taken home wiggling or be expertly gutted and cleaned on the spot. (Saporito et al. 2003)

A great deal of confusion surrounds the issue of standardization versus specialization, in part because of the various terms employed. Marketing standardization has also been called globalization, while marketing specialization has been referred to as localization as well as customization. Regardless of the terminology, too often the issue of standardization versus specialization of international marketing is perceived as an either/or proposition. In fact, standardization versus specialization of the marketing mix may be seen as the end points on a continuum, with many possible approaches between these two extremes. A company may choose to standardize one element while customizing another. For example, Mars sells an identical product to consumers all over Europe, but modifies the advertising message content. As part of a major rebranding push for the Mars bar across Europe, Mars created a mixed campaign that pays unprecedented detail to local habits and tastes. The "think local" strategy is the product of new creative thinking by Grey Worldwide, which picked up the business in 2002 from the incumbent of 40 years, D'Arcy. While in the United Kingdom the tagline for the Mars bar is "Pleasure you can't measure," in Germany it is "Mars—Das hat was" (that's it), and in France: "Mars: Que du bonheur" (Mars: what happiness). Outdoor executions that aim to trigger feelings of pleasure differ in each market as well. For instance, in the United Kingdom, the slogan is "Saturday 3 P.M.," referring to the much anticipated soccer kick-off time during the weekend. The phrase "Saturday 3 P.M." has no meaning whatsoever in any country outside the United Kingdom. In France, the simple word "August" appears, evoking the month of the year when the whole country goes on holiday; and the words "the last parking space" have a particular appeal to the Germans. The agency has adapted this strategy to take into consideration the specific market and culture (Mussey 2002).

The issue of marketing standardization versus specialization, as it pertains to product, price, and distribution, will be addressed in this chapter. Globalization versus localization of advertising will be discussed in detail in Chapters 5 and 6.

Product

The American Marketing Association defines a product as "anything that can be offered to a market for attention, acquisition, use, or consumption that might satisfy a want or need" (American Marketing Association 1960). A product can be thought of in terms of three levels. These three levels, as outlined by Philip Kotler and Gary Armstrong (Kotler 1990, 221), are illustrated in Figure 2.2.

The *core product* refers to the bundle of benefits the consumer expects to receive from purchasing the item. These benefits can be functional, psychological, social, or economic in nature. For example, consumers may purchase an automobile for purposes of transportation (functional benefit), select a specific style because it is currently in fashion among their group of

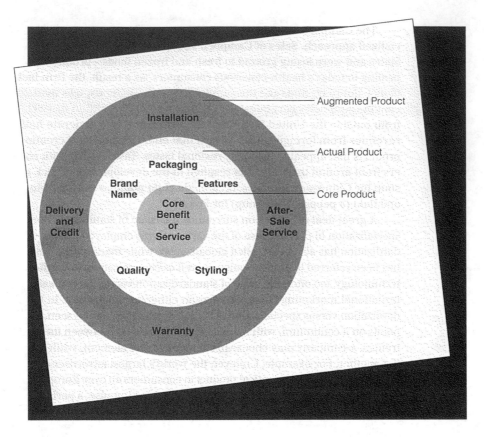

Figure 2.2 Three levels of a product.

friends (social benefit), opt for a stick shift over an automatic because it provides better mileage (economic benefit), and choose the color red because it's their favorite (psychological benefit).

The *actual product* includes the specific features and styling of the product, its quality, the brand name, and its packaging; and the *augmented product* refers to product installation, delivery and credit provided to consumers, warranty, and postpurchase servicing.

Most products can be classified as durable goods, nondurable goods, or services. *Durable goods* are major products, often high-ticket items that tend to last for an extended period of time and, as a result, are purchased rather infrequently. Automobiles, appliances, and furniture are examples of durable goods. *Nondurable goods* are typically lower in price, consumed in a relatively short period of time, and thus purchased frequently. Examples of nondurable goods include food products and personal care items such as shampoos and toothpaste. *Services* are defined as activities or benefits offered by one party to another that are essentially intangible and do not result in the transfer of ownership of any kind. Obtaining health insurance, getting a haircut, or having an auto repaired are examples of services that consumers may purchase.

Products can be further distinguished between consumer goods and industrial goods. *Consumer goods* are items purchased by the end consumer for personal consumption. In contrast,

industrial goods are items a firm purchases so that it may engage in business. Industrial goods include raw materials that actually become part of the end product (for example, in the garment industry, textiles purchased by a garment manufacturer that become part of its line of clothing), goods such as equipment and machinery used in the manufacturing process itself (for instance, industrial-quality sewing machines purchased to enable the creation of the fashions), and supplies and services (such as photocopier paper and long distance telephone service).

Product planning in the international setting requires that marketers explore the needs and wants of consumers in different markets and determine how those needs and wants might be satisfied by the firm's products. In addition to deciding which products should be offered, the international marketer must determine whether product modifications are necessary.

Product Standardization

One option available to the international marketer is to sell exactly the same product abroad as is sold in the home market—what is known as product standardization. The advantages to this strategy are numerous. Selling an identical product in a number of markets eliminates duplication of costs related to research and development, product design, and package design. Consider the case of Black & Decker, a classic example of the benefits of product standardization. In 1982, Black & Decker operated 25 plants in 13 countries on 6 continents, which led to considerable duplication of effort. Indeed, Black & Decker produced 260 different motor sizes before it undertook global restructuring of its operations. Employing the same raw materials, equipment, plants, and processes typically leads to manufacturing economies of scale. A standardized product also increases the potential for economies of scale related to promotional efforts. Coca-Cola, Kellogg's corn flakes, Perrier bottled water, Pond's cold cream, Mitsubishi autos, Gillette razor blades, Birkenstock sandals, and Colgate toothpaste are examples of products that are available in the same form in markets around the globe.

Studies have revealed that the feasibility of product standardization may depend on the specific product category. Among consumer goods, nondurables generally are believed to require greater customization than durable goods because they appeal more directly to tastes, habits, and customs, which tend to be country-specific (Douglas and Urban 1977, 53; Hoevell and Walters 1972, 69). Some research has indicated that industrial products are more amenable to standardization than are consumer goods (Boddewyn et al. 1986, 69; Cahn and Mauborgne 1987). Product standardization also may be effective for markets with highly similar target audiences (Sheth 1986, 9; Kahle and Sudharshan 1987, 60). For example, the youth market around the world is said to be surprisingly similar. Marketers of jeans, records, and soft drinks find that they can sell essentially identical products to teens in Peoria and Paris. And marketers of "global village products"—essentially goods and services targeted to international travelers, such as hotels and rental cars—also find similarities in their target audience. Teresa Domzal and Lynette Unger propose that product standardization appears most feasible when products approach either end of the "high-tech/high-touch" spectrum:

Consumers around the world who are interested in high-tech products share a common language, in bytes or other technical features, which enable global strategies to be successful. The hypothesized success of global marketing of "high-touch" products is more difficult to explain beyond the fact that products such as fragrance, fashion, or jewelry, for example, simply touch on universal emotional themes or needs. The high-tech/high-touch hypothesis appears to be borne out in the recent success of certain global products. High-tech products such as personal computers, video and stereo equipment and automobiles, and high-touch categories such as health food, fitness clothing, mineral water and fragrances are popular the world over. (Domzal and Unger 1987, 23)

 Product Adaptation

Although product standardization is the less costly approach, the international marketer may choose to engage in product adaptation for a variety of reasons. Marketing environments vary from country to country, and as a result, a product designed and developed for consumers in one market may not match needs in another.

Mandatory Product Adaptation Mandatory adaptation refers to situations in which the international firm adapts its products because it literally has no other choice. Differing levels of technical sophistication may necessitate product simplification. For example, frozen foods cannot be marketed in countries where retailers do not have freezer storage facilities. Likewise, if consumers in these markets typically do not own refrigerators, demand for frozen foods is likely to be quite limited. Variations in electrical systems from one country to the next (and even within countries) must also be considered when marketing consumer or industrial electrical appliances. A television designed for the U.S. market simply will not run in Mexico or Germany because of differences in both the frequency and voltage of the electrical power supply and the broadcast standards in these countries. In addition, the United States still relies on the American/British measurement system, while almost every other country has converted to the metric system. Any American firm attempting to sell a product abroad for which measurement is an important variable must go metric. For example, as Louis Kraar recounts, Hewlett-Packard had little choice—and lots of incentive—but to modify one of its products for the Asian market:

> The firm introduced its first Japanese-language computer printer. The Japanese version of the popular DeskJet 500 machine was followed by similar models with built-in software to print in Chinese characters and the Hankul alphabet of Korea. Localizing products is well worth the trouble and considerable expense. Hewlett-Packard's sales of $2 billion in Asia and the Pacific last year represent 16 percent of the corporate total. (Kraar 1991, 133)

Governmental regulations often present formidable barriers to product standardization. These regulations relate to product standards as well as testing and approval procedures. Each country has different product requirements designed to protect its citizens and its environment. The German government, for example, has strict guidelines regarding the purity of beers sold in that country, which prevents many brands from entering the market. Similarly, the United States has very specific safety restrictions on auto emissions that must be met by both foreign and domestic automobiles sold in this country. If such government-mandated standards force international firms to spend additional time and money modifying products, they can function as a nontariff barrier and, in discouraging imports, help protect domestic manufacturers.

Discretionary Product Adaptation When faced with technical differences or governmental restrictions, the international firm has little choice but to adapt its product. In other instances the decision to standardize or adapt is not nearly so clear-cut. In these cases the international marketer must explore differences in consumption patterns, such as whether the product is purchased by relatively the same consumer income group from one country to another, whether most consumers use the product or service for the same purpose, and whether the method of preparation is the same for all target countries. In addition, the marketer must consider the psychosocial characteristics of consumers, such as whether the same basic psychological, social, and economic factors motivate the purchase and use of the product in all target countries; and whether the advantages and disadvantages of the product or service in the minds of consumers are basically the same from one country to another. Finally, the marketer must take into account more general cultural criteria, such as whether some stigma is attached to the product or service, or whether the product or service interferes with tradition in one or more of the targeted markets (Britt 1974, 32).

Campbell Soup has clearly learned valuable lessons from their early mistakes. The firm would have benefited from a more in-depth analysis of both consumption and psychosocial factors when they initially moved overseas in the late 1950s. During the decade that followed, the company recorded some $30 million in losses in its overseas operations. The firm's difficulties stemmed mainly from its failure to adapt its product to suit local preferences (Ricks et al. 1974, 16; Sales Management, 1967, 31). England comprised Campbell's most important foreign market. A primary mistake was the failure to explain to the English housewife how to prepare the soup. The English, accustomed to the ready-to-eat Heinz soups but unfamiliar with the concept of condensed soups, were unable to justify the cost of the smaller Campbell's soup can compared to the larger Heinz can. It took two years for Campbell to provide the necessary explanations and to promote the idea of condensed soups. Failure to adapt the taste of their soups to local palates was another problem. The taste of established local varieties of tomato soup so differed from Campbell's that it was not until Campbell made significant changes in its flavors that sales picked up. As a result, Campbell's now creates new products to appeal to distinctly regional tastes. Taste-testing with consumers from around the world have resulted in the development of duck gizzard soup for Chinese consumers, *creama de chile poblano* soup for Mexicans, and *flaki* (a peppery tripe soup) for Poles (Weber 1993, 52).

McDonald's has successfully marketed its fast food worldwide for decades. While the restaurant provides its customers with nearly an identical eating experience wherever the Golden

Figure 2.3 In Hong Kong, it's McRice.

Arches appear, it also pays very close attention to local tastes and customs. For example, in catering to Singaporeans' penchant for spaghetti and preference for chicken, McDonald's has launched McSpaghetti—a pasta-based meal served in a tangy chicken pomodoro sauce. Retailing for $2.20, and including a garlic McMuffin, McSpaghetti is served at all McDonald's islandwide, along with traditional McDonald's fare. This follows other product innovations like the savory breakfast item chicken SingaPorridge. Porridge is a popular local breakfast item and is widely considered a comfort food in Singapore. McDonald's research clearly paid off, given that weekend breakfast now accounts for half of the chain's entire business across Singapore's 126 outlets. Menu tailoring is not unique to Singapore. In Japan, teriyaki burgers often appear alongside the Big Mac, and in Hong Kong, McDonald's has begun offering customers a rice-based alternative (see Figure 2.3).

Regardless of the source of pressure for product modification, the international marketer must attempt to measure the costs and revenues associated with marketing a standardized product and compare them with the costs and revenues expected in a product adaption strategy. Further complicating the decision to standardize or adapt is the fact that this formula may vary on a market-by-market basis. As a case in point, two years after Mattel allowed its Japanese affiliate to "Japanize" Barbie Doll's features, sales blossomed from near zero to 2 million units. Interestingly, Barbie sold well without modification in 60 other countries (Kotler 1986, 13).

New Product Development

Too often marketers have attempted to export products that, while appropriate to the home market, were not particularly well suited to the needs of consumers in other countries without significant modifications. In some instances product modifications may be so extensive that it is no longer profitable to market the item. Here marketers may find that creating a completely new product is the best way to meet the needs of a foreign market. For example, Heinz developed a special line of rice-based baby foods for the Chinese market, and a fruit-based drink for children called Frutsi for the Mexican market. More recently, Martha Stewart has found great success catering to Japanese tastes. Pairing with local retailer Seiyu, she has opened more than 200 outlets and annually sells over $1 million worth of products to women who want to bring a piece of New England to their crowded Japanese apartments. But products intended for the American market did not appeal to Japanese consumers. Towels targeted at American women in reds and browns, for example, were deemed "muddy." Instead, Martha sells linens in vibrant colors, along with chopsticks in pastels, square frying pans for making traditional cube-shaped omelettes, and bedroom slippers—a must in every Japanese home (Dawson and Brady 2002).

Country-of-Origin Effect

Consumers base their product evaluations on a variety of criteria, including the country in which the product is produced. Marlboro is an American cigarette, Chanel No. 5 is a French perfume, Buitoni is an Italian pasta, and Johnny Walker is a Scotch whiskey. Each of these brands has national credentials, and anyone attempting to market worldwide a Scottish pasta or an Italian whiskey probably would have serious credibility problems because of this country-of-origin effect (Shalofsky 1987, 88). Some countries have particularly positive associations with specific product categories. For example, Germany and Japan are stereotypically seen as producing high-quality autos while France and Italy are typically associated with fine wines. A plausible national base or home market appears to be an important characteristic of the overall product and may influence perceptions of the product's quality. Figure 2.4 shows an example of an advertisement highlighting the country of origin.

Bozell Worldwide, a major advertising agency, commissioned a study to determine how consumers in 20 countries rate the quality of goods from some major exporting nations. At the top of the list was Japan, with 38.5 percent of respondents rating manufactured goods "excellent" or "very good." Germany came in second (36.0 percent), the United States third (34.3 percent), and Britain fourth (21.9 percent). At the bottom of the list were Spain (10.3 percent), China (9.2 percent), and Taiwan (9.0 percent) (*Adweek* 1994).

In some instances a firm may wish to downplay a product's country of origin. Research has revealed that antiglobalism exists in many Asian countries, and this trend has gathered momentum over the past five years. Nestlé, which sells a product called Milo with the same winning positioning all around the world, has repositioned the product for Malaysia. In Malaysia the slogan "Malaysia boleh" is employed—which means Malaysia can win. For all

Figure 2.4 French advertisement for Martini highlighting the country of origin.

intents and purposes, Milo is perceived as a Malaysian rather than a Swiss brand in this market. What this suggests is that "repressing" or reframing (rather than emphasizing) provenance can be a smart neoglobal strategy (Young 2001).

Given the increasingly multinational corporate world, it is often difficult to determine exactly where a product comes from. Because they build their products all over the world, companies like IBM, Mitsubishi, and Siemens AG are in fact American, Japanese, and German in name only. For example, IBM manufactures products in 12 countries, and their IBM PS-1 personal computer—stamped "Made in U.S.A."—might be assembled in Raleigh, North Carolina, yet contain a floppy disk drive from IBM's Japanese plants, a monitor from Korea, and a mixture of imported and domestic computer chips (*San Diego Union-Tribune* 1992a). "Almost any one product weighing more than 10 pounds and costing more than $10 these days is a global composite, combining parts or services from many different nations," notes Robert B. Reich, Harvard political economist and current secretary of labor (*San Diego Union-Tribune* 1992b).

Branding and Trademark Decisions

Branding decisions are an important part of international product marketing strategy. A brand is any name, term, sign, symbol, or design—or combination of these—intended to differentiate the goods or services of one seller from those of another. A trademark is a brand or part of a brand that is given legal protection. Registering a trademark protects the seller's exclusive rights to the use of that brand name. From the consumer's perspective, trademarks help to identify the origin of the product and provide a guarantee of consistent quality.

Protection of successful and well-known trademarks is challenging in the home market, and doubly so internationally. Marketers may protect their trademarks in each nation in which they operate as well as internationally. Most countries offer some system of trademark registration and protection for both foreign and national firms. There are two basic systems of trademark registration:

1. Priority in registration: In Europe and elsewhere, the first firm to register a trademark is considered the rightful owner of that trademark.
2. Priority in use: In the United States and Britain, rights to a trademark are established and maintained through use. In order for a brand to be protected, it must both be registered and have, in fact, been sold in that particular country. "Use" is defined legally and varies from one country to the next. In some countries, the export sale of several cases of a product is sufficient to be defined as use; in others, the product might have to be manufactured locally.

The Madrid Protocol for International Registration of Trademarks allows a marketer to obtain international protection of a trademark. After 13 years, the United States has finally joined this one-stop-shopping system for managing trademarks that more than 65 other countries have adopted since 1989. Under this system, a U.S. applicant, for example, can file an application with the U.S. Patent and Trademark Office. On the form, the applicant would indicate

the countries belonging to the Madrid Protocol in which they wanted protection. The form can be submitted in French or English, eliminating the need for applying in multiple languages. The Patent and Trademark Office then forwards the application to the World Intellectual Property Organization (WIPO), and WIPO sends out an international registration for the mark. WIPO then sends the application to the relevant countries, where trademark examiners will analyze the application. Each country may take 18 months to make a final decision, or longer if the application is opposed. If the trademark is approved, the Madrid Protocol gives it a lifespan of 10 years plus one renewal, for which the owner must pay a $100 renewal fee. It is an easier, cheaper, and more efficient way for trademark holders to secure worldwide protection than submitting separate applications to each country involved. For small companies and independent inventors, the rule makes it feasible to invest in international trademarks by significantly reducing the red tape, local agents, language, and fees involved. For example, in 2000 the U.S. government estimated that a U.S. trademark owner who wanted to register his mark in 10 countries faced $14,000 in fees for 10 separate applications. The Madrid Protocol brings that cost down to about $4,700. But the new rule means that trademark applicants will have to search not only U.S. trademark archives but an international register of archives from all Madrid Protocol countries when checking whether the mark they want already belongs to someone else (Chartrand 2002).

In some countries the international marketer is required to periodically renew registration rights and pay a renewal fee. Registration fees typically are modest, but the associated legal fees can raise costs significantly. Given the costs and efforts required to register trademarks, the international marketer must carefully evaluate each market in order to determine whether to seek protection. The marketer must also continually monitor the foreign markets in which it operates to ensure that trademark infringement does not become a problem. For example, Xerox is one of 13,000 legally registered foreign trademarks in the Commonwealth of Independent States (CIS). With the disintegration of the Soviet Union, however, protection of these trademarks has become problematic. Manufacturers of other copy machines, such as Canon, often use the Xerox name to advertise their machines. As a result, consumers in the CIS are apparently confusing the name *Xerox* with the generic term. Therefore Xerox has undertaken a year-long TV and radio advertising campaign to combat the problem (McCay 1992).

The international marketer must also decide whether to promote a single product brand worldwide—commonly referred to as a *global brand*—or to promote different brands for different regions or even individual markets. Certain advantages are associated with registering a single brand in all countries in which the firm operates. There is often a certain level of prestige associated with an international brand. A recent survey of the world's most valuable brands, conducted annually by *Business Week*, found Coca-Cola to be the top brand worldwide:

> Brands usually aren't listed on corporate balance sheets, but they can go further in determining a company's success than a new factory or technological breakthrough. That's because nurturing a strong brand, even in bad times, can allow companies to command premium prices. A strong brand also can open the door when growth depends on breaking into new markets. (Khermouch 2002, 93)

TABLE 2.1 World's 25 Most Valuable Brands, 2001, U.S. billion $

Rank	Brand	2002 Brand Value	Country of Ownership
1.	Coca-Cola	69.64	U.S.
2.	Microsoft	64.09	U.S.
3.	IBM	51.19	U.S.
4.	GE	41.31	U.S.
5.	INTEL	30.86	U.S.
6.	NOKIA	29.97	Finland
7.	Disney	29.26	U.S.
8.	McDonald's	26.38	U.S.
9.	Marlboro	24.15	U.S.
10.	Mercedes	21.01	Germany
11.	Ford	20.40	U.S.
12.	Toyota	19.45	Japan
13.	Citibank	18.07	U.S.
14.	Hewlett-Packard	16.78	U.S.
15.	American Express	16.29	U.S.
16.	Cisco	16.22	U.S.
17.	AT&T	16.06	U.S.
18.	Honda	15.06	Japan
19.	Gillette	14.96	U.S.
20.	BMW	14.43	Germany
21.	Sony	13.90	Japan
22.	Nescafe	12.84	Switzerland
23.	Oracle	11.51	U.S.
24.	Budweiser	11.35	U.S.
25.	Merrill Lynch	11.23	U.S.

Source: Kermonch (2002).

To determine which global brands are the most valuable, *Business Week* and Interbrand, a unit of Omnicom Group Inc., ranked brands by dollar value, based on the idea that strong brands have the power to lift sales and earnings. Interbrand attempts to figure out how much of a boost each brand delivers, how stable the boost is likely to be, and how much those future earnings are worth today. The value that is assigned is strictly for the products with the brand on them, not for others sold by the company. Therefore, Coca-Cola—with a value approaching $70 billion—is ranked just on those products carrying the Coke name, not Sprite or Powerade. Table 2.1 lists the top 25 global brands.

It is clearly less costly to prepare advertising campaigns and promotional literature for a single brand than for several. A single brand also allows the marketer to utilize international media and reap the benefits where media spill over national borders, such as in Europe. With increasing international travel, a single trademark will ensure that consumers recognize a firm's products, thereby eliminating brand confusion.

However, certain factors may necessitate modification of the brand name or trademark. Some brand names simply do not translate well. In other cases, a brand name in one market may mean something entirely different in another. Consider the case of the Japanese car manufacturer Mitsubishi Corp., which wanted to name one of its models Pajero. In certain Latin American countries, the term is slang for compulsive sexual behavior. Instead Mitsubishi adopted the name Montero for most markets around the world (Asher 2001). Also, different countries often prefer different types of brand names. For example, there is a pronounced difference in the names Americans and Japanese give to their cars. Whereas the Japanese lean toward pastoral names or names of girls—Bluebird, Bluebonnet, Sunny, Violet, Gloria—American cars have names such as Mustang, Cougar, Thunderbird, and Cutlass. The first sports car Nissan sent to the United States was named the Datsun Fair Lady. Nissan's head of sales for all the western United States was so convinced that such a name would not sell cars in this country that he replaced it with one using the company's internal name for the car, the 240Z. The auto went on to become a big seller for Nissan (Johnston 1988, 33).

Governmental restrictions may prohibit the use of a brand name. For example, in marketing Diet Coca-Cola to a number of European countries, the Coca-Cola company encountered restrictions regarding use of the word "diet." As shown in Figure 2.5, Coca-Cola solved the problem by changing the product name to Coca-Cola Light. However, packaging and graphics are standardized so despite the name change, the product is quite familiar and reassuring to U.S. consumers travelling abroad.

Target audience preferences may also influence the brand name selected. The Coca-Cola Light name was also used for the Japanese market because Japanese consumers tend not to be overweight and do not like to admit they are dieting by purchasing products labeled as dietetic. Accompanying this new brand name was a shift in promotional strategy, which emphasized "figure maintenance" rather than "weight loss."

Brand Piracy

A problem that many well-known brands face in foreign markets is brand piracy. Like many U.S. companies, Microsoft is mesmerized by the dream of capturing its share of business in China—if only it could overcome piracy, which is rampant. More than 90 percent of the application software used in China comes from illegal copies. It has been 13 years since China adopted its first copyright law, and it later tightened the rules only reluctantly, mostly to win admission to the World Trade Organization. Now comfortably in the WTO and enjoying a $30 billion trade surplus with the United States, China scarcely bothers to enforce the laws. Although Microsoft software by far is the most popular, with 60 percent of Chinese computers running on Microsoft operating systems, few consumers or businesses shell out for the real thing. Microsoft's China revenue was only $85 million in 2002, as estimated by International Data Corp. Microsoft would have taken in $400 billion had it been paid only for its share of software in brand-new computers (Chen and Quin 2003).

Paus.

Figure 2.5 Diet Coca-Cola renamed Coca-Cola Light for the Swedish market.

There are three distinct forms of piracy: imitation, faking, and preemption. *Imitation* basically involves copying an established brand. For instance, LaCoste, manufacturer of the popular jerseys with the alligator logo, must combat knockoffs of its product sold in numerous countries. *Faking* refers to identifying the fraudulent product with a symbol, logo, or brand name that is very similar to the famous brand. For example, preference for foreign brands in Vietnam has led to knockoffs such as Volgate toothpaste and Lix soap. Coca-Cola, which manufactures the soft drink Sprite, asked a South Korean court to ban the production and sale in South Korea of Sprint, which was introduced with a name, logo, and taste much like Sprite's.

Preemption of brand names occurs in those countries where the law permits wholesale registration of brand names. In such countries a person may register, in his or her name, a large number of well-known brand names and then sell them either to those interested in counterfeiting or, better still, to the multinational when it is ready to move into that country.

 Packaging and Labeling Decisions

Packaging refers to the design and production of product containers or wrappings. Packaging includes the immediate container (for example, the plastic container surrounding Sure deodorant), a secondary package that is discarded after purchase (the cardboard box that a container of Sure is sold in), and any packaging necessary to ship the product to retailers (such as a cardboard carton containing dozens of packages of Sure deodorant). Labeling is also considered part of the packaging, and consists of printed information appearing on or along with the packaging.

Packaging has both protective and promotional aspects. In determining whether the same packaging can be used for foreign markets, marketers must consider a variety of marketplace conditions. Packaging must allow the product to reach its destination without damage. Markets with long, slow, or poor distribution channels may require sturdier packaging. Climatic extremes may necessitate packaging modifications. For example, Quaker Oats adopted special vacuum-sealed tins to protect its products in hot and humid climates. Consumption rates directly influence storage time and may vary from one market to the next.

Packaging is often determined by the income level of a market. Unilever attempted to reach consumers in emerging markets by both modifying the packaging and using less expensive formulations. Using a concept with the code name "Project Everyman," Unilever added new customers too poor to regularly buy standard versions of the company's detergent or shampoo. For example, in Brazil, Unilever's research revealed that many Brazilians could not afford washing machines or Unilever's Omo brand of detergent, which was way beyond their household income. Instead, many poorer Brazilians purchased bars of soap to wash clothes in rivers and lakes. The lack of washing machines made a simpler soap formula an option. And, because many consumers washed their clothes in rivers, the powder was packaged in plastic instead of paper that would get soggy. The newly developed detergent, named Ala, was also produced locally to cut transportation costs, further lowering product price. Within three months after its launch, Ala had captured at least 15 percent of the test market. Developing and emerging markets account for 28 percent of total Unilever sales, up from just 16 percent

in 1985. However, Unilever expects developing and emerging markets to approach 50 percent of the company's sales within the coming decade (Britt and Maqbool 1997, 3).

Lower per capita income usually translates into lower usage rates and smaller purchase amounts, and it might even suggest that products such as razor blades, chewing gum, and cigarettes be individually packaged, so that consumers with limited incomes can afford them. Coca-Cola, for example, began testing 200-milliliter bottles in several rural areas. Coke's normal size bottle is 300 milliliters, and the lower price for the smaller size bottle aimed to increase consumption.

Smaller sizes also may be more appropriate for countries where consumers shop daily or have smaller homes and thus fewer storage facilities. For example, superconcentrated versions of laundry detergents (Fab Ultra and Wisk Power Scoop) introduced to the U.S. marketplace have sold successfully for well over a decade in Europe and Japan, where space in both the supermarket and the home is at a premium. Larger packages are appropriate for markets where shopping is conducted on a weekly basis and storage space is ample.

The type of retail outlet in which the product is sold may further influence the packaging. Self-service retailing, which plays an increasingly important role in most developed countries, dictates that packaging perform a multitude of promotional functions as well—from attracting the consumer's attention, to describing product features, to making the ultimate sale. In markets with predominantly small retail outlets, with limited floor or shelf space, it may be appropriate to modify the packaging. In terms of legal restrictions, some countries do not allow the promotional tactics commonly employed in other markets.

Customer preferences, often shaped by culture, may influence whether packaging is persuasive to consumers in various markets. Utilizing the same or similar packaging employed in the home market may prove ineffective. It could be that a particular visual resonates well with consumers in one market but not another. For the introduction of cholesterol-lowering Benecol margarine, designers created a package that included a mountain scene to communicate cross-culturally that the product's key ingredient is natural. But designers left considerable room for differences in the product shot to accommodate local needs. For example, in the U.S. market the package for the spread featured an English muffin, as opposed to Europe, where rolls, which are more commonly consumed, were depicted (Asher 2001). Even the color of a product's packaging may prove problematic for a marketer. For example, while white connotes purity and cleanliness in many regions and cultures, in the Far East it is also associated with mourning. Likewise, red is a positive color in Denmark as well as many Asian countries, but it represents witchcraft and death in a number of African nations. Using the colors of the national flag may be perceived as patriotic in some countries, yet disallowed in others.

In many countries—both developing and developed—the usefulness of the packaging plays a greater role. Often the package will be kept and reused as a container. Lego, the Danish toy manufacturer, employed a standardized marketing philosophy in over 100 countries to sell its building blocks. In recent years, however, Lego has encountered stiff competition from look-alike and lower-priced rival products from Japan, the United States, and elsewhere. The *Harvard Business Review* describes Lego's dilemma—and its response:

In the United States, where the competition has been the fiercest, Tyco, a leading competitor, began putting its toys in plastic buckets that could be used for storage after each play. This utilitarian approach contrasted with Lego's elegant see-through cartons standardized worldwide. But American parents seemed to prefer the functional toys-in-a-bucket idea over cartons. Seeing a potential for serious damage, Lego's alarmed U.S. management sought permission from Denmark to package Lego toys in buckets. The head office flatly refused the request. The denial was based on seemingly sound arguments. The bucket idea could cheapen Lego's reputation for high quality. Moreover, the Lego bucket would rightly be seen as a "me too" defensive reaction from a renowned innovator. Finally, and perhaps most important, buckets would be a radical deviation from the company's policy of standardized marketing everywhere. Even U.S. consumer survey results comparing buckets favorably with cartons weren't considered a good enough reason for change from the global concept. Two years later, however, headquarters in Billund reversed itself. The impetus was a massive loss of U.S. market share to competitive goods sold in buckets. Soon after, the American subsidiary began marketing some of its toys in a newly designed bucket of its own. Now to the delight of many in Billund, the buckets are outselling the cartons, and the share erosion has reassuringly halted. Recently, the bucket was introduced worldwide and was a smashing success. (Kashani 1989, 91)

Ecological concerns are an additional variable that must be considered in evaluating product packaging. In some countries certain forms of packaging are either banned or not condoned by consumers, or else there is a market preference for specific packaging materials, such as glass instead of aluminum or tin, or paper rather than plastic. In Denmark, for instance, soft drinks may be sold only in glass bottles with refundable deposits, and in the United States consumers have been critical of styrofoam packaging used by fast food outlets. Virtually all deodorant manufacturers have done away with the secondary cardboard packaging to cut down on unnecessary packaging material. And consumers in many foreign markets are not accustomed to the elaborate packaging so commonly used in the United States, considering it quite wasteful. In many European countries, for example, shoppers bring their canvas or string totes to the grocery store in order to carry home purchases.

Labeling laws in many foreign countries are even more stringent than those in the United States. Governmental regulations may affect labeling with regard to a product's origin, name of the producer, weight, description of contents and ingredients, use of additives and preservatives, and dietetic information. Twice per year, the European Union issues "Designation of Origin" labels. To qualify, products must come from a specific geographic region. For example, only cows that graze within 75 miles of Parma can provide the raw materials for "real" Parmesan cheese. Bresse chickens must come from France's Bresse region, and Jamon Serrano (ham) can only be cured in Spain's Serrano. Supporters argue that the labels safeguard against fraud, such as when the Dutch sell grated gouda cheese as Parmesan. In addition, the labels also allow small-scale "artisan" producers to stay in business. "We want to protect traditional foods against imitators," notes Martine Poudelet, the European Union's Food Label Director (Echikson 1998). To enforce the laws, the government created a division of the Ministry of Agriculture called the Institut National de Appellations d' Origine (INAO). To date, there are

41 wines, cheeses, and other products on the EU's list of goods to be protected, but it has plans to seek protection at a later stage for 600 more regional quality products. On top of these, the EU awaits submissions of products peculiar to Cyprus, Malta, and Egypt as well as the Eastern European nations that will join the EU in mid 2004 (Ames, 2003).

The EU further plans to create a global register of geographically defined products that would ban producers from outside the traditional regions from using these names. Perhaps the most bitter trademark problems concern the United States. "Americans can call any fizzy white wine 'Champagne,' any white wine 'Chablis,' and any red wine 'Burgundy.' They must stop or we'll take legal action," notes Poudelet. The threats are serious. Major U.S. food and wine producers counter that the changes are unreasonable and don't come with reciprocal promises to protect U.S. designations, such as Idaho potatoes (Locke, 2003). The EU, however, is not alone in its attempts to protect regionally produced goods. India is keen to protect Darjeeling tea, Sri Lanka its Ceylon tea, Guatemala its Antigua coffee, and Switzerland its Etivaz cheese (Ames, 2003). Regardless of governmental restrictions, the label must be written in a language that local consumers will understand—and this typically means different labels for different markets. Marketers may attempt to get around this by printing multilingual labels. Many companies are trying to maximize profits by selling the same product in the same package in as many different countries as they can. Product information on a package of Procter & Gamble's (P&G) Ariel Futur laundry detergent, sold across the European continent, now appears in 10 languages, with English at the bottom of the list. As a result, it takes 10 times as many words to convey information to consumers. However, a package of P&G's Pampers diapers contains information in up to 20 languages, ranging from Hungarian to Hebrew. P&G has tried to ease the pressure on space by substituting pictograms for some of the information (Tomkins 2000). In some instances, bilinguality is legally mandated. For instance, products destined for Canada must carry product information in both English and French.

Differing levels of literacy may necessitate greater use of visuals rather than extensive copy. This commonplace practice proved to be quite perplexing for one major marketer. As David Ricks explains, the firm attempted to sell baby food to the indigenous peoples of one developing country by using its regular label showing a baby and stating the type of baby food in the jar. "Unfortunately, the local population took one look at the labels and interpreted them to mean the jars contained ground-up babies. Sales, of course, were terrible" (Ricks 1983, 34).

Place

Once foreign markets have been selected, the international marketer must determine the appropriate channels of distribution. These channels essentially connect the producer of the goods with the end consumer. Firms operating internationally must determine appropriate channels between nations—commonly called market entry channels—which involve movement of the product to the borders of foreign countries, as well as channels within nations—those that move the product from the foreign entry point to the final consumer. Channels between nations include indirect export, direct export, and manufacture abroad (which includes licensing, franchising, management contracting, foreign assembly, joint ventures, and direct investment). Channels within nations involve decisions regarding wholesalers and retailers.

Channels between Nations: Indirect Export

Exporting is the most common as well as the simplest means of foreign market entry. Firms lacking the resources to build or acquire factories abroad can penetrate foreign markets via this method, in which all goods are produced in the home market, and the international marketer may or may not choose to modify the product for consumers abroad. In indirect export the firm works with independent international marketing middlemen who are responsible for the distribution process. Because a wide variety of middlemen providing these services exists, only the most common methods of indirect exporting will be discussed.

Firms unwilling or unable to establish their own export departments may opt to enter foreign markets with the assistance of domestic sales organizations, better known as *export management companies* (EMCs). EMCs produce no goods of their own; instead, they act as export departments for several manufacturers of unrelated products. They may operate in one of two ways: (1) functioning as a distributor for the manufacturer or (2) serving as an agent of the domestic firm. As a distributor the EMC actually purchases products (takes title) from the domestic firm and then operates abroad on its own behalf. In an agency capacity the EMC's role is limited to establishing foreign contacts and developing foreign marketing strategies. As a distributor the EMC assumes greater risk but also has the opportunity to reap greater profits than it does acting as an agent. Because EMCs service a variety of clients, their mode of operation may vary from one domestic client to the next. Payment for services is made through commission, salary, or retainer plus commission. EMCs often specialize in a particular geographic area, enabling them to offer expertise to domestic corporations. More than 1,000 such firms currently operate in the United States.

Firms planning to conduct business abroad may also deal with *international trading companies,* which buy, sell, transport, and distribute goods. They may also provide financing, assist in the development of joint ventures, provide technical assistance, and even produce goods. They are typically the major suppliers of goods to the markets they serve. Trading companies hail from a number of different countries, including Japan, the United States, and even the CIS. Some of these trading companies were designed primarily for export, while others were originally developed to supply import services. Among the most famous export trading companies are the *sogo shosha* of Japan. Contrary to what most Americans believe, these firms actually import more into Japan from the United States than they export from Japan into the United States. Mitsui and Mitsubishi alone account for well over half of all Japan's imports. Some trading companies are region-specific, handling commodities produced in only one geographic area. Others are product-specific, handling only a limited variety of goods. Still others are industry-oriented, handling only goods specific to a particular industry, such as pharmaceuticals or chemicals.

There are certain advantages associated with utilizing the services of independent middlemen. A firm commits neither time nor money to set up an overseas sales force, and it can rely on the established contacts and marketing know-how of the middlemen operating within foreign markets. And because the indirect approach involves a good deal less investment on the part of the exporting company, it faces considerably less risk. On the downside, the exporter typically has little or no control over the distribution process. Should a product more profitable to the marketing middleman come along, the manufacturer's product may simply be dropped. Also, should sales in a market expand significantly, the exporting firm may find itself without the services of an EMC.

Channels between Nations: Direct Export

In contrast to indirect export, when a firm engages in direct export it does so without the assistance of intermediaries. The manufacturer is responsible for conducting any necessary market research; identifying, evaluating, and selecting foreign markets as well as agents or distributors to represent the firm in those markets; setting product prices; handling international shipping and insurance and preparing export documentation; and coordinating international promotional activities. While both the investment and the risk involved in direct export are greater, the marketer also has more control over the distribution process, which typically results in increased sales and higher profits. For example, bottlers of Equil, Indonesia's only natural mineral water, export their product to Singapore and even Australia. The water is bottled at the source from a mountain spring at the foot of a West Java mountain. Marketed in both sparkling and still varieties, the water is claimed to be free of contaminants and undergoes no processing. The product is said to have particular appeal among expatriates.

Channels between Nations: Manufacture Abroad

A variety of circumstances may prevent the international marketer from engaging in direct export. For example, tariffs or quotas may prevent a firm from selling its products in specific countries, or transportation costs may make products noncompetitive. Positive factors may also encourage a firm to produce its goods abroad. For instance, the size of some markets may justify setting up a plant in a foreign country, or local manufacture may allow the marketer to better respond to local market needs, or manufacturing costs may be lower in foreign markets. Foreign production can take the form of licensing, management contracting, foreign assembly, contract manufacturing, joint ownership, and direct investment.

Licensing One method of market entry is licensing, in which a company offers a licensee in the foreign market rights to a trademark or patent, the use of a manufacturing process, technical advice, or marketing skills. In exchange for the rights or know-how provided by the licensor, the licensee produces and markets the product and pays the licensor a fee or royalty, typically

TABLE 2.2 Top 10 Global Franchises

Rank	Franchise
1.	Subway
2.	Curves for Women
3.	McDonald's
4.	GNC Franchising Inc.
5.	Jani-King
6.	Baskin-Robbins USA Co.
7.	Taco Bell Corp.
8.	Mail Boxes Etc.
9.	Quizno's Franchise Co.
10.	Burger King Corp.

Source: Top Global Franchises, *Entrepreneur Magazine* (*http://www.entrepreneur.com/franzone/listings/topglobal/*).

related to the sales volume of the product. Franchising is a particular type of licensing agreement in which the franchisee typically operates under the name of the franchisor, who provides the franchisee with not only trademarks and know-how but also management and financial assistance. Table 2.2 lists the world's top 10 franchises.

Franchises have spread around the globe, and are affected by the same economic variables as domestic firms. The recent economic crisis in Russia prompted several major franchisors, such as Pizza Hut, Kentucky Fried Chicken, and Dunkin' Donuts, to scale back or leave the market. Yet at the same time, other franchisors reaffirmed their commitment to the market by investing even more money rather than divesting their ventures in the country. McDonald's invested $43 million in 1998 and earmarked an additional $100 million over the next three years—planning a total of 100 outlets.

To effectively penetrate the Russian market, McDonald's made a substantial investment in infrastructure and distribution channels. McDonald's invested in ancillary industries, including food processing facilities, a meat plant, a bakery, a potato plant, a dairy, and quality assurance labs, before opening its first store. Such investment ensures reliable sources of suppliers and proper channels of distribution. Clearly, McDonald's is showing a long-term investment perspective. U.S. franchisors are not alone in Russia. A large British-based pizza parlor chain, Pizza Express, also opened additional outlets in Moscow, and the Great Canadian Bagel Co., operating more than 200 outlets in North America, opened its first store in the same city (Alon and Banai 2000, 104).

A number of advantages are associated with licensing. It offers a quick and easy means of entry into foreign markets. It requires neither capital investment nor an in-depth understanding of the foreign market. In some instances licensing permits entry into markets that might otherwise be closed to imports or direct foreign investments. It can negate high transportation costs, which may make exports noncompetitive. Finally, it offers an alternate means to enter markets with high duty rates or import quotas. For many firms, licensing serves as an intermediate step in the road toward internationalization by providing a means to test foreign markets without an actual outlay of capital or management time.

However, licensing also entails potential disadvantages. The manufacturer has little control over the licensee or its production, distribution, or marketing of the product. From a revenue standpoint, licensing is unlikely to be as profitable as the returns that could be generated from a firm's own operations, as license fees are typically only a small percentage of sales— generally 3–5 percent. Licensing in no way guarantees a basis for future expansion into a market. In fact, when a licensing agreement expires, a firm may find it has created a competitor not only in the markets for which agreements were made but possibly in other markets as well. Firms intending to engage in licensing agreements also need to be aware that licensing regulations vary dramatically from country to country. Finally, there may be variations in restrictions regarding registration requirements, royalty and fee payments, and applicable taxes.

Management Contracting A firm may choose to enter a foreign market via management contracting. Here the domestic firm supplies the management know-how to a foreign firm willing to invest the capital. The domestic firm is compensated via management fees, a share of the profits, and sometimes the option to buy some share in the managed firm at a later date. Management contracting is a low-risk means of market entry that requires no capital investment, capitalizes on the domestic firm's management skills, and assures a quick return. Here, the local investor has a greater say in how the investment is managed. Profits, however, are not likely to be as great as if the firm were to undertake the entire venture. Management contracting is most commonly used in the following sectors: public utilities, tourism (hotels, for example), and agriculture in developing countries.

Foreign Assembly In foreign assembly a firm produces all or most of the product's components or ingredients domestically and then ships them to foreign markets for final assembly. Many products may be more easily shipped broken down, and transportation costs may also be lower as a result. In some instances tariffs prevent a firm from shipping a fully assembled product. By forcing assembly in the local markets, foreign governments increase local employment.

Contract Manufacturing Another option is contract manufacturing, which involves the actual production of a firm's product in a foreign market by another producer. Typically, the company placing the contract retains full control over both distribution and marketing of the goods. Benefits associated with contract manufacturing include limited local investment, potentially cheaper local labor, and the positive image associated with being locally produced. A marketer may also manufacture goods in one foreign country to be sold in yet another. Consider the case of Hennes & Mauritz (H&M), the Swedish retailer. H&M began its international expansion in 1976, the year it opened its store in London. By the end of 2002, H&M boasted 844 stores worldwide— 45 of which are located in the United States. The stores are geared to young, fashion-conscious females. H&M's formula for success is that they keep their fashions fresh and affordable. "That means spotting the trends even before the trendoids, turning ideas into affordable clothes and making apparel fly off the racks" (Capell and Khermouch 2002, 106). All merchandise is designed in-house. To keep costs down, the company outsources manufacturing to a network

of 900 garment shops located in 21 mostly low-wage countries, primarily Bangladesh, China, and Turkey. H&M constantly shifts production to ensure they get the best deals on manufacturing (Capel and Khermouch 2002, 106). On the downside, in some cases it may prove difficult to locate a foreign firm with the capability of manufacturing the product to the domestic firm's specifications. Extensive technical training of the subcontractor may be necessary, and even then, the firm has limited control over product quality. Here, too, at the end of a contract, the subcontractor may become a competitor. Types of products generally involved in such arrangements include electronics, textiles, and clothing.

Joint Ownership When two or more firms, in different countries, join forces to create a local business in which they share ownership and control of management, manufacturing, and marketing, they have joint ownership. An international firm may purchase interest in a foreign company, or the two parties may form an entirely new business venture. In some joint ventures each partner holds an equal share; in others, one partner holds the majority share. Equity can range anywhere between 10 and 90 percent.

Joint ownership offers the potential for greater profits as compared to contract manufacturing or licensing, and may also afford the international marketer greater control over production, distribution, and marketing activities. The national partner in a joint venture can offer the international marketer valuable knowledge about the local marketplace. The joint venture may also lead to better relationships with local organizations—government, local authorities, or labor unions. Finally, it may be the preferred option if 100 percent foreign equity ownership is not permitted by foreign governments. Mexico and India have traditionally been particularly restrictive about foreign firms owning more than 50 percent of any venture in their countries. In instances where political or other uncertainties call for some limitation of investment risks, joint ventures may be an appropriate entry method.

General Motors, which has long preferred solo operations abroad, has entered several joint ventures around the world, including one with Russia's top automaker, Avtovaz. The goal is to produce 75,000 sport-utility vehicles for local and international markets. Under a $388 million deal to manufacture Chevrolet Nivas, Avtovaz provided facilities, equipment, and know-how, while GM contributed mostly cash and some equipment. GM and Avtovaz each get a 41.5 percent stake in the joint venture, and the European Bank for Reconstruction and Development owns the remaining 17 percent of stock. The project is seen as a major victory for Russia's obsolescent auto industry, which has long been clamoring for foreign investment to help modernize aging equipment and develop new products to replace designs several decades old. The new Chevrolet Niva is a Russian-designed product, which will be sold at Avtovaz dealerships in Russia and GM dealerships abroad. There are plans to export the vehicle to Europe, the Middle East, Asia, and Latin America. No exports are planned for the United States or Canada. The least expensive Niva will cost about $8,000. The joint venture will employ 1,200 Russians and is set to reach full capacity by 2005 (Isachenkov 2002).

Certain drawbacks are associated with joint ownership. When compared with contract manufacturing or licensing, there is a greater investment of capital and management resources,

Figure 2.6 Russian Orthodox priests prepare to bless the assembly line for Chevy Niva sport-utility vehicles at the GM-Avtovaz joint venture in Togliatti, Russia.

as well as an increased level of risk. And, as with any partnership, the potential for conflict of interest always exists. The two parties may disagree about any or all of the marketing mix elements, as well as management style, research and development, personnel requirements, and the accumulation and distribution of profits. What is good for the national firms may not always be beneficial to the international company, and vice versa.

Direct Investment The greatest commitment a firm can make to a foreign market is direct investment, which involves entering a foreign market by developing foreign-based manufacturing facilities. The international firm has the option of obtaining foreign production facilities by acquiring an existing foreign producer or by establishing its own facilities. Acquisition is typically a quicker way for a firm to move into a new market, and it also offers the firm benefits such as built-in political know-how and expertise. For example, when Procter & Gamble first entered the Japanese market by absorbing a soap company, it also acquired a well-trained Japanese sales staff. Because it had, in fact, saved the Japanese firm from bankruptcy, P&G immediately established good relations with not only the staff but also the Japanese government. However, establishing a new facility may be preferable if the international firm is unable to find a national company willing to sell, or if the national government prohibits the sale of domestic companies. Establishing a new facility also allows the international firm to incorporate the most up-to-date technology and equipment.

Regardless of how acquired, foreign production facilities offer numerous advantages. Complete ownership means that 100 percent of the profits goes directly to the international firm. The firm keeps full control over its investment, and there is no possibility for conflict with a national partner. Foreign direct investment also allows corporations to sidestep trade barriers or tariffs and operate abroad as a domestic firm. Nationalism may also lead foreign customers to prefer locally produced goods and services. And, while some governments limit foreign investments, others actually offer incentives to international firms. For example, many governments are under increasing pressure to provide jobs for their citizens. As compared to direct or indirect exporting, the international firm may benefit from lower costs or increased availability in terms of natural or human resources. Mineral or agricultural resources may be more available in some foreign markets, and/or their costs may be lower than they are domestically. Similarly, a skilled work force may be more readily available and/or less costly. Figure 2.7 presents an advertisement that encourages international marketers to consider Singapore.

The major disadvantage associated with direct investment is that it requires substantial investments in terms of capital and management resources. This factor typically prevents smaller firms from engaging in this mode of market entry. The international firm also faces increased risks, such as devalued currencies or even expropriation, which is more likely to happen to wholly owned firms. The international environment is growing increasingly hostile toward full ownership by multinational companies. A major concern is equitable profit repatriation. Therefore, many governments insist that foreign firms engage in licensing or even joint ventures as a means of sharing in the profits obtained in the local market.

Channels within Nations: Distribution to Consumers

The particular market entry strategy a firm selects will impact its decisions about distribution channels within nations. On the one hand, firms that make their products available in foreign markets via indirect exporting and some forms of direct exporting must rely on the distribution channels selected by their intermediaries. Firms engaging in joint ventures or direct investments, on the other hand, will be responsible for evaluating and selecting from among the available channels of distribution within those nations. The specific distribution channels a firm selects within a particular country will impact many of the other marketing elements. For example, product prices will need to reflect markups allowed to middlemen; where and how the product is available to the end user will impact promotional tactics. Channel decisions also involve long-term commitments to foreign organizations that are often difficult to change.

In some instances the international marketer will be faced with distribution channels that are a good deal more complex than those in the home market. For example, a U.S. company marketing in Japan will need to deal with a frustrating maze of middlemen. Larry Rosenberg explains that, historically, Japan has been a country of numerous small retailers, typically located in residential areas and near train stations where local people could shop daily for food and other necessities. Dependency relationships developed between consumers and retailers, and patronage was rewarded by guarantees of a constant supply of high-quality products and good

Figure 2.7 Advertisement encouraging multinationals to consider Singapore as a destination for foreign production facilities.

service. Each retailer obtained goods from a long chain of middlemen, who in turn assured retailers of personalized service in exchange for continued patronage. Thus, dependency relationships developed along the entire chain from producer to consumer. The number of wholesalers and retailers is five times greater than in the United States. The sheer number of middlemen, in addition to the dependency relationships that have developed among them, makes it very difficult for foreigners to distribute goods in Japan (Rosenberg 1980, 47).

At the other extreme, an international marketer operating in a less developed country may well find that channels taken for granted in the home market simply do not exist. Or channels may have already been contracted on an exclusive basis to competitors. Under such circumstances the foreign investor may choose to lure away distributors by offering extra-high margins or other financial incentives. Other options include buying out local distributors or even building up parallel distribution channels from scratch. Finally, an international marketer may be forced to develop original methods of distribution.

Within-country channels of distribution—both wholesaling and retailing—vary greatly from one market to the next. These channels have typically evolved over many years and reflect differences not only in economic development but in culture as well. Each country poses a unique situation, and no general rules can be applied. The international marketer must carefully analyze the established distribution systems in order to uncover differences in the number, size, and types of middlemen, as well as the services they provide.

Channels within Nations: Wholesaling Abroad

Wholesaling patterns are typically reflective of the cultures and economies in which they operate. As a general rule, industrialized countries have many large-scale wholesaling organizations serving a large number of retailers. In contrast, in developing countries wholesaling is likely to be far more fragmented—smaller firms with fewer employees serving a limited number of retailers.

The spectrum of services offered by wholesalers typically relates to the size of their operations: the larger the wholesaler, the greater the variety of services it can provide. Larger wholesalers also generally have larger staffs available to assist the international firm. If it is necessary to utilize the services of a smaller wholesaler, this typically translates into greater responsibility for the international firm. Smaller wholesalers tend to carry less inventory, are less likely to provide adequate promotional efforts, and offer more limited geographic coverage than their larger counterparts.

Channels within Nations: Retailing Abroad

Differences in retailing from one international market to the next are at least as extensive as those in wholesaling. Here, too, the international marketer must carefully analyze each country to assess retailing opportunities as well as constraints. As with wholesaling, there is great variation in the number and size of retail operations in foreign markets and in the services they provide. Overall, the more developed the country, the more likely it is to have larger retail outlets. For

example, supermarkets and department stores are the norm in the United States, while hyper-markets—huge facilities stocked with thousands of products—are popular in many European countries. Carrefour, a French retailer that once had plans to open ten such hypermarkets in the United States, closed its superstores. Wal-Mart and Kmart also experimented with and then abandoned hypermarkets (Denitto 1993). Apparently, the seven-acre hypermarket that sells everything from groceries to auto supplies to refrigerators is just too large for U.S. consumers. In response to weary consumers who complained that the size of hypermarkets made it too difficult to go in and get just one item, Wal-Mart has built 49 "neighborhood markets"—gro-cery and general merchandise outlets covering a mere 39,000 square feet—in contrast to ear-lier mega-stores which were upward of 230,000 square feet (see Figure 2.8). Neighborhood markets are quick-stop stores with additional checkouts and nearby parking. Other retailers, including Home Depot and Staples, are also following suit. Another reason retailers are scal-ing down the size of their stores in the United States is because the number of good locations to position oversize outlets in many major markets is disappearing. Also, in some areas there may not be a large enough customer base to support the superstore concept (Green 2003).

Typically, the number of retail outlets per capita in developed countries is limited. However, even here there is variation. The United States and Germany both have approximately 6 shops per 1,000 people, while France has about 11 and Japan has 13. Developing countries have a much larger number of overall outlets, but these tend to be significantly smaller in size. Mom-and-pop outlets, open-air markets, or peddlers may be the norm. For example, retail outlets in many African countries may consist of no more than 200 square feet of selling space (*Advertising Age* 1992, 1). Table 2.3 shows some sample data on the number of retail outlets in both developed and developing markets. These charts demonstrate the significant variation in retailing from market to market.

In most developed countries, international firms can expect to receive the following ser-vices from retailers: stocking the product, displaying and promoting the merchandise, extend-ing credit to customers, providing service, and gathering market information. Because retail outlets are significantly smaller in developing countries, they typically carry very limited inven-tories. This may mean that the international firm cannot sell its full range of products, that

Figure 2.8 U.S. retail trend: Not-so-superstores.

TABLE 2.3 Total Number of Retail Outlets in Developed and Developing Markets, 2000

Developed Markets	No. of Markets	Developing Markets	No. of Markets
Canada	104,844	Brazil	1,595,062
France	369,609	China	19,306,801
Germany	419,229	Egypt	509,366
Japan	1,240,237	India	10,537,079
United Kingdom	311,844	Mexico	737,895
United States	685,367	Vietnam	727,269

Source: Euromonitor, International Marketing Data and Statistics 2002, 408; and *Euromonitor,* European Marketing Data and Statistics 2002, 266.

adequate display of products may be a challenge, and that the use of point-of-purchase displays will be limited. The smaller the retailer, the less likely it is to be able to offer customers credit or to service the product.

An ever-increasing number of retailers are operating at an international level. Although Woolworth's and Sears are considered the "old-timers" of international retailing, in recent years Wal-Mart, J. C. Penney, Home Depot, Kmart, Safeway, and Target have also ventured overseas. Table 2.4 lists the world's top 25 retailers, ranked by sales.

As of 2003, Wal-Mart is ranked the largest retailer in the world. Wal-Mart is mounting an audacious expansion that could double its sales within just five years, to $480 billion. Some of that growth will come in new markets abroad, where 1,200 stores in nine countries already account for about 16 percent of the chain store's sales. Even more growth will be won as the chain insinuates itself into more U.S. neighborhoods and invades more product categories. The chain has plans to expand from 3,400 U.S. locations today—half of them in the South—to a nationwide network approaching 5,000 stores within five years. While many consumers already think Wal-Mart sells just about everything already, the retailer is planning to add personal computers, ceiling fans, more fashionable clothing, gasoline, and even cars. "The goal is to have a 30 percent share of every major business they are in," notes Linda Kristiansen, a retail analyst for UBS Warbung Equity Research (Saporito et al. 2003).

Foreign retailers are also exploring U.S. soil, as U.S. consumer familiarity with brands like Benneton, Laura Ashley, and Ikea indicates. European grocery chains are also conquering the U.S. Belgian-based Delhaize Group operates more than 1,400 supermarkets along the U.S. east coast under the Food Lion, Hannaford, and Kash 'n' Karry store banners. Hot on the heels of Delhaize is Dutch-based Royal Ahold. In recent years, Ahold added Giant Food to its stable of stores, which includes Stop & Shop, BI-LO, Tops Markets, and Giant-Carlisle chains, totalling over 1,000 U.S. locations. Several other European firms have found niches in the United States. Aldi, a deep-discount grocery chain owned by Germany's Albrecht family, began operating in the Midwest in 1976, and now have 578 stores in 21 states. In the Internet grocery business, Italy's Parmalat, a food processing group known for its long-conservation milk and tomato products, purchased a 20 percent stake in NetGrocer and thereby established an outlet for selling some of its products (Lever 2001). The success of these international retailers suggests that this trend will continue.

Dynamics of International Advertising

TABLE 2.4 World's 25 Largest Retailers Ranked by Sales, 2001

Rank	Company Name	Country	Sector	Sales (U.S. million $)
1.	Wal-Mart	U.S.	Discount store/Wholesale Club	217,800
2.	Carrefour	France	Hypermarket	67,721
3.	Ahold	Netherlands	Supermarket/Hypermarket	64,902
4.	Home Depot	U.S.	Home Improvement	53,553
5.	Kroger	U.S.	Supermarket	50,098
6.	Metro AG	Germany	Diversified	48,264
7.	Target	U.S.	Discount Store/Department Store	39,175
8.	Albertson's	U.S.	Supermarket	37,931
9.	Tesco	U.K.	Supermarket/Hypermarket	37,378
10.	Sears, Roebuck	U.S.	Department Store/General	35,847
11.	Safeway	U.S.	Supermarket	34,301
12.	Costco	U.S.	Wholesale Club	34,137
13.	Rewe Gruppe	Germany	Diversified	33,640
14.	ITM Enterprises	France	Diversified	32,922
15.	J.C. Penney	U.S.	Department Store	32,004
16.	Aldi Gruppe	Germany	Food/Discount Store	30,000
17.	Edeka Gruppe (Ava)	Germany	Diversified	29,392
18.	J Sainsbury	U.K.	Supermarket/Hypermarket/DIY	27,121
19.	Pinault-Printemps Redoute	France	Diversified	27,079
20.	Walgreen	U.S.	Drug Store	24,623
21.	Leclerc	France	Diversified	24,195
22.	Auchan	France	Hypermarket/Diversified	23,478
23.	Tengleman Gruppe	Germany	Diversified	23,393
24.	CVS	U.S.	Drug Store	22,241
25.	Lowe's	U.S.	Home Improvement	22,111

Source: Chain Store Age, December 2002, 50.

Distribution Standardization versus Specialization

An international marketer will need to determine whether factors favor the utilization of uniform distribution patterns in foreign markets or whether a more specialized approach will be more profitable. A standardized approach may offer certain economies of scale. For example, if markets are sufficiently similar, the international marketing manager's skills in one market may be transferred to another. However, given the variation in the number, size, and nature of wholesalers and retailers described previously, a specialized approach may be the only viable option. And, if the market entry approaches vary from one market to another, the international marketer may have little choice but to adapt distribution efforts. For example, Kentucky Fried Chicken (KFC) was the first fast food outlet to enter the Japanese market. KFC and Mitsubishi established a 50–50 joint venture and opened the first KFC in 1970 at the Osaka Exposition; several additional restaurants were opened shortly thereafter. However, within a year after opening its doors, the local chain almost went bankrupt. KFC had made the mistake of locating its outlets in the suburbs and on highways, mimicking the U.S. model, only to learn that few Japanese had cars at the time. Only after putting aside the American distribution approach and beginning to open downtown outlets did KFC experience steady growth.

 Price

In pricing products, international marketers must determine whether to standardize prices in markets worldwide or to differentiate prices among countries. In setting a standard worldwide price, a firm establishes a uniform price for its product all around the world. However, that price may be too high for consumers in less-developed countries. For example, Western brands are usually higher-priced than domestic brands in transition economies. A pair of glasses at VisionExpress, now operating in Russia, costs about $60—half of what it costs in the United States, but more than 60 times what government stores charge (Alon and Banai 2000, 104). Starbucks recently opened its first store in Mexico. A major challenge will be getting Mexican consumers to pay U.S. style prices for coffee. A small cup of coffee at Starbucks's Mexico City store costs 16 pesos ($1.60) and specialty coffee drinks can run more than 50 pesos ($5). Mexicans are used to far lower prices, with a cup of coffee at a corner café usually costing less than 50 cents. Mexico's minimum wage is 43 pesos ($4.30) per day (Weissart 2002). Despite a high degree of price sensitivity in many developing markets, foreign brands nonetheless often remain competitive because of the high level of perceived quality and status that is associated with Western goods.

At other times the price may not be high enough for consumers in wealthier countries with higher levels of income. Here a marketer may opt to use a *differentiated pricing strategy,* in which price is based on a number of factors and not determined in isolation from the other marketing mix elements. For example, the prices of well-known household brands vary significantly across Europe, according to a major European commissioned study. The Internal Market Scoreboard Survey looked at 11 branded products in each of the 15 European Union countries. British consumers spend 70 percent more for a tube of Colgate toothpaste than do shoppers in Portugal and Spain, and they pay 80 percent more for Nivea shaving foam than the French. In Denmark, which along with Sweden is one of the most expensive European Union countries for grocery items, a Mars chocolate bar costs double what people pay in Belgium, and a bottle of Coca-Cola costs double the price in Germany. Heinz ketchup is twice as expensive in Italy as in Germany, and a bottle of Evian water costs four times as much in Finland as in France. The introduction of the euro has only highlighted these differences. No country is consistently expensive or cheap, but overall, Spain ranks the cheapest, followed by the Netherlands, Germany, and France. The United Kingdom is one of the more expensive countries, but Kellogg's cornflakes is a real bargain there, costing half what it does in Greece. In general, the richest countries tend to charge the most. However, Germany and the Netherlands, both with high per capita incomes, are exceptions. The survey found prices are influenced strongly by what type of retail outlet has a big market share. Countries such as Spain, France, and Germany, in which hypermarkets have a relatively

high market share, charge less. While variables such as market size, consumer tastes, landscape, and climate can explain some of the discrepancies, the survey concluded that the price differences are too large to be explained away by natural factors. Instead, the survey claims that the very large price differences for specific items suggest that producers exploit market fragmentation by operating different pricing policies in different national markets. There is still considerable scope for price convergence in the European Union (Bowes 2002).

A classic investigation found that, among U.S. multinational corporations, over two-thirds of consumer-nondurables marketers and almost 50 percent of industrial-products manufacturers adapted pricing to local conditions (Boddewyn 1976, 1).

This adaptation is justified on the grounds that local market considerations play such a significant role in setting product prices. Among the factors influencing pricing are corporate objectives, competition, consumer demand, and governmental and regulatory considerations.

Pricing Objectives and Strategies

International marketers may adjust pricing objectives based on the specific conditions of the markets they enter. Typical pricing objectives include profit maximization, return on an investment, and increases in total sales volume or market share. In pursuing pricing objectives, a firm may select from a variety of pricing strategies. The pricing strategy adopted will, in turn, impact the other marketing factors. A firm might engage in a market penetration strategy, which entails establishing a relatively low price with the goal of stimulating consumer interest. The firm accepts a lower per unit return in hopes of capturing a large share of the market and discouraging competition. Once a satisfactory level of market share is obtained, the firm typically raises prices to increase profitability. Penetration pricing is commonly employed with low-cost consumer products and tends to be most effective with price-sensitive consumers and in countries with significant manufacturing economies of scale.

In a situation in which either no or very few competitors exist, or in which consumers are willing to pay a high price, perhaps because a product is unique or innovative, marketers may opt to "skim the cream" from the market. The aim of a *market skimming* strategy is to obtain a premium price for a product—at least initially. This approach allows marketers to recoup research and development costs quickly as well as generate profits. Prices are typically reduced once competitors enter the market or in order to attract more price-conscious consumers.

If a number of competitors already exists in a given market or if a product is essentially undistinguishable from the competition, a firm may engage in *competitive pricing*. Here, a manufacturer sets product prices at or just below those of competitors. This approach requires constant monitoring of competitors' prices so the marketer can prominently display a lower price in promotional messages. In contrast, with a *prestige pricing* strategy, product prices are set high and remain high. Promotional messages are aimed at a select clientele who can afford to pay the higher prices, and product quality and service are highlighted.

Clearly, the actual cost involved in manufacturing, distributing, and promoting a product will play a role in the price charged. The actual costs may vary from country to country. If specific markets require product modifications, these will need to be calculated into the price of the product. The manufacturer will also need to calculate into the price any additional operational costs related to the export operation, such as transportation and insurance costs. Further, costs incurred in entering the foreign market—including taxes, duties, and tariffs—must also be taken into account. Finally, wholesaler and retailer markups must be considered.

The number and nature of competitors' manufacturing similar products or providing similar services will influence pricing decisions. The fewer the competitors, the greater the pricing flexibility. The intensity of demand for a certain product also impacts its price. Higher prices may be charged where demand is buoyant, and lower prices charged where demand is weak— even if production costs are the same in both instances. Total demand for a product is the net result of the combination of (1) consumer satisfaction derived from the product's "bundle of benefits," (2) the size of the market, and (3) the market's ability to purchase the product. Not only must consumers be willing to purchase a product, they must also be able to.

Governmental Influences on Pricing

Pricing is often one of the most heavily regulated areas in international marketing. Host countries have a variety of means to influence pricing. International marketers frequently encounter specified price markups, price ceilings, price freezes, restrictions on price changes, restrictions on acceptable profit margins, and government subsidies. The international marketer may also encounter governmental monopolies that control all international selling and buying. Further, tariffs and other government-controlled barriers force prices up for selected goods. Drug prices are often cheaper in Canada than in the United States—even for drugs produced by U.S. manufacturers. This is because pharmaceutical prices are governed by a governmental price ceiling. For example, Vioxx, a popular arthritis pain treatment, sells for 43 percent less in Canada. As a result, for the past few years, bands of renegade U.S. shoppers have piled onto buses to stock up on medications across the border. This has raised the issue of permitting drugs from U.S. manufacturers to be literally reimported into the United States from Canada, and the debate over whether reimportation would, in fact, reduce costs without compromising safety. The U.S. Congress is expected to take up the issue of cross-border sales late in 2003 (Calfee 2002).

Export Pricing

When U.S. firms export products to international markets, costs associated with freight and shipping, insurance, tariffs, taxes, storage fees, documentation costs, and middleman margins must all be added to the domestic price of the product. These costs typically inflate the final price to a level significantly higher than the price charged in domestic markets for the same product, in what is commonly known as price escalation. This higher price for the product may mean that it is out of line with domestically available substitutes—which, in turn, may have a negative impact on consumer demand. In some instances this may be offset by the fact that the foreign goods are perceived as exclusive. For example, U.S. consumers generally pay more for

French perfumes, German beers, and Italian leather shoes than for their domestic counterparts, yet demand still remains high.

On the other hand, a variety of factors may lead to a situation in which the imported product costs less than domestic goods. As noted previously, a desire to price products competitively may result in lower prices. In some instances, overproduction may necessitate moving product inventories; storage space may not be available, or products may be perishable. This may result in a price lower than that charged in the home market.

Numerous international firms also have been accused of dumping goods on foreign markets. *Dumping* refers to the selling of goods in foreign markets for less than they are sold in the home market or to setting the product price below the cost of production. In some cases this may be unintentional on the part of the international marketer. Some firms, however, intentionally sell at a loss in foreign markets in order to increase their market share. In many countries—including the United States—domestic firms may petition their governments to impose antidumping duties on imports alleged to be dumped. In another case where the United States and Canada are at odds, the issue is softwood, which is used to build houses. In the United States, about 30 percent of such softwood comes from Canada. In March 2002, the U.S. Department of Commerce announced it would slap a tariff of 29 percent on Canadian softwood, claiming that Canada subsidized its timber industry and dumped wood at prices that did not even cover production costs. Canada, of course, hotly denied this, arguing that they simply priced their timber competitively. While lower prices may be seen as a plus for consumers, dumping tends to have a devastating effect on domestic industries. When low-priced foreign goods flood a market, consumers purchase the imports and neglect domestic products. As a result, domestic manufacturers may be driven out of business, so that the home country loses a supplier in addition to jobs and tax revenues. Thus, while an industry may be protected via tariffs, consumers ultimately end up paying higher prices. As a result of the tariff on Canadian softwood, industry experts reckon the price of new homes in the United States will increase by as much as $1,500 (*Economist* 2002a, 26). In the first half of the 1990s, developed countries such as the United States, European Union members, and Australia and New Zealand initiated 63 percent of all antidumping proceedings worldwide, according to a recent study. However, from 1995–1999, the situation reversed, and developing countries initiated 59 percent of all antidumping proceedings (Lynch 2001). India, for example, initiated 170 antidumping investigations since 1999, one short of the United States's total. By contrast, it initiated a mere 15 investigations in the first half of the 1990s. This proliferation is unlikely to abate. Most observers reckon that China will become a big user of antidumping actions, as well as being on the receiving end (*Economist* 2002b).

Pricing and Manufacture Abroad

When goods are both produced and distributed within the foreign country, the various marketing objectives and strategies discussed previously apply as well. The marketer must take into account consumer demand and the competitive environment. However, firms must take additional factors into consideration in pricing goods. When goods are manufactured abroad,

foreign labor and material costs may be lower or higher than those in the home market, directly affecting overall production costs and, ultimately, product price.

Foreign governments in both developed and developing countries may impose price controls on goods produced within their borders. Should a firm wish to raise product prices, it typically must apply for a price increase and provide documentation supporting the request, which may or may not be granted. Such price controls can jeopardize not only the financial well-being but even the survival of a company. For example, Gerber began operations in Venezuela in the 1960s. Unprofitable operations forced the firm to close its doors in 1979. Gerber blamed price controls for its failure in the market—some of Gerber's products were still being sold at prices set more than 10 years earlier because the Venezuelan government had refused repeated requests for price increases.

Inflation rates around the world vary dramatically. In many foreign countries the rate is similar to that in the United States, or perhaps even lower. According to Globastat, the U.S. inflation rate is about 3.3 percent, while the inflation rate of Italy is 2.5 percent, and Taiwan's inflation rate is a mere 1.3 percent. However, in other countries, double- or even triple-figure inflation rates are not uncommon. In Venezuela inflation stands at 13.4 percent, in Yugoslavia 42 percent, and in the Congo an unbelievable 540 percent (Globastat 2003). Firms operating in such markets face a definite challenge in terms of pricing products. In countries with no price controls, pricing strategy involves raising prices frequently enough to keep pace with inflation. The situation becomes even more problematic when price controls are also imposed.

Promotion

Promotion is the fourth and final component in the marketing mix. Promotion includes advertising, sales promotion, public relations and publicity, and personal selling. In addition, the areas of direct marketing, sponsorships, trade fairs, and product integrations will be addressed.

Advertising

Advertising, according to the Definitions Committee of the American Marketing Association, "is any paid form of non-personal presentation and promotion of ideas, goods or services by an identified sponsor" (*Journal of Marketing* 1948, 202).

Several aspects of this definition deserve further explanation. The "paid" aspect refers to the fact that the advertiser must purchase time and space for the message. "Non-personal" indicates that the message appears in the mass media, which means there is little opportunity for feedback from the message receiver. Because of this, advertisers utilize research to determine how a specific target audience might interpret and respond to a message prior to its distribution. Finally, the "identified" aspect refers to the fact that the media require sponsors to identify themselves.

The role that advertising plays in a society differs from one market to the next. In Chapter 1 we examined countries in terms of their total advertising expenditures. In comparing the role

TABLE 2.5   Per Capita Advertising Expenditures in Selected Countries

Countries with Highest Spending	Per Capita (U.S. million $)	Countries with Lowest Spending	Per Capita (U.S. million $)
United States	534.8	Laos	0.9
Hong Kong	510.9	Pakistan	1.0
Puerto Rico	428.4	India	1.6
Switzerland	352.8	Vietnam	1.8
Japan	331.8	Cambodia	2.4
Norway	326.8	China	3.7
United Kingdom	270.6	Indonesia	4.9
Denmark	252.8	Philippines	6.5
Australia	235.8	Romania	7.9
Singapore	222.0	Saudi Arabia	7.5

Source: Zenith Media 2002.

of advertising in various nations, it is also useful to examine per capita advertising expenditures. Table 2.5 presents this measure for 2002—the most recent year for which data were collected. These figures demonstrate the significant variation from one country to the next. Advertising expenditures per capita range from a high of $534 for the United States and $510 for Hong Kong, to a low of $1.60 per person in India and a mere 90 cents per person in Laos.

As with the other marketing mix elements, advertising can be standardized (whereby the same advertising theme is employed for each foreign market) or specialized (in which case the messages are adapted for local markets). Agencies and advertisers alike are divided over the issue. While some agencies have jumped on the "globalization bandwagon," others remain committed to localization. Both Saatchi & Saatchi and BBD&O are believers in the global approach. Grey Advertising, on the other hand, suggests that each world business challenge is unique and, as a result, espouses "global vision with a local touch." Views regarding the effectiveness and practicality of the global approach to marketing messages are mixed. Exxon's "Put a tiger in your tank" theme, employed in many different markets, provided the firm with a uniform positioning across markets. Marlboro cigarettes are also advertised in much the same fashion around the globe. Other marketers, due to a variety of constraints, opt to modify their advertising campaigns. Often, themes or appeals used in the home market may not be appropriate for specific foreign audiences. In a classic example, Pepsodent attempted to sell its toothpaste in a remote area of Southeast Asia via a message that stressed how the toothpaste helped whiten teeth. Unfortunately, this campaign had little effect, as this was an area where many local people deliberately chewed betel nut in order to achieve darkly stained teeth—a sign of prestige. A variety of other factors may also limit the feasibility of standardized campaigns. The issue of standardization versus specialization of advertising will be dealt with in greater detail in Chapters 5 and 6. It should be noted here, however, that of all the elements of the marketing mix, advertising is generally acknowledged to be the most difficult to standardize (Boddewyn et al. 1986, 69).

In addition to strategic decisions, such as whether to standardize or specialize campaigns, the international marketer must decide on the appropriate message content. Advertising is

effective only if it is able to both gain the attention of the target audience and communicate the product benefits clearly. Creative considerations will be addressed in Chapter 6. If the target audience is to receive the advertising message, it must appear in the appropriate medium. Media decisions include whether to employ local or international media. Advertising media will be discussed in Chapter 7. Research guides both whom the advertising should be targeted to and what the content of the message should be. Creative appeals may be evaluated prior to dissemination to help predict whether the message appeals to the correct audience. Research is also undertaken after a campaign has run to determine whether objectives have been met. Research in the international setting is the focus of Chapter 8.

Sales Promotion

Sales promotion consists of a variety of techniques designed to support and complement both advertising and personal selling. The goal of sales promotion is to stimulate immediate consumer purchasing or dealer effectiveness. Cents-off coupons, premiums, samples, and point-of-purchase displays may induce trial purchase of products as well as maintain consumer loyalty. See Figure 2.9 for an example of an M&M's sales promotion effort for the Hong Kong marketplace. Sweepstakes and contests can create interest in and excitement about a company's product or service and increase the likelihood that its advertising campaigns will receive attention. Price deals, trade shows, and contests are typical trade promotion activities that may be directed at wholesalers, distributors, and retailers. The overall use of sales promotion efforts appears to be on the increase worldwide.

Here are just a few examples of successful, award-winning promotions from around the world:

- To fend off competition from top rival Kellogg's and increase its market share, Telma, Israel's No. 1 cornflakes brand, enlisted Israeli basketball star Oded Katash in its "Cornflakes for Champions" campaign. The athlete greeted consumers at family basketball competitions held in local youth centers. From the hundreds of families who entered, the winners advanced to play each other, and the ultimate winner played Katash in the finals at Superland amusement park in front of more than 10,000 spectators. The winning family provided a testimonial for boxes of Telma, with Katash appearing on the front. The cereal's sales rose almost 20 percent as a result of the promotion.
- Marketers hit Brazilian bars and clubs to promote Johnnie Walker, the country's best-selling whisky. In addition to on-premise samples, they placed an alphanumeric pager at each table. Every 30 minutes, calls were made to the pagers, awarding prizes to some Johnnie Walker drinkers and telling others to wait for a chance to win. The four-month promotion also used e-mail to spread the word about participating bars, a Web site with screensavers, virtual postcards, event photos, and a blind-date service that electronically matched up cybersurfers' profiles. The promotion generated 7,000 e-mail addresses and peaked consumption levels by as much as 120 percent.

Figure 2.9 M&M's sales-promotion effort appealing to consumers in Hong Kong.

- To create awareness for the relaunch of Philips' Softone colored light bulbs while boosting trial among young homeowners and generating repair purchases, marketers distributed two million "Yes Please" promotional bags to British households. The bags contained a glossy, 16-page brochure, a coupon, a questionnaire, and a creative offer for a free Softone light bulb. Recipients filled out the questionnaire, which included a spot for them to select one of the seven colored bulbs. They then hung the bag and questionnaire outside their front door. The next morning, the questionnaire was withdrawn from the bag and the desired light bulb—a short-life, 10 hour bulb made just for the promotion, was left behind. The 700,000 bulb requests resulted in a 35 percent response rate. Another eight percent of respondents redeemed the coupon, and 27 percent filled out the survey, supplying Philips with solid marketing information on a crop of new prospects. Brand awareness increased from 9 to 82 percent. (Estell 2001, 13)

While many companies effectively utilize sales promotion tools to help sell their products in foreign markets, marketers must be aware of potential pitfalls. Because of cultural differences among consumers, promotional incentives that have proven successful in the home market may not be as effective in foreign markets. For example, when Procter & Gamble mailed 580,000 free samples of Vidal Sassoon Wash & Go shampoo to consumers in Warsaw, it never expected an adverse reaction. The samples were in such demand that some Poles wrecked mailboxes to steal them. Following what was believed to be the first mass mailing of free samples in Poland, about 2,000 mailboxes—mostly in large urban areas—were broken into by people who wanted the samples either to use or to sell. The samples turned up at open markets, selling for 60 cents each. P&G has assured the Polish post office that it will pay for the damages (Gajewski 1991).

Differing legal restrictions and regulations from one country to the next may render some promotional efforts impossible while requiring that others be modified significantly. Such restrictions often mean that marketers must develop separate promotions for each country. Over the past few years, marketers and their agencies have experienced increasing frustration at the complex web of regulations regarding sales promotions in Europe. For example, in Germany, considered one of the most restrictive of the European Union nations, buy-one-get-one-free offers are illegal, and U.S. retailer Wal-Mart has already had to retreat on its favorite strategy of deep price cuts in this market. In France, on-pack premiums are restricted to seven percent of the product's value. In Belgium, retail sales can run only for a month and prices must not be cut by more than one-third. The European Commission is due to recommend a basis for a legal framework governing promotional marketing across the 15 members of the Union. There are two views on how the Commission will achieve its desired legal framework. One path would be mutual recognition, meaning that any promotion produced in one member country would be accepted as lawful throughout the European Union. The alternative would be harmonization—a common set of rules for the whole European Union (Gofton 2000, 60). The outcome still remains to be seen. The following are perceived to be quite liberal with regard to the regulation of premiums, gifts, and competitions: Australia, Canada, France, Hong Kong, Ireland, Malaysia, New Zealand, the Philippines, Singapore, Spain, Sweden, the United

Kingdom, and the United States. In contrast, Austria, Belgium, Denmark, Germany, Italy, Japan, Korea, Mexico, the Netherlands, Switzerland, and Venezuela are seen as significantly more restrictive. Because both industrialized and developing countries appear on each list, any attempt to generalize some meaning is useless.

Because distribution channels in foreign markets generally are different from those in the United States, promotions that rely heavily on retailer involvement and cooperation may not be effective. For example, while U.S. retailers commonly handle processing of coupons and the display of point-of-purchase materials, international marketers cannot assume that this level of assistance exists in foreign markets. In the United States, 70 percent of dollars spent on consumer promotions go into coupons. This is not the case in most foreign markets. Coupons are far less common—or even nonexistent—in other countries simply because the cultures don't accept them. For example, coupons are just now emerging in the United Kingdom, and retailers are being made aware of how to process them. In contrast, in Russia, coupons are still a few years down the road because there are no fulfilment houses to deal with them. As a result, sweepstakes tend to play a greater role in Russian promotional programs (Ryan 1995). Also, retailers in many foreign markets may be smaller in size or greater in number, and as a result it may be more difficult to contact them. With regard to promotions directed at both consumers and the trade, international marketers must study each country separately.

Public Relations

Public relations involves a variety of efforts to create and maintain a positive image of an organization with its various constituencies. Corporate public relations typically focuses on an organization's noncustomer constituencies, such as employees, stockholders, suppliers/distributors, governmental agencies, labor unions, the media, and various activist groups, as well as with the public at large. When the focus is specifically an organization's interactions with current and potential consumers, this marketing-oriented aspect of public relations is called marketing public relations, or MPR for short. MPR is defined as "the process of planning, executing and evaluating programs that encourage purchase and consumer satisfaction through credible communication of information and impressions that identify companies and their products with the needs, wants, concerns and interests of consumers" (Harris 1993, 12). In short, MPR supports marketing's product and sales focus by increasing the brand and company's credibility with consumers.

MPR is often further delineated as involving either proactive or reactive public relations (Goldman 1984, 16). *Proactive MPR* is offensively rather than defensively oriented and opportunistic rather than remedial. Proactive MPR is a tool for communicating a brand's merits, and is typically used in conjunction with advertising, sales promotion, and personal selling. Proactive MPR is typically employed when introducing a new product and announcing product revisions. Unilever provides an excellent example of proactive MPR. The company markets Cif, a household cleaning product, in 52 countries. In introducing Cif to the Argentine market, the manufacturer demonstrated the product's effectiveness by scrubbing clean the 35-year-old planetarium located in the city of Buenos Aires. Nueva Comunicacion, the brand's press and

public relations agency, organized the event. It included a print campaign. "Imagine what you can do in your home," the ads boasted below a picture of a sparkling-clean planetarium.

In contrast, reactive MPR is undertaken as a result of external pressures and challenges that might be brought on by competitive actions, shifts in consumer attitudes, changes in government policy, or other external influences. *Reactive MPR* generally deals with changes that have negative consequences for a company. An unanticipated marketplace event can place an organization in a vulnerable position, requiring reactive MPR (Shimp 2003, 569). One such event was Coca-Cola's contamination scare in Belgium in 1999. Up to 250 people became ill after consuming the allegedly contaminated soft drink. Coca-Cola's initial—and unfortunate—response was to deny the allegations. The public outcry was immediate. The media were no more supportive, claiming that Coca-Cola has literally poisoned its consumers. Coca-Cola's brand reputation and profitability were at stake. Coca-Cola finally admitted manufacturing mistakes at its bottling plants—apparently tainted carbon has been introduced into bottles of the product. Five countries—Belgium, France, Germany, Luxembourg, and the Netherlands—banned the product. Before the scare in Europe was over, millions of cans and bottles of Coke were taken off store shelves, a bottling plant in France was shut down, and the company lost up to $200 million. Management finally took action. Press releases touted the purity of the product and Coke distributed coupons for a free 1.5-liter bottle of the beverage to each of Belgium's 4 million households. Road shows, beach parties, and rock concerts followed. Interestingly, a subsequent European Union report found that neither carbon dioxide nor fungicide nor insecticide nor rat poison showed up in large enough amounts to cause health problems. Some researchers in the United States suspected that the symptoms suffered by the European consumers were partly in their heads. The EU, understandably loath to label its citizens hysterical, rejected this explanation, arguing instead that Coca-Cola had destroyed evidence. In turn, Coke denied the claim, pointing to their full cooperation with authorities (Goldman 1999). The issue remains unresolved. Clearly, even seemingly invincible brands aren't immune to disaster. And when a major crisis strikes, judicious public relations strategies are essential to saving the brand's image. A mismanaged crisis brings on the dreaded "Seven Plagues of Unhappy Repercussions": extended duration/negative press, angry customers and shareholders, lawsuits, government investigations, public interest groups, low employee morale/productivity, and a drop in stock price and earnings (Cohn 2000, 16).

Each plague begets another. The longer the story is covered, the bigger the hit to a company's reputation and bottom line. While a company doesn't necessarily get off scot-free when it manages a crisis well, the damage is relatively short-term in contrast to damage caused by a problem that is poorly managed.

Publicity, as part of the broader function of public relations, involves seeking favorable comments on the product/service or firm itself via news stories, editorials, or announcements in the mass media. In contrast to advertising, publicity is not directly paid for by the company, nor does the company have control over the content or frequency of the coverage. The advantages of such "free publicity" are both credibility and message length. Information conveyed through nonadvertising media are generally considered more credible by the public. In addition, a news or feature treatment of an issue is typically longer than a 30-second spot or an

advertisement in the print media. While publicity is an important communication technique employed in public relations, public relations practitioners have a number of additional tools at their disposal, such as newsletters and other publications, press conferences, company-sponsored events, and participation in community activities.

Public relations often plays a more critical role for a firm operating abroad than it does domestically. Clearly, international marketers face fewer problems if their firm is perceived positively in the country in which it operates. A variety of groups, including local governments, local media, and the general public, for example, may feel threatened by the presence of a foreign multinational in their country. Thus it is the responsibility of public relations personnel to position the firm as a good corporate citizen that is involved with and concerned about the future of the host country. This is often best accomplished via community involvement. Company management and employees may contribute to the community's social and economic development through participation in a variety of activities: civic and youth groups, cultural or recreational activities, charitable fundraising events, and so on.

Increasingly, companies involved in international marketing recognize the value of incorporating public relations to support and enhance their promotional efforts. Avon, Du Pont, G. D. Searle (manufacturer of NutraSweet), Johnson & Johnson, Combustion Engineering, and Union Carbide all have enlisted the aid of international public relations specialists. To meet this demand, public relations firms—like advertising agencies—are busy merging with or acquiring offices outside the United States. Table 2.6 ranks public relations companies by worldwide fee income.

Personal Selling

Personal selling involves individual, personal contact with the customer, with the intent of either making an immediate sale or developing a long-term relationship that will eventually result in a sale. Personal selling can take a variety of forms, including sales calls at a customer's place of business or a consumer's home, or customer assistance at a retail outlet. As such, it is often the most expensive element in the promotion mix on a per customer basis. In addition to such face-to-face contact, personal selling may also include contact through some form of telecommunication, such as telephone sales, which can help to reduce costs. Personal selling generally involves a greater degree of feedback than advertising, as the impact of the sales presentation often can be assessed directly through consumers' reactions. This provides a sales representative with the opportunity to tailor the presentation.

The international marketer may choose to utilize a traveling sales force based at the company headquarters or perhaps to manage a team of expatriates based abroad. This approach tends to be expensive and is often challenging. While the global marketplace has somewhat narrowed the differences in business culture between the United States and the rest of the world, key differences remain for salespersons. U.S.-based salespersons operating overseas must often contend with longer sales cycles in nearly every country. Even within the European continent, there are variations, which tend to delay the closing of sales. For example, German customers

TABLE 2.6 Top 25 Public Relations Firms

Rank	Public Relations Agency	Worldwide Fees (U.S. million $)
1.	Weber Shandwick Worldwide	$ 426.6
2.	Fleishman-Hillard	345.1
3.	Hill & Knowlton	325.1
4.	Incepta	266.0
5.	Burson-Marsteller	259.1
6.	Edelman Public Relations Worldwide	223.7
7.	Ketchem	185.2
8.	Porter Novelli	179.3
9.	GCI Group/APCO Worldwide	151.1
10.	Ogilvy Public Relations Worldwide	145.9
11.	Euro RSCG Corporate Communications	124.2
12.	Manning, Selvage & Lee	116.0
13.	Golin/Harris International	113.2
14.	Cordiant Communications Group	90.7
15.	Ruder Finn Group	80.3
16.	Brodeur Worldwide	70.0
17.	Waggener Edstrom	59.9
18.	Cohn and Wolfe	57.8
19.	Rowland Communications Worldwide	42.7
20.	Text 100 Public Relations	33.7
21.	Schwartz Communications	30.4
22.	MWW Group	29.3
23.	Publicis Dialog	28.6
24.	FitzGerald Communications	22.8
25.	Campbell & Co.	20.0

Source: Agency Report, *Advertising Age,* 22 April 2002.

tend to need strong reassurances in everything. They don't like risk. Notes Ute Zimmerman, president and founder of euroPRenence, a public relations firm with offices in Frankfurt and Boston:

> Forget about pointing out the product's new bells and whistles. Germans only want to hear about three product features: its bottom line benefits and how it will make life easier; that there will be strong service support for the product; and that the product is guaranteed. Germans are also fanatical when it comes to references. Instead of the two or three checks that an American executive would typically seek, Germans demand four, five, or six. As for closing a sale, all contracts are thoroughly reviewed by lawyers for both sides. In contrast, further south, in Spain and Italy, a salesperson should expect to spend more time on the social aspects of selling. U.S. salespeople may find themselves schmoozing not only the company decision maker, but his spouse, perhaps the children, and possibly even the extended family members, such as siblings, parents, aunts and uncles. (Bertagnoli 2001)

Because it typically involves both communication and personal contact, personal selling is closely linked to national or even regional cultural characteristics. As a result, personal selling activities are often conducted on a national basis. Most companies, regardless of their size, prefer to use sales representatives from the host country to staff their sales force. Even in the European Union, personal selling is slow to cross national borders. With few exceptions, a German salesperson will not be particularly effective in Holland, nor will a French salesperson have much luck persuading a Swiss consumer. Nationals are quite simply more readily accepted than foreigners, and they also are more familiar with their country. The challenge in utilizing a national sales force lies in recruitment and training, as well as in adapting personal selling activities to fit the local market.

Personal selling often plays a greater role in foreign than in domestic markets. Government restrictions on advertising, limitations in available media, and low literacy rates may cause marketers to turn to personal selling as a means of communicating with foreign customers. Lower wages in many developing countries may make personal selling a more cost-efficient method of selling as well. However, in other instances, personal selling, and in particular door-to-door sales, may be less acceptable abroad. Amway distributes home and personal care products in more than 80 countries, normally via its door-to-door sales force. For example, in the Japanese market, Amway's sales force of 800,000 generate yearly sales of ¥130 billion—or about $1.25 billion. However, in China, Amway sells its 112 types of cosmetics, nutritional, and personal care products in 58 outlets in 26 of the country's provinces and municipalities because Beijing authorities banned direct selling in 1998 in response to a growing number of illegal selling schemes and get-rich-quick scams. The Chinese government is drafting legislation to reintroduce direct selling by foreign companies following China's entry into the World Trade Organization. The rules are expected to go into effect in 2004. In the meantime, Amway has changed its distribution system in China, incorporating distributors into the company's service and training team and opening retail outlets. Goods are sold by "sales representatives," many of whom are former distributors (Madden 2001).

Direct Marketing

Traditionally, direct marketing has not been considered an element in the promotions mix. However, because of the increasingly important role direct marketing plays in the communications programs of many different kinds of organizations, it is included here. Indeed, direct marketing is currently growing faster than virtually any other form of promotion. The reasons for this are numerous. The widespread use of credit cards and the convenience of toll-free numbers have made it significantly easier for consumers in most markets to respond to direct marketing offers. From the marketer's perspective, the desire for greater accountability of the effectiveness of a promotional effort has encouraged the use of this approach. In most instances, messages are sent to a known individual, making it possible to track whether that customer did or did not respond. This is clearly a benefit that most advertising and promotions cannot offer. But probably the most significant recent advance has been the ability of firms to collect massive amounts of information about their customers via computer databases. The data are used to help marketers understand who their customers are and determine their likes and

dislikes and when they are most likely to purchase. Such information, of course, helps to increase the likelihood that those receiving a direct marketing offer will indeed respond.

Direct marketing refers to a way of doing business—one in which the marketer attempts to sell goods directly to the consumer without the aid of a wholesaler or retailer. Messages are designed to solicit a measurable response or transaction from the target audience. Direct marketing is seen as much more personal than advertising because it incorporates a degree of two-way communication. Direct marketers may employ a variety of media, placing such messages on the Internet, on radio and television, and in newspapers and magazines. Procter & Gamble, for example, launched a general-interest women's magazine in the French market, demonstrating the household giant's intention to diversify product advertising away from mass-media campaigns and toward greater use of direct marketing. P&G has mailed out 2.7 million copies of the new 52-page French-language magazine, titled *Mieux* (Better). It has announced tentative plans to publish the magazine twice yearly. Editorial content in *Mieux* mimics the conventional subjects of women's magazines, with articles on children, decoration, entertaining, and the kitchen. The magazine is heavy on product placement (which will be discussed in the following pages), with frequent mention of leading P&G brands such as Ariel, Dash, Mr. Clean, Swiffer, and Tampax. A coupon booklet distributed with the magazine offers about $20 of savings on P&G products, which provides ample opportunity for follow-up on the effectiveness of the mailing. "We definitely want to see how many of the coupons were used, for which products, and where," notes P&G Communications Director Christian Vivier de Vaugouin. This is the sort of information that allows us to move toward more of a one-to-one relationship with our consumers" (*Advertising Age Global Daily News* 2001).

Direct selling, direct mail, telemarketing, and catalog sales are also commonly employed in direct response campaigns. Otto Versand, the world's largest mail order retailer, for example, publishes more than 600 different catalogues each year for consumers around the globe. Together, the international fashion design house owned by Otto Versand, has launched a new women's clothing line called "Pure." Aimed at women older than 35 who appreciate fine, tailored clothing, Pure rolled out in the spring of 2003 with a 32-page catalogue that was distributed in 16 markets, including the United Kingdom, the United States, France, Germany, and Japan.

While direct marketing techniques may be quite sophisticated in many markets, in others they may play a minimal role or even be nonexistent. For example, direct marketing is a relatively new and as yet underdeveloped promotional tool in the Middle East. One of the real obstacles to the growth of direct marketing in the Middle East is the problem of names. Some Arabs don't use surnames in the Western sense; others describe themselves one way for ordinary purposes but use other names, including tribal connections and family antecedents, for official purposes. Another challenge relates to mailing lists. While there are many list owners in the region (such as shops, banks, airlines, and conference organizers), not much effort is put into updating or cleaning files. Although direct mailing to the general public may still be some way off as a viable promotional tool, it appears that business-to-business offers a significant opportunity. Directories of businesses and chamber of commerce membership lists are a good deal easier to come by than data on individual consumers.

 Sponsorships

Sponsorships are one of the fastest-growing forms of marketing today. Indeed, it is estimated that well over $20 billion are spent annually around the globe on sponsorships. Sponsorship marketing expanded by 10 percent worldwide in 2002 and expected to grow by a further 14 percent in 2003 (Costello 2003).

A number of reasons have been given for this tremendous growth in sponsorship activities: the escalating costs of traditional advertising media, the fragmentation of media audiences, the growing diversity in leisure activities, and the ability to reach targeted groups of people economically (Arens 2002, 248).

In addition, by attaching their names to special events and causes, companies are able to avoid the clutter inherent in traditional advertising media.

> Sponsorship involves two main activities: 1) an exchange between a sponsor (such as a brand) and a sponsee (such as a sporting event) whereby the latter receives a fee and the former obtains the right to associate itself with the activity sponsored and 2) the marketing of the association by the sponsor. Both activities are necessary if the sponsorship fee is to be a meaningful investment. (Cornwell and Maignan 1998)

The objectives of sponsorships include: increasing the awareness of a company and its brands, enhancing the corporate or brand image, and showing corporate responsibility. While the primary audience of current and potential consumers may be valuable, even more important may be the secondary audience. Sponsorships can be a powerful public relations tool. The company sponsoring an event may also be communicating with stockholders, community leaders, and employees.

The benefits of sponsorships were examined in a recent global study by WPP Group's Mediaedge:cia. The survey polled 12,000 consumers in 18 countries by telephone and over the Internet. Respondents were asked how much they notice sponsorships, whether they are influenced by them, and what their perceptions are about companies that do sponsorships. Fifty-three percent of male respondents said sports sponsorships strongly influence their buying habits; only 26 percent of women concurred. However, nearly 70 percent of women said they would buy a product if its maker sponsored a good cause, compared with 46 percent of men. Age also played a role. Slightly more than 40 percent of people aged 25–34 cited sports sponsorships as influencing purchases, and nearly 35 percent in that age group said sponsors are a factor in buying decisions. By contrast, 25 percent of respondents aged 35–44 and only 18 percent aged 45–55 said sponsorships were an influencing factor for them. Income was also a differentiator. Half of the respondents in households with incomes of more than $50,000 were aware of sponsors. However, mid-market households ($40,000–$50,000) were most likely to act on that awareness, with 40 percent indicating they would purchase products in response to a sponsorship (Kaplan 2002).

Sponsorships can take a variety of forms. The bulk of sponsorship dollars go to sports events (such as golf and tennis tournaments, motor sports, professional sports leagues or teams,

and, of course, the Olympics). Consider the Swatch Group, which recently signed an agreement with the International Olympic Committee to become its eighth Olympic Partners sponsor. The deal makes Swatch the official timing supplier, competition-results manager, and licensed merchandised sponsor for the period 2005–2008, which covers the 2006 Winter Games in Torino, Italy, and the 2008 Summer Games in Beijing. A sponsorship in the timekeeping category is generally considered the most visible, as the marketer's name is splashed across scoring devices everywhere from the ski slopes in winter to the swimming pool in summer. But, sports marketing expert David Carter, president of Los Angeles–based Sports Business Group, notes this sponsorship means even more to Swatch: "It gives them further legitimacy as a reliable timekeeper. In North America, people think of Swatch as a trendy watch from a decade ago. Clearly, it's about getting the message out on a global basis but it also helps authenticate their line as a reliable timepiece" (Thomaselli 2002). Like the seven other Olympic Partners sponsors—Coca-Cola Co., John Hancock, Eastman Kodak Co., Panasonic, Samsung Electronics, Schlumberger-Sema, and Visa USA, Swatch has global marketing rights and is expected to pay $50–$75 million per four-year Olympic cycle. Sponsorship of this event highlights two of the primary drawbacks of sponsorships in general. First, sponsorships can be quite costly—even in instances where events are cosponsored. Second, while cosponsoring an event may prove less expensive, a marketer must then contend with clutter. Indeed, some events have so many sponsors that no single sponsor's message ends up standing out.

Sponsors may also support entertainment attractions (rock concerts, for example, or the theater) or festivals, fairs, and annual events (such as the Macy's Thanksgiving Day Parade). Or companies may choose to form an alliance with a nonprofit organization. This is also known as *cause-related marketing*. Cause-related marketing allows firms to enhance their brands' images and sales while allowing nonprofit partners to obtain additional funding by aligning their causes with corporate sponsors. While the sponsored event or organization may be nonprofit, cause-related sponsorships are not the same as philanthropy. Philanthropy is support of a cause without any commercial incentive. Cause-related marketing is used to achieve specific commercial objectives.

Though there are several varieties of cause-related marketing, the most common form involves a company contributing to a designated cause every time a customer undertakes some action (such as buying a product or redeeming a coupon) that supports the company and its brands (Varadarajan and Menon 1988, 58). A fashionable brand of cosmetics provides an excellent example. M-A-C cosmetics, a unit of Estee Lauder, has distributed money to charities assisting people living with HIV/AIDS since the 1990s. As a by-product of its AIDS efforts, M-A-C has a best-selling lipstick, known as Viva Glam. All proceeds from Viva Glam sales, including counter reps' commissions, go to the M-A-C AIDS Fund, which has raised $16 million over the past four years—a tie M-A-C also promotes in its advertising. "We definitely believe the reason Viva Glam is our best seller is because it supports a charity," notes a M-A-C executive. "People care about being able to make a difference, even if they're just choosing one lipstick over another. As the face of AIDS has evolved, M-A-C now spends more time on the crisis outside the United States, targeting young people with education and prevention messages" (Bittar 2002, 18). Although cause-related marketing was initiated in the

United States during the early 1980s, marketers around the globe have become active participants in supporting causes.

Regardless of the form that a sponsorship takes, successful sponsorships require a meaningful fit among the brand, the event or cause, and the target market. Avon provides an excellent example. Avon, the world's leading direct seller of beauty and related products—with $5.7 billion in annual revenues—currently markets in 139 countries through 3.4 million independent sales representatives. Avon is committed to women through programs such the Avon Worldwide Fund for Women's Health, the Avon Global Women's Walking-Running Wellness Program, and Avon's Breast Cancer Crusade. Launched in 1993, the mission of the Avon Breast Cancer Crusade is to fund medical research into the possible prevention, diagnosis, treatment, and cure of breast cancer, and to provide women, particularly those who are medically underserved, with access to breast cancer education, early detection screening services, clinical care, financial assistance, and support services. The crusade has raised more than $250 million worldwide since 1993. Avon provides an industry model in terms of its visibility, continuity, and reinforcement of its mission as the "company for women." Notes Susan Heaney, director of Avon's crusade, "there should be a relationship or correlation between your business and the cause. Any kind of cause marketing needs to make sense; there needs to be a link to the core business" (Bittar 2002, 19). As a result of Avon's efforts, other advertisers have chosen to support the cause. See Figure 2.10 for a joint sponsorship encouraging consumers to purchase a 2002 Fold silk scarf, designed by Kate Spade and available at Bloomingdale's, to show their support.

Trade Fairs

Trade fairs or trade shows, as they are also known, are a temporary forum (usually lasting from several days to up to a month) for sellers of a product category to exhibit and demonstrate their wares to prospective buyers. Thousands of trade fairs are conducted annually around the world. Trade fairs play an even larger role abroad than they do in the United States—indeed, some of the world's largest trade fairs take place overseas (the Paris Air Show is an example). Trade fairs account for up to one-third of a typical Europeans firm's marketing budget. *Business America* publishes an annual listing of international trade fares where U.S. manufacturers can exhibit their products. Trade fairs have many functions, including:

1. servicing present customers;
2. identifying prospects;
3. introducing new or modified products;
4. gathering information about competitor's new products;
5. taking product orders;
6. enhancing the company's image. (Kerin & Cron 1987)

In addition, at the international level, trade fairs can prove invaluable to firms in the early stages of internationalizing their business, such as in exporting, as they offer a means of

Get Tied To The Cause

A Ford and Kate Spade Exclusive: Only at Bloomingdale's

You don't have to be a celebrity to get tied to the cause. Don't wait to join the fight against breast cancer—purchase your limited-edition 2002 Ford silk scarf (22″ x 22″), designed by **Kate Spade:**

- **online** at Bloomingdales.com
- **by phone** at (800) 777-0000
- **in-store** at Bloomingdale's department stores nationwide

Ford will donate all proceeds from each $25 scarf to the Susan G. Komen Breast Cancer Foundation (www.komen.org) and The Breast Cancer Research Foundation (www.bcrfcure.org).

Plus, free cotton bandannas featuring the Kate Spade breast cancer awareness design will continue to be available at the Ford tent at Susan G. Komen Breast Cancer Foundation Race for the Cure® events across the country (while supplies last). For more information and Race dates, visit www.fordvehicles.com/fordforce.

Win a Fashion Fantasy Weekend

Ford invites you to enter for a chance to submerge yourself in style on a trip for two to the fashion capital, New York City. Prize package includes:

- Behind-the-scenes tour of Kate Spade's studio
- Shopping spree at Bloomingdale's
- Tickets to a Broadway show
- Two nights' stay at the hip downtown hotel, The Mercer
- Plus, a Kate Spade carry-on and pajamas for the trip

To enter and for complete rules, visit www.fordvehicles.com/fordforce.

NO PURCHASE NECESSARY. Open to U.S. residents, age 18 and older who have Internet access as of August 8, 2002. Sweepstakes starts on August 8, 2002 and ends on December 31, 2002. Void where prohibited.

Ford: Putting the Brakes on Breast Cancer

Ford Division and its dealers are leaders in the drive to survive and taking a stand against breast cancer. Over the past eight years, Ford has dedicated more than $50 million toward awareness, education and survivor support programs. Please join Ford in its mission to help find a cure.

bloomingdale's

Figure 2.10 Ford, Kate Spade, and Bloomingdale's get tied to the cause.

checking out foreign markets. Exhibiting at trade fairs provides firms with a chance to explore market possibilities before making a commitment to an export country—particularly a developing country. Also, many countries offer subsidies to firms participating in joint sales efforts (de Mooij 1994, 371).

Potential distributors and agents are also likely to attend such fairs.

There are two main types of trade fairs. Some trade fairs are broad, general exhibitions, such as the Hanover Fair in Germany, with thousands of exhibitors in more than 20 industry categories, encompassing both consumer and industrial goods. These are considered "horizontal" trade fairs. In contrast, "vertical" trade fairs are often sponsored by a specific industry group or field (such as food products, automobiles, or toys). For example, at the Frankfurt Book Fair, over 300,000 titles are on display each year. The fair typically occupies about a dozen floors of five huge halls. In 2002, the space housed 6,375 exhibitor booths from 110 countries, with well over 250,000 visitors in attendance (Ashling 2002).

Trade fairs are not the only means of exhibiting products overseas. Manufacturers may also rent space in trade centers to display their merchandise on a more permanent basis. Vienna and Taipei are examples of two such trade centers. Figure 2.11 shows an advertisement promoting the Taipei World Trade Center.

A recent innovation is the online trade fair or digital trade fair. "The traditional trade show is typically conducted at a convention center in a major city. As noted in the example above, representatives for the multitude of exhibitors along with hundreds, if not thousands, of potential customers travel to the trade show site to participate in the event. Needless to say, millions of dollars are invested in renting space, setting up exhibits, travelling, lodging, dining, and so on. The online trade show eliminates most of these expenses, a significant benefit. On the downside, such online trade fairs lack the opportunity for physically inspecting products and interacting with trade-show exhibitors on a personal, one-to-one basis. Online trade shows will not eliminate their traditional counterparts, but this would appear to be a growth area" (Shimp 2003, 514).

Product Integration

Heralded by many as the next big development in marketing, consumer-product integration into media content, such as TV, films, video games, and even music, is showing increasingly positive results. Originally known as product placement, the tactic is now beginning to go under the moniker of "product integration" (Fitzgerald 2003). In the United States, product placement in television literally dates back to the 1940s, when shows such as Texaco Star Theatre and The Colgate Comedy Hour were funded by advertisers. Back then, there were no separate commercials. Instead, the star of the show would break off to plug the sponsor's product. The system worked well as long as there were only three television networks because advertisers were rewarded with enormous viewing figures. But as more channels were created, the economics of solo sponsorship were undermined by fragmenting audiences and rising production costs. Eventually the networks took over program production and introduced the concept of the multi-advertiser commercial break. Now, economics are undermining the system again. With hundreds

Figure 2.11 Print advertisement promoting the Taipei World Trade Center.

of channels being created, heavy demand for programming is raising the cost of advertising while audiences per channel decline. As a result, the financially squeezed networks are having to rethink the rules that until recently kept advertisers out of programs (Tomkins 2002).

Product placement is also being driven by advertisers' concerns. Advertisers' confidence in the effectiveness of the traditional 30-second spot is waning, based in good part on the findings of a recent Roper poll. The Roper survey revealed that 39 percent of Americans said they "often" switch to another channel when ads come on, a figure that is up 25 points from 1985. Another 19 percent said they turn down the TV or mute it, a 10-point increase. In fact, one of the fastest growing gadgets respondents said they can't live without is the remote control, which 44 percent consider a necessity (only 23 percent did in 1992). And 76 percent feel advertising is "shown in far too many places now, you can't get away from it," a response that jumped 10 points since just 1998 (Ebenkamp 2001). Sprinkled into the mix is the fear of new technology that allows viewers to eliminate television commercials altogether. TiVo and Sonicblue of the United States have introduced digital videocassette recorders with internal hard drives instead of cassette tapes, allowing commercials to be skipped or eliminated with a click or two of the remote control. So far, only 1.3 million U.S. households have digital VCRs, but analysts predict the number could soar to 38.9 million—or 35 percent of U.S. households by 2007, as satellite and cable operators incorporate the technology into their set-top boxes (Tomkins 2002).

While permissible in films, technically, payment in exchange for product placement on television is illegal. The federal communication code requires broadcasters to acknowledge any paid promotions in their program credits. Brand name products can appear in TV shows without acknowledgement only if the manufacturer has not paid for airtime and if the products are "reasonably related" to the content of the show (Jacobson and Mazur 1995, 71). But advertisers have found ways to get around the rules. Today the deals are coming in under the euphemisms of product integration and marketing partnerships. In ABC's version of the British quiz show *Who Wants to Be a Millionaire?*, for example, AT&T sponsored the program and bought advertising spots during the commercial breaks. Host Regis Philbin even invoked "our friends at AT&T" when contestants phoned a friend for help in answering a question and an AT&T clock timed the 30-second call.

Some advertisers are not only placing their products in television programs but also making the programs. For example, Johnson & Johnson premiered *Door to Door*, a two-hour, made-for-television film on Turner Network Television. For advertisers, the benefits of creating a program go beyond simply having their name on it. They can interweave their products subtly into the plot, take the best advertising spots for themselves, bar rivals from taking any of the rest, and, above all, make sure the program projects positive values and thereby reinforces their brand values in consumer's minds. The question is whether product placement has any measurable effect on sales. New York–based iTVX uses a system of variables to measure product placement's impact, which can range from 20 percent of the impact of a TV spot to five times higher than a viewer's impression of an average spot.

Product placements have also appeared in films for decades. However, until relatively recently, product plugs were the result of an informal barter system between advertisers and film

producers. In exchange for featuring a particular brand of auto in a movie, for example, the auto manufacturer would provide wheels for the film's stars during the shoot. However, paid product placements were pioneered in the 1980s, and Steven Spielberg's 1982 film *E.T.* is widely credited with starting the trend—a trend that turned out to be quite profitable to the advertiser. When the alien in *E.T.* nibbled on Reese's Pieces onscreen, sales of the candy soared by over 60 percent. While in the past, a film might have one or two such "sponsors," today's films boast literally dozens. The recent James Bond film *Die Another Day* features James Bond driving an Aston Martin, checking the time on his Omeda Seamaster, mixing his martini with Finlandia, flying on British Airways, and toasting with Bollinger champagne—risking allegations that the Bond films are becoming little more than extended product ads.

But for many companies seeking to reach a global audience, an international box office smash can prove far more effective and efficient than domestically produced ads. Today there are dozens of agencies—both in the United States and abroad—that arrange cash deals between filmmakers and corporate sponsors. A corporation will typically retain a product-placement agency for an annual fee, then pay for each placement in a film. Placement fees vary according to the prominence of the plug. Variables include whether the product is used in the background or foreground, whether a character in the program touches the product, wears the product, or talks about the product, and whether it is featured in a product-centered episode (such as the *Seinfeld* Junior Mint episode) (Fitzgerald 2003). Clearly, the more prominent the placement, the greater the impact on brand name awareness and recall.

A number of factors are driving the trend toward product integration in Latin America, Asia, and Europe, but these factors vary on a market-by-market basis. For example, in Argentina, ad spending is down 50 percent, and broadcasters are having trouble paying for programs to fill their schedules. In this economy, branded content ideas are inspired by survival as much as by a commitment to innovation. Brazil is using product placements in TV shows to hype products for export to other countries. The idea is to use Brazil's soap operas, which are shown around the world, to promote Brazilian coffee and soft drinks, clothing, and even jet planes. The soap opera *Esperanca* (Portuguese for "hope") already incorporates the quality of Brazilian coffee in its plot and is slated for international program sales. The cost of such initiatives is split between industry trade associations and the government's Agency of Export Promotion.

Marketers in India face an entirely different challenge. Here, many rural consumers lack TV reception, making it difficult to reach them with this medium. However, the country boasts the world's largest movie industry, with more than 1,000 films being produced each year. Thus it makes sense for marketers to focus on placement in films. In 2001 Publicis Group's Leo Burnett Worldwide opened Leo Entertainment, specializing in creating ads to promote films and arranging product placement in movies. One of Leo Entertainment's first big projects was the film *Kaante* (Hindi for "thorns"). It was a natural fit for Burnett client Coca-Cola Co., which had been looking for ways to enhance the macho image of Thums Up, India's leading cola brand. *Kaante,* in which a gang of six Indians plan the perfect bank robbery in Los Angeles, has the image Thums Up wanted. Thums Up has a more macho, rugged appeal than Coca-Cola or Pepsi.

During the movie, the bank robbers drink Thums Up, the cola's logo is visible on a tote bag used in the heist, and the robbers use the "thumbs up" gesture. According to Leo Entertainment, "it is very subliminal, very natural in the film." In Europe, a number of countries, such as Britain and Germany, forbid product placements in regular TV shows. As a result, agencies and advertisers have been busy creating ideas for program specials, which are permitted (Britt 2002, 18). So far, the blurring of advertising with programming worldwide is in its infancy, but all indications suggest that consumers will be seeing a lot more product integration in the future.

IIII Integrated Marketing Communications

Until quite recently, most firms planned and managed their marketing and promotions functions separately. Increasingly, however, companies are moving toward integrated marketing communications. The American Association of Advertising Agencies defines integrated marketing communications (IMC) as:

> a concept of marketing communications planning that recognizes the added value of a comprehensive plan that evaluates the strategic roles of a variety of communication disciplines, e.g., general advertising, direct response, sales promotion and public relations—and combines these disciplines to provide clarity, consistency and maximum impact. (Duncan and Everett 1993, 30)

A major benefit associated with IMC is synergism, "meaning that the individual efforts are mutually reinforced with the resulting effect being greater than if each functional area had selected its own targets, chosen its own message strategy, and set its own media schedule and timing" (Novelli 1990, 7).

However, even this view of IMC is too narrow. Researchers and practitioners alike have noted that the messages consumers receive about a company and its products are not limited to advertisements, direct marketing efforts, publicity, and sales promotions. Rather, claim Don Schultz and colleagues, "almost everything the marketer does relates to or provides some form of communication to customers and prospects, from the design of the product through the packaging and distribution channel selected. These product contacts communicate something about the value and the person for whom the product was designed" (Schultz et al. 1994, 45).

The kind of customer service that is provided after the product is purchased also sends a message to consumers. Thus the other elements of the marketing mix—which have typically been isolated from the communication strategy—are, in fact, sources of information for the consumer as well. In addition, the target audience may gather information about a product or service from conversations with friends, relatives, and co-workers. Even retailers and the media have something to say about a manufacturer's product. According to Schultz and colleagues, "The marketer has very limited control over much of the information and data that the consumer receives. . . . That's why it's so critical for marketers to maintain some sort of control over the communication they initiate or influence" (Schultz et al. 1994, 45).

IMC, then, is all about managing the various contacts a firm has with its customers, since each of these contacts potentially influences consumer behavior. In order to better manage these contacts, the firm actively solicits responses from consumers. Response solicitation devices may include a telephone call, a direct mail flyer, a purchase warranty card, or some other form through which the consumer can engage in two-way communications with the manufacturer. Response information is then stored in a database (along with demographic and psychographic data), providing the marketer with the necessary feedback to adjust future communications.

Schultz and colleagues note: "In short, marketing is communication and communication is marketing. The two are inseparable. And, for that reason, the proper integration of all marketing messages is that much more important" (Schultz et al. 1994, 45).

Because IMC was developed in the United States, initially it was predominantly practiced by innovative American firms such as IBM and Eastman Kodak. Today, an ever-increasing number of marketers are exploring the benefits that IMC has to offer. However, respondents to a recent survey conducted for *Advertising Age* reveal that few have actually achieved integration in practice (Atkinson 2003, 1).

The survey, which polled 208 judges of the Effies—an award presented to the most effective marketing campaigns of the year—gathered the views of ad agencies, major marketers, media companies, and specialist-marketing firms. The respondents agreed that cross-discipline strategies are often a nightmare to execute and difficult to measure effectively. Interestingly, most ad agencies cited consistent execution as the biggest problem, while most clients pointed to measurement as their biggest headache.

Despite the challenges associated with implementing a fully integrated marketing communications program, most marketers today consider themselves proponents of the approach, and the benefits of IMC are just as applicable when operating in the global marketplace as in the domestic marketplace. In *Communicating Globally: An Integrated Marketing Approach*, authors Don Schultz and Philip Kitchen outline an eight-step integrated global marketing communication planning process:

Step 1: Global Customer/Prospect Databases. The authors note that a key ingredient in this approach to developing effective and efficient global marketing communication programs is substantive, continually updated knowledge about customers and prospects. Such information typically comes from databases that the organization maintains. Of particular value is capturing and using information that describes or illustrates the relationship the corporation has with a customer (this includes data on purchases, inquiries, responses to promotions, and any other behavioral data).

Step 2: Customer Prospect Valuation. Ideally, an organization should invest its finite resources in cultivating its best prospects. Thus some means of valuing each prospect is essential, and Schultz and Kitchen propose that the best way to value such potential consumers is financially. If the marketer has a sense of how much income a prospect might generate in the future, it can determine how much it is willing to invest to acquire that prospect and turn him or her into a customer.

Step 3: Contact Points and Preferences. The marketer should attempt to audit and value the various ways in which customers come into contact with an organization. Such contacts can come about not only through traditional advertising, but also through employees, channel partners, or other means. Then each of those contact points can be viewed as useful methods of communicating in the future.

Step 4: Brand or Organization Relationships. The authors note a common practice for many global organizations to treat every customer as if they were the same—for example, by preparing a single advertisement and, using a variety of media, sending it out to everyone in the target audience. But relationships with customers vary, so the astute marketer will understand these differing relationships and apply this information in developing effective marketing communication programs.

Step 5: Message and Incentive Development and Delivery. At the heart of integrated marketing communication is the premise that you can't develop effective communications unless you understand the audience you are trying to communicate with. And these messages must be communicated via appropriate delivery systems—which may be the traditional forms of media (print, broadcast, direct mail, etc.), but should be looked at more broadly to include unique forms of delivery as well.

Step 6: Estimate on Return on Customer Investment. A marketer's next step is to estimate what type of return or response might be generated from the firm's marketing activities. Clearly, the better the customers or prospects the marketer chooses to invest in, the better the return will be. By knowing the value of the prospects (Step 2) and what the investments in communications are, it becomes possible to estimate what type of return might be generated.

Step 7: Investment and Allocation. The next step in the process is the actual determination of financial investment the firm plans to make in customers and prospects. This involves matching up the costs of various marketing communication activities and testing them against estimated returns. For example, if a message needs to be delivered to a specific group, the marketer must determine whether media advertising, direct marketing approaches, or in-store point-of-purchase efforts will provide the best returns on investment.

Step 8: Marketplace Measurement. The final step is to set up systems of measurement to determine marketplace results. This involves determining what the marketer got back for its investment in various prospects and just how long it took to achieve those returns. This information is then input back into the customer/prospect database. Schultz and Kitchen note that this closed-loop, circular system is what really differentiates the integrated marketing communication approach. "Only by using actual marketplace results as the basis for our next planning cycle can we truly become a learning organization. Knowing what worked and what didn't work, knowing what performed up to expectations and what didn't enables us to become better, more effective integrated global marketing communication managers. We can't succeed unless we close the loop." (Schultz and Kitchen 2000, 85)

Royal Caribbean International provides an example of a savvy marketer employing an integrated marketing effort. Their IMC program is designed to support Royal Caribbean's

expanded cruise vacation offerings in Europe in 2003 and further reinforce the company's leadership in the region. The campaign features a series of print advertisements that humorously connect onshore and onboard experiences available to Royal Caribbean guests by depicting well-known sites in Europe along with paper stubs from ship activities. One ad pairs a photo of the Sistine Chapel's famed ceiling with an appointment card for a neck massage in the ship's spa. Another matches the sculpted backside of a Michelangelo statue in the Louvre with a reminder to attend a spinning class in the ship's fitness center. Beyond the print ads, the campaign also includes consumer outreach through direct mail, Royal Caribbean's Crown and Anchor loyalty program newsletter, and public relations efforts. Guests cruising with Royal Caribbean are able to learn more about the European itineraries through an in-stateroom video. In addition, interactive aspects of the European campaign appear on Royal Caribbean's Web site. For the trade, Royal Caribbean is conducting a travel agent sweepstakes in which agents can win a variety of prizes, including a 12-night Mediterranean cruise-tour, a 12-night Mediterranean/ Greek Isles or Scandinavia/Russia cruise, a 7-night Mediterranean cruise, or a $200 MasterCard Web certificate. Trade ads, retail posters, a video, and e-mail communications further reinforce Royal Caribbean's European offerings with agents (*PR Newswire* 2002).

Summary

Although the focus of this text is on advertising, the international marketer must realize that decisions relating to advertising in the international arena cannot be made without regard to other promotions efforts or the remaining elements of the marketing mix. From the international marketer's perspective the elements of the marketing mix are generally seen as the "controllable elements" of the marketing decision. This is the case with both domestic and international marketing. However, international marketers must also deal with a number of elements outside their control when they enter a foreign market. Product, price, distribution, and promotion decisions must be made within a framework of several uncontrollable elements of the specific marketplace—what is commonly known as the marketing environment. Although marketing principles are universally applicable, the environment within which the marketer must implement the marketing plan can and usually does change dramatically from country to country. Thus we turn our attention to this topic in Chapter 3.

References

Advertising Age. 1992. Ad Age International and Audits & Surveys examine retail distribution patterns around the world. 22 June, 1–12.

Advertising Age Global Daily News. 2001. P&G launches women's magazine in France. 10 January. < www.adageglobal.com/cgi-bin/daily.pl?daily_id=4187&post_date=2001–01–10>

Advertising Age. 2002. Agency Report. 22 April.

Adweek. 1994. We're Number 1—At least we are in Nicaragua. 21 February, 15.

Alon, Ilan, and Moshe Banai. 2000. Executive insights: Franchising opportunities and threats in Russia. *Journal of International Marketing.* 8(3): 104–19.

American Marketing Association. 1960. *Marketing definitions: A glossary of marketing terms.* Compiled by the Committee on Definitions. Chicago.

Ames, Paul. 2003 EU proposes regional food list. *San Diego Union Tribune.* 29 August, C-3.

Arens, William F. 2002. *Contemporary Advertising.* Boston: McGraw-Hill Irwin. 8th ed.

Asher, Jonathan. 2001. Global branding: Same but different. *Brandweek,* 9 April, 25.

Ashling, Jim. 2002. The world's largest book fair. *Information Today,* December, 50.

Atkinson, Claire 2003. Integration still a pipe dream for many. *Advertising Age,* 10 March, 1.

Bertagnoli, Lisa. 2001. Selling overseas complex endeavor. *Marketing News,* 30 July, 4.

Bittar, Christine. 2002. Seeking cause and effect. *Brandweek,* 11 November, 18–24.

Boddewyn, J.J. 1976. American marketing in the European Common Market 1963–1973. In *Multicultural Product Management.* Cambridge: Marketing Science Institute, 1–25.

Boddewyn, J. J., Robin Soehl, and Jacques Picard. 1986. Standardization in international marketing: Is Ted Levitt in fact right? *Business Horizons.* 29: (November/December): 69–75.

Bowes, Elena. 2002. Where's the cheapest Coke in Europe? EC study investigates. *Advertising Age Global Daily News,* 30 May. <www.adageglobal.com/cgi-bin/daily.pl?daily_id=7663&post_date=2002–05–30.>

Britt, Bill and Mir Maqboll. 1997. Unilever tests small sizes. *Advertising Age,* 10 March, 3.

Britt, Bill. 2002. Content, commerce deals offer answers in overseas markets. *Advertising Age,* 21 October, 18.

Britt, Stuart Henderson. 1974. Standardizing marketing for the international market. *Columbia Journal of World Business* 9 (Winter): 32–40.

Buzzell, Robert D. 1968. Can you standardize multinational marketing? *Harvard Business Review* 6 (November/December):

Cahn, Kim, and R.A. Mauborgne. 1987. Cross cultural strategies. *Journal of Business Strategy* 7 (Spring): 31.

Calfee, John. 2002. Why drugs from Canada won't cut prices. *Consumer's Research Magazine,* November, 10.

Capell, Kerry, and Gerry Khermouch. 2002. Hip H & M. *Business Week,* 11 November, 106–10.

Chain Store Age. 2002. World's 25 largest Retailers Ranked by Sales. December. 50.

Chartrand, Sabra. 2002. After 13 years of ruminating, the U.S. agrees to join a global trademark system. *New York Times,* 16 December, C-16.

Chen, Wu, and Ya Quin. 2003. Microsoft's long march. *Forbes,* 17 February, 78.

Cohn, Robin. 2000. Crisis readiness: Insurance for your reputation. *Directorship,* September, 16.

Cornwell, Bettina, and Isabelle Maignan. 1998. An international review of sponsorship research. *Journal of Advertising.* 27 (1): (Spring): 11.

Costello, Rose. 2003. And now, a word from the sponsors. *Sunday Times* (London), 19 January, 12.

Dawson, Chester, and Dianne Brady. 2002. Land of the rising glue gun. *Business Week,* 7 January, 14.

De Mooij, Marieke. 1994. *Advertising Worldwide.* 2nd ed. New York: Prentice Hall.

Denitto, Emily. 1993. Hyper markets seem to be big flop in U.S. *Advertising Age,* 4 October, 20.

Domzal, Teresa, and Lynette Unger. 1987. Emerging positioning strategies in global marketing. *Journal of Consumer Marketing* 4(4) (Fall): 23–40.

Douglas, Susan P., and Christine Urban. 1977. Lifestyle analysis to profile women in international markets. *Journal of Marketing* 61(3): (July): 53–54.

Duncan, Thomas R., and Stephen E Everett. 1993. Client perceptions of integrated marketing communications. *Journal of Advertising Research* 33(3): (May/June): 30–39.

Ebenkamp, Becky. 2001. Return to Peyton placement. *Brandweek,* 4 June, S-10.

Echikson, William. 1998. When cheese is not just cheese: Getting picky about origin. *Christian Science Monitor,* 22 January, 1.

Economist. 2002a. North America's neighbours look woodenly at each other. March 30, 26.

———. 2002b. The dumping dilemma. 1 June, 71.

Entrepreneur Magazine. 2003. Top Global Franchises. <www.entrepreneur.com/franzone/listings/topglobal>

Estell, Libby. 2001. Going global. *Incentive,* January, 13.

Euromonitor. 2002. International Marketing Data and Statistics. 408.

Euromonitor. 2002. European Marketing Data and Statistics. 266.

Fitzgerald, Kate. 2003. Growing pains for placements. *Advertising Age,* 3 February, S-2.

Gajewski, Maciek. 1991. Samples: A steal in Poland. *Advertising Age,* 4 November, 54.

Globastat. 2003. Inflation rate (consumer prices). <www.globastat.com/e10.htm>

Gofton, Ken. 2000. How Euro rules will change sales promotion. *Marketing,* 5 October, 60.

Goldman, Jordan. 1984. *Public relations in the marketing mix.* Lincolnwood, Ill.: NTC Business Books.

Goldman, Debra. 1999. Consumer republic. *Adweek,* 23 August, 16.

Green, Frank. 2003. Retail trend: Not-so-superstores. *San Diego Union-Tribune,* 22 February, C-1.

Harris, Thomas. 1993. *The marketer's guide to public relations.* New York: Wiley.

———. 1994. PR gets personal. *Direct marketing,* April, 29–32.

Hoevell, P. J., and P. G. Walters. 1972. International marketing presentations: Some options. *European Journal of Marketing* (Summer): 69–79.

Isachenkov, Vladimir. 2002. GM joint-venture in SUV plant buoys Russian auto industry. *San Diego Union-Tribune,* 24 September, C-2.

Jacobson, Michael, and Laurie Ann Mazur. 1995. *Marketing madness: A survival guide for consumer society.* Boulder, Colo.: Westview Press.

Johnston, Jean. 1988. Japanese firms in the U.S.: Adapting the persuasive message. *Bulletin for the Association for Business Communications* 51(3) (September): 33–34.

Journal of Marketing. 1948. Report of the Definitions Committee. 12 October.

Kale, Sudhir, and D. Sudharshan. 1987. A strategic approach to international segmentation. *International Marketing Review* 4(2): (Summer): 60–71.

Kaplan, David. 2002. How to play the name game with women, men. *Adweek*, 9 September, 3.

Kashani, Kamran. 1989. Beware the pitfalls of global marketing. *Harvard Business Review* 67(5) (September/October): 91–98.

Kerin, Rover A., and William Cron. 1987. Assessing trade show functions and performance. *Journal of Marketing* 51(3): (July): 88.

Khermouch, Gerry. 2002. The best global brands. *Business Week*, 5 August, 92–99.

Kotler, Philip. 1986. Global standardization—Courting danger. *Journal of Consumer Marketing* 3(2) (Spring): 13–15.

Kotler, Philip, and Gary Armstrong. 1990. *Marketing: An introduction.* Englewood Cliffs, N.J.: Prentice Hall.

Kraar, Louis. 1991. How Americans win in Asia. *Fortune,* 7 October, 133–40.

Lever, Robert. 2001. Delivering the goods. *Europe* (407): (June), 20.

Levitt, Theodore. 1983. The globalization of markets. *Harvard Business Review* (May/June): 92–102.

Locke, Michelle. 2003. European effort to protect food names leaves bad taste. *San Diego Union Tribune.* 13 August, C-4.

Lynch, Michael. 2001. Global dumping. *Reason* 33 (November): 15.

McCarthy, Jerome. 1960. *Basic marketing: A managerial approach.* Homewood, Ill: Irwin.

McCay, Betsy. 1992. Xerox fights trademark battle. *Advertising Age,* 27 April, 139.

MacIntyre, Donald. 2002. Eric Kom: Global marketing chief of Samsung. *Time,* 2 December, 54.

Madden, Normandy. 2001. Amway taps Leo Burnett for China biz. *Advertising Age Global Daily News,* 18 December. <www.adageglobal.com/cgi-bin/daily.pl?daily_id=6452&post_date=2002-12-18>

Mussey, Dagmar. 2002. New Mars bar ads in Europe are sensitive to local tastes. *Advertising Age Global Daily News,* 16 April. <www.adageglobal.com/cgi-bin/article.pl?article_id=247>

Novelli, William D. 1989/1990. One-stop shopping: Some thoughts on integrated marketing communication. *Public Relations Quarterly.* 34(4), 7–9.

PR Newswire. 2002. Royal Caribbean International launches Europe-focused integrated marketing campaign. 5 November, 1.

Ricks, David. 1983. *Big business blunders: Mistakes in multinational marketing.* Homewood, Ill: Dow Jones-Irwin.

Ricks, David A., Marilyn Fu, and Jeffrey S. Arpan. 1974. *International business blunders.* Columbus, Ohio.

Rosenberg, Larry 1980. Deciphering the Japanese cultural code. *International Marketing Review* (Autumn): 47–57.

Ryan, Leslie. 1995. Sales promotion: Made in America. *Brandweek,* 31 July, 28.

Sales Management. 1967. The $30 million lesson. 1 March, 31–38.

San Diego Union-Tribune. 1992a. With multinational ties, it's difficult to tell where products really came from. 2 February, A36.

———. 1992b. Made in America gets tougher to determine. 2 February, A33.

Saporito, Bill, William Boston, Neil Gough, and Rita Healy. 2003. Can Wal-Mart get any bigger? *Time,* 13 January, 38.

Schultz, Don E., Stanley L. Tannenbaum, and Robert E. Lauterborn. 1994. *The new marketing paradigm: Integrated marketing communications.* Lincolnwood, Ill: NTC Business Books.

Schultz, Don E., and Philip J. Kitchen. 2000. *Communicating globally: An integrated marketing approach.* Lincolnwood: Ill: NTC Business Books.

Shalofsky, Ivor. 1987. Research for global brands. *European Research* (May): 88–93.

Sheth, Hagdish. 1986. Global markets or global competition? *Journal of Consumer Marketing* 3(2): (Spring): 9–11.

Shimp, Terence. 2003. *Advertising, promotion & supplemental aspects of integrated marketing communications.* Mason, Ohio: Thompson-Southwestern.

Thomaselli, Rich. 2002. Swatch Group signs on as Olympic partner sponsor. *Advertising Age,* 25 November, 6.

Tomkins, Richard. 2000. Laundry, with a minor in linguistics: Once informative, product packaging has gone global and now offers lessons in a dozen different languages. *Financial Times* (London), 10 June, 13.

———. 2002. As television audiences tire of commercials, advertisers move into programs. *Financial Times* (London), 5 November, 21.

Varadarajan, P. Rajan, and Anil Menon. 1988. Cause-related marketing: A coalignment of marketing strategy and corporate philanthropy. *Journal of Marketing* 52(3): (July): 58–74.

Weber, Joseph. 1993. Campbell: Now it's M-m global. *Business Week,* 15 March, 52–56.

Weissart, Will. 2002. Starbucks set for Mexico debut. *San Diego Union-Tribune,* 6 September, C-2.

Young, Miles. 2001. Brand building vs. flag burning. Speech presented at the Asia Society luncheon, 12 November, New York. Miles Young is chairman of Ogilvy & Mather Asia <www.adageglobal.com/cgi-bin/pages.pl?link=496>

Zenith Media. 2002. Per Capita Advertising Expenditures in Selected Countries.

CHAPTER THREE

The International Marketing and Advertising Environment

Demographic and geographic characteristics, and economic and political-legal factors, all are important not only in evaluating a country's potential as a market but also in designing and implementing the marketing mix for a specific market. Thus, each of these environmental factors will be analyzed in this chapter. The international marketer must consider demographic characteristics (size of the population, rate of population growth, education, population density, and age structure and composition of population), economic factors (GNP per capita, income distribution, and rate of GNP growth), geographic characteristics (size of the country, topographical characteristics, and climate conditions), and the political-legal environment (political stability, laws and regulations, and the degree of nationalism). Clearly, cultural characteristics also play an influential role. However, this aspect of the international marketing and advertising environment will be dealt with separately in Chapter 4. Figure 3.1 shows the relationship of these environmental factors to the marketing mix.

The international marketer generally has very limited, if any, control over these environmental factors. The marketer's task is to assess these factors in order to identify potential barriers to doing business. Firms operating in affluent markets are accustomed to having extensive secondary data available, but obtaining similar data in developing markets can prove quite a challenge. Often, data are inaccurate or simply not available. If no insurmountable barriers are detected, the research on these uncontrollable environmental elements will provide information that allows the international marketer to adapt the marketing mix to the specific market.

Demographic Characteristics

Just as the demographic characteristics of various segments within the U.S. population make them more or less appealing to marketers, so, too, do demographic characteristics of foreign

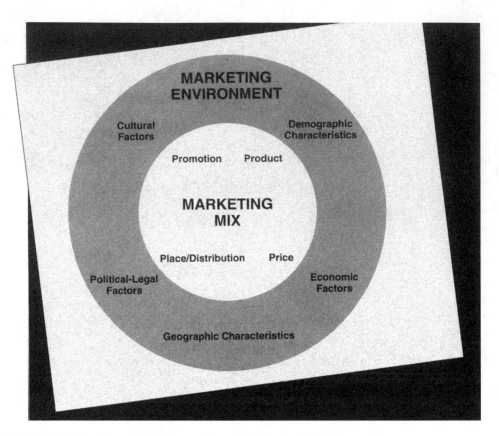

Figure 3.1 Relationship of environmental factors to the marketing mix.

countries—such as market size, population growth and distribution, and education—influence a marketer's decision regarding whether and how to enter a market.

Market Size

The current world population is estimated at 6.1 billion—already more than twice the 1950 figure—and it is expected to grow by another 3 billion in the next half century, according to recently released United Nations projections (Hagmann 2001). How these 6 billion or so potential consumers are distributed around the globe is of intense interest to the international marketer. Knowing a market's size is essential in determining whether to enter a market, and a country's population provides one basic indicator of market size. Generally, the larger the population of a market, the greater its potential, all other things being equal. However, population figures alone are usually not a sufficient guide to market size. Population size must typically be combined with many other factors, such as population growth rates, distribution patterns, and available income.

There is enormous variation in the population of countries around the globe, as Table 3.1 shows. The table reveals that well over half the people in the world live in only 10 countries and

TABLE 3.1 2000 Population Figures (in millions)

Country	Population	Country	Population
China	1,262	Cambodia	12
India	1,016	Greece	11
United States	282	Guatemala	11
Indonesia	210	Yugoslavia	11
Brazil	170	Belgium	10
Russian Federation	146	Portugal	10
Pakistan	138	Zambia	10
Japan	127	Sweden	9
Mexico	98	Austria	8
Germany	82	Bolivia	8
Philippines	76	Dominican Republic	8
Egypt	64	Switzerland	7
Thailand	61	Hong Kong	7
United Kingdom	60	Israel	6
France	59	Denmark	5
Italy	58	Finland	5
South Korea	47	Jordan	5
South Africa	43	Norway	4
Columbia	42	Puerto Rico	4
Spain	39	Ireland	4
Argentina	37	Lebanon	4
Canada	31	New Zealand	4
Kenya	30	Costa Rica	4
Venezuela	24	Singapore	4
Malaysia	23	Panama	3
Saudi Arabia	21	United Arab Emirates	3
Australia	19	Oman	2
Sri Lanka	19	Mongolia	2
Yemen	18	Slovenia	2
Netherlands	16	Kuwait	2
Ecuador	13	Trinidad & Tobago	1
Zimbabwe	13	Swaziland	1

Source: World Bank 2002.

that the world's largest nation has a population approximately *10,000* times the population of some of the smallest countries.

Population Growth

Most international marketers are also concerned with population growth rates. The world's population is currently growing at a rate of 1.2 percent, or 77 million people per year.

Six countries account for half of this growth: India (21 percent), China (12 percent), Pakistan (5 percent), Nigeria (4 percent), Bangladesh (4 percent), and Indonesia (3 percent). By 2050, nearly 9 out of every 10 people will be living in a developing country—1 out of 6 in India alone, which will replace China as the most populous nation (Hagmann 2001). Other countries' growth rates are more moderate—such as Mexico (1.9 percent), Thailand (1.3 percent), Canada (1.1 percent), and the United States (1.1 percent). Some countries even report declining growth rates: Bulgaria (-0.4 percent), Hungary (-0.3 percent), and the Ukraine (-0.1 percent). Overall, wealthier countries tend to have more stable populations while developing countries have rapidly expanding populations.

From the perspective of the international marketer, high population growth rates may indicate the formation of new households, and therefore increased demand for a variety of consumer goods. However, rapidly expanding populations also may have a negative effect on per capita income, translating into more limited purchasing power. Even in countries with stagnant or declining population growth rates, potential exists for the international marketer.

IIIII Population Distribution

Along with population growth rates, the international marketer will need to evaluate the distribution of the population. Three important population distribution characteristics are density, age and age structure, and household size.

Density As with population size, there is a great deal of variation in population density among nations. In 2000, for example, the United States had a population density of 31 persons per square kilometer, as contrasted to the 3 persons per square kilometer in Canada. Note, however, that most Canadians live within 150 miles of the U.S. border and that the population density is actually much lower in the predominantly uninhabited Yukon and Northwest territories. On the high end of the scale, Bangladesh has an almost unbelievable 1,007 persons per square kilometer, and Singapore a staggering 6,587 persons per square kilometer (World Bank 2002, 14).

Age One important aspect of age is the average life expectancy of consumers in various markets. In most Western countries, the average life expectancy is quite similar (for example, 77 for the United States, 78 for France, 79 for Canada, and 80 for Japan). In contrast, most people living in developing nations have a relatively short life expectancy (for example, 60 in Bangladesh, 51 in Nigeria, 44 in Ethiopia, and only 38 in Angola) (Globalstat 2003, 1).

Markets also vary in their age structure. Markets with varying age groupings reflect consumers with both differing needs and differing levels of purchasing power. The lower life expectancy in many countries also means their populations are comparatively young. As Table 3.2 shows, a significantly larger percentage of the population in many lower-income countries falls into the 0–14 age grouping than in the higher-income ones. However, even within these groupings variation exists.

TABLE 3.2 Economic Development and Age Structure (percentage 0–14 years)

Low-Income Economies (36.9%)		Lower-Middle Income Economies (26.9%)		Upper-Middle Income Economies (29.1%)		High-Income Economies (18.5%)	
Uganda	49.2%	Algeria	34.8%	Venezuela	36.5%	United States	21.5%
Kenya	43.5	Peru	33.4	Brazil	28.8	France	18.7
India	33.5	Thailand	26.7	Hungary	19.9	Germany	15.4
China	24.8	Poland	19.2	Portugal	16.7	Japan	14.7

Source: World Bank (2002).

Nearly half of Uganda's population is currently under 14 years of age. One-third of India's population and one-fourth of China's is currently 14 years or younger. Savvy marketers keep an eye to the future—in 15 to 20 years, these citizens will be in their late 20s to late 30s, the prime earning and spending years—which make these countries particularly appealing to international marketers. However, a profound trend is sweeping the industrialized world: due to plunging birth rates, an ever-increasing percentage of the population is graying. In virtually all countries of the more developed regions, fertility is currently below the replacement level of 2.1 children per woman—the level needed to ensure that a population will replace itself in the long run. The birth rate in European countries has dropped significantly and the number of children under 15 has shrunk by 23 percent since 1970. The pattern is just as dramatic in Japan and Korea, and to a lesser extent in the United States. This shift is expected to continue. A few decades hence, even large developing nations like Russia, Brazil, and Thailand will see a surge of retirees. By 2050, the average age of the world is expected to rise from the current 26 to 36. In Spain, the average by mid-century should hit 55. Globally, we will see a tripling in the number of people 60 years or older, increasing from 606 million today to nearly 2 billion by 2050. On the plus side, these older consumer segments tend to be more affluent—having reached the peak of their earning potential—and as a result have greater amounts of disposable income available. However, there are negative implications as well. Who will do the work in geriatric societies? Who will support the burgeoning class of pensioners? And what will happen to growth? After all, in addition to productivity, a rising labor force is the key ingredient of economic expansion (Baker 2002, 138).

Household Size A *household* refers to all persons, both related and unrelated, who occupy a housing unit (Engel and Blackwell 1982, 20). The term means very different things in different countries. A household in Thailand typically consists of an extended family, with grandparents and grandchildren, aunts and uncles, and cousins all living under one roof. The typical household in the United States, in contrast, is generally limited to the nuclear family. Also, in many parts of the world, households pool their incomes, which slightly distorts per capita income figures. While population figures in many developed countries remain stable, the number of households has increased while the average household size has decreased. This can be attributed to two factors: increases in both the divorce rate and the number of sole-survivor households.

Smaller-sized households have direct implications for the marketers of consumer goods. For example, package sizes may need to be smaller or prepackaged for single servings. This, in turn, impacts advertising message content.

Education Another demographic variable of interest to international marketers is education. The education information available is largely limited to the national enrollments in the various levels of education—primary, secondary, and university or college. A fairly close relationship seems to exist between economic development and educational attainment, with individuals in the more developed countries generally completing more years of education. As one might expect, education is also highly correlated with literacy. From an international marketer's standpoint, consumers must be able to read advertising messages and product labels as well as understand warranty and guarantee information. If large percentages of consumers are illiterate in certain markets, advertising programs and product packaging may need to be modified. Level of education is also of interest because it reflects the degree of consumer sophistication. Complex messages and products that require instructions may need to be adapted depending on educational trends in a particular country. Table 3.3 lists sample rates of illiteracy by country.

Economic Factors

In addition to demographic information, international marketers require economic data in order to assess market potential. This is because the attractiveness of a market goes beyond sheer numbers of people—a nation's current and future attractiveness is also based on the willingness and ability of those people to spend. A clear understanding of a host country's economic environment—including type of economy, per capita income, and level of urbanization—is also essential in developing an appropriate marketing and communications strategy.

TABLE 3.3 Illiteracy Rates by Country

Country	Rate	Country	Rate
Niger	86.4%	Mexico	10.4%
Sierra Leone	68.6	Yugoslavia	7.0
Afghanistan	68.5	Vietnam	6.3
Pakistan	57.3	Philippines	5.4
India	48.0	Chile	4.8
Uganda	38.2	United States	3.0
Guatemala	36.4	Russia	2.0
China	18.5	Japan	1.0
Malaysia	16.5	Czech Republic	0.1
Zimbabwe	15.0	Norway	0.0

Source: 2003 Literacy Rate, *Globastat (http://www.globastat.com/p22.htm).*

▐▐▐▐ Classification Systems

Classifications of economic systems vary depending on the originator of the classification system as well as its intended use. The following system is commonly employed in the marketing literature:

- *Subsistence economies:* includes countries in which the vast majority of citizens are engaged in agriculture. They tend to consume much of what they produce and to barter any excess production. Overall, market opportunities here are still rather limited.
- *Raw-material–exporting economies:* includes countries that are rich in one or more natural resources but considered poor in most other ways. Their revenues generally come from exporting these resources—for example, Saudi Arabia (oil) and Zaire (copper and coffee). Such countries tend to be good markets for heavy machinery and tools.
- *Industrializing economies:* includes countries in which manufacturing accounts for roughly 10–20 percent of the national economy—for example, Brazil, Egypt, and the Philippines. As manufacturing increases, these countries may require imports of raw materials and heavy machinery. Industrialization often creates a new rich class as well as a growing middle class, both of which demand a variety of consumer goods.
- *Industrial economies:* includes countries that are major exporters of manufactured goods as well as investment funds. Industrial economies trade goods among themselves as well as export them to industrializing and raw-material–exporting economies. Industrial economies generally have large middle classes, making them ideal for most categories of consumer goods.

Historically, industrial economies have represented the greatest marketing opportunities for corporations, because consumers in these countries typically have the capacity to purchase goods offered by international marketers. In addition, the communications, transportation, financial, and distribution networks necessary to conduct business are in place. However, such markets also tend to have stable or, as noted previously, even shrinking population bases, and as a result, markets for many goods and services may already be saturated. Thus, marketers are increasingly turning to less developed nations, which tend to have expanding populations and therefore potentially greater growth opportunities. For Unilever, the poor already are a huge market. The consumer goods giant has made an art of selling its products in tiny packages costing a few cents each. The conglomerate's Indian subsidiary, Hindustan Lever Ltd., knew that many Indians could not afford to buy a large bottle of shampoo—a product typically used only on special occasions anyway. So it created single-use packets (in three sizes, according to hair length) that go for a few cents—and now sells 4.5 billion of them a year (Murphy 2002, 169). The strategy has gone global. Unilever's Rexona brand deodorant sticks sell for 16 cents and up. They are big hits in India, the Philippines, Bolivia, and Peru—where Unilever has grabbed 60 percent of the deodorant market. A nickel-size Vaseline package and a tube containing enough Close Up toothpaste for 20 brushings sell for about 8 cents each. In Nigeria, Unilever sells 3-inch-square packets of margarine that don't need refrigeration (Kripalani and Engardio 2002, 112).

▍▍▍ Income

A statistic commonly used to describe the economic condition of a country is per capita income, a widely accepted indicator of a country's economic development as well as the potential purchasing power of its individuals. Per capita income is often stated in relation to a country's total income, or gross national product (GNP). The World Bank Atlas method of calculating gross national product (also known as GNI for gross national income) per capita converts national currency units to dollars at prevailing exchange rates, adjusted for inflation and averaged over three years. Because those rates do not always reflect differences in prices, purchasing power parities are united to convert GNP per capita estimates into international dollars. An international dollar buys the same amount of goods and services in a country's domestic market as one dollar would buy in the United States. Table 3.4 shows the wide range in the per capita income figures (both GNP per capita and purchase power parity) among nations of the world. For example, in 2000, Switzerland had a GNP per capita of U.S. $38,140, while Ethiopia has a GNP per capita of little more than U.S. $100. In 1998, the 20 percent of the world's people who live in the high-income countries had 82 times the income of the lowest 20 percent. Statistics show 60 percent of the world's population receives only 6 percent of the world's income. The high-income nations contain 17 percent of the world's population, yet receive 78 percent of world income (Ausaid 2001, 1).

Note that per capita figures are averages and give no indication of income distribution. Typically, the more developed the country, the more even the distribution of income. In many developing countries, however, there is a bimodal distribution of income—a very rich segment of the population and a very large, very poor segment with literally no middle class. The following serves as a useful classification system:

- *Very low family incomes:* subsistence economies characterized by rural populations in which consumption relies on personal output or barter. Some urban centers may provide markets.

TABLE 3.4 2000 GNP per Capita and Purchasing Power Parity

Country	GNP per Capita	Purchasing Power Parity
Switzerland	$38,140	$30,450
Japan	35,620	27,080
United States	34,100	34,100
Germany	25,120	24,920
Singapore	24,740	24,910
India	450	2,340
Bangladesh	370	1,590
Zambia	300	750
Niger	180	740
Ethiopia	100	660

Source: World Bank (2002).

- *Mostly low family incomes:* economies that are beginning to industrialize. Most goods are produced domestically.
- *Very low, very high family incomes:* economies that exhibit strongly bimodal income distributions. The majority of the population may live barely above the subsistence level, while a minority provides a strong market for imported or luxury items. The affluent are truly affluent and will consume accordingly.
- *Low, medium, and high family incomes:* economies in which industrialization has produced an emerging middle class with increasing disposable income. However, due to traditional social class barriers, the very low– and very high–income classes tend to remain.
- *Mostly medium family incomes:* advanced industrial economies with institutions and policies that reduce extremes in income distribution. The result is a large and comfortable middle class able to purchase a wide array of both domestic and imported products and services. (Kotler 1988, 383)

Household income may be a more telling statistic than GNP per capita. In many developing countries, the extended family rather than the nuclear family is the norm. For example, in Latin American countries the typical household includes aunts, uncles, cousins, grandparents, and sometimes even great-grandparents. Several family members may be wage earners, directly impacting the buying power of the family unit. And while the nuclear family is still the norm in the United States, today that unit typically includes two wage earners. As a result, international marketers often pair household income with household size in analyzing a market's willingness and ability to spend. Clearly, available income directly influences what individuals are capable of purchasing. Table 3.5 reveals the varying degrees to which consumers possess various goods in both developed and developing countries.

TABLE 3.5 Possession of Goods (per 100 households)

	Shower	Washing Machine	Refrigerator	Auto	Telephone	CD Player
Argentina	92.3%	49.1%	83.3%	57.4%	66.3%	24.0%
Canada	99.1	84.2	99.0	85.9	88.8	76.1
China	41.7	2.4	6.3	2.9	24.6	2.0
India	41.3	4.7	13.3	0.6	15.1	1.4
Japan	99.9	99.0	97.4	81.5	86.8	65.8
Mexico	67.0	40.3	67.8	22.5	30.7	9.6
Philippines	82.8	8.0	41.0	7.7	10.8	3.6
Singapore	99.6	93.8	99.2	41.2	96.0	56.4
South Africa	58.9	24.2	79.2	8.9	28.5	6.8
Thailand	64.3	5.0	69.3	35.8	26.8	5.1
U.S.	99.5	80.1	99.6	92.9	85.5	56.8
Venezuela	91.8	38.7	81.7	47.4	42.3	9.5

Source: International Marketing Forecasts, *Euromonitor* (2002).

As can be seen from the figures above, there is a great deal of variation in the ownership of durable goods. Automobile ownership ranges from nearly 93 cars for every 100 households in the United States to fewer than 4 cars per 100 households in China. Indeed, for years, most cars in China were sold to state institutions and companies, or ended up in taxi fleets. This is now changing. According to Automotive Resources in Asia, a Beijing consultancy, car sales will grow 15 percent annually and could more than double to 2.5 million by 2010. In the coming years, more and more Chinese will purchase their first automobile. Until recently, cars were out of reach of ordinary Chinese, including even members of the new middle class. But as tariffs on imported cars dropped in the wake of China's accession to the World Trade Organization, and a slew of new models came on the market, domestic auto makers were forced to drop their prices. Currently, the price for a small domestic vehicle is about $4,700. Private citizens, armed with savings and aided by a variety of installment plans, are flocking to dealerships. Clearly, this has whetted the appetite of foreign manufacturers—Ford Motor Co. and Volkswagen are just two of the firms actively wooing Chinese consumers. But there are still roadblocks. Duties on imported cars are still between 44 and 51 percent, and Beijing has not allowed foreign auto makers to offer car loans, despite its WTO commitment to do so. Nonetheless, most foreign manufacturers are betting that China will continue to open up (Roberts and Webb 2002, 45).

Critics of globalization note that free trade and cross-border investment have benefited the rich at the expensive of the poor. They argue that the ranks of the poor are growing, and that the disparity between rich and poor has grown. However, recent research has shown that, contrary to popular belief, it is precisely during the recent period of increased globalization of the world economy that poverty rates and global income inequality have most diminished (Globalization 2003). Economist Xavier Sala-i-Martin of Columbia University calculates that the fraction of the world's population below the poverty line (defined as an income of $2 a day in constant 1985 dollars) fell to 19 percent in 1998, down from 41 percent in 1970. Rising incomes since 1980 in China and India account for most of the improvement. In Latin America, poverty decreased in the 1970s but has changed little since then. In contrast, poverty worsened in Africa. In 1970, 11 percent of the world's poor were in Africa and 76 percent were in Asia. By 1998, Africa's share of the poor had risen to 66 percent and Asia's had fallen to 15 percent (Coy 2002, 22). Nonetheless, corporations have continued to operate in just such markets. Coca-Cola has been operating in Africa for almost 60 years—though the entire continent still brings in only 3 to 4 percent of its profits. To make the product as affordable as possible in African markets such as Zimbabwe, Coke uses local inputs and distribution, offers a break on the price of the formula to operations, and reduces recurring costs, such as packaging (Coke uses returnable glass bottles in most poor markets, for example).

Many multinationals, driven by conscience, have signed on to the idea that they have to do more in poor countries than slurp up profits and spit them out back home in the form of dividends (Murphy 2002, 164). London's Freeplay Energy Group proves that good corporate citizenship can also be good business. In 1996, Freeplay helped to pioneer the windup radio, which can be charged by cranking a handle. In the West, where they sell for up to $100,

they are especially popular among campers. But Freeplay has found a much more rewarding market in sub-Saharan Africa, where only 30 percent of homes have electricity, and per capita incomes are $100 to $300 a year, prohibiting the regular purchase of batteries. Here Freeplay sells their radios at a discount to aid agencies and governments, so that Africans can listen to public-service broadcasts of health and agriculture information and school lessons. In Rwanda, Freeplay's radios went to 65,000 teenagers who are heads of their households because their parents died in civil strife. A private company, Freeplay says its radio business is profitable (Kripalani and Engardio 2002, 112). Corporate social responsibility will be addressed in detail in Chapter 10.

Urbanization

One of the most telling economic indicators is the degree to which a country is urbanized. Table 3.6 shows the degree of urbanization for the world's four broad economic groupings. The averages for these groupings reveal a strong correlation between degree of urbanization and level of economic development. However, even within the broad economic groupings, there is significant variation. Typically, the more urbanized markets tend to be more appealing to international marketers. Developing countries are generally much less urbanized and, as a result, tend to be less attractive markets, particularly for consumer goods. Even less developed countries, however, may contain sizable pockets of high-income consumers. Products targeted to the urban markets in such countries may need only minimal changes from those marketed in developed countries. However, if the marketer is attempting to reach both the rural and urban populations in developing countries, a greater degree of product specialization is likely to be required (Hill and Still 1984, 62). In any case, whether consumers live in predominantly urban or rural areas directly influences the media selected to disseminate advertising messages.

TABLE 3.6 Economic Development and Urban Population (as percentage of total population), 2001

Low-income Economies—32%		Upper-middle Income Economies—76%	
Ethiopia	18%	Portugal	64%
Bangladesh	25	Mexico	74
India	28	Brazil	81
China	32	Venezuela	87
Lower-middle Income Economies—42%		High-income Economies—79%	
Thailand	23%	Ireland	59%
Cameroon	49	United States	77
Romania	56	United Kingdom	90
Philippines	59	Hong Kong	100

Source: World Bank (2002)

Geographic Characteristics

Geography, which refers to the earth's surface, climate, continents, countries, and available resources, is an uncontrollable environmental element that the international marketer cannot ignore. Topography and climate are of particular interest here. A market's physical characteristics may affect the international marketer's appraisal of a market and may well influence a number of the marketing mix factors.

Topography refers to the surface features of a country—its rivers, lakes, deserts, forests, and mountains. These characteristics are of interest to the international marketer in that they may impact product distribution. For example, large mountain ranges or bodies of water may complicate the physical distribution of products. In contrast, predominantly flat surface areas typically translate into easy transportation by road or rail, and navigable rivers likewise enable economical transportation. Further, the topography may serve to separate groups within the larger market. For example, consumers living in the highland regions of a country may display differing consumption behavior from those living in the valleys or flatlands.

Altitude, humidity, and temperature are all features of a country's climate. The climate and its degree of variation throughout the year can potentially impact what products a firm offers for sale, how they are distributed, and even how they are priced. The products that consumers may need will vary, depending on whether they live in tropical, temperate, desert, or arctic regions. For example, whether an automobile manufacturer equips vehicles with air conditioners or heaters depends on where those autos are being shipped.

The Political-Legal Environment

International marketers must have a good understanding of the political systems as well as the laws and regulations of the market in which they operate. Both the political system and local laws shape a given country's business environment and may directly impact various aspects of the marketing program, including whether a product can be sold in a particular country and how it will be distributed, priced, and, in particular, advertised. Legal and political constraints can be particularly challenging for the international marketer to overcome. A variety of factors influence the political-legal relationship between an international firm, its home country, and the host country in which it hopes to operate.

Political-Legal Environment of the Home Country

The political environment in most countries typically provides support for the international marketing efforts of firms located in that country. Governments may engage in efforts to reduce trade barriers or to increase trade opportunities. The United States, for example, has traditionally had a liberal attitude toward exports and imports. In other instances, however, foreign policy or national security concerns may result in constraints on free trade.

Trade Sanctions Governmental actions that restrict the free flow of goods and services between countries are known as *trade sanctions.* Sanctions often are used during times of war as a means of forcing countries to behave peacefully. In the 1992 Gulf War, for example, the United States imposed severe trade sanctions against Iraq and encouraged other countries to do the same. Trade sanctions may also be employed in the hopes of changing a nation's government or its policies. Reasons for the imposition of trade sanctions have varied, ranging from violations of human rights to terrorist activities and even nuclear armament. For instance, in 1994, President Clinton lifted a 19-year trade embargo against Vietnam. In anticipation of the lifting of the ban, at least six advertising agencies moved to establish relationships in the market. U.S. businesses cheered because the move immediately created sales opportunities for companies hungry to catch up with their foreign competitors in Vietnam, a market of over 70 million potential consumers. Much like the advertising agencies, many U.S. corporations, including Motorola, Microsoft, Coca-Cola, and Caterpillar had already laid the groundwork during the embargo. Caterpillar opened two sales offices and even began taking orders—but was forbidden from actually making transactions. Caterpillar's plans included building roads and sewage systems. With regard to South Africa, against which the United States imposed economic sanctions in 1988, Steven Burgess, a marketing professor at the Witwatersrand University School of Business Economics, noted: "If we have a nonracial government here tomorrow morning, South Africa becomes a boom town" (Barnes 1993). Burgess's prophecy has proven correct. Despite continued outbursts of violence, multinational firms have returned to South Africa in record numbers since the fall of apartheid and the subsequent lifting of the economic sanctions. For example, PepsiCo, which divested in protest against apartheid in the mid-1980s, is once again selling its products in this nation. Following the decision by Pepsi to re-enter South Africa, its worldwide lead agency, BBD&O, also announced its return. BBD&O was one of South Africa's biggest shops until it was liquidated when the ban was imposed (Koenderman 1994). Multinationals such as Eastman Kodak, General Motors, Honeywell, IBM, Procter & Gamble, and Sony see this nation of 35 million potential consumers as an appealing starting point for the rest of southern Africa.

The United States currently prohibits firms from dealing with Cuba and Iraq, among others, and is considering imposing sanctions on North Korea. The United States instituted a trade embargo against Cuba in 1962 when dictator Fidel Castro seized power. In November 2001, when Hurricane Michelle devastated parts of Cuba, the United States responded with aid. The Trade Sanctions Reform and Export Enhancement Act of 2000 permit shipments of humanitarian cargo such as food and medicine. Thus the United States's first commercial shipment of food to Cuba in nearly 40 years was delivered—nearly 96,000 metric tons of food. Many marketers expressed hope that this signalled a shift in U.S. policy. Indeed, by the end of 2001, the U.S. Congress began allowing food and agricultural exports. "The trade door was opened a crack, and now products are flowing through that crack," said Steve Appel, vice president of the American Farm Bureau. We expect that crack to grow wider and wider" (Case 2003). Indeed, since late 2001, U.S. companies have signed contracts worth more than $250 million with Cuba. Of that total, goods worth $210 million have been delivered and paid for. Optimism grows and many believe that eventually, the United States could account for more than half of Cuba's food imports. Cuban officials said that U.S. good shipments could total $1 billion in just a few years. Cuba could eventually become the second largest Latin American market for U.S. farm exports, trailing only Mexico. But staunch supporters of the embargo remain. U.S. law stipulates that farmers can be paid only in cash, but some European and Canadian investors have reportedly grown frustrated with their ventures in Cuba—the communist regime apparently owes billions of dollars to non-U.S. suppliers Then there are the concerns over Castro's alleged links to international terrorism (Gyan 2001). President Bush has refused to lift the trade embargo until democratic and economic reforms are made.

Clearly, if trade with certain countries or regions is cut off, the international firm may incur significant loss of business. Therefore, international firms must actively monitor the political climate in the countries in which they do business in order to anticipate potential sanctions and prepare for the consequences.

Export and Import Controls Two additional governmental activities that may directly impact the international marketer are export controls and import controls. *Export controls* are usually designed to prevent adversaries from acquiring strategically important goods, or at least to delay their acquisition. In the United States, exporters of defense-related equipment, for example, must obtain a license from the U.S. Department of Commerce permitting shipment. In fact, in order for any good, service, or idea to be exported from the United States, the exporter must obtain an export license from the Department of Commerce, which administers the Export Administration Act (Springer 1986, 10). The Department of Commerce has a list of commodities available whose export is considered sensitive. Goods may be ranked high on this list due to concerns over national security, foreign policy, limitations in supply, or nuclear proliferation. An additional list ranks countries according to their political relationship with the United States.

If an industry—particularly a strategic industry—faces strong competition from imports, it may pressure government for protection against foreign goods. It is often argued that such protection is necessary to save jobs and that increased imports may further worsen the U.S. balance of payments. In response to such pressure, minimum prices may be set for imported goods. While import barriers often encourage foreign firms to invest in the domestic market, resulting in capital inflows, all too often, consumers bear the brunt of protective measures—paying higher prices for goods and finding fewer choices available.

 Political-Legal Environment of the Host Country

In evaluating a host country, the international marketer also must gauge its degree of economic, as well as political stability. Because entering a foreign market generally translates into a long-term commitment, firms seek assurance of relatively stable governmental policies regarding foreign business. In most countries, the political environment is relatively stable. However, a glance at world headlines in recent years, and even recent months, reveals that political environments can change rapidly. In 1990 the Soviet Union was a socialist country; today, Russia and most of the republics are taking steps toward capitalism. Similarly, East Germany no longer exists, and the nations of Eastern Europe are evolving before our very eyes from Soviet satellites to viable political and economic entities—even members of the European Union.

 Political Risk

Should a firm choose to operate in a country where the political risk is high, it may face civil disturbances, terrorism, and possibly even warfare. Political unrest is often associated with an anti-industry element, making the company and its employees potential targets for violence. Even when such violence seems unlikely, the international marketer may still be faced with adverse governmental actions, which include expropriation, confiscation, domestication, and a variety of other impediments to trade.

Expropriation refers to the takeover of a foreign investment by the host government. While it does not relieve the host government from providing some compensation to the former owners, compensation negotiations are often protracted and often result in settlements unsatisfactory to the owners. Moreover, if expropriation occurs, it can ward off other foreign firms. *Confiscation* is similar to expropriation in that ownership of the firm is transferred to the host country. However, when a firm is confiscated, no compensation is forthcoming. Certain industries are more prone than others to expropriation or confiscation—particularly those considered by the host nation to be critical to national defense or national wealth. Many countries, however, are turning from expropriation and confiscation to *domestication.* Here, the host government demands partial transfer of ownership and management responsibility and imposes regulations to ensure that a large share of the product is locally produced and a large share of the profit is retained in the country.

Restrictions affecting imports can be classified as tariff and nontariff barriers. A *tariff* is simply a tax imposed by a government on goods entering its borders. A tariff may be imposed either to generate revenues or to discourage the importation of goods in an attempt to protect domestic products from being outpriced by cheaper imports. As such, tariffs can serve as a very effective form of protectionism. Worldwide, tariffs range from minimal to quite hefty.

The average tariff on manufactured goods around the world is 40 percent. Canadian tariffs average 10 percent, but range from 0 to 27 percent. The European Union has tariffs ranging from 0 to 30 percent, and the Saudi tariff averages 12 percent. U.S. tariffs on manufactured goods are already quite low, at just 4 percent. The U.S. administration is pushing global free trade with a proposal that would eliminate tariffs on all manufactured goods from World Trade Organization countries by 2015. The elimination process would be a gradual reduction; by 2010, WTO members would pledge to reduce tariffs to below 8 percent and phase out those that had been 5 percent. Tariff-free trade worldwide would lift some 300 million people in developing countries out of poverty, according to World Bank estimates. However, this estimate presupposes that agricultural goods are included in the equation. Worldwide tariffs on agriculture average 62 percent, and such tariffs, whether in Europe, the United States, India, or Japan,

are fiercely defended. In the United States, for example, in accordance with the farm bill passed in 2002, American farmers stand to receive $271 billion in subsidies over the next decade (Dale 2002). Between the American farm lobby and the European Union's Common Agricultural Policy, the prospects for agricultural tariff reforms are rather dim. Countries around the world must examine their policies, because when trade flows, consumers and exporters alike benefit.

Nontariff barriers are equally serious impediments to trade. One form of nontariff barrier is the *quota*—a numerical or dollar limit applied to a specific category of goods. Quotas are not something only other countries do. The automobile industry provides a classic example. In the early 1980s, the United States government imposed quotas on Japanese auto imports in order to reduce the number of autos shipped to this country. Standards are another form of nontariff barrier. Whether imposed by design or accident, stringent requirements affecting the product, its packaging and labeling, and testing methods serve to restrict the entry of foreign goods. Bureaucratic red tape (such as customs guidelines or extensive documentation) also may effectively serve to discourage imports.

In addition to controlling the movement of goods across borders, host countries also influence the movement of capital into and out of their markets. *Exchange controls* may be employed by host governments that face a shortage of foreign currency; such controls can make it difficult for the international firm to remove its profits and investments from a country. When a country's balance of payments is unfavorable or unstable, it will not want precious capital to cross its borders. Thus, for instance, rather than selling Pepsi to the former Soviet Union, PepsiCo engages in barter—trading Pepsi for vodka.

Foreign countries may also exercise control over exchange rates. Currency needed to purchase foreign luxuries often carries high exchange rates while necessities receive more favorable rates. Such controls may be implemented in an effort to reduce the importation of goods that are considered unnecessary. Countries may also raise the tax rates applied to foreign investors in an effort to control the firms and their capital. Such tax increases may result in much-needed revenue for the host country, but they can severely damage the operations of the foreign investors.

In order to reduce the risk of adverse governmental actions, the international firm must demonstrate genuine concern for the welfare of the host country and not simply for its own profits. International firms can convey this message in a variety of ways. They can employ locals, particularly in management and decision-making positions, and offer fair pay and favorable working conditions. Local production of goods, production utilizing local materials, and the use of local suppliers all help to strengthen the image of the firm as a good corporate citizen.

While international marketers may still find it profitable to do business with an unstable country, the situation will certainly affect how business is conducted. International marketers must assess the economic and political risk of each country the firm considers entering and, once operations have been set up, must continually monitor the risk level.

A few major corporations have a separate office or staff assigned to evaluating risk in foreign markets they plan to enter, as well as dealing with crises in countries in which they already operate. For example, in Indonesia—which ranks high in terms of political risk—Nike's local factories produce 31 percent of the footwear it sells worldwide. At the firm's Jakarta

headquarters, Nike has a full-time labor-relations manager whose job it is to prevent disruptions of the company's operations due to strikes or other unrest (Shari 2001). However, for most small- and medium-sized companies, such an undertaking is unrealistic because of the cost, expertise, and resources required. These firms have a number of alternatives. One option is to hire a firm specializing in this area. For a fee (often ranging upward of $10,000), such firms advise their clients on the risks of doing business abroad as well as provide training for executives on how to protect themselves, cope with potential kidnapping and extortion, and guide their employees in political crises. Another alternative is to utilize one of a number of risk-assessment reports available to assist such international marketers in determining which countries are likely to prove most hazardous. Some of these measurement techniques focus very narrowly on whether a country has an open or closed political system. A political system is considered open "when nongovernmental actors can shape events by voicing their approval or discontent in the form of voting, protests, boycotts, and so on. In closed systems, a government does not allow these forms of expression publicly and the repression of the populace can lead to violent encounters" (Onkvisit and Shaw 1997, 150). Others are broader, examining not only the political risk, but the country risk in general. For example, to obtain an overall country risk score, *Euromoney* magazine assigns a weighting to a variety of categories in addition to political risk: economic performance, debt indicators, credit ratings, access to bank finance, access to short-term finance, and access to capital markets (O'Leary 2002, 208). Another valuable resource is the country credit rating, which is prepared by *Institutional Investor* magazine. This report is based on a survey of 100 leading international banks concerning a country's credit worthiness and the chance of payment default. As an alternative to subscribing to such reports, major banks can provide assistance to clients in assessing business risks overseas. Bank of America, for example, uses a ranking system based on a common set of economic and financial criteria to evaluate eight countries for business risk.

Nationalism The degree of nationalism a foreign market exhibits may make it more or less appealing to the international marketer. Some nations are quite receptive to foreign firms and may actively encourage investment from abroad, while others are quite hostile. Firms will clearly receive a better reception from a host country that has positive relations with its own country. A wide spectrum of factors can impact these relations. For example, if a host country is critical of some aspect of the foreign policy of the international firm's home country, the firm may be subject to fallout from this criticism. Another factor is whether the home country has particularly friendly or antagonistic relations with either the host country or even other nations. In such a case, a number of elements of the marketing mix may require modification. For example, products might be adapted, and commercial messages may play down rather than emphasize the advertised product's country of origin. McDonald's provides an excellent example. During most of the 78-day air war against Yugoslavia in the fall of 1999, McDonald's kept the burgers flipping while NATO kept the bombs dropping. Vandalized at the outset by angry mobs, McDonald's Corp. was forced to close its 15 restaurants in Yugoslavia temporarily. But when local managers again opened their doors, they accomplished an extraordinary comeback using an unusual marketing strategy: they put McDonald's U.S. origins on the back burner.

> To help overcome animosity toward a quintessential American trademark, the local restaurants promoted the McCountry, a domestic pork burger with paprika garnish. As a national flourish to evoke Serbian identity and pride, they produced posters and lapel buttons showing the golden arches topped with a traditional Serbian cap called the sajkaca (pronounced shy-KACH-a). They also handed out free cheeseburgers at anti-NATO rallies. The basement of one restaurant in the Serbian capital even served as a bomb shelter. Now that the war is over, the company is basking in its success. Cash registers are ringing at prewar levels. In spite of falling wages, rising prices and lingering anger at the United States, McDonald's restaurants around the country are thronged with Serbs hungry for Big Macs and fries. (Block 1999)

Though they are registered as local businesses, every restaurant in Yugoslavia is in fact 100 percent owned and operated by McDonald's. Key to the success of the campaign was presenting McDonald's as a Yugoslav company.

Nationalism is often cyclical. Back in the early 1990s, everything Western was embraced in Russia. President Boris Yeltsin even complained to the Russian Duma about the "Snickerization" of his country's economy, referring to the phenomenal success Mars Inc. had in penetrating the market. A newspaper poll in 1994 revealed that only 15 percent of Russians had never sampled a Snickers bar. Amaretto, a novelty liqueur from the West, was the in-drink in bars, and everyone watched the latest Sylvester Stallone movie. At the time it was very uncool to be Russian. Today, along with the rise in political nationalism under President Vladimir Putin, consumer nationalism has also risen. Now radio stations play all-Russian rock and the "made-in-Russia" labels are increasingly showing up a supermarkets. Russian bars sell beer and kerchiefed babushkas star in cutting-edge music videos. The trademark onion domes of Russian churches decorate labels for chocolate bars and dumplings. Marketing surveys confirm how dramatic the turnabout has been. Before 1998, according to the firm Comcon, only 48 percent of Russians said they preferred to buy domestic goods when considering quality and not just price. By 1999, that figure had jumped to 90 percent (Glasser 2001).

The striking change was clearly accelerated by the 1998 ruble devaluation that made many imported goods inaccessibly expensive for Russians. But some say the change suggests something deeper—perhaps the wounded pride of an ex-superpower struggling to reassert itself. Western companies once found it easy to sell anything with English on the package. Now, if a product isn't *nasha*—Russian for "ours"—it's simply harder to sell. "The most successful products today are local ones created by Western companies and promoted using Western techniques—but aimed at Russian patriotism," notes Alexander Gromov, managing director of the Moscow office of the ad agency Saatchi & Saatchi. "They are talking to Russians speaking their language—but using all the tricks of western advertising" (Glasser 2001).

Mars has responded successfully to this "Russification." When the U.S. confectionary giant started a new candy bar in the country, they named it Derzhava—a politically loaded word that translates literally as "power," and is the unofficial slogan of Russian's strong-state crowd. The Derzhava television ad campaign appeals directly to Russians who believe they have been left behind by capitalism: a husband, his wife, and her mother sit at their modest country dacha

watching in disgust as their nouveau-riche neighbors haul in tacky statues to adorn their glitzy new palace. As the husband bites into his chocolate, he reassures the tea-drinking mother and daughter: "Forget about money; taste is everything."

International Law

A variety of international laws and agencies regulate business across national boundaries.

The International Monetary Fund (IMF) Marketers typically exchange goods and services for money. Either gold or an internationally acceptable currency is necessary for this exchange. Currently, U.S. dollars are by far the most widely used medium of exchange in international trade, followed by the euro and the yen. There is some speculation that the euro has the potential of replacing the U.S. dollar as the world's major currency. The IMF, created at the end of World War II, promotes international monetary cooperation and facilitates the expansion of trade among member countries. It works to diminish the degree of nationalistic actions taken by countries, thereby decreasing financial barriers to international trade. The IMF also lends money to member countries facing deficits in their international debt payments, allowing them to continue trading on the world market, until they can correct their payment problems. At present the fund has over 140 member countries, accounting for about 80 percent of total world production and 90 percent of world trade.

World Bank Membership in the World Bank is open to all members of the IMF, and the bank is owned and controlled by its 129 member governments. Each member country subscribes to shares for an amount reflecting its relative economic strength. The United States is the bank's largest shareholder, providing 25.3 percent of the subscription capital. The primary purpose of the bank is to provide both financial and technical assistance to developing countries. The World Bank currently lends about $8 billion a year to help raise the standard of living in poor countries. The bank provides loans for a variety of projects related to agriculture, rural development, education, population planning, electrical power, transportation, telecommunications, and water supply. The bank evaluates the prospects for repayment before granting loans. Loans are usually repayable over a 20-year period.

General Agreement on Tariffs and Trade (GATT) The General Agreement on Tariffs and Trade was initially set up in 1948 as a temporary body to ensure that the discriminatory trade practices of the 1920s and 1930s would not again plague international business. The United States and 22 other countries signed this agreement. The multinational, intergovernmental treaty, which operated within the framework of the United Nations, had approximately the same membership as the IMF. GATT's rules governed trade relations between member countries, the goal of which was the reduction of trade barriers and the further liberalization of world trade. The growth achieved during the past 20 years in the world economy is due in no small part to the efforts of GATT.

World Trade Organization (WTO) Even though GATT was successful in reducing tariff barriers around the globe, the increased use of nontariff barriers such as quotas and subsidies went largely ignored. GATT also focused primarily on manufactured goods, and yet trade in services—such as banking, insurance, and accounting—has also increased globally. Further, a number of countries have become increasingly concerned about the lack of intellectual property protection and the lax enforcement of existing patent, trademark, and copyright laws. Using GATT as its foundation, the World Trade Organization was created in 1995 in order to address these issues (Terpstra and Russow 2000). Initially GATT and WTO coexisted, but GATT ceased to exist after 1996. WTO, being more permanent than GATT, will have greater authority to settle trade disputes, and will serve along with the IMF and the World Bank to monitor trade and resolve disputes.

Summary

The international marketing environment contains a variety of elements: demographic characteristics (market size, population growth and distribution, education), geographic characteristics (topography and climate), economic factors (per capita income, GNP, distribution of income, household income, education), and the political-legal system (tariff and nontariff barriers, exchange controls, political risks, degree of nationalism). Acquiring and interpreting marketplace information relating to each of these areas are of fundamental importance to the development of marketing and advertising strategies. The one key area that we have not yet addressed is the cultural environment. Chapter 4 will be devoted to exploring this topic.

References

Ausaid. 2001. Global income and income distribution, 15 August. <globaledge.ausaid.gov.au/secondary/casestud/economics/I/glob-inc.html>

Baker, Stephen. 2002. The coming battle for immigrants. *Business Week,* 26 August, 138–40.

Barnes, Kathleen. 1993. Big marketers poised to flood into South Africa. *Advertising Age,* 17 May, 11.

Block, Robert. 1999. How big mac kept from becoming a Serb archenemy. *Wall Street Journal,* 3 September, B-1.

Case, Brendan. 2003. Exports to Cuba a booming business for U.S. farmers, Ranchers. *Knight Ridder Tribune News Service,* 17 February, 1.

Coy, Peter. 2002. Poverty: The news brightens. *Business Week,* 17 June, 22.

Dale, Helle. 2002. Zoellick's return: U.S. trade rep's bold tariff proposal. *Washington Times,* 4 December, A-19.

Engel, James F., and Rodger E. Blackwell. 1982. *Consumer behavior.* Chicago, Ill.: Dryden Press.

Euromonitor. 2002. International Marketing Forecasts.

Glasser, Susan. 2001. Patriotism, selling like hot cakes. *Washington Post,* 9 May, C-1.

Globalization is narrowing the poverty gap 2003. 2 March. <www.iccwbo.org/home/news_archives/2003/stories/globalization.asp>

Globalstat. 2003. Life expectancy at birth. <www.globalstat.com/p15.htm.>

Globalstat. 2003. Literacy Rates. <www.globalstat.com/p22.htm.>

Gyan, Jr., Joe. 2001. U.S. corn leaves N.O. for Cuba. *Advocate* (Baton Rouge, La.), 15 December, 12-A.

Hagmann, Michael. 2001. The world in 2050: More crowded, urban and aged. *Bulletin of the World Health Organization* 79(5): 484.

Hill, John, and Richard Still. 1984. Effects of urbanization on multinational product planning: Markets in lesser developed countries. *Columbia Journal of World Business* 19 (Summer): 62–67.

Koenderman, Tony. 1994. Pepsi, BBD&O thirst for S. Africa. *Adweek,* 4 July, 12.

Kotler, Philip. 1988. *Marketing management.* Englewood Cliffs, N.J.: Prentice Hall.

Kripalani, Manjeet, and Pete Engardio. 2002. Small is profitable: What will work in developing world is a focus on inexpensive, downsized, simple-to-use products. *Business Week,* 26 August, 112–14.

Murphy, Cait. 2002. The hunt for globalization that works. *Fortune,* 28 October, 163–76.

O'Leary, Michael. 2002. Analysts take an optimistic view. *Euromoney,* September, 208–15.

Onkvisit, Sak, and John Shaw. 1997. *International marketing: Analysis and strategy.* Upper Saddle River, N.J.: Prentice Hall.

Roberts, Dexter, and Alysha Webb. 2002. Motor nation: Finally, China's middle classes can afford the family car. *Business Week,* 17 June, 44–48.

Shari, Michael. 2001. Staying the course. *Business Week,* 24 September, 112.

Springer, Jr., Robert. 1986. New export laws and aid to international marketers. *Marketing News,* 3 January, 10, 67.

Terpstra, Vern, and Lloyd Russow. 2000. *International dimensions of marketing.* Cincinnati: Southwestern College Publishing.

World Bank. 2002. *World Development Indicators.*

CHAPTER FOUR

The Cultural Environment

The final aspect of the marketing and advertising environment that the international marketer must consider is the culture of a particular country. Marketers have traditionally examined a potential market's demographic and geographic characteristics, as well as economic and political factors, in order to determine if and how they might impact the marketing mix. However, only in recent years has greater attention been paid to the cultural environment. Each country exhibits cultural differences that influence the consumers' needs and wants, their methods of satisfying them, and the messages they are most likely to respond to. The international business literature reveals hundreds of blunders that have resulted from miscalculating—or simply ignoring—the cultural environment. This chapter explores the concept of culture and its various elements, and discusses tools potentially useful to international marketers attempting to analyze foreign cultures and penetrate foreign markets.

 Concept of Culture

Culture can be conceptualized in many ways. Indeed, in the early 1950s, Kroeber and Kluckhohn (1952) identified well over 160 different definitions of culture in the anthropological literature. Of course, many new definitions have appeared since. A classic definition is provided by E. B. Taylor, who defined culture as "a complex whole, which includes knowledge, beliefs, art, morals, law, custom, and any other capabilities and habits acquired by individuals as members of a society" (Taylor 1871, 1). Adamson Hoebel referred to culture as the "integrated sum total of learned behavioral traits that are manifest and shared by members of society" (Hoebel 1960, 168). Culture has also been defined as a "learned, shared, compelling, interrelated set of symbols whose meaning provides a set of orientations for members of a society" (Terpstra and David 1991, 12).

Even the three definitions provided here reveal some commonalities. It is generally agreed that culture is not inherent or innate, but rather is learned. Learning typically takes place in institutions, such as the family, church, and school. Samovar, Porter, and Stefani (1998, 39) note that, in addition to these formalized institutions, we also learn culture from more invisible instructors, such as proverbs, folktales, legends, art forms, and, of course, the mass media. Most definitions of culture also emphasize that culture is shared by members of a group. It is this shared aspect that enables communication between individuals within that culture. Because culture is shared, it defines the boundaries between different groups. Cross-cultural communication is so difficult, in large part, because of the lack of shared symbols. Finally, all facets of culture are interrelated—if one aspect of culture is changed, all else will be influenced as well. As Edward T. Hall notes, "you touch a culture in one place and everything else is affected" (Hall 1976, 13).

 Self-Reference Criterion and Ethnocentrism

When we examine other cultures, we tend to view them through "culturally tinted glasses." For example, if our own culture places a high value on education or cleanliness, we may assume—correctly or incorrectly—that other cultures share these same values. James Lee terms this unconscious reference to one's own culture the *self-reference criterion* (Lee 1966, 47). Because of this unconscious reference to one's own cultural values, marketers operating abroad may behave in a culturally myopic fashion.

Ethnocentrism poses another obstacle to understanding foreign cultures. Literally defined, *ethnocentrism* means "culturally centered"; it refers to people's tendency to place themselves at the center of the universe and not only evaluate others by the standards of their own culture but also believe that their own culture is superior to all others. A fundamental assumption of ethnocentric people is that their way of doing things is right, proper, and normal, and that the ways of culturally different people are wrong and inferior (Ferraro 1990, 34). Not surprisingly, this tendency toward an "us versus them" mentality is universal. People in all cultures, to some degree, display ethnocentric behaviors. Ethnocentrism limits our ability to accept cultural differences, which diminishes the chance of developing effective marketing programs. For example, the Body Shop's expansion into the United States has proved so far to be an unprofitable venture, primarily because of the ethnocentric assumption by the organization's senior management that their corporate identify strategy, which promotes the virtues of environmental friendliness and which has been highly successful within the United Kingdom, would be just as readily accepted in markets within the United States (Thomas and Hill 1999, 377). Gap has experienced similar challenges in moving abroad. Sales in Gap's 525 international stores have been so poor that the firm cut international store growth to 20 percent (down from 41 percent in the previous year). Gap's failing may be in believing that just because its merchandising and marketing is effective in the United States, it will surely be effective everywhere else. For example, in Japan the tags on Gap clothing are in English and Gap employees cheerfully greet customers with the casual Japanese version of "hi," an unaccustomed

informality for the mannerly Japanese (Barron and Ito 2001, 62). The best defense against ethnocentrism is an awareness of the tendency toward ethnocentrism.

Subcultures

While the focus of this text is international in scope, it is important to recognize that variations within cultures may be even greater than variations among cultures. In each culture there exist *subcultures*—groups of people with shared value systems based on common experiences. People belonging to various nationality groups (Italian, Polish, and Scandinavian Americans), religious groups (Protestants, Jews, Catholics), ethnic groups (blacks, Asians, Hispanics), political groups (Democrats, Republicans, socialists), and geographic groups (westerners, easterners, southerners) may well exhibit characteristic patterns of behavior that serve to distinguish them from other subgroups within a country. The same can be said about people who belong to specific age or income groups. Clearly, an individual can belong to more than one subculture. To the extent that these patterns of behavior impact wants and needs, these subcultures can be targeted by marketers.

The 2000 Census has boosted interest in a number of subcultures in the United States. Table 4.1 presents population figures for 2000 and projections for 2006 for blacks, Hispanics, and Asian Americans. All told, these three groups comprise close to 30 percent of the U.S. population and, by 2050, they are projected to make up half of the total U.S. population (Raugust 2002a, M-2). Each of these groups is currently more youthful than the general population. Over the coming decade, the multicultural population will not only continue to grow but will also be at their wage-earning peak and have incomes nearly equal to the general market. These developments, combined with the aging demographics of the white population, will make multicultural consumers of increasing interest to marketers.

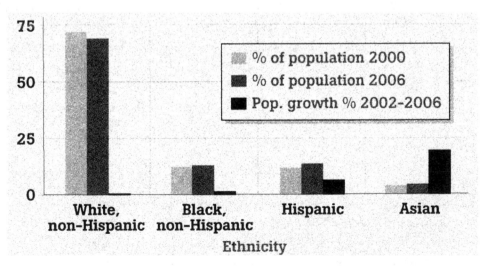

Figure 4.1 2000 Census.

TABLE 4.1 2000 Census

Ethnicity	2000 Population	2006 Estimated Population
White, non-Hispanic	196,929,000	199,923, 000
Black, non-Hispanic	33,619,000	35,845, 000
Hispanic	32,832,000	39,307, 000
Asian	10,620,000	12,879, 000

Source: U.S. Census Bureau, 2000.

African Americans are the largest segment of the multicultural market. They control more than $550 billion in purchasing power and are responsible for two out of every three dollars spent by ethnic consumers (Raugust 2002b, M-1). They are prime prospects for marketers of products such as films, active footwear, and soft drinks, where their share of market is at least twice as high as their 13 percent representation within the total population. See Figure 4.2 for a Pepsi-Cola advertisement targeting black consumers.

Perhaps the hottest group is the Hispanic market, which accounted for nearly 12 percent of the U.S. population in 2000. Conservative analysts predict that Hispanics will outnumber African Americans by the end of the decade. Others, pointing to high birthrate and immigration, expect Hispanics will become the number one ethnic group by the time this text goes to press. Indeed, the market is anticipated to balloon to somewhere between 23 and 35 percent of the U.S. population by 2050. It is estimated that Hispanics' purchasing power surpassed $630 billion in 2002 (Raugust 2002b, M-1). Hispanics outspend the general market in certain categories. For example, they purchase 48 percent more food for at-home consumption than the average U.S. household and twice as much premium-priced fish and seafood. See Figure 4.3 for an example of Wal-Mart's efforts to target Hispanics. Note the family orientation of the message.

Asian Americans are a relatively small and fragmented market, with six different ethnic groups accounting for 90 percent of the total, but their numbers are also growing. In 1990, just 2.9 percent of the U.S. population identified themselves as Asian or Pacific Islander. By 2007, nearly 5 percent of the U.S. population will be of Asian ethnicity. Asian Americans tend to be better educated and have higher incomes than the other ethnic groups.

A 2002 survey revealed that most advertisers market to Hispanics and African Americans (70 percent and 59 percent respectively), but only 27 percent target Asian Americans (Wentz 2002, 6). As multicultural markets continue to grow in scope and buying power, an ever-increasing number of marketers will attempt to reach these consumers. Marketers typically look to advertising agencies that understand the opportunities as well as difficulties in reaching ethnic consumers. Research has consistently shown that multicultural consumers respond best to messages and images that reflect a deep insight into their culture and the unique ways they perceive and use a product. Table 4.2 lists the top multicultural agencies by gross income.

Marketing to African Americans, Hispanics, and Asian Americans means much more than simply replacing a Caucasian model with an ethnic model. Much as with marketing to Caucasian

Figure 4.2 Pepsi-Cola Targets African American consumers.

Ilusiones

"Al año de casados, recibimos la gran noticia: ¡íbamos a ser padres! Y, desde ese momento, Wal-Mart ha sido nuestro secreto para hacer que el presupuesto rinda mas allá de lo esperado."

— Raquel Martínez

Desde que Raquel Martínez supo que esperaba una visita de la cigüeña, se pasó horas enteras en Wal-Mart, buscando y comprando de todo para su nueva bebita: biberones, chupones, pañales… ¡hasta el trajecito con el que la vistió para llevársela del hospital! "Con precios tan razonables y con gente amable para ayudarnos como Patricio Parras, en Wal-Mart nos alcanzó para todo lo que necesitábamos… y ahora, tres años después, sigo viniendo y, claro, sigo ahorrando."

WAL★MART
Para Su Familia, De Todo Corazón.

Siempre.

wal-mart.com

Figure 4.3 Wal-Mart ad targeting Hispanics.

TABLE 4.2 Top Multicultural Agencies, 2002 (U.S. million $)

Rank	Agency	U.S. Gross Income		Rank	Agency	U.S. Gross Income
Marketing to African Americans				*Marketing to Hispanics*		
1.	Burrell Communications Group	24.8		1.	Bravo Group	27.9
2.	UniWorld Group	23.7		2.	Bromley Communications	17.7
3.	Carol H. Williams Advertising	19.6		3.	CreativeOnDemand	15.0
4.	Images USA	12.0		4.	Zubi Advertising Services	14.9
5.	Chisholm-Mingo	7.1		5.	La Agencia de Orci & Associates	13.4
6.	Fuse	5.0		6.	Dieste, Harmel & Partners	13.0
7.	Correct Communications	3.8		7.	Mendoza Dillon & Asociados	12.9
8.	RJ Dale Advertising & PR	3.6		8.	Publicis Sanchez & Levitan	12.2
9.	Matlock Advertising & Public Relations	3.2		9.	Lapiz	11.2
10.	Anderson Communications	3.1		10.	Del Rivero Messianu DDB	10.0

Rank	Agency	U.S. Gross Income
Marketing to Asian Americans		
1.	A Partnership	6.6
2.	Kang & Lee	6.5
3.	Time Advertising	6.0
4.	PanCom	5.7
5.	IW Group	5.6
6.	InterTrend Communications	5.0
7.	Admerasia	4.0
8.	Adasia Communications	2.5
9.	Dae Advertising	1.6
10.	Saeshe Advertising	1.0

Source: Agency Report, *Advertising Age,* 21 April 2003, S-12.

consumers, advertisers that succeed in multicultural marketing tailor their messages to their audience and integrate advertising, public relations, promotions, direct marketing, sponsorships, and community events. For example, Heineken Beer launched a totally integrated marketing program created specifically for the Hispanic market. The $11 billion campaign included three lavishly produced 30-second commercials that aired on Spanish-language television stations. According to Heineken's brand manager, Pepe Carreras, "although the commercials follow the same creative style as Heineken's general market TV spots, they have been tailored to the sensibilities of Hispanic Americans—featuring Hispanic actors and situations with which the Hispanic audience can identify" (*Business Wire* 1999a, 1).

In addition to the television ads, seven radio spots aired that revolved around Hispanic consumers telling "real stories" about their favorite beer. In addition to broadcasting, Heineken's effort in the Hispanic community included out-of-home advertising (bus shelters, billboards, and phone kiosks). Rounding out the marketing campaign was an expansion of a

series of local Latin music concerts in Hispanic bars—including local grassroots concerts in city parks as well as major stars at Radio City Music Hall in New York. Heineken was also one of the first corporations to donate money to Hispanic Hurricane Relief and has been involved in a number of charitable and civic endeavors in the Hispanic community. "There is a real feeling of 'community' among Latinos and through our integrated advertising and marketing program, Heineken is a vital member of that community—both in bringing fun and entertainment and providing aid where needed," Carreras emphasized.

An understanding of subcultures is essential, because the failure to recognize distinctive subcultures can lead to an illusion of sameness within a market that simply does not exist. Additionally, understanding a subculture in one country may also help the marketer to understand a similar subculture in a foreign market. Knowing what motivates a New York businessman who earns $100,000 annually may well assist in the understanding of his counterpart abroad. A Paris businesswoman is likely to be much more similar to her colleague across the ocean than she is to a fellow French woman who works in the vineyards of Burgundy.

Culture and Communication

Many cultural differences, and their impact on elements of the marketing mix, are obvious. Clearly, if one wishes to communicate with consumers in Kenya, language differences must be taken into account, and all promotional materials must be translated into the local tongue. Many cultural differences are, however, quite subtle. For example, one American shoe manufacturer promoted its product through advertisements with photos of bare feet. Although such a message would pose no problem in most countries, the campaign failed miserably in Southeast Asia, where exposure of the foot is considered an insult. The problem of communicating to people in diverse cultures has been called one of the greatest challenges in marketing communications (Ricks 1988, 11). International marketers, if they are to be successful in their efforts, must become culturally sensitive—that is, tuned to the nuances of culture. Indeed, they must become students of culture.

Among the important elements of culture marketers must take into consideration are verbal communication (both spoken and written) and the various forms of nonverbal communication (among them gestures, space, time, and other signs and symbols).

Verbal Communication

In deciding which markets to enter and how to enter them, the international marketer must speak with governmental and business leaders in foreign countries as well as with potential employees and suppliers. Marketers probably will deal with the local language when collecting market data. Also, in attempting to communicate with potential customers, marketers are faced with choosing a brand name, selecting copy or text to be included on product packaging, developing advertising slogans, and creating advertising messages.

Because language plays such a central role in international marketing, it is crucial to understand the close relationship between culture and language. Culture and communication are inextricably linked. It has been said that it is impossible to truly understand a culture without understanding the language spoken by its people (Whorf 1956, 212). Conversely, a language cannot be fully understood outside its cultural context. As Gerhard Maletzke explains:

> The art and manner in which one understands the world is determined to a large extent by language; but language, at the same time, is an expression of a specific group-experiencing of the world, and therefore may itself be shaped by the Weltanschauung as well as the wishes, expectations, and motivations of the group using it. (Maletzke 1976, 74)

Put more simply, culture both influences and is influenced by language.

Linguists claim that up to 5,000 different languages are spoken around the globe—some spoken by millions, others by no more than several hundred. Table 4.3 lists the leading languages spoken around the world. Chinese tops the list as the most spoken language, but although the written language is uniform, there are literally hundreds of local dialects in China. Multilingual societies constitute the majority of the world's nations. For example, Zaire has over 100 different tribal languages, and in India over 200 languages and dialects are spoken. Any country in which a number of different languages are spoken undoubtedly will also have a number of different cultures. Consider Canada, where citizens speak predominantly English or French; or Belgium, where French and Flemish are spoken. In both Canada and Belgium, the differing linguistic groups have clashed on occasion. In Zaire and India, such confrontations have even resulted in violence.

A debate continues regarding whether English can be considered the world's first genuinely global language. To be worthy of the designation "global," a language needs to be present in every country in the world. English now probably is; it is the first language for about 340 million people, mainly in the United States, Canada, Britain, Ireland, Australia, New Zealand, and South Africa. It has achieved special status as a second language spoken by another 375 million in more than 70 countries, such as China, Nigeria, India, Singapore, and Vanuatu. And in most—perhaps all—of the remaining countries, it is the foreign language children are most likely to learn at school. Foreign English language learners may now exceed 1 billion. Although estimates vary greatly, some 1.5 billion people are thought to be competent communicators in English. That is a quarter of the world's population. The question is, how can English be a global language when three out of four people never use it? The answer is that English is now the dominant tongue in international politics, banking, the press, news agencies, broadcasting, the recording industry, movies, travel, science and technology, knowledge management, communications—and, of course, advertising (Crystal 1999, 4).

But even English is not universally embraced. The French have a long reputation for being monolingual and quite defensive about their language. French officials have been waging an increasingly aggressive war against English creeping into common usage. French, as well as international, advertisers have come under fire for using English words in advertising copy. The advertising standards regulator (BVP) argues that only 35 percent of the population speak

TABLE 4.3 Languages Spoken Around the World

Language	Hub	Countries	Speakers (millions)
Chinese, Mandarin	China	16	874
Hindi	India	17	366
English	United Kingdom	104	341
Spanish	Spain	43	322–58
Bengali	Bangladesh	9	207
Portuguese	Portugal	33	176
Russian	Russia	30	167
Japanese	Japan	26	125
German, Standard	Germany	40	100
Korea	South	31	78

Source: World Almanac and Book of Facts, 2003, 633.

enough English to be able to follow such English language slogans as Nike's "Just do it" and Apple's "Think different." So, in line with a 1994 law, Nike, Apple, and a string of other companies are supposed to include a French translation equal in size and prominence and with exactly the same meaning. But the BVP notes that the rules are often bent, and "English first" appears to be the order of the day (King 2000, 18). France is not alone in its mission to protect its language; current laws regarding foreign-language use in Korea are designed essentially to protect the sovereignty of the Korean language. Foreign languages must be translated into Korean, if a translation is at all possible. "Unnecessary" use of foreign languages and mixing Korean with foreign languages is prohibited. However, there is no regulatory framework spelling out exactly what "unnecessary" use is (Ambler 2000, 1). And a recent study (Gerritsen et al. 2000, 17) found that while one-third of the commercials on Dutch television contain English words and phrases, Dutch consumers neither understand nor appreciate them.

While language helps to define a cultural group, as Table 4.3 revealed, the same language can be spoken in a number of different countries. For example, Spanish is spoken in Spain, Mexico, Argentina, and Peru. English is spoken in the United States, England, much of Canada, Australia, and Ireland. Nonetheless, marketers must use caution when employing the same language in two or more markets. For example, there are significant differences between American English and British English. Often the same word or phrase may mean different things. A billion means a thousand million to an American, but a million million to a Brit. Also, different words may also be used for the same thing, as Table 4.4 illustrates.

Languages differ in their levels of formality. In English, there is only one word for "you." In contrast, the French use the informal *tu* for family and friends, and the formal *vous* for people they do not know well. Similarly, Germans use *du* for informal and personal settings, and *Sie* in formal settings.

This situation is significantly more complicated in Japanese. In the Japanese language the level of formality depends on the gender and status of the speaker and listener as well as the

TABLE 4.4 American English vs. British English

American	British	American	British
aisle	gangway	baby carriage	pram
bacon	gammon	checkers	draughts
diaper	nappy	druggist	chemist
elevator	lift	flashlight	torch
French fries	chips	lawyer	solicitor
line	queue	mail box	pillar box
radio	wireless	second floor	first floor
sidewalk	pavement	toilet	W.C.
truck	lorry	two weeks	fortnight
underwear	smalls	vacation	holiday

context of the conversation. This has a number of implications for marketing communications. For example, the language used by the seller is much more deferential than that of the buyer—the buyer is always placed in the position of superior status. Moreover, the female speaker is always required to use more polite, deferential language. As a result, saleswomen or female characters in broadcast advertisements tend to give a product a "feminine" image. While this association may be beneficial for certain kinds of products, such as household items, for others it may hurt sales (Shane 1988, 155).

Language and Context The concept of high and low context provides an understanding of different cultural orientations and explains how communication is conveyed and perceived. As defined by Edward T. Hall, low-context cultures place high value on words, and communicators are encouraged to be direct, exact, and unambiguous. What is important is what is said, not how it is said or the environment in which it is said. In contrast, high-context cultures consider verbal communications to be only a part of the overall message, and communicators rely much more heavily on contextual cues. Edward and Mildred Hall wrote: "Context is the information that surrounds an event and is inextricably bound up with the meaning of that event. The elements that combine to produce a given meaning—events and context—are in different proportions depending on culture" (Hall and Hall 1987, 7). Thus, messages in high-context cultures tend to be a good deal more implicit and ambiguous, with communicators relying much more on nonverbal behavior, the physical setting, social circumstances, and the nature of interpersonal relationships. The Halls further explain that "a high context communication or message is one in which most of the information is already in the person, while very little is in the coded, explicit, transmitted part of the message. A low-context communication is vested in the explicit code" (Hall 1976, 16). Cultures typically are not perceived as either high- or low-context but, as Figure 4.4 shows, are arranged along a continuum. Note that this continuum should not give the impression of equal intervals. In part, contextuality of communication is related to whether the language itself expresses ideas and facts more or less explicitly. As Jean-Claude Usunier explains:

```
High Context
   ↑   Japanese
       Chinese
       Arab
       Greek
       Spanish
       Italian
       English
       French
       United States
       Scandinavian
       German
   ↓   Swiss German
Low Context
```

Figure 4.4 High-context versus low-context cultures.

Japanese, for instance, is on average less precise than English or French. For example, personal pronouns are often not explicitly expressed in Japanese, and the number of tenses is largely reduced (especially in comparison to French). In Japanese, both spoken words (that is sounds) and written words (based on *kanjis*, that is pictograms) often have multiple meanings, so that the listener needs some kind of contextual clarification. Sometimes, Japanese people write the *kanjis* (ideographs) briefly on their hand to make clear what they are saying. Naturally it would be a mistake to say that certain languages are vague and others precise. The real world is more complex. This has to be strongly nuanced when one looks more carefully at the structure of the language. For instance, German has many verbs that have quite different meanings according to context. It is easy to discover such examples just by consulting a German-English dictionary. For instance, the verb *absetzen* means, according to context, to deposit or deduct a sum, to take off a hat, to dismiss an official, to depose a king, to drop a passenger, to sell goods, to stop or pause, or to take off (a play). The same holds true for the Finnish language, even though the Finns may have a reputation, like many northern Europeans for their explicitness in communication. Finnish has a very special language structure which renders the use of context useful in communication, that of Finno-Ugrian languages, really only shared with Estonia and Hungary. The Finnish language uses sixteen cases which virtually replace all prepositions used in other languages. Even proper nouns can be declined using these cases. (Usunier 1966, 371)

The differences between communications styles in high- versus low-context cultures have direct implications for the international advertiser. Messages constructed by writers from high-context cultures might be difficult to understand in low-context cultures because they do not come to the point. Similarly, messages constructed by writers from low-context cultures may be difficult to understand in high-context cultures because they omit essential contextual material (Wells 1987, 18). For example, the United States is considered to be a low-context culture while Japan is considered a high-context culture. American marketers tend to be more logical, scientific, and oriented toward data, systems, and procedures, while Japanese marketers tend to be more intuitive, subjective, and oriented toward communications and human relations (Lazer 1995, 69). As might be expected, the advertising messages created in these two markets differ dramatically. American consumers are known for their interest in product information and precise details (Biswas et al. 1992, 73).

Consumers in the United States look to advertising messages for just such information. Thus commercial communications tend to emphasize the merits of the product clearly, logically, and reasonably by directly presenting information, facts, and evidence related to the product (Hong et al. 1987, 55).

A number of studies have documented that Japanese ads, both broadcast and print, contain fewer information cues than ads appearing in the United States and many other countries (Lyn 1992, 1; Ramaprasad and Hasegawa 1990, 1025). Japanese advertising is less likely to focus on the product's merits; the direct or hard-sell approach so common in American advertising seems to leave the Japanese consumer cold (Mueller 1992, 22). Comparative claims, a mainstay in American advertising, are almost unheard of in Japan. Instead, note Edward and Mildred Hall, "Japanese advertising evokes a mood and is designed to appeal to emotions, produce good feelings, and create a happy atmosphere. The approach is soft-sell" (Hall and Hall 1987, 139). Indeed, much of Japanese advertising is so soft-sell that it is often difficult to determine what the product is from viewing an advertisement. For example, a quick glimpse at the Japanese advertisement in Figure 4.5 would probably not reveal that this is a message promoting mayonnaise. Indeed, even reading the copy probably wouldn't help much. The headline (in English) is simply "Speed." The single line of body copy tells the consumer that salads are as quick to prepare as prepackaged foods. The only hint that this is an ad for Kewpie mayonnaise is the trade figure in the center of the ad and the product name in the lower right hand corner. The suggestion that salads be prepared with Kewpie mayonnaise is implied.

Translations No discussion of language in international commercial communications would be complete without addressing the importance of translations. Errors in the translation of brand names, packaging copy, and advertising messages have cost businesses millions of dollars, not to mention damaging their credibility and reputation. It is not enough for translators merely to be familiar with the native tongue. In order to avoid translation blunders, translators must also be familiar with nuances, idioms, and slang. Consider the following:

- The American Dairy Association experienced tremendous success with the campaign "Got Milk?" (see Figure 4.6). It was decided to extend the ads to Mexico. Unfortunately, the Spanish translation was "Are you lactating?"
- Coors translated its slogan, "Turn it loose," into Spanish, where it was read as "Suffer from diarrhea."
- Bacardi concocted a fruity drink with the name "Pavian" to suggest French chic . . . but "Pavian" means "baboon" in German.
- When Kentucky Fried Chicken entered the Chinese market, to their horror they discovered that their slogan "finger lickin' good" came out as "eat your fingers off."
- When Vicks first introduced its cough drops in the German market, they were chagrined to learn that the German pronunciation of v is f—which in German is the vulgar equivalent of "sexual penetration."
- In Italy, a campaign for "Schweppes Tonic Water" translated the name into the much less thirst-quenching "Schweppes Toilet Water."
- Puffs tissues proved challenging to introduce into the German market because "Puff" in

Figure 4.5 Soft-sell Japanese advertisement for mayonnaise.

You should see what's underneath.
The calcium in milk keeps bones strong and helps prevent osteoporosis.

got milk?

American Heart Association
Fat Free and 1/2% Lowfat Milk meet American Heart Association food
criteria for saturated fat and cholesterol for healthy people over age 2.

Figure 4.6 The "Got Milk?" campaign got into trouble in Mexico.

German is the colloquial term for a whorehouse. The English weren't too fond of the name either, as it is a highly derogatory term for a homosexual.

- Ford introduced the Pinto in Brazil. After watching sales go nowhere, the company learned that "Pinto" is Brazilian slang for "tiny male genitals." Ford pried the nameplates off all the cars and changed them to read "Corcel," which means horse.

One useful technique in revealing translation errors is called back-translation (Miracle 1988, RC-51). One individual is responsible for the initial translation of the message. A second individual then translates the message back into the original language. If the message does not translate back, it's likely that there is a translation problem. While back-translation is a helpful tool, it's no guarantee against translation bloopers. Hiring only native speakers of the language into which the message is to be translated also helps to reduce problems, as does acknowledging that some words and phrases simply cannot be translated. Translation techniques will be discussed in greater detail in Chapter 6. A final caution with regard to language—international marketers must recognize that writing and reading rules differ from culture to culture as well. Americans simply take it for granted that when they read or write, they move from left to right. Failure to recognize that this is not the case everywhere can result in marketing disasters. For example, a print ad for a laundry detergent appeared in the United States and featured a classic product demonstration. Laundry detergent was poured onto soiled clothing, which was soaking in a washing machine. After laundering, the clothing looked clean as new. The execution was so straightforward that the New York agency team responsible for it sent it directly to their Arabic agency's traffic person, suitably translated, for placement in local media. Unfortunately, the American advertising professionals were unaware that Arabic is read from right to left. The result: the ad showed laundry becoming soiled as a result of the detergent being added (Caporimo 1995, 16).

Nonverbal Communication

We communicate not only through spoken language but also through nonverbal language. Indeed, it has been estimated that approximately 70 percent of all communication between two individuals within the same culture is nonverbal in nature. Nonverbal communication, often referred to as the silent language, can pose serious problems for international marketers and advertisers.

A number of classification systems of nonverbal language exist, some containing up to 24 different categories of behaviors (Hall 1976; Condon and Yousef 1975). Most classification systems include facial expressions, eye contact and gaze, body movement (such as hand gestures and posture), touching, smell, space usage, time symbolism, appearance or dress, color symbolism, and even silence. It is important to note that nonverbal methods of communication are no more universal than verbal methods.

Nonverbal communication regulates human interaction in several important ways: (1) it sends messages about our attitudes and feelings, (2) it elaborates on our verbal messages, and

(3) it governs the timing and turn-taking between communicators (Ferraro 1990, 34). A thorough discussion of all of the aspects of the silent language, as it is often called, is beyond the scope of this text. However, because of their importance to the international marketer, four areas will be addressed briefly: gestures, space usage, time symbolism, and signs and colors.

Gestures Thousands of cross-cultural examples prove that the meaning of gestures shift from culture to culture. Gestures refer to any movement of the fingers, hands, or arms. Just as one word can mean different things in different countries, so, too, nonverbal cues vary in their meaning. The American "OK" gesture communicated by making a circle with one's thumb and index finger means zero or worthless in France and signifies money in Japan and Korea. In Greece and Brazil, it carries a quite vulgar connotation. However in Arab countries, paired with a baring of the teeth, it suggests extreme hostility. Caution is advised using this gesture in Tunisia, because there it means "I'll kill you." The "thumbs up" sign used in an AT&T campaign presented a problem when it had to be translated into other languages. For most Americans this gesture signifies positive affirmation. But to Russians and Poles, because the palm of the hand was visible, it gave the print advertisement, produced by N. W. Ayer, an entirely different— even offensive—meaning. YAR Communications, an agency specializing in translations, was engaged to reshoot the graphic element of the advertisement so that only the back of the hand was seen, thereby conveying the intended meaning (Davis 1993, 50).

There are also different gestures that convey the same message from market to market. Consider how men in different parts of the world show their appreciation of an attractive female via gestures:

- *The waist curve* (common in English-speaking cultures): hands sweep down to make the curvaceous outline of the female body.
- *The cheek screw* (Italy and Sardinia): the forefinger is pressed into the cheek and rotated.
- *The hand on the heart* (South America): the right hand is placed over the heart, signifying a heart throb.
- *The eye touch* (Italy and South America): a straight forefinger is placed on the lower eyelid and pulled down slightly.
- *The cheek pinch* (Sicily): a man pinches his own cheek.
- *The breast cup* (Europe in general): both hands make a cupping movement in the air, simulating the squeezing of the woman's breast.

Gestures used in greetings also vary from one culture to the next. In the United States, the hand wave is a common form of greeting. Hence, at McDonald's restaurants across the country, life-size Ronald McDonald statues have their hands raised in a friendly wave. However, operators of McDonald's restaurants in Thailand were required to modify the figure to display the unique Thai greeting gesture, the "Wai." The traditional greeting consists of the palms of both hands placed together and raised in front of the head as a sign of humility and respect. This is the first time that Ronald McDonald—the fast food chain's mascot—has displayed a culture-

specific gesture such as this one. Usually, the rather neutral and internationalized statue is distributed from the United States to franchises around the globe. In this case, Thai operators had to custom-manufacture the molded fiberglass and resin stature. The end result? The mascot has become genuinely Thai (*Advertising Age* 2002).

There are also cultural differences regarding the amount and size of gestures employed during communication. Some cultures are quite animated. Middle Easterners, South Americans, Greeks, and, in particular, Italians employ a wide variety of gestures quite frequently. Indeed, there is even a stereotype that suggests Italians would be unable to explain themselves if their hands were tied behind their backs. Other cultures—Americans and Northern Europeans, for example—are more restrained in their gestures. These cultures place a higher value on verbal communication and consider excessive gesturing to be overly emotional or irrational.

Space Usage How humans use space is referred to as *proxemics.* Edward and Mildred Hall suggest that "each person has around him an invisible bubble of space which expands and contracts depending on his relationship to those around him, his emotional state, and the activity he is performing" (Hall and Hall 1987, 12). Based on his observations of North Americans, Edward Hall developed four categories of distance in human interactions:

1. *Intimate distance:* ranging from body contact to 18 inches, this distance is used for personal contact, comforting, and protecting. Here, olfactory and thermal sensations are at their highest.
2. *Personal distance:* from 18 inches to 4 feet, depending on the closeness of the relationship, in this distancing mode people have an invisible "space bubble" separating themselves from others.
3. *Social distance:* from 4 to 12 feet, this distance is used by acquaintances and strangers in business meetings and classrooms.
4. *Public distance:* from 12 to 25 feet, at this distance recognition of others is not mandatory, and the subtle shades of meaning of voice, gesture, and facial expression are lost. (Hall 1966, 177)

However, the use of space is culture-bound—members of different cultures do not necessarily conform to Hall's four categories of distance. Americans are said to demonstrate a particularly high level of territoriality when compared with members of other cultures. In contrasting Europeans and Americans, Hall and Hall note:

> In Northern Europe the bubbles are quite large; moving south to France, Italy, Greece and Spain, the bubbles get smaller and smaller so that the distance that is perceived as intimate in the north overlaps personal distance in the south, which means that Mediterranean Europeans get too close to the Germans, Scandinavians, English, and Americans of northern European ancestry. (Hall and Hall 1987, 113)

Imagine the diversity when we compare how space is used in Africa or Asia. For example, most Americans feel quite uncomfortable when trapped on a crowded commuter train or in a full elevator. However, space is used differently by members of Japanese society. Japanese tend

to stand and sit much closer together than Americans and appear to endure crowded conditions in public areas without much discomfort. As further evidence that Japanese and Americans use space differently, consider that in the United States top executives are typically separated from their employees—often inhabiting the top floor of the company building or, at the very least, sequestered in private offices. Because the Japanese are a group-oriented people, top executives rarely occupy private offices, preferring instead to work shoulder to shoulder with their employees. Clearly, each culture develops its own set of rules for space, and proper usage of space must be employed when developing visuals for advertising messages destined for foreign markets. Space usage also has implications for personal selling. A salesperson who does not understand the appropriate use of space in a given market may find it difficult to sell his or her product line.

Time Symbolism Just as the use of space is culturally influenced, so, too, is our use of time. A culture's concept of time refers to the relative importance it places on time. Edward T. Hall noted that "two time systems have evolved—monochronic and polychronic. "Monochronic time means paying attention to and doing only one thing at a time. Polychronic time means being involved with many things at once. Like oil and water, the two systems do not mix" (Hall 1966, 16). In a *monochronic* time (M-time) system, schedules often take priority over everything else and are treated as sacred and unalterable. Planes and trains must always run on time. Individuals raised in M-time systems constantly check their calendars and watches, worry about being prompt for appointments, and take it as an insult if kept waiting by others. Although this may seem natural and logical, it is merely a learned product of northern European culture. Hall explains that M-time systems grew out of the Industrial Revolution in England, wherein the factory labor force was required to be on hand and in place at the appointed hour. While examples of purely monochronic societies are rare, it can safely be said that Western cultures, in particular the United States, Switzerland, Germany, and Scandinavia, are dominated by M-time.

Polychronic time (P-time) systems are the antithesis of M-time systems. P-time is characterized by the simultaneous occurrence of many things and by a much greater involvement with people. In P-time systems, schedules and agendas mean very little, and appointments are often forgotten or rearranged at the last minute. No eyebrows are raised if one arrives at a meeting 45 minutes late. Middle Eastern and Latin American cultures often exhibit P-time behaviors. Indonesians have an expression for polychronic time: they call it *jam karet* or "rubber time"—flexible, stretchable meeting times, schedules, and agendas. Indonesians tend to place a higher value on human relationships than on arbitrary schedules and deadlines.

What does all this mean for businesses operating in the international arena? Consider the agency–client relationship—and the confusion that might result if each participant in the relationship is operating on a different time system. A Western client might rush to ensure arriving on time for a meeting with a Middle Eastern agency executive—and feel quite irritated if left sitting for nearly an hour in an outer office. Consider the potential impact on advertising message content. A telephone company did not take time orientation into account when developing a television spot for its Latin American audience. In the ad, the wife told her husband to "run downstairs and phone

Mary. Tell her we'll be a little late." In fact, this commercial contained two major cultural errors. First, almost no Latin American would feel obligated to phone to warn of tardiness because it is expected. Second, Latin American wives seldom dare to order their husbands around (Ricks 1983, 70). It is impossible to estimate how much business has been lost because marketers failed to take into account differences between monochronic and polychronic peoples.

Colors and Other Signs and Symbols International marketers may encounter problems with the connotative meanings of colors and other signs and symbols as they vary from culture to culture. Laurence Jacobs and colleagues note: "Like language, marketers in a particular nation often take color for granted, having experienced certain color associations all their lives, and do not even question whether other associations may exist in different societies" (Jacobs et al. 1991, 21). However, the significance of and meanings associated with specific colors vary from culture to culture. For example, while black signifies mourning in many Western cultures, white is the color most associated with death in Japan, Hong Kong, and India. White lilies are the appropriate flower for funerals in England, Canada, and Sweden, yet in Mexico white flowers are said to lift the spirits. Yellow flowers connote death in both Mexico and Taiwan, while purple is the color of death in Brazil and purple flowers are considered most appropriate for funerals. In the former Soviet Union, yellow flowers are considered a sign of disrespect to a woman, and in Taiwan, wearing a green hat signifies an unfaithful wife. Red is considered a positive color in Denmark but associated with the occult in many African countries.

International marketers need to know what associations a culture has in terms of colors and how they might affect product design, packaging, logos, advertisements, and other collaterals. When color meanings are similar across markets, a standardized strategy may be viable. A recent study by Madden, Hewett, and Roth (2000) found that blue, green, and white tend to be well liked across many countries and have similar meanings. However, the meanings associated with black and red varied considerably. Despite such generalizations, a thorough understanding of how colors are perceived in each country a marketer is planning to enter is clearly advisable. When the meaning associated with a color is different across cultures, marketers benefit from pursuing a customized strategy. David Ricks points out that the "choice of package and product coloring is very tricky. Sometimes companies have failed to sell their products overseas and have never known why. Often the reason was a simple one; the product or its container was merely an inappropriate color" (Ricks 1983, 32). For example, a number of years ago a leading U.S. golf ball manufacturer targeted Japan as an important new market for its product. However, sales of the company's golf balls were well below average. As it turned out, the firm had offered its product in white packaging—a color often associated with mourning. To make matters worse, it had packaged the balls in groups of four—the number signifying death in Japan (Glover 1994, 2). While the number 4 sounds like the word "death" in both Japanese and Chinese, it also happens to sound like "loin" in other languages. Numbers and shapes both mean different things to different peoples. While Americans associate misfortune with the number 13, it has no particular meaning in most other cultures. The number 7 is considered bad luck in Kenya and good luck in the former Czechoslovakia, and it has magical connotations in Benin.

Even the use of animals can prove problematic. The owl in both the United States and United Kingdom symbolizes wisdom; in France the bird is considered to have rather limited intelligence, while in the Middle East it is seen as a bad omen. Not knowing the symbolism associated with a particular animal in various cultures can directly affect the bottom line. A well-known marketer of eyeglasses initiated a campaign in Thailand with billboards showing cute pictures of animals wearing eyeglasses. Sales, however, failed to materialize. The marketer only later discovered that the Thais regarded animals as a lower level of creation and found advertising using animal themes to be unappealing. In another example of an advertising faux pas, a print ad for a men's cologne pictured a man and his dog in a rural American setting. This ad worked well in America but failed in Northern Africa. The advertiser simply assumed that "man's best friend" was loved everywhere and failed to recognize that Muslims usually consider dogs to be either signs of bad luck or symbols of uncleanliness.

The Influence of Culture on Marketing and Advertising

Religion, Morals, and Ethical Standards

Robert Bartels notes that "the foundation of a nation's culture and the most important determinant of social and business conduct are the religious and philosophic beliefs of a people. From them spring role perceptions, behavior patterns, codes of ethics and the institutionalized manner in which economic activities are performed" (Bartels 1982, 5). As such, knowledge of the moral and religious traditions of a country are essential to the international marketer's understanding of why consumers behave the way they do in a particular market.

Although numerous religious groups exist in the world today, Buddhism, Christianity, Hinduism, Islam, and Shinto are considered the major religions in terms of numbers of adherents. The influences of religion on international marketing are manifold. In some countries references to God or religion are taken very seriously. In cultures practicing Islam, it is considered highly inappropriate to use quranic quotations, the Prophet's name, God's name, or pictures of Islamic shrines on products or in promotional materials (Hashmi 1987). In a marketing blunder tied to religion, a shipment of Nike shoes featured a logo that resembled the word "Allah" in Arabic script. Allah is Islam's word for God. Nike said the logo (see Figure 4.7) was meant to look like flames, for a line of shoes to be sold during the summer with names such as Air Bakin', Air Melt, Air Grill, and Air-B-Que. When Nike's eastern European office discovered that the original logo could be insulting to Muslim consumers, they immediately changed the design—but not before the Islamic Council loudly criticized the product (Abu-Nasr 1997, A-11). Other marketers tread lightly when it comes to religion. When Hyatt Hotels enters a new market, it takes religious customs very seriously. In Singapore ceiling arrows point in the direction of Mecca. The Grand Hyatt in Bangkok boasts both a house god and a house temple. In Bali, Hyatt asked religious leaders for help in approving the artwork before the hotel opened. Artifacts the hotel had purchased to be placed near the restaurant were repositioned elsewhere when company of-

Figure 4.7 Nihad Awad, executive director of the Islamic Council, displays Nike shoes he says are insulting to Muslims.

ficials were informed that the artifacts were too holy to be close to an area where people eat (Greenberg 1993, F4).

Religion directly impacts the way its adherents feel about work and the value they place on material goods. At the heart of Buddhism, for example, is the belief that suffering is caused by attachment to material possessions and selfish enjoyment of any kind. Islam also considers an emphasis on material wealth immoral. Such views stand in direct contrast to the Protestant work ethic, wherein acquisition of wealth is a measure of achievement. The doctrine "for the good of all" is at the heart of the Shinto religion, practiced extensively in Japan. This doctrine is reflected in the Japanese work ethic: to live is to work and to work is to be conscientious and to make everyone proud. The Japanese dedication to hard work has resulted in twelve-hour work days, often six days per week.

Religious traditions may forbid altogether the sale, or at least the advertising, of various products. There are about 320 million consumers in North Africa and the Middle East and most do not consume alcoholic beverages for religious reasons. In some countries, such as Saudi Arabia, alcohol is even outlawed. For most brewers this would seem an insurmountable obstacle. How-

Figure 4.8 Strong demand in Muslim regions for nonalcoholic malt beverages

ever, Heineken and Carlsberg, two international brewers, have found it quite lucrative to sell nonalcoholic beers to consumers in such markets (Mortimer 2003, H-2). In Egypt, two Heineken products have become particularly successful. Each year, the company sells over 11 million gallons of Fayrouz, a fruit-flavored malt beverage that produces a head of foam when poured into a glass but contains no alcohol. A second product does nearly as well—over 9.2 million gallons of Birell, a beer-flavored nonalcoholic drink, are sold to consumers each year (see Figure 4.8).

While some product categories, such as alcoholic beverages and cigarettes obviously have the potential to cause difficulties in foreign markets, sometimes quite benign products come up against obstacles related to religion as well. Gillette faced quite a challenge in promoting its razors to consumers in Iran because Islam discourages followers from shaving. As Laurel Wentz relates, in attempting to obtain media space for Gillette's Blue II advertisements, a representative from an affiliate agency went from one paper to the next. Finally, he came across a newspaper advertising manager without a beard and noted that "shaving is not just for your face . . . if you have a car accident and someone has to shave your head, Gillette Blue II is the best" (Wentz 1992, 140). Using this argument, the newspaper advertising manager consulted his clergyman and returned with permission to run the ad. Other products that are banned in this market because of the very conservative application of Islamic teachings include cigarettes, lighters, and even candy and chocolates. Islam also forbids the consumption of pork, while followers of the Hindu religion don't eat beef. An advertising blunder occurred some years ago when an appliance manufacturer ran an advertisement depicting an open refrigerator containing a centrally placed chunk of ham. Ads often feature a refrigerator stocked with delicious food, and because such photos are rather difficult to shoot, they generally are used for as many promotional purposes as possible. Unfortunately, the company used the stock photo in an ad headed for the Middle East. Locals considered the portrayal of pork to be insensitive and unappealing.

Religion may influence male/female roles, which may, in turn, impact various aspects of the marketing program—everything from the product to be promoted, to marketing research, and even creative expression. The Arabic culture, which is grounded in the Islamic religion, provides an excellent example. Historically, sales of cameras in Saudi Arabia have been quite limited, because Islamic tradition requires that women be veiled. However, Polaroid instant photography allowed Arab men to photograph their wives and daughters in the privacy of their homes, without the need for strangers to handle the film in a processing lab. Polaroid cameras became a great success in this market. In attempting to gather market information on female consumers in the Middle East, one marketer planned to conduct a series of focus group interviews. But because of the very secluded role of women in this society, which is a direct outgrowth of the dominant religion, the marketer had to invite husbands and brothers to the focus group sessions instead. Similarly, hiring men to conduct face-to-face interviews with or even telephone surveys of women, or addressing mailed questionnaires to women for the purpose of collecting market data, would be considered highly inappropriate (Hashmi 1987). Even though the guidelines provided in the Quran may not be strictly followed by all Arabs, public expectations about modesty in dressing by women are still strongly influenced by the Quran. And advertisers are not advised to deviate from these public expectations. In Arabic advertising today, female

models are only portrayed if their presence relates directly to the product category (such as cosmetics or household products), and when they do appear, they are appropriately dressed—that is, wearing a long dress and a head covering that does not expose any hair (Al-Makaty et al 1996, 16). Indeed, many international advertisers have been forced to modify their print campaigns by superimposing long dresses on any scantily clad models. The only acceptable role that female models may portray is that of mother/caretaker.

What is considered moral behavior is also directly influenced by religion. Warner Lambert had its share of marketing problems in the late 1960s when it attempted to introduce Listerine to Thai consumers. In Thailand, Warner Lambert produced commercials fashioned after a well-known American TV spot showing a young man and woman kissing and otherwise expressing affection. Sales remained minimal, and company executives were puzzled by the turn of events. Finally, the problem was discovered: such public portrayals of male–female relationships was objectionable to the Thai people. The commercial was quickly reshot to show two young women instead. The ad caught on, and increased sales confirmed the effectiveness of the modifications (Diamond 1969, 50). In developing commercial messages for the Muslim world, human nudity is to be avoided at all costs as it is regarded as highly offensive. In other countries, such as France and, increasingly, the United States, nude models in advertisements hardly raise an eyebrow.

Many major holidays are also closely tied to religion. We are all familiar with the fervor with which American businesses gear up for the Christmas season. As early as September, many retailers begin to decorate their stores and shops with garlands and Christmas trees to stimulate holiday shopping. In December retailers generally extend their business hours in response to dramatic increases in consumer purchases. In many countries where Christianity plays a major role, Sundays are considered a type of holiday, and no or very few business establishments are open for business. In the Muslim world the entire month of Ramadan is a religious holiday, and Muslims are required to fast from dawn to dusk. Because of the rigors of such fasting, there is a marked drop-off in productivity during this period. At the same time, Ramadan is a significant holiday in terms of marketing and advertising because, at the end of the holiday, Idul Fitri is celebrated, and every man, woman, and child receives a gift of clothing. Religious holidays can present real marketing opportunities to savvy international marketers. Consider the following example. The Hindu festival Kumbh Mela takes place every three years, rotating between four locations. However, the Kumbh Mela at Allahabad, at the confluence of three of India's holiest rivers (Ganges, Yamuna, and Saraswati) is considered the most important and is known as the Maha Kumbh Mela. A holy dip in the Ganges at Prayag is believed to wash the bather of all sins and grant salvation. Indians from all over the country join the pilgrimage, and in 2001 the religious event delivered a 70 million-strong audience over a period of 42 days. Those companies providing pilgrims with a "brand experience" include international marketers such as Unilever, SmithKline Beecham, Coca-Cola Co., PepsiCo, and Colgate-Palmolive. Specialist rural marketing agencies, such as Interpublic Group of Cos.' Linteractive and WWP Group's HTA Rural and Ogilvy Outreach, helped clients reach Indian consumers at the event. They mounted product sampling blitzes and product demonstrations, and flaunted brands using novel ad media such as rail stations, kiosks, hoardings, giant screens, glow signs, handcarts, and even boats. HTA Rural coordinated stalls for product sales and demonstrations. To reinforce brand recognition for the Unilever cream Fair 'N Lovely, a logo game was included, and consumers who bought a large tube at the stall got a free photo of themselves with the brand and the event as a backdrop. The photo was processed on the spot and provided a permanent reminder of the brand's tie to the event. Ogilvy Outreach conducted "live" product demos for Hindustan Levers's Lifebuoy soap. Villagers tended to wash in muddy water and they were shown how Lifebuoy kills germs while mud multiplies them. Branded hand-carts then moved around the Mela selling products at a discount (*Advertising Age* 2001). For global marketers seeking a deeper rural penetration into the Indian market, the Mela is indeed a blessing.

Expressions of Culture

Geert Hofstede proposed that the four basic expressions of culture are symbols, heroes, rituals, and values (see Figure 4.9). These expressions are depicted by Hofstede much like the layers of an onion, suggesting that symbols represent the most superficial and values the deepest manifestations of culture, with heroes and rituals falling in between. Marieke de Mooij (1994, 123) does a fine job of defining these layers.

Symbols can be words, gestures, pictures, and objects that carry a specific meaning recognized only by members of a particular culture. Included here are the latest status symbol, the newest fashion trend, and the hippest hairstyle. New symbols are quickly developed and old ones fade away. Often, the symbols from one cultural group are adopted by another. For these reasons, symbols are shown in the outer, most superficial layer of the diagram. *Heroes* are persons, alive or dead, real or imaginary, who possess characteristics prized in a particular culture. Thus heroes serve as models for members of a society. Political figures (from Abraham Lincoln to George W. Bush) can be upheld as heroes by a specific group, as can film and television stars (such as Brad Pitt and Jennifer Aniston). Even cartoon characters can be perceived as heroes (whether it be Superman or Snoopy). *Rituals* are collective activities considered essential within a culture. Social and religious ceremonies, business and political meetings, even sporting events, are all rituals. Consider the ritualistic behavior associated with football games in the United States. Tickets are purchased months in advance. Fans often paint themselves with the team's colors to show support in the stands. Before the event itself, tailgate parties take place in the stadium parking lot. In the diagram, symbols, heroes, and rituals are intersected with the term *practices*. While practices are visible to non-members of a culture, their cultural meaning is invisible. The true meaning of practices lies in how they are interpreted by members of the culture. At the core of culture lie *values*. Values are broad tendencies to prefer certain states of affairs over others, and typically embody contrasts (what is good versus what is evil, what is

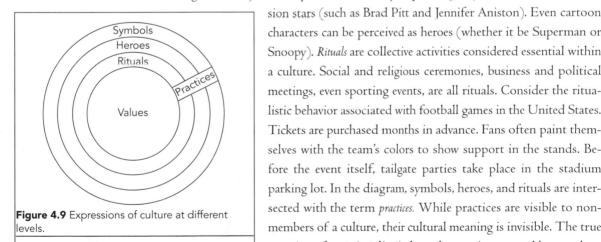

Figure 4.9 Expressions of culture at different levels.

Source: Hofstede (1990).

beautiful versus what is ugly) (Hofstede 1990). Because cultural values are of critical importance to the international marketer and advertiser, they will be discussed in greater detail below.

 Values

To maximize the chances of success, marketers must examine cultural values. Milton Rokeach provides a classic definition of a value: "an enduring belief that a specific mode of conduct or end state of existence is personally and socially preferable to an opposite or converse mode of conduct or end state of existence" (Rokeach 1973, 27). Put more simply, Edward C. Steward states that values "represent a learned organization of rules for making choices and for resolving conflicts" (Steward 1972, 74). Articles on values and consumer behavior in scholarly journals suggest that values may indeed be one of the most powerful explanations of and influences on consumer behavior (Rokeach 1968).

While an examination of value systems can prove quite beneficial to a marketer, it is often fraught with problems. A major stumbling block in analyzing value systems is that many nations are multicultural. The United States, though often called a cultural melting pot, is an example of a particularly heterogeneous culture. If we state that a particular value is characteristic of the United States, it is not to say that each and every member of this society will possess that value. Rather, the concept of values should be used to assist in identifying the primary differences among consumers in different societies. Thus it is possible to make broad statements regarding the value systems that tend to dominate in a particular society.

Classifying and Assessing Values Several classification systems have been devised for assessing the dominant values of a culture. For example, Rokeach developed a means of quantifying personal value systems (Rokeach 1968). As shown in Table 4.5, the Rokeach value survey identifies 18 terminal and 18 instrumental values. Terminal values concern desired end states of existence that are socially and personally worth striving for. Instrumental values relate to modes of conduct, and represent beliefs that are socially and personally preferable in all situations with respect to all objects. Value systems are identified by having individuals complete a survey that asks them to arrange all 36 values in order of their importance as guiding principles in their lives.

This framework is effective in discriminating between people of culturally diverse backgrounds (Munson and McIntyre 1978, 103). For example, the instrumental value of "ambitious" means hardworking and aspiring. The degree to which consumers perceive themselves as hardworking (or aspiring to this value) may differ from one culture to the next, and this may have implications for promotional efforts. A recent survey of young people around the world found significant differences in the percentage of those describing themselves as "hardworking" versus "into having a good time." The "work hard/play hard" ethic appears to be most common in English-speaking countries. While 93 percent of American respondents, 84 percent of Australian respondents, and 61 percent of British respondents perceived themselves

TABLE 4.5 Terminal and Instrumental Values

Terminal Values	Instrumental Values
A comfortable life (a prosperous life)	Ambitious (hardworking, aspiring)
An exciting life (a stimulating active life)	Broadminded (open-minded)
A sense of accomplishment (a lasting contribution)	Capable (competent, effective)
A world at peace (free of war and conflict)	Cheerful (lighthearted, joyful)
A world of beauty (beauty of nature and the arts)	Clean (neat, tidy)
Equality (brotherhood, equal opportunity for all)	Courageous (standing up for your beliefs)
Family security (taking care of loved ones)	Forgiving (willing to pardon others)
Freedom (independence, free choice)	Helpful (working for welfare of others)
Happiness (contentedness)	Honest (sincere, truthful)
Inner harmony (freedom from inner conflict)	Imaginative (daring, creative)
Mature love (sexual and spiritual intimacy)	Independent (self-sufficient)
National security (protection from attack)	Intellectual (intelligent, reflective)
Pleasure (an enjoyable leisurely life)	Logical (consistent, rational)
Salvation (saved, eternal life)	Loving (affectionate, tender)
Self-respect (respect, admiration)	Obedient (dutiful, respectful)
Social recognition (respect, admiration)	Polite (courteous, well-mannered)
True friendship (close companionship)	Responsible (dependent, reliable)
Wisdom (mature understanding of life)	Self-controlled (restrained, self-disciplined)

Source: Rokeach (1973), 28.

as hard workers, a mere 34 percent of German and 30 percent of Brazilian respondents gave themselves credit for working hard, indicating that instead they value having a good time. Surprisingly, Japanese youth are the least likely to describe themselves as either hardworking or fun-loving (Yankelovich Partners 1992, 62). Such insights clearly have implications for designing advertising message content targeted to this segment in various markets.

Core values go much deeper than behavior or attitudes, and they determine, at a basic level, people's choices and desires. Behavior changes with amazing speed in response to outside forces of all kinds, such as whether a person had a good night's sleep or how long the line at the grocery store was. Although slower to change, attitudes are also prone to external forces, such as the beliefs of one's peer group. Core values, however, are intrinsic to a person's identity. By appealing to people's inner selves, it is possible to influence their outer selves—their purchase behavior (Miller 1998, 11).

An examination of cultural values can do more than assist marketers in segmenting consumers. With regard to the relationship between values and advertising, values may be among the major influences on human behavior. As noted in *Social Values and Social Change*, "Value-linked advertisements may animate affect, creating an affective response closer to the value-induced affect than to the product or advertisement without the value link. To the extent that affective advertisements are more influential than bland ads, values may be a mechanism to explore when

trying to understand the sources of affect" (Kahle, 1983). Indeed, numerous empirical studies have found that advertisements reflecting local cultural values are, in fact, more persuasive than those that ignore them (Gregory and Munch 1997; Taylor and Wilson 1997; Han and Shavitt 1994). If marketers hope to formulate more effective messages for foreign markets, they must become sensitive to the core values of a given country.

IIIII Hofstede's Dimensions of Culture

One of the most important frameworks for understanding culture in the past two decades has been Geert Hofstede's typology of cultural dimensions (Hofstede 1980). Based on 117,000 questionnaires from 88,000 respondents in 20 languages reflecting 66 countries, Hofstede delineated four important dimensions that can be used to classify countries: Power distance, societal desire for hierarchy or egalitarianism; individualism, society's preference for a group or individual orientation; masculinity versus femininity, a sex-role dimension; and uncertainty avoidance, a culture's tolerance for uncertainty. Later research resulted in the addition of a fifth dimension, long-term orientation (Hofstede and Bond 1988), the cultural perspective on a long-term versus a short-term basis. Each of the five dimensions is measured on a scale from 0 to 100. The scores indicate the relative differences between cultures. An increasing number of marketing and advertising researchers have recognized the potential applicability of Hofstede's dimensions to marketing research problems (for example, Albers-Miller 1996, 59; de Mooij 1998, 186; and Milner and Collins 2000, 67). As with time orientation and context, differences in the following five dimensions impact both the content of commercial messages and the creative strategies most likely to be employed.

IIIII Power Distance

Power Distance in Hofstede's typology focuses on the degree of equality or inequality among people in a country's society. Cultures with a high power distance index (PDI) tend to be more accepting of hierarchies and autocratic leadership. Everyone has their rightful place in the social hierarchy, and the acceptance and giving of authority is considered normal. Individuals tend to obey the recommendations of authority figures such as parents, teachers, or bosses. Dependency is also an element of hierarchical relationships among people. Dependency can be used to a marketer's advantage, as the following example related to personal selling shows. An export manager for an Australian manufacturer of manhole covers, when visiting Malaysia (ranked high in PDI) never raised the issue of business when calling on prospective or regular clients. Rather, he ascertained whether there were relatives living in Australia or children pursuing studies there. On his return to Australia, he would contact these relations or students and look after them so as to create obligations. These obligations would be discharged by the Malaysian firms placing orders with his company without his ever having to solicit business (Fletcher and Melewar 2001, 10). In high power distance markets, commercial messages

should avoid egalitarian appeals. Consumers in such cultures are more likely to expect clear directions in communications. Zandpour and Campos (1994) found that testimonials by a celebrity, a credible source, or a user of the product were a distinct feature of ads in cultures with high power distance.

In cultures ranking lower on the power distance index, such as the United States, authority has a negative connotation. Low power distance cultures stress equality and opportunity for everyone. In the United States, for example, it is assumed that superiors and subordinates are basically equal, and employees will quite readily approach and even contradict their bosses. Americans avoid becoming dependent upon others and don't want others to become dependent upon them. Indeed, children in the United States are raised to be independent at a relatively young age (deMoog, 1998). In low power distance cultures, there is little tolerance for authority, and consumers are more likely to make their decisions on the basis of facts and reasoning.

Individualism versus Collectivism

Hofstede's *individualism versus collectivism* dimension pertains to the importance of the group rather than the individual. A high individualism ranking indicates that individuality and individual rights are paramount within the society. Ties between individuals are loose, and everyone is expected to look after themselves. Laws, rules, and regulations are institutionalized to protect the rights of the individual.

Americans are considered highly individualistic. Indeed, it is said that both the best and worst features of American culture can be attributed to individualism. Proponents of individualism have argued that it is the basis of liberty, democracy, and freedom, and serves as a protection against tyranny. On the other hand, individualism has been blamed for alienation from one another, loneliness, selfishness, and narcissism. As one might expect, advertisements in individualistic cultures place a high value on individuality (or being unique), independence, success, and self-realization. As an example of such an orientation, consider the advertisement in Figure 4.10 for the U.S. Army. This ad is part of an on-going campaign entitled "An Army of One" (although the U.S. Army is 1,045,690 strong). The headline reads: "This uniform didn't change me. Earning the right to wear it did." In addition, ads targeting individualistic consumers are more likely to provide detailed, factual information needed for decision making.

A low individualism ranking indicates a country tends to be collectivistic. In collectivistic societies, social ties are much tighter. One owes one's lifelong loyalty to one's in-group, and breaking this loyalty has dire consequences. The supreme value is the welfare of the group. Japan is considered a collectivistic society where the concern for belonging plays a critical role. Japanese belong to reference groups, which vary from small to large, formal to informal, and intimate to impersonal. In identifying themselves, the Japanese stress their position in a social frame rather than their individualistic attributes. The Japanese approach to the group role is to perceive oneself as an integral part of the whole. The individual does not interact as an individual, but as the son in a parent-child relationship or as a worker in an employee-employer relationship.

Figure 4.10 U.S. Army ad portraying individualism.

A high value is placed on the harmonious integration of group members and on consensus. It is emphasized that opinions should always be held unanimously. The Japanese see all decisions and actions as part of group consensus. The individual is not held morally responsible for such decisions. When a person commits a wrongful act, it is the group that is embarrassed and, in the final analysis, responsible for the misdeed. Among the Japanese, this generates pressures for conformity to group norms and pressures to be like everyone else. The sense of identity anchored to in-group belongingness is sustained by going along with peers. There is a restraint from expressing disagreement with whatever appears to be the majority opinion.

This strong sense of belongingness as a state of self-identity calls for the individual's total commitment and loyalty to the group. This also means that the group is responsible for taking care of all the needs of its members. Mutual obligations of loyalty and total protection are established in Japanese employment practices. Although the current economic crisis in Asia has challenged the concept of lifetime employment, promotion and wage-rank based on length of service, and paternalistic relationships between employer and employee, most companies still try to provide employees with basic needs such as housing, medical care, education, and recreational facilities.

Japanese advertising, as well as advertising in other collectivistic cultures, reflects this group orientation. The majority of ads in such cultures tend to show people in groups rather than as individuals. "We" and "us" are popular pronouns. Message content tends to emphasize interdependence, family, group well-being, and concern for others. It is important to note that the group orientation dominates—between 70 and 80 percent of the world's population is more or less collectivistic.

Masculinity versus Femininity

Cultures which rank high in *masculinity* emphasize stereotypical "masculine" traits—such as achievement, assertiveness, dominance, success, competition, and heroism. Those ranking low on masculinity emphasize "feminine" traits, such as a preference for relationships, modesty, caring for the weak, and quality of life. A fundamental issue addressed by this dimension is the way a society allocates social (as opposed to biological) roles to the sexes. Masculine societies tend to strive for maximum social differentiation between the sexes. The norm is that men are given the more outgoing, assertive roles, and women the caring, nurturing roles. Minimum social-differentiation societies, in comparison with maximum social-differentiation societies, permeate their institutions with a quality-of-life–oriented mentality. Such societies become "welfare societies," in which caring for all members, even the weakest, is an important goal for men as well as women (Milner and Collins 2000).

Venezuela has one of the highest masculinity rankings in Latin America. This indicates that the country experiences a high degree of gender differentiation of roles. Even today, males play the dominant role in society. Sweden, in contrast, has one of the lowest masculinity rankings. For more than two decades, Swedish women have earned as much as 90 percent as their

male counterparts. And more than one-third of parliamentary seats are held by women. Whether masculine or feminine values dominate in a particular culture is reflected in a country's advertisements. For example, traditional sex roles do not play well in Swedish ads. Figure 4.11 is a Swedish ad for Knorr sauce mixes. Note the inset at the top left side of the page—the male partner is setting the table rather than the female. Examining television ads from a range of countries that Hofstede designated as masculine and feminine, Milner and Collins (2000) found that ads produced for consumers in countries at the feminine end of the continuum also feature a greater proportion of characters in relationships than those at the masculine end. The researchers propose that this finding has practical implications in determining the types of ad appeals that might be appropriate in a specific country. For example, a firm providing cellular phone service in Sweden might find it effective to develop messages that show cell phones being used in nurturing relationships in Sweden (for example, developing closer bonds between grandparents and grandchildren) whereas it might use nonpersonal situations (such as dial-ups to a financial news provider) in the United States, which tends to be a more masculine country. Further, in cultures characterized as predominantly masculine, winning, achievement, performance, success, and status are much used in advertising appeals, and comparison advertising is common.

Uncertainty Avoidance

Uncertainty avoidance focuses on the degree to which society reinforces or does not reinforce uncertainty and ambiguity. People in countries low in uncertainty avoidance are relatively comfortable with ambiguity and are tolerant of others' behaviors and views. Weak uncertainty avoidance cultures feel that there should be as few rules as possible. They believe more in generalities and common sense, and exhibit less ritual behavior. Conflict and competition are not threatening. Consumers in such cultures more readily accept change and take on greater risks.

Where uncertainty avoidance is high, there is a need for rules, regulations, and controls. Formality and structure are central. This often translates into a search for truth and a belief in experts. The implication for communication is that uncertainty reduction requires explicit, logical, and direct information on the part of the communicator. Conflict and competition are avoided. People in strong uncertainty avoidance cultures have higher levels of anxiety, and the show of emotions is accepted. People living in such societies are likely to build up tension and stress that must be released. This is done in different ways: They may talk louder, use their hands while speaking, drive more aggressively, or embrace more emotionally (deMoog, 1998).

Consumers in high uncertainty avoidance cultures are likely to be drawn to products that emphasize low risk or safety features. In terms of creative strategy, the "argument" provides an audience with facts and reasons why they should purchase the advertised product or service. Zandpour and Campos (1994) found arguments and explicit conclusions to be the strategy of choice among cultures with a low tolerance for ambiguity and uncertainty. Uncertainty reduction requires explicit, logical, and direct information on the part of the communicator. In contrast,

Lyxa till det med
något enkelt

På finare restauranger finns det speciella kockar som enbart ägnar sig
åt att laga olika såser. En stor konst i sig själv med andra ord.
 Nu kan du också lyxa till det hemma med en riktigt god sås. Utan att
anlita en speciell såskock. Prova Sauce Raffinesse, en ny serie smak-
rika såser av hög kvalitet. Sauce Raffinesse finns i sju varianter, alla är
lika enkla att laga, alla lika välsmakande till både fest och vardag.

Knorr Mer smak på livet

Figure 4.11 Differentiation between the sexes is minimized in this Swedish ad for Knorr sauce mixes.

"symbolic association" as an advertising strategy (utilizing subtle presentations linking the product to a symbol with minimal and implicit information about the product) was found to be uncommon in high uncertainty avoidance cultures.

Long-term/Short-term Orientation

Hofstede identified his four cultural dimensions using a survey developed from a Western perspective. To examine culture from an Eastern perspective, a group of researchers, the Chinese Culture Connection (1987), developed a survey based on Chinese values. This instrument revealed a fifth cultural dimension: *long-term/short-term orientation.*

A high long-term orientation ranking indicates that the country prescribes values of long-term commitment and respect for tradition. This is thought to support a strong work ethic where long-term rewards are expected as a result of today's hard work. A low long-term orientation ranking indicates that the country does not reinforce the concept of long-term traditional orientation. In this culture, change can occur more rapidly as long-term traditions and commitments do not become an impediment to change.

In general, people from East Asian countries, such as China, Japan, and Korea, tend to score high on the long-term index. Those with a long-term orientation value tradition and history and tend to look to the past for inspiration. By comparison, many Westerners, such as Americans and northern Europeans, are said to have a short-term orientation. People with a short-term orientation are more likely to perceive that the past is over and done with. The old is easily discarded and the new is quickly embraced, and there is an emphasis on planning for the future.

Table 4.6 below presents scores for Hofstede's five dimensions for 25 national cultures.

Influence of Culture on Consumer Behavior

The culture of a society affects the kinds of products that are consumed as well as when and how they are consumed, by whom they are purchased and consumed, and how much is consumed.

Why Consumers Buy

Anthropologists, psychologists, and sociologists all have been attempting to explain why individuals engage in consumption behavior. It is difficult enough to answer this question in the domestic market, but it becomes truly challenging in the international environment. In attempting to understand consumers, both domestic and foreign, marketers may look at the needs that motivate purchase behavior. A useful theory of human motivation was developed by Abraham Maslow (1964), who hypothesized that people's needs can be arranged in a hierarchy reflecting their relative potency. At the base of the hierarchy are physiological needs. As

TABLE 4.6 Country Scores on Hofstede's Five Dimensions

Country	PDI	IDV	MAS	UAI	LTO
Argentina	49	46	56	86	*
Australia	36	90	61	51	31
Belgium	65	75	54	94	*
Brazil	69	38	49	76	65
China	80	15	55	40	100
Czech Republic	35	60	45	60	*
East Africa	64	27	41	52	25
Germany	35	67	66	65	31
Hong Kong	68	25	57	29	96
India	77	48	56	40	61
Indonesia	78	14	46	48	*
Italy	50	76	70	75	*
Japan	54	46	95	92	80
Mexico	81	30	69	82	*
Norway	31	69	8	50	*
Pakistan	55	14	50	70	0
Poland	55	60	65	78	37
Singapore	74	20	48	8	48
South Africa	49	65	63	49	*
South Korea	60	18	39	85	75
Spain	57	51	42	86	*
Sweden	31	71	5	29	33
Thailand	64	20	34	64	56
United Kingdom	35	89	66	35	25
United States	40	91	62	46	29

PDI = Power Distance Index

IDV = Individualism

MAS = Masculinity

UAI = Uncertainty Avoidance Index

LTO = Long Term Orientation

* = Not available

humans, our need for food, water, and shelter from the elements dominates our behavior. As these fundamental or "lower" needs are met, higher needs emerge, such as the need for safety—for security and protection from dangers in the environment. Once this need has been provided for, social needs arise—for affection from family and friends and to belong to a group. Higher-order needs include the need for esteem (self-respect, prestige, success, and achievement) and, finally, the need for self-actualization (self-fulfillment). People are not, however, locked into a particular level; clearly, an individual attempting to fulfill esteem needs also must address basic physiological needs.

Maslow's model has relevance to the international marketer in that the needs that dominate a particular culture are closely tied to that country's level of development. Apparently, the more highly developed the market, the greater the proportion of goods and products devoted to filling social and esteem needs as opposed to physiological needs. An examination of American advertisements reveals this to be the case in this country. Consider the many products promoted as status-enhancing goods—from automobiles to clothing to bottled water. The advertising appeals employed in cultures at different stages of economic development are likely to be quite different. While Maslow's hierarchy of needs is a useful tool, and presumably applies to consumer buying behavior in many different countries, caution should be exercised when employing it in a cross-cultural setting. The hierarchy is a theory based on Western behavior and has not been proven applicable to non-Western or developing countries.

What Consumers Buy

People around the globe purchase goods and services to meet the various needs outlined in Maslow's model above. But as Terpstra and Russow (2000) note, the exact contents of the particular market basket will differ from country to country. Of concern to international marketers is whether their product can find a place in the market basket of a particular group of foreign consumers. It should come as no great surprise that because they are dictated by culture, consumption habits vary greatly from one market to the next. While there are numerous examples of products that have been sold successfully around the globe, other products face nearly insurmountable challenges. Consumption of beef provides an excellent example. In some cultures beef consumption ranges from minimal to nonexistant. Many Thai and Chinese do not consume beef, believing it is improper to eat cattle that work on farms and help to produce other foodstuffs such as rice and vegetables. Religious taboos prohibit Hindus from eating beef. No amount of advertising would sway such consumers to eat it. In contrast, Americans eat a whopping 100 pounds of beef per capita annually. American beef producers have been running a longstanding campaign under the banner "Beef—It's What's For Dinner (see Figure 4.12 for a sample ad with the headline "All of a sudden a $2,000 grill seems perfectly reasonable"). Clearly, this ad would have little relevance to a Thai consumer. There is no shortage of examples of how culture directly impacts consumption. Laundry-product manufacturers have had little success in introducing dryer-activated fabric softeners in many European countries because of the custom of hanging out clothes to dry on a clothesline. Demand for products that a marketer fails to provide can cause headaches as well. For example, after successfully opening a park in Tokyo, Disney decided to expand to the European market, opening Euro-Disney just outside Paris. Just as with the parks in the United States and Tokyo, all alcoholic beverages were banned. However, Disney failed to consider the European penchant for drinking wine and beer with meals. In addition, the park did not offer sufficient restaurant seating for European customers, who expected to sit down at the accustomed dining time and enjoy a leisurely meal. Disney was criticized strongly for sticking too closely to its homogeneous "It's A Small World After All" philosophy. Euro-Disney estimated that it would lose almost $350 million

WWW.BEEFITSWHATSFORDINNER.COM

BEEF
IT'S WHAT'S FOR DINNER®

FUNDED BY AMERICA'S BEEF PRODUCERS

ALL OF A SUDDEN,

A $2,000 GRILL SEEMS PERFECTLY REASONABLE.

Figure 4.12 While beef is popular in the United States, consumption in other markets is minimal.

during its first year of operations. Disney has since introduced both beer and wine at all park restaurants (Wentz 1992, 140).

Who Makes Purchase Decisions

The marketer must know who in the family is the primary decision maker, and for which products. In some cultures the female holds the purse strings, while in others it is the male. In Japan, for example,

> [the] housewife makes most of the major purchases for the family and buys the family's food, household supplies and clothing. Usually, she receives her husband's paycheck, manages the household budget, and allocates funds for different categories of expenses, including savings for children's education, vacations, leisure activities, and retirement. She is the person advertisers must try to reach. (Hall and Hall 1987, 137)

In contrast, in many fundamental Islamic markets, such as Libya, household purchasing is most often undertaken by men.

In the United States, for an increasing number of product categories, children, teens, and young adults are the primary decision makers. Gen Y is the label given to America's 71 million 8- to 25-year-olds. These young people represent roughly 26 percent of the population, and their spending power exceeds $200 billion a year. They influence another $200–$400 billion of their parent's money annually as well. But this new generation of big spenders is not responding to the traditional media—not even MTV. Frustrated market researchers have concocted their own name for Gen Y: the Unreachables. This is the first generation of Americans to grow up online. They resist reading and increasingly keep the TV off. The smartest marketers have given up trying to reach them in a mass way. Here's how some marketers are attempting to reach this lucrative audience:

- *Online hype:* Hydrogen Records directs its fans into popular chat rooms to talk up new records. And Arista Records sends targeted e-mails to teens.
- *Skate parks:* Vans, the sneaker maker, cosies up to teens by building zippy skateboard parks.
- *Student fans:* Red Bull enlists students for promotions and hires squadrons of teens to hand out the energy drink on the street.
- *Hip events:* IMG, the sports marketing giant, purchased the U.S. Open of Surfing in order to link some of its clients with the event.
- *Computer games:* Such familiar names as Mountain Dew, Oakley, and Hurley made deals to place their logos on Tony Hawk's Pro Skater 3 from Activision.
- *Videos:* Burton, the snowboard king, constantly maneuvers to get its boards and riders into snowboarding videos. (Horovitz 2002, B-01)

Of course, not all young people around the world display such consumer clout. Many cultures place much greater value on the elders in the community and emphasize the wisdom that comes with age. This respect for the elderly stands in marked contrast to the extreme youth orientation in the United States.

 How Much Consumers Buy

Even the amount or quantity of a product that consumers in different cultures purchase is not constant. In the United States, shoppers typically purchase the economy size of products, as shopping is typically done on a weekly basis. In both Europe and Japan, where shopping is often done on a daily basis and where household storage space is more limited, consumers tend to purchase smaller-sized packages. Once Philips introduced a smaller version of its coffee makers to fit into smaller-sized Japanese kitchens, sales took off. Two-liter bottles of Coca-Cola failed to move from retail shelves in Spain because few consumers had refrigerators with large enough compartments to store the beverage container. In contrast, in Mexico Campbell sells its soup in cans large enough to serve four or more, as families in this market are typically larger. Even deodorant consumption varies dramatically (*Advertising Age* 1992). Americans consume almost twice as much deodorant as the French and nearly four times as much as Italians. Consumers in the United States are perceived by much of the rest of the world as quite fanatical with regard to personal hygiene.

Consumption patterns clearly have importance for advertisers in deciding how to introduce a brand. Where a group of products enjoys widespread acceptance, the message will likely be directed toward obtaining the largest share of the market. Where consumption is low or nonexistent, the marketing communications will have an educational character.

With regard to breakfast cereal, for example, U.S. citizens consume 9.3 pounds per person, while the British consume 12.9 pounds and the Irish a whopping 13.3 pounds. When Kellogg runs ads for Frosted Flakes and Corn Flakes in these markets, it is competing with other brands of cereals. In contrast, the German and Japanese cereal markets are comparatively undeveloped. Per capita cereal consumption is a mere 1.6 pounds in Germany and an almost negligible 0.1 pound in Japan. Traditionally, Germans eat bread with cheese or meat in the mornings or, occasionally, a type of whole-grain cereal, while the Japanese eat primarily rice-based breakfasts. It is also important to note that many Japanese suffer from lactose intolerance, which further complicates the promotion of a breakfast consisting of cereal and milk. Kellogg initially faced quite a challenge in marketing its cereals in Germany and, in particular, in Japan, where they are only now making a serious breakthrough. Early messages for both Frosted Flakes and Corn Flakes tended to be predominantly educational in nature. Interestingly, even in the 1960s, Western-style soups had little trouble making it to the Japanese table—even the breakfast table. George Fields notes: "It was easier for soup to be served for the Japanese breakfast than cereal, because, traditionally, Japanese bean-paste soup (misoshiru) was always served for breakfast; thus, when breakfast started to turn Western, with toast and margarine, etc., Western-style soup had no conceptual problems being positioned. In a traditionally salt-oriented Japanese breakfast, cereals with milk and sugar had problems in this respect" (Fields 1989, 115).

Cultural Universals

Much attention has been given in this chapter to the differences between cultures. Some suggest focusing instead on the similarities between cultures. Theodore Levitt, often called the global marketing guru, proposes that the "world is becoming a common marketplace in which people—no matter where they live—desire the same products and life-styles. Global companies must forget idiosyncratic differences between countries and cultures and instead concentrate on satisfying universal drives" (Lynch, 1984, 49).

Cultural universals are defined as modes of behavior common to all cultures. George Murdock (1945) developed a list of cultural universals that includes athletic sports, bodily adornments, calendars, cooking, courtship, education, etiquette, family, folklore, funeral rites, gestures, gift giving, incest taboos, joking, kin groups, law, magic, marriage, mealtimes, mourning, mythology, property rights, religious rituals, tool making, and weather control. Proponents of globalization argue that, to the extent that some aspects of the cultural environment may be perceived as universal as opposed to unique to each distinct society, it may be possible for international marketers and advertisers to standardize various aspects of the marketing mix.

Granted, as human beings, we all share basic biological similarities. For example, all humans sense hunger, and the eating of food to ensure survival is a universal behavior. However, just how we respond to this biological drive—what we eat, as well as when, how, where, and with whom we eat—is shaped by culture. Beyond biological drives, humans are confronted with universal needs, as outlined by Maslow above. But once again, the manner in which consumers in different markets address these needs can vary substantially. While consumers in the United States and Japan both experience "social needs," Americans nonetheless identify themselves as individuals whereas Japanese identify themselves by their associations with various groups. This is not to suggest that standardization of the marketing mix is not possible or not desirable. The benefits associated with this approach are many, and examples of successful global products speak to its viability. Rather, this should serve as a warning that what might appear to be a cultural universal is often no more than an illusion of similarity. Prior to attempting to sell the same product in the same fashion abroad, the international marketer must carefully examine the various elements of the marketing environment (demographic, economic, geographic, political-legal, and cultural) for potential pitfalls.

Tools for Understanding Cross-Cultural Communication

Many firms, especially smaller ones, or those entering foreign markets for the first time, do not have the resources, time, or personnel required to assess all the elements of the marketing environment that might potentially influence the marketing mix. Nevertheless, the international marketer can draw on various tools in comparing the foreign market with the firm's domestic market for the purpose of making promotional decisions.

Market Distance

The concept of market distance has its origins in early international trade theory as an explanation for why trade tended to be concentrated in foreign markets most similar to domestic markets. Migration patterns are at the core of this concept. When migrant groups settle in foreign countries, they carry with them their culture—their language, religion, values, and learned behaviors—all of which affect the goods and services they tend to purchase. Marketers in the host country thus acquire knowledge with regard to these consumption styles and habits, and this information influences their views on other foreign markets. Foreign markets are then seen as more or less similar to what the marketers know about their home market. In turn, this perceived similarity influences managerial preferences and choices of foreign markets, the international expansion strategies firms select, and the magnitude and direction of international trade (Reid 1986, 22).

In communicating with consumers in foreign countries, regardless of perceived market distance, messages encoded in one country must be decoded in another. However, when messages are communicated cross-nationally between similar markets, the decoding effect of the receiver produces results more nearly like those intended in the original message encoding by the sender. Conversely, when messages are communicated cross-nationally between highly dissimilar—or distant—markets, the decoding effect of the receiver may not produce the intended results. The model of cross-cultural communication outlined in Figure 4.13 incorporates economic, political-legal, and demographic differences in addition to cultural differences. This model is useful in that it refers to the degree of homogeneity or heterogeneity between markets in general. Clearly, the greater the degree of homogeneity, the greater the potential for a standardized approach. Greater heterogeneity suggests that one or more of the elements of the marketing mix (the product, price, distribution, and promotion) may require modification.

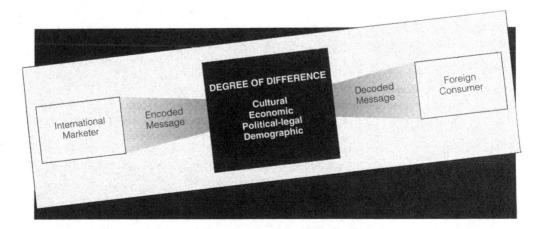

Figure 4.13 Cross-cultural communications model.

Source: Adapted from Vern Terpstra, International Dimensions of Marketing, 3d ed. (Chicago: Dryden, 1983), 413.

Larry Samovar and Richard Porter propose that the degree of similarity or dissimilarity between senders and receivers may be viewed on a continuum of compared cultures, as shown in Figure 4.14. The authors explain the scale as follows:

If we imagine differences varying along a minimum-maximum dimension, the degree of difference between two groups depends on their relative social uniqueness. Although this scale is unrefined, it allows us to examine intercultural communication acts and gain insight into the effect cultural differences have on communication. To see how this dimensional scale helps us understand intercultural communication we can look at some examples of cultural differences positioned along the scale.

The first example represents a case of maximum differences—those found between Asian and Western cultures. This may be typified as an interaction between two farmers, one who works on a communal farm on the outskirts of Beijing in China and the other who operates a large mechanized and automated wheat, corn and dairy farm in Michigan. In this situation we should expect to find the greatest number of diverse cultural factors. Physical appearance, religion, philosophy, economic systems, social attitudes, language, heritage, basic conceptualization of self and the universe, and the degree of technological development are cultural factors that differ sharply. We must recognize, however, that these two farmers also share the commonality of farming, with its rural life-style and love of the land. In some respects, they may be more closely related than they are to members of their own cultures who live in large urban settings. In other words, across some cultural dimensions, the Michigan farmer may have more in common with the Chinese farmer than with a Wall Street securities broker.

Another example nearer the center of the scale is the difference between American culture and German culture. Less variation is found: Physical characteristics are similar, and the English language is derived in part from German and its ancestor languages. The roots of both German and American philosophy are found in ancient Greece, and most Americans and Germans share some form of the Judeo-Christian tradition. Yet there are some significant differences. Germans have political and economic systems that are different from those found in the United States. German society tends toward formality while in the United States we tend toward informality. Germans have memories of local warfare and the destruction of their cities and economy, of having been a defeated nation on more than one occasion. The United States has never lost a war on its own territory.

Examples near the minimal ends of the dimension can be characterized in two ways. First are variations found between members of separate but similar cultures— for instance, between U.S. Americans and English-Canadians. These differences are less than those found between American and German cultures, between American and Greek cultures, between American and British cultures, or even between American and French-Canadian cultures, but greater than generally found within a single

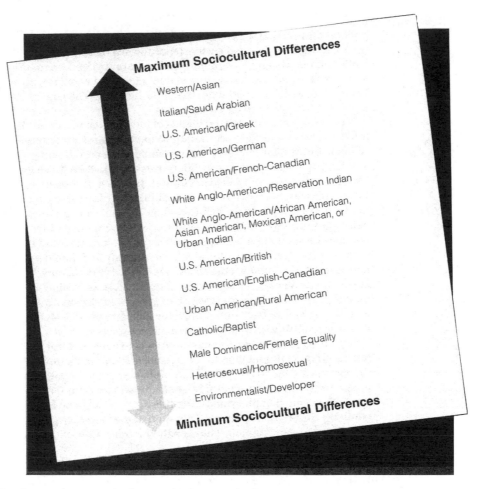

Figure 4.14 Continuum of compared cultures, subcultures, and subgroups.

Source: Samovar and Porter (1994), 22.

culture. Second, minimal differences also may be seen in the variation between co-cultures, within the same dominant culture. Socio-cultural differences may be found between members of the Catholic church and the Baptist church; environmentalists and advocates of further development of Alaskan oil resources; middle-class Americans and the urban poor; mainstream Americans and the gay and lesbian community; the able and the disabled; or male dominance advocates and female equality advocates.

In both these categorizations, members of each cultural group have more in common than in the examples found in the middle or at the maximum end of the scale. They probably speak the same language, share the same general religion, attend the same schools, and live in the same neighborhoods. Yet, these groups to some extent are culturally different; they do not fully share the experiences, nor do they share the same perception. They see their worlds differently. (Samovar and Porter 1994, 22)

Profiles of values clusters or segments around the world can help marketers to determine the appropriate approach to the elements of the marketing mix. The Roper Organization conducts Worldwide Consumer Surveys, interviewing 30,000 consumers in over 30 countries. The face-to-face interviews with 1,000 consumers in each of those countries can be projected to 1.39 billion people (*Business Wire* 1999b).

Survey respondents rank 56 values by the importance they hold as guiding principles in their lives. Among adults, six global values segments, residing in all countries—but to varying degrees—were found. Interestingly, the largest segment focuses on the material world, while the second largest centers on the soul. Roper's six global values segments are as follows:

Strivers: The largest group, strivers are slightly more likely to be men than women and place more emphasis on material and professional goals than other groups. Strivers are ambitious, status-conscious, and power-seeking. One in three people living in developing Asia are strivers, as is about one-fourth of the population in Russia and developed Asia. Strivers account for 23 percent of the world's population.

Devouts: This group comprises 22 percent of adults. For devouts, which includes more women than men, tradition and duty are very important. This group values faith and respect for elders. devouts are most common in developing Asia and the Middle Eastern and African countries. They are least common in developed Asia and Western Europe.

Altruists: This group accounts for 18 percent of adults, with a slightly higher percentage of females. Altruists are proponents of social issues and causes and are concerned with the welfare of society. With a median age of 44, this group is somewhat older than the other groups. More altruists live in Latin America and Russia than in other countries.

Intimates: Intimates, comprising 15 percent of the world's population, value close personal relationships, family, and home above all else. They are almost as likely to be men as women. One in four Europeans and Americans are intimates, as compared with just 7 percent of developing Asia.

Fun Seekers: Fun seekers focus on excitement, recreation, and enjoyment. Although found in disproportionate numbers in developed Asia, this group accounts for 12 percent of the global population. Not surprisingly, fun seekers are the youngest group, with a male to female ratio of 54 to 46 percent.

Creatives: This group is the smallest, at 10 percent worldwide. Their hallmark trait is a strong interest in education, knowledge, and technology. Creatives are more common in Latin America and Western Europe. Along with intimates, this group has the most balanced gender mix. (Miller 1998 and *Business Wire* 1999b)

Although most people fall into a particular category, some values cut across many categories and countries. For example, "protecting the family" ranks in the top 10 values for all six groups. All countries surveyed rank family in their top five guiding principles except Indonesia, which ranks

"respecting ancestors" as number 1. All the Asian countries place family in their top two values. Protecting the family was given the top value in 22 countries, including the United States.

The Roper research shows that people in different segments generally pursue different activities, buy different products, and use different media. For instance, fun seekers like to frequent restaurants, bars, and movies, making products or services related to these activities a good marketing bet wherever fun seekers abound. Intimates enjoy cooking and gardening. They spend a good deal of time with television and radio, so broadcast media are excellent choices for reaching them. Clearly, an understanding of which segments dominate in a country helps with marketing efforts and enables advertisers to tailor their messages to those parts of the population most likely to buy.

Summary

To operate effectively in foreign markets, international marketers and advertisers must recognize the pervasive influence of culture. Failure to understand the cultural environment can lead and has led to misunderstandings, miscommunications, and marketing failures. In this chapter we examined only a few of the more prominent elements of culture—including verbal language, nonverbal communications, signs and symbols, needs and values, religion, and customs—as they impact consumer behavior. In addition, we outlined a number of tools for assessing foreign cultures. In the next chapter we turn to the standardization-versus-specialization controversy.

References

Abu-Nasr, Donna. 1997. Muslim group demands apology from Nike. *San Diego Union-Tribune*, 10 April, A-11.

Advertising Age. 1992. Orbit international database. 27 April, I30.

———. 2001. Marketing to the masses: Uniliver, Pepsi among those targeting 70 m pilgrims at Hindu event. 17 January. <www.adageglobal.com/cgi-bin/daily.pl?daily_id=4215&post_date=2001-01-17>

———. 2002. Ronald McDonald statues greet customers in true Thai style. 20 September. <www.adageglobal.com/cgi-bin/daily.pl?daily_id=8410&post_date=2002-09-20>

Advertising Age. 2003. Agency Report. 21 April. S-12.

Al-Makaty, Safran, G. Tubergen, S. Whitlow, and Douglas Doyd. 1996. Attitudes toward advertising in Islam. *Journal of Advertising Research* 36 (May/June): 16–26.

Albers-Miller, Nancy. 1996. Designing cross-cultural advertising research: A closer look at paired comparisons. *International Marketing Review* 13(5): 59–75.

Ambler, Chris. 2000. Restrictions on the use of English paradoxical to some firms. *Korea Herald,* 6 July, 1.

Barron, Kelly and Shiyori Ito. 2001. Culture Gap. *Forbes,* 19 March, 62.

Bartels, Robert. 1982. National culture—Business relations: United States and Japan contrasted. *Management International Review* 22(2): 5.

Biswas, Abhigit, Janeen Olsen, and Valerie Carlet. 1992. A comparison of print advertisements from the United States and France. *Journal of Advertising* 21(4): December, 73–81.

Business Wire. 1999a. Heineken launches integrated marketing effort targeted at Hispanic America. 12 April, 1.

———. 1999b. Roper reports worldwide; global consumer 2000 study. 23 March, 1.

Chinese Culture Connection. 1987. Chinese values and the search for culture-free dimensions of culture. *Journal of Cross-Cultural Psychology* 18(2): 143–64.

Condon, John, and Merrill Rathi Yousef. 1975. *Introduction to intercultural communication.* Indianapolis, Ind.: Bobbs-Merrill.

Caporimo, James. 1995. Worldwide advertising has benefits, but one size doesn't always fit all. *Brandweek,* 17 July, 16.

Crystal, David. 1999. English as she is spoke in the world: Why our tongue qualifies as the first ever global language. *Financial Times* (London), 6 December, 4.

Davis, Riccardo. 1993. Many languages—1 ad message. *Advertising Age,* 20 September, 50.

de Mooij, Marieke. 1994. *Advertising worldwide.* 2d. ed. New York: Prentice Hall.

———. 1998. *Global marketing and advertising: Understanding cultural paradoxes.* Thousand Oaks, Calif.: Sage Publications.

Diamond, R. S. 1969. Managers away from home. *Fortune,* 15 August, 50.

Ferraro, Gary P. 1990. *The cultural dimension of international business.* Englewood Cliffs, N.J.: Prentice Hall.

Fields, George. 1989. *Gucci on the Ginza: Japan's new consumer generation.* Tokyo: Kodansha International.

Fletcher, Richard, and C. Melewar. 2001. The complexities of communicating to customers in emerging markets. *Journal of Communication Management* 6(1) (September): 9–23.

Gerritsen, Marinel, Hubert Korzilius, Frank van Meurs, and Inge Gijsbers. 2000. English in Dutch commercials: Not understood and not appreciated. *Journal of Advertising Research* 40(4): July/August, 17–29.

Glover, Katherine. 1994. Do's and taboos: Cultural aspects of international business. *Business America* 8(15): 2–6.

Greenberg, Peter. 1993. Cultural sensitivity is becoming new aim for international hotels. *San Diego Union-Tribune,* 3 October, F4.

Gregory, Gary, and James Munch. 1997. Cultural values in international advertising: An examination of familial norms and roles in Mexico. *Psychology & Marketing* 14(2): March, 99–119.

Hall, Edward T. 1966. *The hidden dimension.* Garden City, N.Y.: Anchor Press/Doubleday.

———. 1976. *Beyond culture.* New York: Doubleday.

Hall, Edward T., and Mildred Reed Hall. 1987. *Hidden differences: Doing business with the Japanese.* New York: Anchor Books.

Han, Sang, and Sharon Shavitt. 1994. Persuasion and culture: Advertising appeals in individualistic and collectivistic societies. *Journal of Experimental Social Psychology* 30(4):July, 326–50.

Hashmi, Mahmud S. 1987. Marketing in the Islamic context. Presented to the 6th annual Conference on Languages and Communication for World Business and the Professions, 8 May, Ann Arbor, Michigan.

Hoebel, Adamson. 1960. *Man, culture and society.* New York: Oxford University Press.

Hofstede, Geert. 1980. *Culture's consequences: International differences in work-related values.* Beverly Hills, Calif.: Sage Publications.

———. 1990. Expressions of culture at different levels. Working paper 90–006, University of Limburg, Netherlands.

Hofstede, Geert, and Michael H. Bond. 1988. The Confucius connection: From cultural roots to economic growth. *Organizational Dynamics* 16: Spring, 5–21.

Hong, Jae W., Aydin Muderrisoglu, and George Zinkhan. 1987. Cultural differences and advertising expression: A comparative content analysis of Japanese and U.S. magazine advertising. *Journal of Advertising* 16(1): 55–68.

Horovitz, Bruce. 2002. Gen Y: A tough crowd to sell. *USA Today,* 22 April, B-01.

ITIM Culture and Management Consultants. 2003. National culture. www.itim.org/4aba.html.

Jacobs, Laurence, Charles Keown, and Kyung-Il Ghymn. 1991. Cross-cultural color comparisons: Global marketers beware. *International Marketing Review* 8(3): 21–30.

Kahle, Lynn R. 1983. ed: *Social values and social change: Adaptions to life in America.* New York: Praeger.

King, Samantha. 2000. Language police give billboards in English a pasting. *South China Morning Post,* 30 November, 18.

Kroeber, A. L. & Kluckhohn, C. 1952. Culture: A critical review of concepts and definitions. *Harvard University Peaboby Museum of American Archaeology and Ethnology Papers* 47: 181.

Lazer, William, Shoji Murata, and Hiroshi Kosaka. 1985. Japanese marketing—Toward a better understanding. *Journal of Marketing* 49: Summer, 69–81.

Lee, James A. 1966. Cultural analysis in overseas operations. *Harvard Business Review* (March/April): 47.

Lin, Carolyn. 1992. Cultural differences in message strategies: A comparison between American and Japanese television commercials. Paper presented at the AEJMC Annual Conference, 8–11 April, Montreal.

Lynch, Mitchell. 1984. Harvard's Levitt called global marketing guru. *Advertising Age,* 25 June, 49.

Madden, Thomas, Kelly Hewett, and Martin Roth. 2000. Managing images in different cultures: A cross-national study of color meanings and preferences. *Journal of International Marketing,* 8(4), 90–107.

Maletzke, Gerhard. 1976. Intercultural and international communication. In *International and intercultural communication,* ed. Heinz-Dietrich Fischer and John Calhoun Merrill. New York: Hastings House.

Maslow, Abraham. 1964. A theory of human motivation. In *Readings in managerial psychology*, ed. Harold Leavitt and Louis Pondy, 6–24. Chicago: University of Chicago Press.

Miller, Tom. 1998. Global segments from "strivers" to "creatives." *Marketing News*, 4 July, 11.

Milner, Laura, and James Collins. 2000. Sex-role portrayals and the gender of nations. *Journal of Advertising* 29(1) (Spring): 67–79.

Miracle, Gordon. 1988. An empirical study of the usefulness of the back-translation technique for international advertising messages in print media. In *Proceedings of the 1988 conference of the American Academy of Advertising*, ed. John D. Leckenby, American Academy of Advertising, Austin Texas, RC-51.

Mortimer, Jasper. 2003. Breweries tap Mideast market. *San Diego Union-Tribune*, 16 February, H-2.

Mueller, Barbara. 1992. January/February. Standardization vs. specialization: An examination of westernization in Japanese advertising. *Journal of Advertising Research* 32(1) (January/February): 15–24.

Munson, J. Michael, and Shelby H. McIntyre. 1978. Personal values and values attributed to a distant cultural stereotype. In *Advances in consumer research*, vol. 5, ed. H. Keith Hunt, 103+. Ann Arbor, Mich.: Association for Consumer Research.

Murdock, George P. 1945. The common denominator of cultures. In *The science of man in the world crises*, ed. Ralph Linton, 123–42. New York: Columbia University Press.

Ramaprasad, Preponderant, and Kazumi Hasegawa. 1990. An analysis of Japanese television commercials. *Journalism Quarterly* 67 (Winter): 1025–33.

Raugust, Karen. 2002a. Multicultural goes mainstream. *Advertising Age*, 4 November, M-2.

———. 2002b. Census 2000 boosts interest in multicultural markets. *Advertising Age*, 4 November, M-1.

Reid, Stan. 1986. Migration, cultural distance and international market expansion. In *Research in international marketing*, ed. Peter W. Turnbull and Stanley Paliwoda, 22–33. London: Croom Helm.

Ricks, David. 1983. *Big business blunders: Mistakes in multinational marketing.* Homewood, Ill.: Dow Jones–Irwin.

———. 1988. International business blunders: An update. *Business and Economic Review* 34 (January/February/March): 11–14.

Rokeach, Milton. 1968. *Beliefs, attitudes and values.* San Francisco: Jossey-Bass.

———. 1973. *The nature of human values.* New York: Free Press.

Samovar, Larry, and Richard E. Porter. 1994. *Intercultural communication: A reader.* 7th ed. Belmont, Calif.: Wadsworth.

Samovar, Larry, Richard Porter, and Lisa Stafani. 1998. *Communication between cultures.* 3d ed. Belmont, Calif.: Wadsworth.

Shane, Scott. 1988. Language and marketing in Japan. *International Journal of Advertising* 7: 155–61.

Steward, Edward C. 1972. *American cultural patterns: A cross cultural perspective.* Pittsburgh, Penn.: Intercultural Communications Network.

Taylor, Eda, and Dale R. Wilson. 1997. Impact of information level on the effectiveness of U.S. and Korean television communication. *Journal of Advertising* 20 (Spring): 1–15.

Taylor, Edward B. 1871. *Primitive culture.* London: John Murray.

Terpstra, Vern. 1983. *International dimensions of marketing.* 3rd ed, Chicago, Ohio: Dryden.

Terpstra, Vern, and Kenneth David. 1991. *The cultural environment of international business.* 2d ed. Cincinnati, Ohio: Southwestern.

Terpstra, Vern, and Lloyd Russow. 2000. *International dimensions of marketing.* 4th ed., Cincinnati, Ohio: South-Western College Publishing.

Thomas, Marlo, and Helene Hill. 1999. The impact of ethnocentrism on devising and implementing a corporate identity strategy for new international markets. *Internatinal Marketing Review,* 16(415) 376–90.

Usunier, Jean-Claude. 1996. *Marketing across cultures.* 2d ed. New York: Prentice Hall.

Wells, William. 1987. Global advertisers should pay heed to contextual variations. *Marketing News,* 13 February, 18.

Wentz, Laurel. 1992. Smooth talk wins Gillette ad space in Iran. *Advertising Age,* 27 April, 140.

———. 2002. Marketers will fuel multicultural ad boost. *Advertising Age,* 11 November, 6.

Wentz, Laurel, and Bruce Crumley. 1993. Magic doesn't travel during Euro-Disney visit. *Advertising Age,* 20 September, 1, 3.

Whorf, Benjamin Lee. 1956. *Language, thought, and reality.* Cambridge, Mass.: Technology Press of Massachusetts Institute of Technology.

World Almanac and Book of Facts. 2003. 633.

Yankelovich Partners. 1992. When it comes to pop culture, we are the world. *Adweek,* 2 November, 62.

Zandpour, Fred, and Veronica Campos. 1994. Global reach and local touch: Achieving cultural fitness in TV advertising. *Journal of Advertising Research* 34(5) (September/October): 35.

CHAPTER FIVE

Coordinating and Controlling International Advertising

Chapter 2 focused on the four P's of the marketing mix—product, price, place (distribution), and, briefly, promotion. In Chapter 3 we highlighted the importance of examining various characteristics of foreign markets—demographic and geographic characteristics, economic factors, and the political-legal environment—and in Chapter 4 we explored the cultural environment. Now we turn our attention to the coordination and control of international marketing communications. Once international marketers have developed a product that meets the needs of a specific group in a foreign market, have priced it properly, and have distributed it via the appropriate channels, they must still inform consumers abroad of the product's availability and benefits. Advertising's goal is to generate awareness, interest, desire, and, ultimately, action. In this chapter we will focus on centralized versus decentralized control of international advertising, advertising agency selection, and marketing and advertising strategy options.

Centralized versus Decentralized Control of International Advertising

One of the first decisions a company must make when it decides to communicate with consumers in the various markets in which it intends to do business is how to organize international promotional functions—including advertising, personal selling, direct marketing, publicity, and sales promotions. A critical question relates to the locus of decision making—will it be highly centralized at company headquarters, or will a more decentralized, collaborative, and participatory approach to marketing communications be adopted? It should be noted that there is a close relationship between the decision on centralization and the extent of advertising standardization ultimately employed. In international advertising, Tai and Wong (1998) propose that marketers have four basic options: (1) global approach (centralized decision process, standardized advertising approach), (2) local approach (decentralized decision process,

differentiated advertising approach), (3) "regcal" approach (centralized decision process, regional advertising approach), and (4) "glocal" approach (decentralized decision process, standardized advertising approach).

Global Approach (Centralized Decision Process, Standardized Advertising Approach)

Complete *centralization* of decision making related to international advertising implies a high level of head office control—advertising agency selection, campaign planning, creative strategy and message development, media strategy and selection, budgeting, and sales promotion efforts all are conducted in the country in which the firm's headquarters is situated. One of the major advantages associated with centralization is that it affords the marketer complete control over all promotional efforts. This degree of control is essential if the marketer is planning on integrating marketing communications. In addition, it eases coordination efforts in multiple markets.

A centralized approach is significantly more likely to be employed if the marketing environments of the message sender and receiver(s) are highly similar. In particular, centralization is commonly used if there is little variation in both the media available for advertising and the regulation of advertising from one market to the next. Depending on the foreign market, the international marketer may not feel that local managers possess the management skills necessary to conduct effective research and to develop coherent advertising strategies. Further, subsidiaries often lack the financial resources to produce advertising executions with high production values. In many instances foreign managers are quite relieved to turn over responsibility for advertising decisions to headquarters.

The centralized approach is highly correlated with the use of standardized advertising—employing virtually the same campaign in both domestic and foreign markets. Conversely, a low level of head office control (decentralization) suggests that local development of advertising campaigns is more likely to be employed (Kirpolani et al. 1988, 323). The issue of standardization as it relates to creative strategy will be dealt with in detail in the following chapter. Mattel Inc. is an example of a firm following the global approach. Mattel is the world's largest toy company and the firm's best selling brands include Barbie®, Hot Wheels®, Fisher-Price®, and American Girl®. Headquartered in El Segundo, California, Mattel has offices and facilities in 36 countries and sells its products in more than 150 nations around the world. As part of its continuing globalization strategy, Mattel has consolidated all of its international agencies. Ogilvy & Mather is now responsible for all advertising assignments on a global basis and is responsible for the global coordination, modification, and distribution of Mattel creative materials for all international markets (*PR Newswire* 2002, 1).

However, there are weaknesses associated with highly centralized control as well. For example, a firm employing such an organizational approach may find it lacks (1) the ability to sense changes in market needs occurring away from home, (2) the resources to analyze data and develop strategic responses to competitive challenges emerging in foreign markets, or (3) the

managerial initiative, motivation, and capability in its overseas operations to respond imaginatively to diverse and fast-changing environments (Bartlett and Ghoshal 1986, 87).

Local Approach (Decentralized Decision Process, Differentiated Advertising Approach)

Complete *decentralization* of international advertising means that all, or nearly all, advertising decisions are made by local managers in the foreign markets. The philosophy here, according to Christopher Bartlett and Sumantra Ghoshal, is that international subsidiaries should not be mere "pipelines to move products. Their own special strengths can help build competitive advantage" (Bartlett and Ghoshal 1986, 88). A primary benefit of decentralization is that promotional programs are tailored to the specific needs of each market. Nationals may be perceived as knowing the local market best and thus better equipped to make necessary modifications to advertising campaigns as a result of differences in the local media scene, political-legal environment, or culture. An international marketer may also opt for a decentralized approach if markets are small or the volume of international business and advertising is too limited to warrant close attention from headquarters. Local managers are likely to be more highly motivated when given responsibility for the promotional programs in their market. In some instances this approach is employed because foreign managers can be resentful if the home office centralizes control over advertising functions and then mandates the specific messages to be used in their markets. Certainly, a degree of control over promotional efforts is relinquished if a decentralized approach is adopted. Tai and Wong note that many food brands engage in the local approach. One example is the U.S. company Welch Food Inc., where a team approach is used in order to take advantage of the expertise of both management at the Welch Food company and local distributors, as well as to ensure better coordination between both sides. All advertising decisions are made jointly by headquarters and local distributors. But apart from the target segment, which is kept consistent, all other advertising elements differ from the home market (Tai and Wong 1998, 319).

Regcal Approach (Centralized Decision Process, Regional Approach)

Tai and Wong note that the regcal approach is made up of "reg" (regional) and "cal" (local); that is, it uses a combined approach of centralized decision making and regional—sometimes even local—adaptation. For example, an international or network agency may be designated as the lead agency, responsible for developing what is termed pattern advertising (Tai and Wong 1998, 320). Pattern advertising refers to centralization of the "what" of an ad campaign and regionalization or localization of the "how" (Roth 1982, 290). Thus the basic advertising strategy, general creative, and even media approaches are provided to each subsidiary; however, local managers are then free to select their own media and modify copy, visuals, or other elements of the message to meet regional or local needs. This approach allows for local input and adaptation while still permitting a degree of uniformity in a firm's international promotions. In the past, Ikea, the Swedish furniture giant, has traditionally run its advertising on a strictly country-by-country basis. The firm recently appointed Finnish shop Hasan & Partners to handle its first integrated branding campaign across several European markets. The regional campaign is intended for Finland, Switzerland, the Netherlands, and Belgium (Brikell, 2002). However, the regcal approach is not without problems. A critical question is how much country-to-country autonomy is practical.

Glocal Approach (Decentralized Decision Process, Standardized Approach)

Glocal is a combination of the "glo" (global) and "cal" (local) approaches. Here, the headquarters develops a global campaign, which local offices may or may not choose to follow, but most decisions are determined by local subsidiaries or distributors. Coca-Cola, often cited in the same breath with globalization, has increasingly moved toward the glocal approach. Coca-Cola's CEO, Douglas Daft, allows local people to call the shots. He told the *New York Times:* "To me it was so natural, so logical to let local managers make decisions on products, advertising and other areas heretofore controlled by Atlanta" (Crain 2000). Headquarters develops campaigns for its major brands (Coke, Fanta, and Sprite), which it then provides to its local offices. Local offices, which are responsible for their own profit and loss accounts, often adopt the standardized approach because of similarity in target audiences or attitudes between the domestic and foreign markets. In 2000, Coca-Cola and the Interpublic Group signed an alliance whereby Interpublic acts as "creative consultant and idea generator at the global level." However, while Interpublic will come up with the core message about brand Coca-Cola, local managers at the country level are free to work with Interpublic shops of independent agencies in their region. The decision is likely to lead to agency consolidation on the brand, which spends about $900 million a year on advertising globally. Interpublic's McCann Erickson Worldwide has worked on the flagship brand since 1942 and fields ads for Coke in 89 countries. Although Atlanta's decision to name a global partner appears to be at odds with the marketers to "local" mantra, a company spokesperson says it fits in because local execs will be involved in decisions (*Advertising Age* 2000).

Agency Selection

Firms marketing their goods and services abroad must decide who should plan, prepare, and execute their promotional campaigns. International marketers have a variety of options, including (1) employing their domestic agency (and then exporting advertising messages), (2) using their domestic in-house agency or a foreign subsidiary's in-house agency, (3) calling on the services of an international agency with domestic and overseas offices, or (4) hiring a foreign advertising agency.

Domestic and In-House Agencies

In some instances, firms may choose to simply export advertising campaigns originally created for the domestic market. Indeed, there are numerous examples of campaigns that have been exported quite successfully: the Marlboro man, conceived for the U.S. market, has travelled well all around the world—literally for decades. Other advertisers who have used this approach include IBM, Philips, and Waterman Pens. Firms may also choose to rely on their domestic advertising agency to prepare advertising messages for their foreign markets. A firm's domestic agency may well be affiliated with foreign shops capable of providing necessary translation services and assistance with media planning and buying. A domestic agency might also belong to an international network offering similar services. However, a very real danger of employing a domestic agency is that it may not be familiar with the many pitfalls associated with international advertising.

Some companies rely on their in-house advertising departments for foreign advertising assistance. On the plus side, the in-house agency is likely to be intimately familiar with the product or service to be promoted. Hennes & Mauritz (introduced in Chapter 2) provides an excellent example. In 2001, the Swedish fashion giant announced it was parting company with Finnish creative shop Hasan & Partners, just a year after entrusting it with its estimated $100 million ad account. More than 50 agencies attempted to court H&M, but the firm's new agency was to be neither a top Swedish agency nor one of the international network agencies. Instead, like many haute couture fashion houses and more mass marketers like Benetton, H&M decided to handle its advertising in-house. H&M set up its own ad shop, called the Red Room, to handle the creation of all advertising for over 14 countries (Brikell 2001). On the downside, domestic in-house agencies may lack the necessary experience in dealing with foreign markets. When international advertisers turn to a foreign subsidiary's in-house agency, they may gain familiarity with the local market but lose a degree of control over promotional efforts. Further, there is no guarantee that the quality of the work produced will live up to the firm's expectations.

International Agencies and Global Networks

International firms leaning toward a centralized approach are three times more likely to employ an international agency or global network than they are to use a foreign agency (Kanso 1991, 129). Clearly, it is easier for international marketers to deal with a single international agency than with a separate agency in each market in which they operate. Although agency networks offer multicountry coverage, there is no guarantee that offices in each country will be equally strong. Clients may find agency work in one market of especially high quality, but less so in another market.

It can safely be said that Saatchi & Saatchi was the first of the truly global agencies. In an attempt to become the first advertising agency capable of meeting the needs of increasingly global clients, London-based Saatchi & Saatchi introduced its global orientation in 1984 in an advertisement headlined, "The New Opportunity for World Brands." The advertisement reflected

the philosophy of global marketing outlined by Harvard Business School professor Theodore Levitt, who stated:

> The world's needs and desires have been irrevocably homogenized by technology. The global corporation accepts that technology drives consumers relentlessly towards the same common goals, i.e. the alleviation of life's burdens and the expansion of discretionary time and spending power. . . . Successful global companies sell the same things the same way everywhere and different cultural preferences, national tastes and standards are vestiges of the past. (Wentz 1991)

Not surprisingly, Levitt became a member of the Saatchi board. In late 1991 Saatchi & Saatchi further enhanced its global orientation by restructuring its North American and non–North American operations into a single unit. The agency even offered rewards to employees creating successful international campaigns, a practice reflecting its recognition that major clients, such as Procter & Gamble, look for advertising ideas that can run globally (Wentz, 1991, 49).

Along with the globalization of the advertising business that has occurred since the 1980s has inevitably come consolidation, as agencies without the resources to compete on a full international footing have sought protection within ever-larger holding companies. Indeed, Saatchi & Saatchi, with its more than 130 offices in 80 countries, was acquired by Paris-based Publicis Group in 2000. Corporate clients include General Mills, Procter & Gamble, and Toyota.

By the mid-1990s, the top 10 agency networks' combined share of global advertising spending more than doubled, from 22.9 percent during the previous 10-year period to 48.3 percent. Driving this concentration of power is an assumption that ad agencies must have a global presence, enormous size, and a full range of marketing services to survive. This has led to decades of mergers and acquisitions, during which, for example, Omnicom bought more than 150 agencies. Interpublic grew from two U.S.-based ad agency groups to three worldwide ad agency networks: 30–40 smaller U.S.- and overseas-based ad shops, three global direct-marketing agencies, and 16–18 agencies focused on service such as public relations, health care marketing, entertainment and sports marketing, and consumer research.

In 2001, 95 percent of advertising account reviews were won by agencies of the big four (the Omnicom Group, the Interpublic Group, the WWP Group, and Publicis). Today, agency consolidation has resulted in these four largest agency-holding companies controlling 55 percent of global ad billings and 82 percent of U.S. ad billings (Elliott 2002, 3). Clearly, this alignment fever has spelled success for international agency networks and now is undoubtedly the era of the advertising superpowers: superagencies with superclients.

The megagroups clearly offer opportunities for synergy. They can deliver to their clients the ease of one-stop shopping for all of their marketing and promotional needs. They provide a multitude of marketing service alongside advertising, as they have aligned themselves with a wide variety of communication specialists in order to be able to offer integrated communication services to their clients. Just five years ago, over 90 percent of the revenues of the major holding companies derived from advertising and media services (Sanders and Cuneo 2002, 3).

Today, these "below the line" services, as they have become to be called, account for an ever-increasing percentage of annual revenue. For example, direct marketing, public relations, promotions, event marketing, and consulting combined accounted for 58 percent of revenues at Omnicom, 55 percent at WWP, 40 percent at Interpublic, and 23 percent at Publicis in 2002. These figures are certain to continue their steady rise. For example, WWP expects approximately two-thirds of revenue to come from marketing services in 5–10 years, according to WWP CEO Martin Sorrell. At Interpublic, a 50–50 split between advertising and below-the-line revenue over the next two years is considered a healthy estimate (Van der Pool and Rountree 2003, 9). The change is being encouraged by marketers who are trying to reach consumers through a wide variety of communication channels. For example, Mary Kay Haben, group vice president of Kraft Foods North America, notes that at Kraft:

> we spend almost as much in other forms of marketing as we do on advertising. The goal is to simplify the development of integrated ideas. Agencies capable of providing integrated campaigns in a cost-efficient, time efficient manner have an opportunity for a big win. (Sanders and Cuneo 2002, 3) (See Figure 5.1 for below-the-line revenues as a percentage of total revenues at the Big Four holding companies.)

Indeed, how holding companies handle the integration of these disciplines is expected to go a long way toward determining their performance level in years to come. Notes Lou Schultz, former chairman of Interpublic's Initiative Media Worldwide: "as marketers integrate more programs to communicate with their audiences, the distinction between advertising and below-the-line activities will blur" (Van der Pool and Rountree 2003, 9).

In addition to integrated marketing communications, conglomerates can also offer additional benefit to clients, including a means to consolidate and cut administrative expenses. Size is also of benefit when it comes to securing commodities. For example, a large media buying unit will clearly be able to command greater attention—and better prices—in both national as well as international markets.

On the downside, critics complain that the holding companies have become too large and too complex. See Figure 5.2 for an "anti-conglomerate" ad. The message for Seiter & Miller pokes fun at the conglomerates with a headline that reads: "Inter-Omni-PP . . . Is your ad agency telling you to get lost?" The copy notes:

> how much bigger and bureaucratic can the public agencies get? At Seiters & Miller, there are no divisions, subdivisions, or sub-par work. Here you'll find smart, talented professionals all under one roof, and all dedicated to one mission—working hand in hand with you to build your business.

Many on both the creative and business sides of advertising contend that the expansion of agency companies has smothered originality under a blanket of conformity. Paul Cappelli, a refugee from the Interpublic agency McCann-Erickson, who now runs the Ad Store, a New York–based boutique, notes:

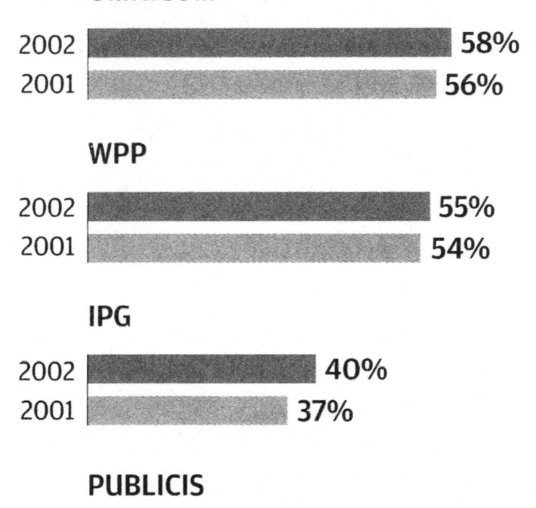

Below-the-Line Revenue as % of Total Revenue

OMNICOM

2002	58%
2001	56%

WPP

2002	55%
2001	54%

IPG

2002	40%
2001	37%

PUBLICIS

2002	23%
2001	24%

Figure 5.1 Below-the-line revenue as percentage of total revenue.

Sources: Company statements, Adweek estimates

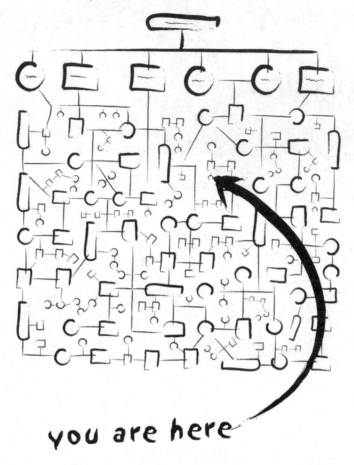

IS YOUR AD AGENCY TELLING YOU TO GET LOST?

(FIND YOURSELF AT A BETTER PLACE)

How much bigger and bureaucratic can the public agencies get? At Seiter & Miller, there are no divisions, subdivisions, subsidiaries, or sub-par work. Here, you'll find smart, talented professionals all

under one roof, and all dedicated to one mission – working hand in hand with you to build your business. If you still remember why advertising used to be called a 'people business', call us.

Contact Steve Seiter: 212-843-9900 or visit www.seitermiller.com

Figure 5.2 Anti-holding company advertisement for Seiter & Miller advertising agency.

You have a holding company dictating what can and can't be done, which stifles creativity, and the corporate culture numbs individuality. We call those agencies "notworks" instead of "networks" because if you're not one of the biggest clients, you get lost in the shuffle. (Elliott 2002, 3)

Another major drawback of such conglomerates is that sometimes agency brands must be sacrificed to benefit another owned by the same holding company. Madison Avenue's history is replete with shuttered agencies whose doors carried the names of former giants—Lintas, Ayer, and Wells, Rich & Green. In October 2002, D'Arcy Masius Benton & Bowels, which began in 1906 and developed into the world's 14th-largest agency brand (and is still reflected in the rankings below), was the latest victim of industry consolidation. Publicis, which became D'Arcy's parent after its merger with Bcom3 group, closed the agency and folded DMB&B clients into the holding company's other agencies. A related disadvantage for holding companies is that as they continue to grow and expand, client conflicts become a critical issue. For example, Interpublic was unable to persuade PepsiCo that "walls" could be constructed in such a way to insure there would be no leaks of confidential PepsiCo information among Interpublic's PepsiCo agency (Foote, Cone & Belding) and Interpublic's Coca-Cola Co. agencies (principally McCann-Erickson Worldwide and Lowe Lintas & Partners Worldwide). In the end, PepsiCo could not see a difference between the Interpublic shops (Kurz 2001, 22).

Table 5.1 lists the top agency networks in Europe, Latin America, Asia/Pacific, and the Middle East in 2001. Note that most of these networks are part of major holding companies. McCann-Erickson Worldwide was the dominant agency in Europe as well as the leading Western agency in Latin America. Dentsu, with over $2 billion in gross income, was the top-ranked agency in the Asia/Pacific region. Fortune Promoseven Group (linked with McCann-Erickson Worldwide) was the top ranked agency in the Middle East. Rankings are based on gross income in dollar amounts that an agency organization derives from the region.

Foreign (Local) Agencies

If the multinational firm adheres to decentralization, giving a good deal of autonomy to foreign managers, the advertiser is significantly more likely to select foreign (local) agencies to coordinate promotional activities for each market in which it operates. The selection of a local agency may even be left to overseas managers. Academics and practitioners who encourage the use of foreign (local) agencies argue that only such agencies can truly appreciate the local culture and, as a result, can develop messages best able to communicate with foreign consumers. A survey undertaken by *Advertising Age*'s Clancy Shulman revealed that while Europeans regularly purchase brands from other countries, when it comes to advertising messages they prefer the home-grown variety (Giges 1992, 11). Foreign agencies thus can act as a cultural bridge between the international firm and the local market (Terpstra 1988, 159).

Because foreign agencies are often independent and typically smaller in size, they may demonstrate an innovativeness that agency networks cannot—and this may be just what a marketer

TABLE 5.1 Top Agency Networks in Europe, Latin America, Asia/Pacific, and the Middle East, 2001 (U.S. million $)

Europe

Rank	Agency	Equity Gross Income	Equity Billings
1.	McCann Erickson Worldwide	$ 856.1	$ 7,586.8
2.	Euro RSCG	815.6	5,315.5
3.	Y & R Advertising	755.3	13,357.6
4.	Publicis Worldwide	741.9	5,266.8
5.	BBDO Worldwide	677.1	4,974.8
6.	Ogilvy & Mather Worldwide	649.6	6,181.5
7.	DDB Wolwide Communications	588.7	4,190.8
8.	J. Walter Thompson Co.	524.5	3,644.6
9.	Grey Worldwide	521.6	3,104.9
10.	TBWA Worldwide	492.1	3,676.4
11.	Lowe & Partners Worldwide	367.5	2,754.8
12.	Leo Burnett Worldwide	331.4	2,914.3
13.	D'Arcy Masius Menton & Bowles	325.2	3,836.C
14.	Bates Worldwide	306.6	2,718.9
15.	Saatchi & Saatshi Worldwide	198.8	1,769.5
16.	Foote, Cone & Belding Worldwide	195.3	1,360.6
17.	Rapp Collins Worldwide	130.2	861.9
18.	Brann Worldwide	122.0	642.6
19.	Arnold Worldwide	116.6	813.9
20.	TMP Worldwide	107.6	485.5

Latin America

Rank	Agency	Equity Gross Income	Equity Billings
1.	McCann-Erickson Worldwide	$ 307.4	$ 2,050.6
2.	J. Walter Thompson Co.	165.4	889.2
3.	Ogilvy & Mather Worldwide	114.5	659.5
4.	Euro RSCG Worldwide	110.3	735.6
5.	Leo Burnett Worldwide	98.8	660.5
6.	Y & R Advertising	93.5	757.7
7.	BBDO	85.3	638.7
8.	D'Arcs Masius Benton & Bowles	70.0	453.6
9.	Foote, Cone & Belding Worldwide	66.2	581.0
10.	DDB Worldwide Communications	60.7	348.9
11.	Grey Worldwide	59.4	397.1
12.	Lowe & Partners Worldwide	57.0	344.7
13.	Publicis Worldwide	48.7	330.8
14.	Fischer America Comunicacao Total	40.0	274.6
15.	DPZ Duailibi Petit Zaragoza Propaganda	39.5	205.3
16.	Grupo Interamericano de Comunicacao	31.8	127.0
17.	Saatchi & Saatchi	30.2	236.0
18.	TalentComunicacao	25.4	103.7
19.	Bates Worldwide	25.0	207.5
20.	TBWA	14.9	98.7

Asia/Pacific

Rank	Agency	Equity Gross Income	Equity Billings
1.	Dentsu	$ 2,028.5	$ 13 937.1
2.	Hakuhodo	861.4	6 796.2
3.	Asatsu-DK	354.4	3,291.4
4.	McCann-Erickson Worldwide	280.5	1,938.0
5.	J. Walter Thompson Co.	250.5	1,72˙.5
6.	Ogilvy & Mather Worldwide	206.8	1,406.1
7.	Bates Worldwide	189.6	1,596.0
8.	Tokyo Agency	186.9	1,684.4
9.	DY&R Partnerships/Y&R	149.0	1,253.0
10.	Cheil Communications America	142.0	796.0
11.	Leo Burnett Worldwide	118.8	794.7
12.	TBWA Worldwide	113.8	841.8
13.	Lowe & Partners Worldwide	109.1	829.3
14.	Grey Worldwide	107.6	717.4
15.	DDB Worldwide Communications	98.2	689.2
16.	Clemenger Group	91.0	606.9
17.	BBDO Worldwide	90.3	7C6.7
18.	Publicis Worldwide	88.1	760.9
19.	Asahi Advertising	84.3	572.0
20.	Euro RSCG Worldwide	79.2	520.9

Middle East

Rank	Agency	Equity Gross Income	Equity Billings
1.	Fortune Promoseven Group (McCann)	$ 41.7	$ 335.5
2.	Leo Burnett Worldwide	31.8	262.4
3.	TMI/JWT	27.3	181.7
4.	Impact/BBDO	25.4	168.4
5.	Publicis-Graphics	24.2	161.0
6.	Team/Y&R Middle East	23.4	309.3
7.	Memac (Ogilvy)	22.2	148.1
8.	MADCO	17.5	67.9
9.	Intermarkets	16.4	110.0
10.	Horizon FCB	9.8	65.1

Source: AdAgeGlobal 2003 (www.adageglobal.com/cgi-bin/pages.pl?link=522). *Advertising Age Global Daily News*, 2003.

is looking for. Pizza Hut, a division of U.S.-based Yum Restaurants International, has allowed its French division to create the first-ever "Made in France" advertising campaign for the introduction of a new, locally sourced specialty item—the Alpine-influenced Tartiflette Pizza. The new television campaign, along with direct marketing and point-of-sale promotions, is the first solo effort for local independent K Agency, Paris, which has until now been responsible for adapting various U.S. campaigns to the French market. Pizza Hut assigned the local campaign with hopes that K Agency's locally sourced ads would tap into French consumers' love of regional cheeses and the national penchant for passing the winter holidays in the Alps, which is the hook behind the new pizza. La Pizza Tarflette is the U.S. restaurant chain's bid to cash in on the winter ski fever which hits city dwellers, the principal customers at the chain's 140 French shops. The new product adapts the traditional Alpine Tartiflette recipe—a combination of potatoes, onions, ham, and local reblochon cheese—into a tasty pizza. Humorous TV spots are set in a typical ski resort restaurant and depict the pleasure skiers often take in munching down a Tartiflette after a hard day on the slopes. Except in this case, it's not a traditional version of the cheese dish, but a Pizza Hut Pizza (Speer 2003).

On the downside, utilizing a separate local agency for each foreign market makes coordinating worldwide campaigns quite challenging. International marketers must be aware, however, that the availability of advertising agencies in various markets varies greatly. Some countries, mostly in Africa, have just a single local agency. At the other end of the spectrum are countries such as the United States and the United Kingdom, each with well over 500 advertising agencies.

A major reason that foreign (local) agencies continue to prosper is nationalism. Many countries resent the role played by foreign firms in their economy and particularly the effect of foreign-produced messages on their culture. Increasingly, countries are mandating local production of advertising messages. For example, Canada, Australia, and Venezuela have laws banning commercials produced outside the native country, while Peru bans advertising messages containing foreign-inspired content or foreign models in an attempt to enhance its own national culture. Not only do such policies promote the local culture, but they also ensure the good health of the local advertising industry and provide employment for nationals.

Agency Selection Criteria

In addition to considering the organizational approach (centralized, decentralized, or combined), the international marketer should focus on a number of additional criteria in selecting the best agency or agencies to help the firm achieve its set goals:

- *Market coverage:* The firm must determine whether the agency or network under consideration provides coverage for all relevant markets.
- *Quality of coverage:* The firm must assess the agency's or network's reputation in each market.
- *Market research, public relations, and other marketing services:* If the firm needs market research, public relations, or other marketing services in addition to advertising, it must compare what the different agencies offer.

- *Relative roles of the firm's in-house advertising department and agency:* Some firms have a large in-house staff that takes on significant portions of advertising campaign development. These firms require fewer services from an advertising agency than do companies that rely on an agency for almost everything relating to advertising.

- *Size of the firm's international business:* The smaller the firm's international advertising expenditures, the less likely it will be to divide up its expenditures among numerous agencies. A firm's advertising volume may determine agency choice to assure some minimum level of service. An advertising budget multiplied by a number of markets may be of interest to an international agency even if it is of little interest to a single agency in any one market.

- *Image:* The firm must decide whether it wishes to project a national or international image. Desire for local identification and good local citizenship might indicate that the firm should select a number of national agencies rather than one international one.

- *Level of involvement:* In joint-venture arrangements the international firm typically shares decision making. The foreign partner may already have established a relationship with a local agency, which would be the decisive factor. In the case of licensing agreements, the licensee is typically responsible for the advertising function. Selling through distributors also reduces the degree of control the international firm has over promotional efforts. Generally, international marketers can choose agencies only for the advertising paid for by their firms. If a firm is engaging in a cooperative program with its distributors, its influence in agency selection may be somewhat greater. (Terpstra 1987, 432)

An international marketer may use different types of agencies for different purposes. For example, a recent study of Fortune 500 firms revealed that the choice of agency employed may vary depending on the stage of the advertising campaign. With regard to campaign development, the study showed that 17.8 percent of the firms used the company's in-house agency, 23.3 percent employed a foreign subsidiary's in-house agency, 24.5 percent turned to an international agency with overseas offices, and 34.4 percent selected the services of a foreign advertising agency. The numbers differed slightly with regard to campaign placement. Here, only 14.4 percent of the firms used the company's in-house agency, 27.8 percent sought out the services of a foreign subsidiary's in-house agency, 22.2 percent used an international agency with overseas branches for placement services, and 35.6 percent requested assistance from a foreign agency. Several of the Fortune 500 firms indicated that they used more than one type of organization, assigning campaign preparation and placement to different agencies (Kanso, 1991, 129).

IIII Marketing and Advertising Strategy Options

Duncan and Ramaprasad (1995) note that the crux of the standardization debates used to be: "Should multinational advertising be standardized or localized?" Today the question is: "In what situations and to what extent should multinational advertising be standardized?" Their international study of advertising agency executives focused on practitioners from the West

TABLE 5.2 Mean* Importance of Reasons for Standardizing Multinational Advertising

Reason	Western	Non-Western	Total
Create a single brand image in all markets	1.5	1.7	1.5
Make full use of a proven, successful idea	1.9	2.1	2.0
Take advantage of the demographic/ psychographic similarity in target audience	2.2	2.0	2.1
Culture is similar between countries	2.3	2.1	2.2
Product usage is similar in all markets**	2.2	2.7	2.4
Research has shown that one campaign will work***	2.2	2.6	2.4
Product is standardized	2.3	2.7	2.5
Pressure from client's headquarters	2.6	2.9	2.7
Saves money (one campaign costs less)	2.7	2.9	2.8
Pressure from other agency branches	3.8	3.6	3.71
Time pressure (one campaign takes less time)	3.0	3.5	3.74

*A 5-point scale was used. A lower score indicates greater importance.

**$t = -2.76$; df $=98$; $p < .01$.

***$t = -2.23$; df $= 98$; $p < .05$.

Source: Duncan and Ramaprasad (1995).

(Europe and the Americas) as well as non-Western regions (Asia, including the Pacific Rim and Australia). Duncan and Ramaprasad distinguished between strategy (the creative selling proposition) versus execution (the actual elements and their structure in an ad). In terms of the amount and type of standardization of multinational brands, the researchers found that 68 percent of the multinationally advertised brands use a standardized *strategy* in all the countries in which their advertising runs, 24 percent in some of the countries, and 7 percent not

TABLE 5.3 Mean* Agreement with Future Trends in the Global Marketplace

Trends	Western	Non-Western	Total
The use of standardized campaigns will increase over the next five years**	1.8	2.5	2.1
Consumer segments of demographically and psychographically similar people that extend across national boundaries are emerging	2.1	2.1	2.1
Consumers who are comparable in their values and demographics but reside in different nations will buy standardized products	2.2	2.1	2.2
Consumers with similar lifestyles and demographics, regardless of nationality, can be motivated by standardized advertising	2.3	2.4	2.3
Clients are increasing pressure on agencies to standardize campaigns***	2.3	2.7	2.4
Most standardized campaigns are successful	2.6	2.9	2.7
In cost benefit terms, the economic benefit of a standardized campaign usually offsets its decrease in communication effectiveness	3.4	3.3	3.4

*A 5-point Likert scale was used. A lower score indicates a higher agreement with the statement.

** $t = -4.49$, df $= 98$; $p < .01$.

*** $t = -2.24$, df $= 98$; $p < .05$.

Source: Duncan and Ramaprasad (1995).

at all. Standardization of execution was surprisingly similar, with 54 percent of the multinational brands using it in all countries, 36 percent in some countries, and 8 percent not at all. They found, however, use of standardized language to be uncommon in all countries.

It appears, however, that western region agencies in general use standardization more than do non-western agencies, but in an interesting reversal for specific elements, western agencies standardize strategy and execution more and language less than do non-western agencies. Interviews with respondents explained that standardization is more appropriate for western and highly industrialized markets and for markets that are contiguous. Apparently, it is more challenging to have a pan-Asian than a pan-European campaign because of the physical distances between Asian countries and their different levels of industrialization which has resulted in less assimilation and homogenisation. (Duncan and Ramaprasad 1995, 59)

Table 5.2 highlights the most important reasons for standardizing multinational advertising. The table reveals that practitioners consider a "single brand image" the most important reason to standardize. They consider reasons related to pressures the least important, and product- and audience-based reasons as having middling importance. The researchers note:

TABLE 5.4 Analysis of Standardization and Specialization of the Marketing Mix and Advertising Program

	STANDARDIZATION		ADAPTION	
	FULL	PARTIAL	FULL	PARTIAL
Product Design				
Brand Name				
Product Positioning				
Packaging				
Distribution				
Price				
Personal Selling				
Publicity				
Sales Promotion				
Advertising Strategy				
Theme/Appeal				
Copy/Dialogue				
Music/visuals				
Models/Spokespersons				
Media Planning				
Media Buying				

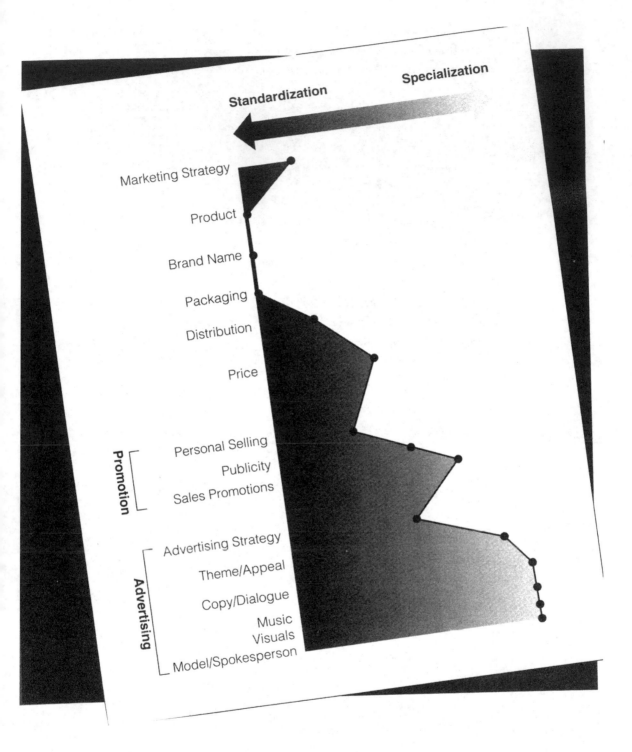

Figure 5.3 Strategic options in the marketing mix: an illustrative mixed strategy.

Source: Adapted from Susan P. Douglas and Yoram Wind, The myth of globalization, Columbia Journal of World Business 22(4) (1987): 19–29.

in their assessment, business efficacy reasons vary in importance, with "exploiting a successful idea" high on the list, "research backing" getting a middling position, and "saving money" placing lower. At the same time, "saving money" and "client pressure" are not unimportant; they have means below 3, suggesting above-average importance. Only "time pressure" and "pressure from other agency branches" have means above 3, indicating smaller importance. In sum, respondents consider creative and advertising fit reasons more important than external pressures. Interestingly, agencies in the western region consider similarity in product use and research backing as significantly more important than do agencies in the non-western region. (Duncan and Ramaprasad 1995, 61)

Table 5.3 reveals that respondents in the Duncan and Ramaprasad investigation agree that clients are increasing pressure to standardize. Western agencies, however, have a significantly different mean, indicating stronger agreement. Respondents also believe that global consumers are emerging who are demographically and psychographically similar, who will buy standardized products, and who will be motivated by standardized advertising. They tend to agree that most standardized campaigns are successful, but tend to disagree that the economic benefits of standardization offset the decrease in communication effectiveness.

The framework outlined in Table 5.4 can assist international marketers in assessing marketing and advertising strategy options. As the diagram shows, marketers must examine each step in a marketing program, taking into consideration the specific product to be marketed as well as the given marketing environment (characterized by its demographic, economic, political-legal, and cultural profile). Only then can the marketer evaluate the potential outcomes of steps taken toward the standardization or specialization end of the continuum. The framework can assist international marketers and advertisers in thinking globally with regard to marketing and advertising strategy, yet acting locally as market circumstances warrant.

Figure 5.3 provides an illustrative mixed strategy and highlights that globalization of both marketing and advertising should be viewed on a continuum.

Summary

Clearly, global marketing and the role of international advertising in selling products in foreign markets is a complex issue. Marketers must decide whether to use a centralized, decentralized, or combination approach with regard to the coordination of promotional programs. A firm planning on selling products abroad may rely on its own in-house agency or on the in-house agency of a foreign subsidiary. Or a marketer may turn to the firm's domestic agency for assistance in preparing marketing communications for foreign markets. Use of a foreign (local) agency or an international agency/network are additional options. A framework outlining the strategic options in the marketing mix can assist the international marketer in making creative decisions for foreign markets—the focus of Chapter 6.

References

Advertising Age Daily News. 2000. Coca-Cola gives global strategy account to Interpublic. 4 December. <www.adageglobal.com/cgi-bin/daily.pl?daily_id=4034&post_date=2000–12–04>

Advertising Age Global Daily News. 2003. Top agency networks in Europe, Latin America. Asia/Pacific, and the Middle East. <www.adageglobal.com/cgi-bin/pages.pl?link=522>

Bartlett, Christopher A., and Sumantra Ghoshal. 1986. Tap your subsidiaries for global reach. *Harvard Business Review* 64 (November/December): 87–94.

Brikell, Pia Grahn. 2001. Hennes & Mauritz makes surprise choise in $100 million global ad review. 11 December. <www.adageglobal.com/cgi-bin/daily.pl?daily_id=6390&post_date=2001–12–11>

Brikell, Pia Grahn. 2002. Ikea awards first multi-market assignments. 16 May. <www.adageglobal.com.cgi-bin/daily.pl?daily_id=7575&post_date=2002–05–16>

Crain, Rance. 2000. Agencies press get-global plans but clients face local realities. *Advertising Age,* 14 February, 32.

Duncan, Tom and Jyotika Ramaprasad. 1995. Standardized multinational advertising: The influencing factors. *Journal of Advertising,* 24(3): Fall, 55–69.

Douglas, Susan P. and Yoram Wind. 1987. The myth of globalization. *Columbia Journal of World Business,* 22(4), 19–29.

Elliott, Stuart. 2002. Advertising's big four: It's their world now. *New York Times,* 31 March, 3.

Giges, Nancy. 1992. Europeans buy outside goods, but like local ads. *Advertising Age,* 27 April, I1.

Kanso, Ali. 1991. The use of advertising agencies for foreign markets: Decentralized decisions and localized approaches? *International Journal of Advertising* 10: 129–36.

Kirpalani, V. H., Michel Laroche, and Rene Darmon. 1988. Role of headquarters control by multinationals in international advertising decisions. *International Journal of Advertising* 7: 323–333.

Kurz, Mitchell. 2001. Holding companies: Size is not a strategy. *Advertising Age,* 26 November, 22.

Levitt, Theodore. 1983. Globalization of markets. *Harvard Business Review* (May/June): 92–102.

PR Newswire. 2002. Mattel, Inc. globalises and consolidates its advertising agency assignments. 14 August, 1.

Quelch, John A. and Edward J. Hoff. 1985. Marketing mix: Analysis of standardization and adaptation. BBDO Worldwide Network meeting.

Roth, Robert F. 1982. *International marketing communications.* Chicago, Ill.: Crain Books.

Sanders, Lisa, and Alice Cuneo. 2002. April 22. 4A's chairman rues multiple assaults. *Advertising Age,* 22 April, 3, 61.

Speer, Lawrence J. 2003. Pizza Hut goes local in France with new menu item, ad campaign. 10 January. <www.adageglobal.com/cgi-bin/daily.pl?daily_id=9086 &post_date=2–003–01010>.

Tai, Susan, and Y. H. Wong. 1998. Advertising decision maing in Asia: "Glocal" versus "reg-cal" approach. *Journal of Managerial Issues* 10(3): Fall, 318–39.

Terpstra, Vern. 1987. *International marketing.* 4th ed. Chicago: Dryden Press.

———. 1988. *International dimensions of marketing.* Boston: PWS-Kent.

Van der Pool, Lisa, and Dristen Rountree. 2003. Below-the-line goes above and beyond. *Ad-week,* 3 February, 9.

Wentz, Laurel. 1991. Saatchi thinks global with international bonuses. *Advertising Age,* 3 June, 49.

CHAPTER SIX

Creative Strategy and Execution

Charles Frazer offers a generally accepted definition of *creative strategy:* "a policy or guiding principle which specifies the general nature and character of messages to be designed. Strategy states the means selected to achieve the desired audience effect over the term of the campaign (Frazer 1983, 36). One of the most important strategic considerations is whether to standardize advertising worldwide or to adapt it to the specific needs of each market. Scholars and practitioners alike are divided with regard to the benefits and disadvantages associated with each strategic approach. It should be reiterated, too, that this debate carries a variety of labels. Standardized campaigns have also been referred to as globalized and universal in the literature; specialized campaigns have been called localized, adapted, and even customized. In this chapter we will use the terms interchangeably in examining standardization versus specialization as it relates to creativity in advertising. We will also touch on the creative development and production of advertisements, examining the use of advertising appeals and both verbal and nonverbal aspects of commercial messages.

IIII Strategic Decisions

IIII Standardization of Advertising

An increasing number of advertising and marketing executives agree with Harvard's Theodore Levitt that the needs and desires of consumers around the world are growing ever more homogenized. These experts contend that the world is one large market and that regional, national, and even international differences are at best superficial. Therefore, the consumer may well be satisfied with similar products and services. There's no arguing with the fact that, today, Campbell soup, Crest toothpaste, and Camel cigarettes are at home in markets around the globe. Levitt went on to note that not only would consumers around the globe be satisfied

with similar products, but advertisers could sell them with similar messages (Levitt 1983, 92). Narrowly defined, *standardized advertising* refers to messages that are used internationally with virtually no change in theme, illustration, or copy—except, perhaps, for translation where needed.

Standardization of international campaigns generally takes one of two routes. One option is to adopt a campaign deemed successful in the national or domestic market for a firm's foreign markets. Esso's "Put a tiger in your tank" campaign is a classic example of a promotional effort that proved effective in the United States and was subsequently exported to numerous other countries. Another option is a preplanned effort to develop a campaign for use in multiple markets.

Advertisers and agencies alike perceive very real benefits associated with this approach. For one thing, coordination and control of marketing and promotional programs is greatly simplified and, as a result, foreign campaigns can be implemented much more quickly. This simplification may assist in faster product rollouts. Anthony Rutigliano notes: "As product life cycles shrink, companies will be hungry for quicker worldwide product roll outs, leaving less time to develop scores of local or national advertising campaigns" (Rutigliano 1986, 27). Indeed, the speed of megabrand launches can be staggering. Ogilvy & Mather introduced Pond's skincare line in 33 markets in a period of 18 months, an American Express testimonial campaign in 18 new markets in 15 months, and Ford's Mondeo in 22 markets within one year. If the drive to market brands appears to be full throttle, it is because competitive conditions warrant it. "The days of testing brands regionally in a single market are practically over," notes Michael Senett, vice-chairman and director of multinational accounts at McCann-Erickson in New York. "Because of the speed of technology, our clients realize they have to launch a brand globally or regionally to pre-empt their competition" (Kaplan 1994).

In addition, fewer marketing and advertising personnel are required at the local level to administer advertising campaigns developed at headquarters than are required to customize promotional efforts. Staff reductions lead to cost savings, and advertising production costs are reduced dramatically. It is certainly much less expensive to produce a single campaign for a number of markets than it is to produce a separate campaign for each specific market. Similarly, the cost associated with developing one television commercial for the European market, for example, and translating the dialogue or dubbing the spot into seven languages is significantly less than it is to develop seven separate television spots. McCann-Erickson claims to have saved Coca-Cola over $90 million in production costs over a 20-year period, during which the company was a staunch supporter of globalization, by producing worldwide commercials.

Further, good ideas can be exploited. If a campaign has proven successful in one market, there may be no need to "reinvent the wheel" in others. Kenneth Robbins, deputy chairman at Interpublic Group company SSC&B Lintas Worldwide, notes that really good ideas are extremely hard to find. As an example, he shares his experiences with Snuggle, introduced in Germany in 1970 as a liquid fabric softener that made clothes incredibly soft. The big idea was the use of a teddy bear as a spokesperson. Research revealed that the depth of feeling for teddy bears was enormous—the stuffed animals personified security, comfort, love, and, most important, softness. Within one year of completing national distribution, the brand claimed a 26

percent market share. The brand was subsequently introduced into 12 additional countries, and the teddy bear spokesperson was dearly loved throughout Europe and the United States (Bowes 1992, 129). That big idea, introduced more than 30 years ago, is still fresh today. Unilever is currently launching Snuggle in Mexico in a bid to enter the country's $250 million fabric softener market—the third largest in the world. Mexican homes consume more than 10 liters of softeners a year, well above the Latin American average of 4 liters. And the Snuggle teddy bear will play center stage in the television, magazine, and outdoor campaigns (Monjaras 2003).

Finally, a consistent international brand or company image can be achieved. A uniform image serves to reduce message confusion in areas where there is media overlap or a good deal of cross-border travel—such as is the case in many European countries. For example, in an attempt to shake off its image as a faceless industrial and electronics giant and to reveal a more innovative and friendly image, Siemens recently unveiled a pan-European corporate advertising campaign. "Siemens. Global network of innovation" is the tagline of the print campaign, developed by Ogilvy & Mather. The copy reads:

> Everyday Siemens' 460,000 employees change the way people live. We create new solutions, ask questions others would never have thought to ask and redefine entire industries from healthcare to energy to transportation. We're able to do this because we bring together extraordinary resources, people and ideas. Siemens is a global network of companies with operations in virtually every country, all with one goal in mind: to make life better.

The regional campaign is expected to run for at least two years (Mussey 2002).

Numerous firms have adopted the standardized approach. L'Oreal provides an excellent example. L'Oreal has been in the beauty business since the early 1900s. A century later it has become the world's largest cosmetics company with $14 billion in annual sales and a long record of double-digit profit growth. Little more than a decade ago, the European market accounted for over 75 percent of its sales; today that figure has dropped to about 50 percent. North America, where L'Oreal is now market leader, now accounts for nearly one third of turnover (Tomlinson 2002). The company has used a standardized approach to sell a wide variety of its products globally. Currently, L'Oreal employs what has been dubbed the "Dream Team"—a stable of dozens of models and actresses to plug its products. The team includes supermodel Claudia Schiffer, Destiny's Child singer Beyoncé Knowles, and actresses Andie MacDowell, Heather Locklear, and Catherine Deneuve (Ellison and Carreyrou 2003). See Figure 6.1 for a German print ad for L'Oreal's Visible Lift make-up featuring Andie MacDowell. The campaign runs in multiple markets.

Products Suitable for Standardization

Standardization of advertising is viewed by many marketers as a challenging task. Clearly, however, some international marketers are successfully employing this approach. Progress has been made in understanding under what conditions standardized advertising works best and for which products global campaigns are particularly well suited (Fannin 1984, 74).

Figure 6.1 German print ad for L'Oreal's Visible Lift make-up featuring Andie MacDowell.

Products for Which Audiences Are Essentially Similar Cross-border consumer segments are emerging. Global youth is a ripe and growing group, which is becoming increasingly similar. In terms of growth, consumers aged 14 and under comprise 21 percent of the U.S. total population, but in other markets, particularly Asia, the percentages are even higher: China, 25 percent; India, 33 percent; Malaysia, 34 percent; Philippines, 36 percent; Vietnam, 32 percent; Brazil, 28 percent; and Argentina, 26 percent. Moreover, global youth represent $100 billion of spending power—certainly an appealing figure to international marketers. Today, there are more similarities than differences among youthful consumers. Elissa Moses, author of *The $100 Billion Allowance: Accessing the Global Teen Market,* notes that teens are simultaneously plugging into two cultural channels: local and global. For global culture, they are a homogeneous target audience. They are plugged into global culture via satellite TV and the Internet (Parmar 2002, 1). Teens around the world increasingly listen to the same music, eat at the same restaurants, and wear the same clothes. Levi-Strauss recently launched a global campaign for its Type 1 jean (see Figure 6.2). With the brand, which features exaggerated details, such as oversized rivets, Levi-Strauss hopes to inject new growth into the product, whose sales have now stabilized following a disastrous period in the late 1990s (Jardine 2002).

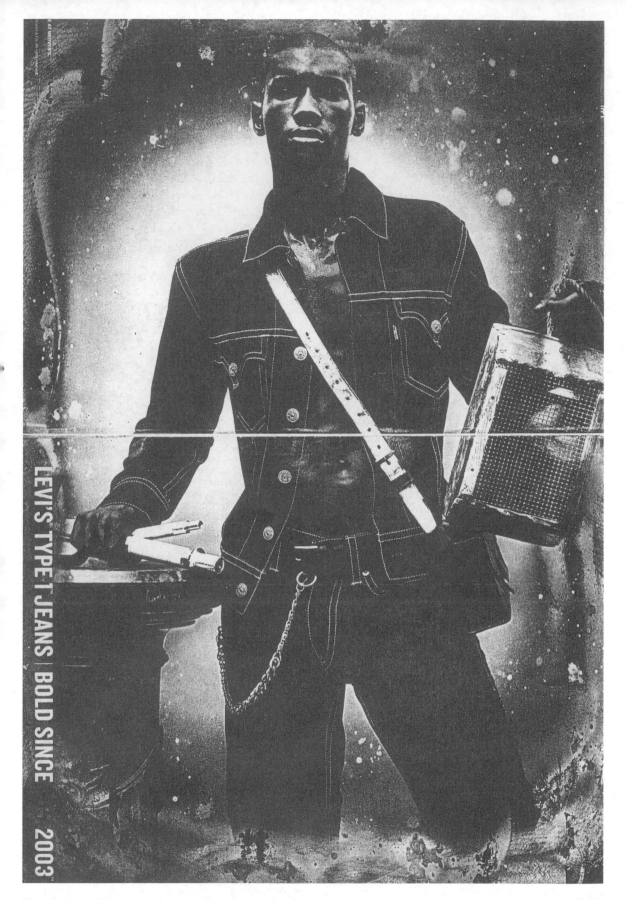

LEVI'S® TYPE 1 JEANS | BOLD SINCE 2003™

Figure 6.2 Levi-Strauss launches New Type 1 jeans globally.

Shared sensibilities are also emerging among social classes across different countries, such as affluent consumers and international business travellers. Upper-class markets have long been targeted globally for upscale products such as jewellery, fine watches, and expensive cars. American Express has found that the market for its Platinum Card, aimed at wealthy consumers, responds to the same type of luxury message, whether it is in Paraguay or Paris (Parmar 2002, 49).

McCann-Erickson's Michael Sennett argues that "a male middle executive in Italy has more in common with a male middle executive in the U.K. than with a farmer in Italy" (Kaplan 1994, 50). InterContinental, which operates 135 hotels in 65 countries, recently introduced a global campaign for the upscale hotel chain featuring photos shot in varied locations, such as in Chicago, Tahiti, London, and Bora Bora. The campaign highlights hotel upgrades and is intended to attract people who frequently take stressful, long-distance business trips. The ads feature the tag "We know what it takes," as well as photos of businessmen. The text on one ad reads: "It doesn't have to be that tough at the top" (Norton 2002).

Products That Can Be Promoted Via Image Campaign

> Many of the packaged goods products that account for much of the advertising dollars spent in the United States are difficult to differentiate on a functional . . . basis. Thus, creative strategy used to sell these products is based on the development of a strong, memorable identity or meaning for the brand through image advertising. (Belch and Belch 1993, 344)

Image advertising has been used successfully around the world to promote a variety of products and services, including liquor, soft drinks, perfumes, clothing, airlines, and financial services. For an example of a successful international image campaign, see two advertisements from the Paco Rabanne campaign for Ultraviolet, a new fragrance for men and women (Figure 6.3). The ad featuring the female was targeted at Russian consumers. The second message, featuring a male model, appeared in Chinese magazines.

High-Tech Products Standardized messages may be appropriate for products coming to the world market for the first time, because such goods generally are not steeped in the cultural heritage of a particular country. Examples of products in this category include camcorders, DVD recorders, plasma TV screens, and computer hardware and software. Recent research shows a definite trend toward standardization in advertising strategy for such products. Bob Nelson explains: "High tech products are purchased and used in the same manner everywhere, are most often standardized and utilitarian, share a common technical language and use information appeals" (Nelson 1994). Figure 6.4 shows an ad for Sony's new plasma television appearing in an Italian publication.

Products with a Nationalistic Flavor If a country has a reputation for producing high-quality goods of a certain type or in a specific field, those goods may well be sold via global advertising messages. Examples of this category include Beck's beer from Germany, Swatch watches from Switzerland, Burgundy wine from France, and the Lexus automobile from Japan. Likewise, products from the

THE NEW PERFUME SYSTEM
ULTRAVIOLET MAN
paco rabanne

The fragrance of a new era
ULTRAVIOLET
paco rabanne

Figure 6.3 Paco Rabanne targets both Russian and Chinese consumers.

United States have been sold on the basis of their country of origin—Levi's blue jeans, Coca-Cola, McDonald's food, and Marlboro cigarettes are all are promoted as fundamentally American. Developed by Leo Burnett in 1955, the Marlboro Man is an archetypal figure, drawn from American history. "The cowboy symbolized the most masculine type of man, and Burnett's ads evoke memorable imagery of real men in a man's world. The campaign became one of the all-time greats in advertising history" (Sivulka 1998, 279). Indeed, after nearly 50 years, the Marlboro man is still being used today, not only in U.S. advertising, but also in campaigns around the globe. See Figure 6.5 for a Marlboro Lights ad appearing in a Polish magazine.

Note that the benefits of employing a standardized approach, whatever the product, accrue to the firm using that approach—not to its customers around the world. For example, consumers of laundry detergent in Bavaria, Germany, are not likely to be overly impressed that they are being exposed to the same television campaign as their counterparts in Beverton, Oregon; however, both groups do care about purchasing a detergent that will get their laundry clean.

Specialization of Advertising

While globalization has been hailed as the new wave in marketing and advertising by some, others contend that while people's basic needs and desires may well be the same all around the

Figure 6.4 Italian ad for Sony's new plasma screen television.

Minister Zdrowia ostrzega: palenie tytoniu jest najczęstszą przyczyną chorób nowotworowych i zawału serca.

Figure 6.5 Polish ad for Marlboro Lights.

world, how they go about satisfying them may vary from country to country. The "global market" still consists of hundreds of nations, each with its own customs, life-styles, economies, and buying habits, and marketers are urged to take these differences into account (Hornick 1980, 36; Green et al. 1975, 25). Advertising has been positioned as one of the most difficult of the marketing-mix elements to standardize. Skeptics note that it is impossible to ascertain whether the success of brands such as Coke, Pepsi, Marlboro, and McDonald's was due to their internationalism or not. The fact is, claims Greg Harris, "one cannot prove in any scientific way . . . the specific contribution that advertising integration has made to the international sales performance of these brands" (Harris 1984, 223). In other words, these brands potentially might have been even more successful had the promotional messages been adapted for each market.

In the case of a fully adapted or "specialized" campaign, the advertiser localizes message content for several countries or even for each country in which the firm operates. Proponents of specialization argue that by concentrating on similarities in geographically divided marketplaces, firms may ignore or oversimplify many significant differences. The primary benefit of specialization is simply that it allows for differences in the international environment. In terms of demographics, for example, the proportion of individuals attending school or having completed various levels of education affects message development and the media employed to disseminate those messages. In many southern African nations, illiteracy rates are particularly high. In these markets an advertising medium was developed that would be considered quite foreign in the eyes of a Madison Avenue advertising executive: boats travel up and down rivers to broadcast product messages to folks standing on shore.

With regard to the political-legal environment, a variety of political issues may present problems for marketing communications. For example, attitudes toward advertising may differ from one market to the next. The Indonesian government commissioned a study of the impact of television and then proceeded to ban TV for a period of 10 years. The government decided that television—and TV ads—could potentially promote consumerism and aggravate tensions between the rich and the poor (Anderson 1984).

In addition, laws and regulations imposed on the advertising industry differ among nations. Legal and regulatory considerations will be addressed in detail in Chapter 9. For now, we will highlight just a few examples to demonstrate that the legal environment has a direct impact on the development of international advertising campaigns. In 1997, in the United States, the Food and Drug Administration relaxed the rules on pharmaceutical product promotion. As a result, U.S. consumers have been bombarded with a plethora of commercial messages for everything from allergy treatments to anti-impotence pills. It should be noted that the United States is on the cutting edge of this trend. At this time, pharmaceutical marketers may not target consumers in Europe—or almost anywhere else. That regulatory environments vary between markets such as the United States and Europe, for example, should come as no great surprise, but variation occurs even within markets. While major steps have been taken over the past few years to harmonize advertising regulation throughout the European Union, marketers still encounter differences in regulatory guidelines from country to country. For example, Sweden bans all television ads for viewers under the age of 12. In Norway, Austria, and the Flemish part of Belgium, advertising

is not allowed around children's programs. Greece does not allow advertisements for toys to be screened between 7:30 A.M. and 10:00 P.M. British advertisers and agencies, however, are quite opposed to any ban on marketing to children.

The media that advertisers are permitted to employ can also vary widely. The media scene abroad may not resemble that in the domestic market. For instance, in the United States, commercial time on television is typically widely available, and on many stations, 24 hours a day. In other markets, however, because some or all of the stations may be state controlled and government operated, television advertising may be banned or severely restricted. In Germany, on many channels, commercial time is limited to 20 minutes per day and typically only in the evenings (5:00 P.M.–8:00 P.M.) in blocks of five to seven minutes. As in many other markets around the world, television advertisements do not interrupt programming—they either run prior to or after. Television advertising content may also be much more closely controlled in foreign markets. An advertiser who wishes to air a television commercial on any of the three Malaysian networks must first submit the script and storyboard for approval to the Ministry of Information at Radio Television Malaysia. Once the script and storyboard have been reviewed by the Advertising Division, they are returned with comments and suggestions for changes to the advertiser or its agency. Only after the client and agency agree to the changes will the script and storyboard receive station approval and proceed to production.

As noted in previous chapters, cultural differences also can pose formidable hurdles to standardization. Erno Laszlo, a U.S. skin-care firm, tried from 1982–1985 to sell its products identically around the world. In contrast to the success L'Oreal experienced in utilizing a standardized approach, Laszlo found it impossible to sell the identical skin-care regimen to fair-skinned Australians, swarthy Italians, and delicate Asians. In Asia, in particular, skin-care customs varied widely from region to region (Bowes 1992, 129).

Just as skin-care habits differ, so do eating customs. McDonald's joint-venture partners, who run the firm's franchises abroad, have complete responsibility for local marketing. Thus McDonald's sells beer along with its hamburgers in Germany, and wine in France. Australian outlets offer mutton pot pie, and in Singapore the fast food restaurant serves up Szechuan burgers. To promote the Szechuan burgers, McDonald's agency in Singapore—10AM—caused quite a stir, as the television spot they created portrayed sweaty men flocking to a brothel fronted by a "mama-san" (madam). 10AM's executive creative director dismissed criticism of the ad, noting: "We just had some fun with the Chinese pun on 'Hot 'n' Spicy' (burger), which also means 'naughty girl.'" Apparently, the ads have been popular with consumers, as ad awareness has increased by 20 percent during the campaign and the restaurant has sold more than one million of the Szechuan burgers (Osborne 2002).

If a specific product's brand name differs from one market to the next, the international marketer may have no choice but to employ a specialized approach to advertising. For example, the Japanese company Kao entered its first non-Asian detergent market with the introduction in Australia of the laundry product that leads the Japanese market. The concentrated detergent is marketed as Attack in Japan, Singapore, Hong Kong, Taiwan, Malaysia, and Thailand, but it was renamed Bio-z for the Australian market. "Taking account of history, we felt the name Attack

was not suitable for a Japanese product in Australia; we felt it might sound a little too aggressive. In any case, rights to that name are owned by another company in Australia," a Kao spokesman explained (Kilburn 1992). Western companies experience similar challenges. Out of the 60 countries where Unilever's cleaning liquid is sold, it is branded as Cif in 39 of them and Jif everywhere else. And Unilever's laundry detergent is called OMO pretty much everywhere in Europe, except the United Kingdom, which stubbornly insists on calling it Persil. Procter & Gamble's global marketing officer Jim Stengel notes:

> Developing global brands is not an end in itself, but a means to an end. Our goal is a global brand leadership in the categories in which we choose to compete. Sometimes we can do that with one brand name and brand positioning and sometimes it takes several brands with different positionings. We got on a kick where we tried to go too far on global standardization with some of our brands, even to the point of changing names. Safeguard provides a case in point. Safeguard was a strong bar soap brand in Mexico under the Spanish name Escuda. As we were trying to standardize more, we changed it to Safeguard. Volume dropped precipitously. We changed it back and volume went back up. (Neff 2002, 53)

Finally, if a specific foreign market is in a different stage of market development than the U.S. market, a given product may find itself in a different stage of the life cycle in that country. Professional sport watch Tag Heuer is no stranger to the challenges of communicating its brand to different markets. Tag Heuer has subsidiaries in 12 countries: the United States, the United Kingdom, France, Italy, Spain, Germany, Switzerland, Singapore, Hong Kong, Australia, Japan, and Malaysia. In those markets there are varying degrees of brand acceptance, requiring different approaches to marketing and advertising. Christian Viros, worldwide chief executive officer, notes:

> where the brand is well established and there is a higher degree of brand awareness, there are more opportunities to carry out unconventional advertising. In those markets, the commercials can be more avant garde and above the typical campaign. However, in countries where the brand is just beginning to gain a foothold, a more straightforward and conventional advertising approach is used. (Banoo 1999)

See Figure 6.6 for an example of a Tag Heuer advertisement targeting French consumers. In some markets an international firm will compete against other international marketers; in other markets the competition may be purely national. Sound advertising strategy in one market will not necessarily be appropriate in another market with a different competitive environment.

A number of firms that adopted the global approach have since soured on the concept. In the early 1980s, Parker Pen was manufacturing about 500 styles of pens in 18 plants. Local offices in over 150 countries were responsible for creating their own advertising and packaging. Putting Theodore Levitt's theory into practice, Parker consolidated to 100 pen styles manufactured in only eight plants. It also hired a single advertising agency to create a global advertising campaign, which was then translated into myriad local languages. However, Parker did not anticipate the resistance of local managers, who resented that the U.S. firm was mandating what the

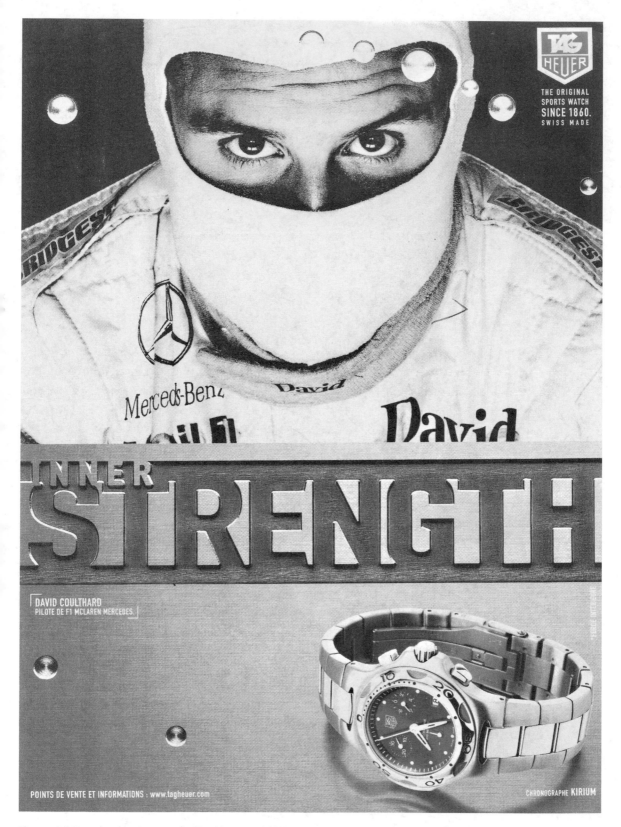

Figure 6.6 French advertisement for Tag Heuer watches.

advertising should be and which advertising agency they should employ. Profits plunged almost immediately—Parker had a $12 million loss for fiscal 1985, and the firm almost went broke. By 1986 a group of its British managers had bought the pen business. Today, the company is once again profitable, and local managers are allowed to select advertising for their own markets (Lipman 1988). Previously committed to a standardized approach, Colgate-Palmolive likewise shifted back to a country-by-country advertising strategy in 1990. As part of the move toward specialization, an approach intended to be a basic element of the firm's long-term growth plans, Colgate-Palmolive decided to decentralize the advertising function and turn over responsibilities to individual operating units. All future advertising will be tailored specifically to local markets and countries (Freemen 1990).

More recently, Coca-Cola has begun to move to an increasingly "think local, act local" approach. In Turkey, the firm recently launched Bibo, a flavored drink for children. Bibo is positioned as "an adventure drink to help children in their development." Ultimately, the product will be marketed in the rest of Eastern Europe and in South Africa as well (*Advertising Age* 2000). Coke already sells Thums Up cola in India and Inca cola in Peru. Not only are products increasingly customized, so too are the advertising messages. Coca-Cola launched a massive campaign across China to boost sales of its products during the Spring Festival—the most important holiday for the Chinese people. In an attempt to reflect Chinese culture, a special TV commercial was produced featuring traditional *Ah Fu* clay dolls, symbols of good luck and fortune. Images of the painted *Ah Fu* dolls also appeared on special packaging (*Advertising Age* 2001a).

In the European market, Coca-Cola unveiled a France-specific campaign. Research revealed that a core value among French youth was optimism. The series of television spots featured young people in a French café setting, discussing topics like love, life after high school, or getting a job. The messages incorporated a French-language slogan "Sourire la Vie" ("Smile through Life"). The slogan was also utilized in a variety of marketing activities, including on-site promotions in cafes and restaurants across France (Speer 2001). And Coca-Cola has gone quite risqué in its Italy-only campaign. In a spot created by the Milan offices of McCann-Erickson Worldwide, nude youth are portrayed frolicking at the beach at midnight. In the spot called "Night Swim," the characters run nude into a lake, which is lit only by the headlights of their cars. In the close-in shots, most of the young women have their arms strategically placed to cover their breasts. Bare buttocks can be seen, but no genitals. A young male remains on shore, in silhouette, dancing in front of the car lights. A female narrator states in a dramatic voice: "It's the first time I've done it, the midnight swim. It's not a problem for me, but there is always something that is a problem for you. Heh, heh—it's so true, sooner or later in life problems undress themselves"—a play on words referring to the nude swimmers (Lyman 2001a). It appears that the most ubiquitous brand of all has left behind both cookie-cutter products and advertising.

The Standardization–Specialization Continuum

Examples of effective standardized campaigns clearly do exist, just as do examples of ineffective ones. Similarly, there are numerous examples of both more- and less-successful specialized campaigns. The pros and cons of both approaches to international advertising will continue to be debated. Many companies have moved away from viewing standardization as an all-or-nothing phenomenon and instead have chosen to employ a modified approach—standardizing some elements of their promotional plan while specializing others. The question is, in fact, one of degree, with standardization and specialization at opposite ends of a continuum, and with many shades of adaptation between the two extremes.

An excellent example of this modified approach is a campaign developed by Coca-Cola. Several years ago, the firm's advertising agency, McCann-Erickson, created an award-winning commercial showing Pittsburgh Steeler football star "Mean" Joe Greene giving his jersey to a young boy who had offered him a bottle of Coke after a tough game. However, the advertisement could not be used outside the United States for two reasons. First, Joe Greene was unknown in foreign markets, and second, American football is not nearly so popular abroad as it is in the United States. Rather than abandon the concept, the agency adapted it to other countries by creating advertisements featuring stars of the more-popular international sport of soccer. Advertisements in South America used the popular Argentinian player Diego Maradona, and those in Asia used Thai star Niwat as the heroes of the spots.

More recently, Nokia employed the modified approach in selling its mobile phones in Asia. The campaign, created by Bates, Singapore, ran in China, Hong Kong, Taiwan, Singapore, Malaysia, Indonesia, Philippines, Thailand, Vietnam, India, Australia, and New Zealand. The overall objective of the campaign was to create brand awareness, and all messages emphasized the importance Nokia places on stylish design. However, elements were adapted to ensure local relevance. "At Nokia, we design products based on our observations of human behavior," noted Nigel Litchfield, senior vice president of Nokia Mobile Phones in Asia Pacific. "Over and above the single common need to be connected, consumers want products that adapt to their own lifestyles and respond intuitively to their personal needs." For example, one spot for China depicts two people who meet for a soccer game thanks to the Chinese-language short messaging capabilities of Nokia phones. Another ad, for the Nokia 9110 Communicator, shows that even in the middle of a power failure, it's still possible to send and receive faxes and e-mails with Nokia's all-in-one communications tool. The ad campaign characterized the many ways in which Nokia's "human technology" simplifies technology, making it readily accessible to consumers in Asia through easy-to-use products that enhance their particular lifestyles (*Advertising Age* 1998).

Execution Decisions

If strategy refers to "what is said" in a campaign, then execution refers to "how it is said." The advertising strategy adopted for a specific international campaign thus guides the execution—the selection of advertising appeals as well as copy and illustrations (Kaynak 1989, 57).

▐▐▐▌ Advertising Appeals

According to George and Michael Belch, advertising appeals "refer to the basis or approach used in the advertisement to attract attention or interest consumers and/or to influence their feelings toward the product, service or cause" (Belch and Belch 1993, 344). The advertising appeals employed should be consistent with the values and tastes of the target audience. Indeed, a recent survey found that, on the whole, consumers seem to prefer domestically generated commercials. Foreign-produced advertisements did not appeal to more than half of European respondents in the three categories surveyed: taste, product differentiation, and likability. The English and French were rated as the most closed cultures toward foreign ads, while the Italians and Germans were rated as the most receptive (Giacomotti 1993). This reinforces the view that advertising carries its culture with it. It is not surprising, then, that commercial messages created in various markets differ significantly. Note Abhijit Biswas and colleagues:

> Cross cultural differences in advertising expression [are] a growing and important area of research, primarily because an understanding of these differences is needed in order to take on the creative challenge of communicating to people of diverse cultural backgrounds. (Biswas et al. 1992, 73)

As highlighted in the continuum of compared cultures shown in Figure 4.14, the United States and Japan fall at the "maximum socio-cultural differences" end of the scale. Japan also offers a prime example of a country that differs significantly from the United States in terms of creative message content. As previously noted, Japanese ads tend to employ indirect communications, and rely on soft sell. They also tend to make greater use of status appeals and demonstrate a greater respect for the elderly than do advertisements in the United States (Mueller 1987, 51). This contrasts sharply with the U.S. emphasis on rational appeals with a focus on presenting features and benefits in order to showcase a product's superiority. In Japanese messages, write C. Anthony Di Benedetto and colleagues:

> The goal is to transfer intended feelings to the consumer rather than detailing specific product attributes and quality. This is because the latter approach can be perceived as an insult to the consumer's intelligence concerning their ability to make a sound judgement about their company preference. (Di Benedetto et al. 1992, 39)

Recall the very soft-sell approach employed in the Japanese mayonnaise ad shown in Figure 4.5. Significant differences are also found in message content when comparing the advertising of European countries with that of the United States. While France and the United States have a good deal more in common, the ads produced in each country are quite distinct. One study found that French ads resorted to more emotional appeals and contained fewer information cues than did U.S. ads. Sex appeals were also employed more frequently—a finding consistent with the perception that France is a more sexually liberated country than the United States. Overall, French ads employed humor appeals to a greater extent than did their U.S.

counterparts (Biswas et al. 1992, 73). Likewise, despite the many cultural similarities between the United States and United Kingdom, substantial differences between U.S. and British advertising exist. Researchers revealed that British ads tend to make frequent use of features inherent in British culture, such as the persistence of class divisions and the affection for eccentricity, and often employ understated humor. In addition, they generally contain less information, employ a softer-sell approach, and attempt to entertain rather than educate the consumer (Nevett 1992, 61). The findings of each of these studies should give pause to practitioners who advocate a complete standardization of commercial messages for international markets.

 Themes and Concepts: Universal versus Culture-Bound

Clearly, standardization of advertising is possible with certain target groups, for certain product categories, and in certain market conditions. At the same time, commercial messages for some audiences require tailoring. Similarly, some products and some market conditions are less suited to the global approach. In terms of creative execution, it appears that there are themes and concepts which tend to have better success at crossing borders, while others are almost guaranteed to cause the marketer headaches. The following list of universal and culture-bound themes and concepts is adapted from de Mooij (1994).

Universal: New or Improved Products Common among consumers around the globe is that they look for new products, new uses for old products, or improvements on old products. Power words that suggest newness have been proven to increase attention—such words include "now," "suddenly," "announcing," "introducing," "it's here," "improved," "at last," "revolutionary," "just arrived," and "important development" (Arens 2002, 15). These words improve the "boom" factor of an ad and can effectively be employed to communicate with consumers in different markets for a wide variety of consumer products, as well as industrial and business-to-business products.

Universal: Basic Everyday Themes Typically, themes based on appeals such as hunger, thirst, affection, motherhood, pride, and jealousy can be used universally. But even here there are potential land mines. A case in point: what could be wrong with a food commercial that shows hungry kids licking their lips in response to a tasty treat? Nothing—unless, of course, the message is aired in a third world country where exposing the tongue is considered obscene.

Universal: The Made-In Concept Recall that in the discussion of products suitable for standardization, products with a nationalistic flavor were highlighted. The tendency for consumers to evaluate goods manufactured in some countries more favorably may encourage a marketer to highlight the country of origin when promoting those goods. The use of "made-in" appeals in advertising fall into three categories (Head 1988, 237):

1. *Appeals to the patriotism or national pride of consumers to motivate the purchase of products manufactured in the home country.* A Molson beer ad that ran in Canada provides an excellent example. To ap-

preciate the success of this message, the reader must understand that many Canadians are frustrated with living in the shadow of the United States and with general misconceptions about their country. Proclaiming Canada as the "best part of North America," the 60-second television spot has an everyman Canadian defiantly expressing the rarely spoken sentiments of a nation that takes pride in its differences from its mighty southern neighbor. The ad consists of a young Canadian called Joe delivering what its creators call "the rant" in front of a large screen showing corresponding images. Dressed in a lumberjack shirt and jeans, Joe starts off slowly by quashing historical images of Canadians, saying: "I'm not a lumberjack or a fur trader. I don't live in an igloo, or eat blubber, or even own a dog sled." He pokes fun at typical misconceptions by Americans and other foreigners of the country's vastness. He notes that he says "about," not "aboot," and pronounces the letter "z" in the British way of "zed" instead of the American style "zee." "I have a prime minister, not a president. I speak English and French, not American," he says, his voice rising and gestures getting more pronounced. The ad ends with Joe raising his arms in triumph as he shouts: "Canada's the second largest land mass, the first nation of hockey and the best part of North America. My name is Joe and I am a Canadian." The spot has become so popular among Canadians that live performances have been scheduled in movie theaters and at sports events—resulting in audiences on their feet, cheering and clapping (Wroughton 2000). The commercial has also received numerous national and international creative awards.

2. *Appeals that highlight for the audience positive and usually stereotypic attributes of another country and then imbue the product or service originating from that country with those image-enhancing qualities.* For example, the Marlboro cigarette campaign portrays the image of the American cowboy and the freedom of the American West to consumers all around the world.

3. *Appeals that allude to a particular expertise that is associated with the country and that, if promoted in advertising messages, might instill confidence in the product.* For example, when we think of pasta, we typically associate it with the birthplace of this cuisine—Italy. Barilla, Italy's largest pasta maker, took advantage of this association. The company markets its products in more than 25 countries. It unveiled its first worldwide campaign with the unified ad slogan, "When you think of Italy, think of pasta. When you think of pasta, think of Barilla" (Lyman 2001b).

Universal: Product Demonstrations Typically straightforward in tone, demonstrations focus on how a brand works and its specific features. Products can be demonstrated in use, in competition with other products, or in before-versus-after scenarios. This technique often helps consumers visualize what the product can do for them. See Figure 6.7 for a Braun Plak Control toothbrush targeting Japanese consumers. Here, the before-versus-after technique is employed to demonstrate just how clean teeth will be as a result of using this product.

Universal: Heroes The reader may recall that in Chapter 4 we discussed heroes as an expression of culture, suggesting that they may be unique to a society. Traditionally, heroes have been culture-bound, for the most part. However, Hollywood has spread the faces of the silver screen around

the globe—and many actors have become international heroes. Film stars are increasingly appearing in international advertising campaigns. Japan has demonstrated a particular fascination with Hollywood stars. Tokyo streets and television screens have been sprinkled with images of Madonna and Takara liquor, Harrison Ford and Karin beer, Peter Falk and Suntory whisky, Eddie Murphy and Saporro canned coffee, Arnold Schwarzenegger and Arinamin vitamins. At one point, one out of every five Japanese television commercials featured a foreign actor or model. This trend has spread to Europe. U.S. actors are now marching westward and directly into Italy, where they are plugging a variety of Italian products, ranging from sunglasses to spumante. Among the actors are Richard Gere, Catherine Zeta-Jones, Harrison Ford, and Bruce Willis. Although some actors and actresses are quite selective about appearing in commercials in their home markets, they apparently welcome overseas opportunities. "Hollywood is the most vigorous industry in the world—on all levels. It influences people's tastes and its events echo throughout the world," notes Silvia Damiani, who hired Brad Pitt to star in ads for her family-run jewelry company (Conti 2000). There are other reasons for Italians' love affair with Hollywood: "with e-commerce and the single currency, Italian companies, which have traditionally used local celebrities, want to appear less provincial, more global. What could be better than trading on the universal, cosmopolitan allure of a Hollywood actor?" explained Luca Vercelloni of GPF & Associati, a research firm (Conti 2000). And while the Italians may not be quite as generous as the Japanese—who pay upward of $7 million for a celebrity-focused campaign, compensation in Italy starts at about six to seven figures and can go up to several million dollars depending on how long the ad is used and in how many countries.

Universal: Lifestyle Concepts To present the user, rather than the product, advertisers may use the lifestyle technique (Arens 2002, 427). Fast food and soft drink advertisers may target their products to young people, focusing on who consumes their products rather than on specific product advantages. Similarly, airlines and hotels often feature the lifestyles of time-challenged business people in their messages. Figure 6.8 is a prime example of an ad that features a lifestyle—the message for Nike targets consumers in the Philippines whose lifestyle evolves around being fit.

Culture-Bound: Sex Appeals There is an old adage in the advertising business: sex sells. In this case, the question is, does sex travel? When it comes to employing sex appeals in advertising messages intended for foreign audiences, marketers are urged to exercise caution. Often, because of increasing advertising clutter, copywriters hope that the use of sex will help their commercial message catch attention. It may well receive attention, but not necessarily the kind the advertiser intended. And what may be considered as perfectly tame in one market can be perceived as downright indecent in another. For example, Leo Burnett Worldwide created a campaign for breast cancer awareness. In the ad, an attractive woman in a sundress draws stares from men on the sidewalk. "If only women paid as much attention to their breasts as men do," said the voice-over. The message was a big hit in Japan, where consumers felt it was a humorous way to draw attention to an important health issue. Surprisingly enough, the campaign flopped in France,

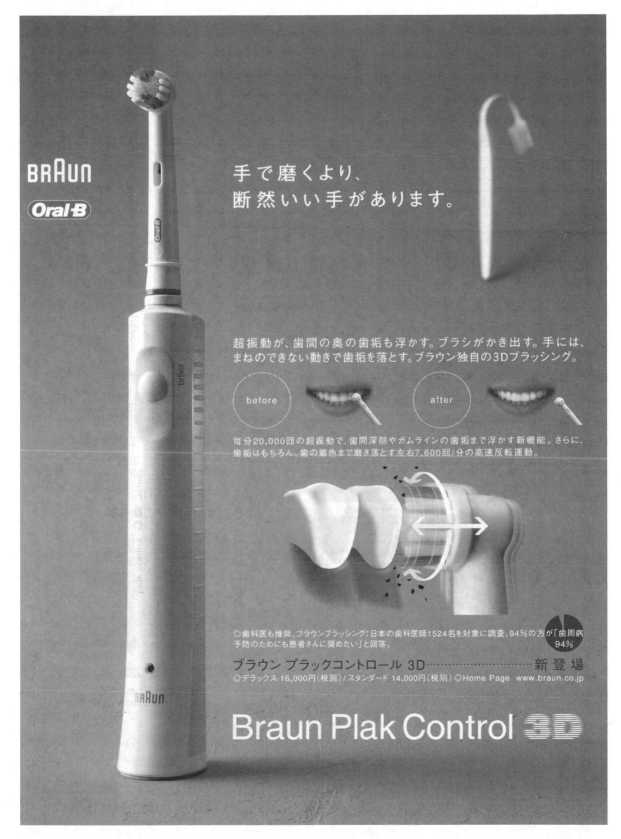

Figure 6.7 Demonstration approach being employed in ad targeted at Japanese consumers.

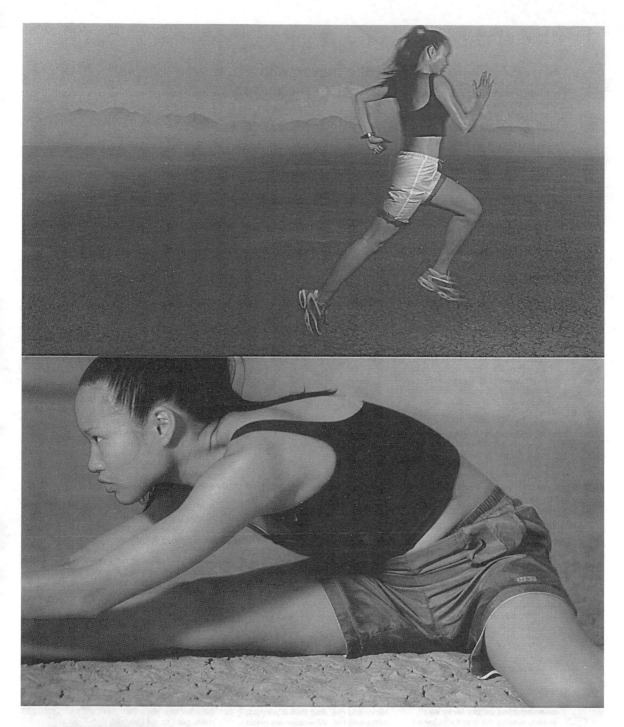

REVERSE IT ✔

TERESA LIN | sprinter, wears the reversible 2 Layer Retro Short.

Figure 6.8 Lifestyle ad for Nike targeting consumers in the Philippines.

despite the fact that in France full frontal nudity in commercial messages hardly raises an eyebrow. Apparently, the use of humor to talk about a serious disease offended French sensibilities (Ellison 2000).

Sometimes the offending campaign will air only once or a few times prior to being pulled. In other instances, the results may be significantly more serious. The agency may be fired from the account, or even brought before a local advertising standards board. Land Rover ran a print campaign in South Africa depicting a seminude African woman whose artificially elongated breasts were blown sideways in the tailwind of a Land Rover Freelander. The campaign caused immediate public outcry. The African Advertising Standards Authority (ASA) subsequently ruled that the ad, created by TBWA Hunt Lascaris, was "irresponsible and exploitive, constituted racial stereotyping, violated human dignity, and that the insensitive portrayal of the woman made a mockery of African culture." The court ordered the advertiser, at their own cost, to place ads containing the ASA ruling in all the publications where the original ads appeared. Land Rover placed the ads, which were seen as a humiliating apology, in over 20 publications, as a cost that exceeded $50,000. Apparently this was the first time the ASA had enforced a disciplinary measure which involved additional costs to the advertiser (Koenderman 2001).

Clearly, cultural norms strongly influence what is considered appropriate in terms of the use of sex appeals in advertising messages. But advertisers can overstep their bounds even in markets that are typically quite liberal with regard to sexual appeals. Benetton, the Italian clothing manufacturer, crossed that line when it employed a visual of a black stallion mounting a white mare in their commercial messages (see Figure 6.9). The outdoor and print campaign ran globally, but few Europeans saw the billboards, as two of Europe's largest billboard contractors imposed a blanket ban on the ad from all their cites within the European Union. Patrick Sion, sales director for the Belgian poster contractor Belgaposter, claims his company's responsibility as good citizens led to the decision. "Local schools, city councils, public transport, they're our business partners too. We have to be careful with the visuals and messages we carry" (*Advertising Age* 1996). A spokesperson for Benetton confirmed that the ad provoked even more initial outcry than the company's typical campaigns.

Culture-Bound: Individuality In Chapter 4 we noted that the majority of the world's cultures tended toward collectivism rather than individualism. Thus, while ads appealing to individuality may prove quite persuasive in some markets, the messages may not resonate with consumers in others. For example, showing a model alone in an advertisement in a highly collectivistic society may be interpreted to mean that they have no identity, because their identity lies in the group. A number of years ago Levi-Strauss ran a campaign for their 501 Blues, which was highly successful in the United States. However the ads didn't click with Hispanic youth. "Why is that guy walking down the street alone?" they asked. "Doesn't he have any friends?" As a result, Levi's changed the advertising for the Hispanic market, downplaying individualism (Mitchell and Oneal 1994, 38). Above and beyond the visual portrayal of individuals versus

Figure 6.9 Benetton campaign crosses the line.

groups in a commercial message, advertisers must consider whether the product it pitched as appealing to individuality versus conformity. In individualistic cultures, products are often promoted as assisting consumers in their goal of standing out from the crowd. Examples abound, such as the classic Reebok "U B U" campaign, which suggested that consumers could demonstrate their individuality simply by purchasing a pair of brand name sneakers.

Culture-Bound: Comparative Advertising Comparative advertising is generally used to claim superiority over competing brands regarding some aspect of the product. In the United States, not only is comparative advertising legal, the Federal Trade Commission actually encourages comparative campaigns because they are seen as providing consumers with much-needed information for making purchase decisions. See Figure 6.10 for French vodka targeting U.S. consumers with a comparative appeal. Not only does Grey Goose position itself as the No. 1 Tasting Vodka in the world, it lists the other 30 brands that simply didn't make the grade. International marketers must understand that the technique is banned in some markets, and in a process of change in others.

Within the European Union, comparative advertising had been allowed in the United Kingdom for more than a quarter of a century (and nearly 30 percent of all ads were comparative in nature), but comparative messages were all but banned in France and Germany. In an attempt to harmonize advertising regulation on the continent, a European Union directive was recently passed whose aim is to promote honesty and fair play by regulating ads that compare one product with another. For the first time, any ads, anywhere in Europe, that in any way, either explicitly or implicitly, identify a competitor or goods and services offered by a competitor are subject to strict legal regulation. Among other things, ads must not create confusion in the marketplace, discredit or denigrate competitors, or take unfair advantage of the reputation of a rival (Staheli 2000). The new legislation has caused a great deal of concern among marketers. A bizarre court case in Germany gives an indication to how the new law is likely to apply, Burger King introduced two advertisements with bar charts, reporting the results of an opinion poll it had commissioned. Most respondents preferred Burger King's products to those of McDonald's. One ad noted: "Full Majority: 62 percent of those tested preferred the taste of the Whopper to the Big Mac." Another message stated "Crisp Difference: 81 percent of all those tested preferred the taste of our new King Pommes to McDonald's French Fries." Both ads were banned by the German government. The court declared that the ads were disallowed under the EU directive. The ads, declared the ruling, are "disparaging and unjustified." The judgment explained:

> Opinion polls carried out by Burger King reflect nothing but a momentary impression which cannot be generalized and which even less can count as verifiable features of hamburgers and fries. In short, it is not an objective fact that Burger King's burgers are tastier—even if people tell pollsters that they think they are. Taste is not a matter of fact. A Whopper for breakfast tastes different from a Whopper had late in the evening with a glass of beer, declare Germany's finest legal minds. (Staheli, 2000, 59)

It will be interesting to see how the issue of comparative advertising plays out in the EU in the years to come. In some markets, while not banned, comparative appeals simply are not employed. In Japan, for example, cultural norms reflect Japanese advertisers' reluctance to use comparative advertising, which connotes a confrontational practice that could make competitor lose face (Lin 1993, 40). In Arabic cultures, behavior toward others is influenced by messages in the Shari'a, the Islamic code, as well as the more collectivistic nature of Arabic people. Arabic culture, in general, encourages people not to compete, to avoid the cost of harming others (Al-Olayan and Karande 2000).

Culture-Bound: Role of Women How women are depicted in advertising messages—as housewives, mothers, domestic workers, consumers, or professionals—is strongly influenced by culture. In the United States, advertisers have been strongly criticized for condoning traditional, out-dated sex roles. In other markets, particularly in Islamic countries, women may only be portrayed in traditional roles—as mothers or as caregivers. A recent study (Milner and Collins 2000, 67) examined television ads from Japan, Russia, Sweden, and the United States. Consistent with Hofstede's framework, which suggests that countries may be characterized along a continuum from masculine to feminine, the study found that television ads from feminine countries featured more depictions of relationships between male and female characters than did masculine countries. For the most part, in feminine cultures, there is minimal social differentiation between the sexes. Women are free to take assertive roles, while men can feel comfortable taking more relationship-oriented, caring roles. Stereotypic roles in feminine cultures are frowned upon. Quite recently (O'Dwyer 2003) Sweden's Marketing Council, composed of a panel of legal and advertising industry professionals, ruled that a McDonald's television spot was gender discriminating and out of order with the country's strict gender equality legislation. The spot, by Publicis Groups' Leo Burnett Worldwide, ran on three Swedish networks but was not allowed to air again after the council's decision. McDonald's apologized to the council and confirmed that it would follow Sweden's gender equality laws in future TV and print advertising. In the controversial commercial, a woman helps a man prepare for work. She hands him a cup of coffee and helps him fasten his tie. In the background, the couple's son and daughter imitate their behavior. According to the council's ruling, the commercial conveyed stereotypical gender roles, with the woman taking care of the home and the man as the family breadwinner. This imbalance violates Sweden's gender equality laws.

Culture-Bound: Humor In general, humor tends not to travel well because it employs cultural conventions that generally are understood only by members of a particular culture. For example, a leading French banking firm, BNP-Paribas, launched a campaign that compared bugs and bankers in a cheeky takedown of stereotypes about the financial services industry. Created by Havas-owned BETC Euro RSCG, Paris, the bugs-versus-bankers campaign used unconventional images of insects to demonstrate the strength of relationships BNP Paribas formed with its clients. One ad in the campaign, which depicted a cartoonish sculpted model locust dressed

Figure 6.10 Ad for French vodka appealing to U.S consumers and employing a comparative appeal.

as a banker photographed next to a luxury sedan parked near a drought-stricken cornfield, asked the question, "What do you want, a banker or a locust?" Accompanying text explained that the staff at BNP Paribas "don't hop from place to place, serving our own interests, like the rapacious locust, but rather seek to build mutually beneficial, long-term relationships." The agency hoped the humor would set BNP Paribas apart from other advertisers in the financial services sector (Speer 2002). Clearly, while the French might find the humor in this message, it would be lost on most consumers in other markets. Interestingly, in individualistic cultures, humorous appeals related to very small groups or individuals tend to be more appropriate, while in collectivistic cultures such as Japan, research has shown that humorous dramatizations of situations involving group members—family, office colleagues or superiors, neighbors, landlords, and so on—are most prevalent (Di Benedetto et al. 1992, 39). However, a study examining commercial messages in Korea, Germany, Thailand, and the United States has shown that one type of humor does appear to have potential across markets. Apparently, creatives in all four countries had developed ads employing incongruity as a humorous appeal. Incongruity, as defined by the researchers (Alden et al. 1993), is based on the contrast between the expected and the unexpected. Thus it is possible that incongruity may appeal to consumers.

Culture-Bound: Opinions and Attitudes Themes based on cultural opinions and attitudes generally do not travel well across borders. Opinions regarding feminine attractiveness provide an excellent example. As de Mooij explains, "in many countries a slim figure is considered attractive, while in others, including some African countries, a plump figure is preferable. In some Asian countries, Caucasian faces are acceptable or even highly valued for some brands, in others not" (de Mooij 1994, 247). Indeed, a major criticism leveled at Western advertising by non-Western nations is that the global messages suggest not only which products to purchase, but how one should look. Western models, by definition, tend to be tall, blond, blue-eyed, and extremely thin. This is an ideal that most women in the world simply cannot live up to—yet continue to aspire to. Consider the message being sent by Pond's in an advertisement currently running in women's magazines in the Philippines:

> I can't believe my rosy white skin caught their eye. It started when I used Pond's skin whitening vitamin cream. I called the Pond's Institute (telephone number is provided) and they told me all about it. It has vitamin B-3 that whitens skin naturally from within and double sunscreen to protect my skin from the sun's harmful rays. Getting rosy white skin was a lot simpler and safer than I thought.

With messages such as these encouraging women in the Philippines to whiten their skin in order to appear more Caucasian, it is no wonder that many nations have imposed mandates that commercial messages be produced domestically, employing local talent rather than Western models. On much stronger footing is a campaign for Avon Basics, a skincare line specially designed for Filipinas. The product line was customized for the Filipina skin, taking into consideration its special needs and characteristics. Advertising, created by Jimenez D'Arcy, featured four local, brown-skinned models as opposed to the fair-complexioned women who tradition-

ally appear in commercials. "We want simple, beautiful models—those that young Filipinas can identify with. No Unreachables please," noted Avon's marketing director (*Advertising Age* 1999).

Verbal Communication: Copy and Dialogue

In Chapter 4 we addressed the cultural aspects of verbal communication. Here, we will focus on challenges in the translation of advertising copy and dialogue. As Barney Raffield points out: "Seemingly harmless brand names and advertising phrases can take on unintended or hidden meanings when translated into other languages, but such errors can make a marketer look somewhat like a buffoon to foreign consumers" (Raffield 1987). While numerous translation blunders have already been highlighted, several more examples drive home the point that even when quickly corrected, such mistakes, at best, result in embarrassment to the company, and, at worst, may lead to long-term losses of sales, market credibility, and international goodwill. Ford Motor goofed when it named its low-cost third world truck Fiera, which means "ugly old woman" in Spanish. Market research showed that American Motor's Matador meant virility and excitement, but when the car was introduced in Puerto Rico, it was discovered that the word meant "killer"—an unfortunate choice for Puerto Rico, which has an unusually high traffic fatality rate. An ad in a Middle Eastern country featured an automobile's new suspension system that, in translation, said the car was "suspended from the ceiling" (Cateora 1990, 468).

The disasters just cited should make advertisers aware that the most effective translation for advertising purposes is not likely to be the most literal one. The task of the advertising translator is to translate thoughts and ideas rather than words. Yuri Radzievsky, president of Euroamerica Translations, notes with amazement that advertisers spend thousands on what something says in one language, but only pennies to ensure that it says the same thing, the same way, when put into another language (Radzievsky 1983/1984).

The most effective approach in preparing copy for foreign markets is to begin from scratch and have all verbal communications entirely rewritten by a speaker of the foreign language who understands the complete marketing plan—including objectives, strategies, and tactics. With regard to translations from one language to another, says Robert Roth, "As far as can be determined, there has never been a 100 percent acceptable translation—certainly not of advertising or public relations material" (Roth 1982, 135). For copy to be translated, advertisers should be aware of some linguistic and managerial guidelines (Roth 1982, 135; Miracle 1988, RC-51).

Linguistic Guidelines

1. Think multilingual. Remember from the start that copy will be translated. Copy should contain neither slang and idioms nor puns, rhymes, figures of speech, similes, or metaphors—all of which are extremely difficult and sometimes impossible to translate.
2. Remember that language is alive and changing. The dictionary should be avoided as a translation tool because the language of the dictionary is not necessarily the language of the people.

3. Recognize that translated words may have different shades of meaning. Some words simply cannot be translated, and others can only be translated in lengthy or awkward forms.

4. Use English at the fifth- or sixth-grade level to ensure ease of translation. Overly technical terms and industry jargon should be avoided.

5. Keep copy for translation relatively short, because many foreign languages invariably take more time or space to say the same thing the English-language copy says.

6. Remember that some languages distinguish between the familiar and the formal (*du/Sie* for "you" in German and *tu/usted* for "you" in Spanish). Others employ honorific expressions depending on the relationship between speakers (inferior/superior in Japanese). Such differences can make translating from one language to another difficult.

Managerial Guidelines

1. Choose translators with care. Use only professional translators, preferably those with advertising copy translation experience. Translators may have specialties—medical, legal, or technical.

2. Use native speakers of the language into which the copy is being translated. Ideally, the translator should currently live in the country where the advertising will appear to ensure both familiarity and currency. Because language evolves, even a native tends to lose track of slang and idioms after being away from home for several years.

3. Examine the region in which translators were born, educated, and resident for significant periods of time. Such exposure may impact dialects. Within Germany, for example, each region speaks its own dialect. Similarly, the French spoken in France, Canada, Belgium, and Switzerland differs significantly.

4. Provide translators with full background on marketing and advertising objectives and strategies.

5. Give translators access to all necessary reference materials dealing with the appropriate subject and industry. Ensure that the translator has an adequate understanding of any required technical terms.

6. Settle on style issues before translation begins. American advertising copy is often considered brusque or staccato, which may not be appropriate for some markets.

7. Allow sufficient time for translations. Forcing translators to work under pressure benefits no one.

8. Don't be stingy—hire the best translators available.

9. Employ the back-translation technique. Here, one individual is responsible for the initial translation of the message, and a second individual then translates the message back into the original language. If the message does not translate back, there is likely a translation problem. Back-translation is a helpful tool; however, it's no guarantee against translation bloopers.

The same translation guidelines apply to both print and broadcast messages. In the production of advertisements for television, it may be preferable to design a spot that does not

TABLE 6.1 Accuracy of Machine Translations

English Phrase	Automatic Translation
Ring around the collar (Wisk Detergent)	Ring around the tension ring (German)
You deserve a break today (McDonald's)	You deserve a rupture today (French and Portuguese)
Silly Rabbit, Trix are for kids (Trix)	Asinine bunny, Trix are prior babies (Swedish)
Pork—the other white meat (Pork Council)	Pig—the other white woman meat (Italian)
Time to make the donuts (Dunkin' Donuts)	Time to form the foam rubber rings (German)
Good to the last drop (Maxwell House)	Bonny to the last bead (Russian).

Source: Recksieck (2003).

employ on-camera sound. While it is possible to dub spots for use in the international arena, the result almost always sounds unnatural, and the technique is not inexpensive.

Clearly, translation done well is both costly and time consuming. International marketers now have at their disposal machine translations. Executives at Lotus, an offshoot of IBM, developed software capable of translating about 15 languages. The primary benefit of machine translations is that they are speedy and, generally, significantly less expensive. However, caution must be exercised, as the translations are not 100 percent accurate. The slogans highlighted in Table 6.1 were fed into an automatic translator—and then translated back into English—with less than successful results. Even the program manufacturers suggest that a professional translator be employed for "clean-up" (Zajc 2000).

Music

Music seems to travel across borders quite well—due, no doubt, to the immense popularity of many international music stars. Table 6.2 presents a chart of albums that have simultaneously attained top-10 chart status in three or more leading world markets (Billboard 2003). This fact has not gone unnoticed by international marketers, who are increasingly employing popular singers and groups in international ad campaigns. Music was the cornerstone of a global Twix Cookie bar campaign in two MTV-style spots. The ads featured musicians Anastacia, Hoku, Boyd Tinsley, and Dean Roland. The singers, from groups such as the Dave Matthews Band and Collective Soul, played to Twix's core target audience: teens and young adults. The quick-cut TV spots combined each of the three singers' different music genres to create one chantlike song. Each music style, such as hip-hop or rock, was paired with a characteristic of a Twix bar: Hoku's music was linked with Twix's chocolate, Roland sang about caramel, and Tinsley touted the cookie. The campaign included TV, radio, print, and Internet ads, plus national and grass-roots promotions, such as tie-ins with concerts. Bob Gamgort, vice president of marketing at Twix parent M&M/Mars, felt the music would help Twix stand out from the clutter of humorous advertisements often used for candy. An additional benefit, Gamgort added, "was that the campaign could easily be tweaked to run overseas. Humor tends to be country-specific, it's hard to translate. Music is transferable across borders" (Petrecca 2000). Clearly, this

TABLE 6.2 Scorecard of Albums Simultaneously Attaining Top 10 Chart Status in Three or More Countries

Artist	U.S.	JPN	U.K.	GER	FRA	CAN	SPN	AUS	ITA	NTH
Phil Collins (Testify)				3	7	3				2
Eminem (The Eminem Show)	9		8		3					
Norah Jones (Come Away With Me)	2					6				3
Avril Lavigne (Let Go)	3		1					1		
Jennifer Lopez (This is Me . . . Then)	6			8		7				10
Soundtrack (8 Mile)	1					4		2		
Shania Twain (Up!)	8					1		10		
U2 (The Best of 1990–2000)								7	5	6
Robbie Williams (Escapology)			2	1				5	4	1

Source: Billboard (2003).

is something the soft drink manufacturers have known for some time. Madonna, the Spice Girls, Ricky Martin, and Britney Spears have all endorsed Pepsi Cola. The latest to join the ranks is Australian pop singer Kylie Minogue, who was featured singing On a Night Like This from her hit album Light Years. Pepsi Cola International's Australian marketing director noted that the commercial aired in 50 countries in regions including Europe, Asia, and Latin America (Advertising Age 2001b).

Nonverbal Communication: Visuals and Illustrations

According to several experts, including Martin Mayer, sight, sound, and motion are the future of international advertising: "Words will become very much less important, especially if the product is standardized, like Coca-Cola, Levi's or Marlboro" (Mayer 1991, 213). The growing use of visual presentation (pictures and illustrations) minimizes the need for translations. Vern Terpstra and Ravi Sarathy write: "More and more European and Japanese ads are purely visual, showing something, evoking a mood and citing the company name. Emphasis on such simple illustrations also avoids part of the problem of illiteracy in poorer nations" (Terpstra and Sarathy 1991). As an example, the many different languages spoken in Europe posed a formidable barrier to Levi's in selling its jeans on the continent. Therefore, the company and its advertising agency created broadcast and movie advertisements that consisted solely of moving pictures and music. Unworried by problems of language or complicated dubbing procedures, Levi's advertising agency in London was able to utilize the Levi's 501 spots for use

throughout Europe (Rijkens 1992, 79). The development of international media is also influencing this trend. Ronald Beatson, director general of the European Association of Advertising Agencies, had this to say:

> What satellite broadcasting is going to mean for us, apart from reach, is greater emphasis on non-verbal communication: the big visual idea, and the use of visual symbols. Where the message transcends national frontiers, it will often transcend national languages. Remember, we have 9 different, national languages within the EU. This is going to put a premium on the visual and musical content of commercials, with less emphasis on verbal communication; and, as brands develop expertise in non-verbal communication, I think we shall see this phenomenon appearing in print media too, with much more emphasis laid on graphics than on copy. (Beatson 1989)

Care should be taken in the selection of visual backgrounds and settings employed in both print and broadcast advertisements destined for foreign markets. These nonverbal communications should either reinforce the local culture in adapted campaigns or remain neutral enough to be accepted in all markets for those campaigns employing a standardized strategy. The creative team must attend to every visual detail in an advertisement. For example, according to Marieke de Mooij and Warren Keegan:

> Landscapes, buildings, traffic signs, etc., must all be neutral. Dutch, Danish and Belgian houses may look similar to the Japanese or Americans, but they look different to the Dutch, the Danish and the Belgians! As soon as they cross each other's borders, they feel they are in a foreign country, not only because of the language, but because of the landscape, houses and churches. (de Mooij and Keegan 1991)

Creativity in the International Arena

The International Advertising Festival, also known as the Cannes Lion Festival, is the largest gathering of international marketing and advertising professionals in the world. In 2003, about 8,000 delegates from the advertising and allied disciplines attended the event to celebrate the best creative work in all major media. The festival showcased over 17,000 ads representing 40 countries. Winning ads are awarded the highly coveted Gold, Silver, and Bronze Lions and the Grand Prix are reserved for the most outstanding creative work. TV and print, outdoors, and on the Web, as well as the most innovative and creative media solutions are all recognized.

In 2003, the top award—the Grand Prix—went to Crispin, Porter & Bogusky, a mid-sized Miami, Florida–based shop for their work on an Ikea campaign. The TV spot—"Lamp"—featured poignant footage of an old lamp being discarded in favor of a newer and nicer one from Ikea. A spokesman interrupts the spot, scolding the viewer for feeling pity for the useless object. The ad taps into the connection consumers have to things for no other reason than they

have been around for a long time. This fact—that people become attached to such household items—is the very problem Ikea faced (Wentz, 2002a). Crispin, Porter & Bogusky won almost enough lions—five plus the Grand Prix—to rank among the top 10 networks (however, Crispin doesn't appear in the rankings in the charts below because it is a two office agency rather than a network).

BBDO Worldwide swept the 2003 festival, winning a total of 22 Gold, Silver, and Bronze Lions in the television and print categories. TBWA Worldwide placed second, with DDB Worldwide coming in third. Table 6.3 lists the international agency networks by Lions won in the TV and print category. Table 6.4 presents global holding companies ranked by Cannes Lions.

Winners of the Grand Prix and Gold Lions receive more than just the praise of their peers. Donald Gunn, director of creative resources worldwide for Leo Burnett, notes:

> Research shows that commercials that win awards are at least twice as likely to be successful in the marketplace as commercials on average. My theory . . . is that there is some definite link between what pleases juries and what pleases viewers when they see advertising in their homes. (Jaffe 1994)

Cannes winners are significantly more likely to report dramatic increases in market shares, sales, volume growth, brand awareness, and favorable image ratings during and after the campaigns' flights" (Tilles 1994).

TABLE 6.3 International Agency Networks Ranked by Lions Won at Cannes in Television and Print, 2002

Network	Holding Company	Grand Prix	Gold	Silver	Bronze	Total
BBDO Worldwide	Omnicom Group		9	6	7	22
TBWA Worldwide	Omnicom Group	1	4	9	5	18*
DDB Worldwide	Omnicom Group		2	4	10	16
Saatchi & Saatchi	Publicis Groupe		4	5	4	13
Wieden & Kennedy	Independent		5	3	2	10
Bartle Bogle Hegarty	Publicis Groupe		5	1	4	10
McCann Erickson	Interpublic Group		5	2	1	8
Leo Burnett	Publicis Groupe			5	5	10
Lowe	Interpublic Group		1	4	3	8
Ogilvy & Mather	WWP Group		2	2	2	6
Young & Rubicam	WWP Group			2	4	6
J. Walter Thompson	WWP Group			3	2	5
Arnold Worldwide	Havas			1	4	5
Grey	Grey	1			2	2*
D'Arcy	Publicis Groupe		1	1	1	3
Foote Cone & Belding	Interpublic Group		1	2		3
Euro RSCG	Havas		1		1	3
Scholz & Friends	Cordiant Comm. Group			2		2

* Plus a Grand Prix

Source: Wentz (2002).

TABLE 6.4 Global Holding Companies Ranked by Cannes Lions, 2002

Holding Company	Total Lions	Holding Company	Total Lions
Omnicom Group	95*	Interpublic Group	32
Publicis Groupe	47	Havas Advertising	14
WWP Group	37*		

Source: Wentz (2002).

Of course, the Cannes Festival is not the only award received for outstanding creativity in advertising. A multitude of other international, national, regional, and local awards are available as well. Wieden & Kennedy was the most awarded advertising agency in the world in 2002, according to the fourth annual Gunn Report, a worldwide league table for the advertising industry that is based on the winners for the most important international and national creative contests. Table 6.5 presents the Gunn Report for 2002, listing the 25 most-awarded agencies in the world.

For decades, New York was known as the center of U.S. advertising creativity. Indeed, the rest of the advertising world took lessons from Madison Avenue. Consumers around the globe read U.S.-produced print advertisements and viewed U.S.-produced television spots. However, during the past two decades, a gradual shift has been taking place. As a creative force, the United States no longer stands alone. As Table 6.5 reveals, the United States accounted for only 6 of the Gunn Report's top 25 ad agencies. England was home to an equal number of award-winning agencies, but an ever-increasing number of agencies hails from Madrid, Tokyo, and Buenos Aires.

Theories abound as to why the United States no longer ranks first in advertising creativity. Alex Biel of the Ogilvy research operation offers one explanation of why European advertising, in particular, has become generally more imaginative than U.S. advertising: "It's because

TABLE 6.5 25 Most-Awarded Ad Agencies in the World, 2002

Rank	Advertising Agency	City	Rank	Advertising Agency	City
1.	Wieden & Kennedy	Portland, Oregon	14.	Springer & Jacoby	Hamburg
2.	Saatchi & Saatchi	London	15.	TBWA Hunt Lascaris	Johannesburg
3.	Dentsu	Tokyo & Osaka	16.	Mother	London
4.	Bartle Bogle	Hegarty London	17.	Tandem DDB	Madrid
5.	Abbott Mead Vickers/BBDO	London	18.	Almap/BBDO	Sao Paulo
6.	BMP DDB	London	19.	Arnold Worldwide	Boston
7.	Lowe	London	20.	Carmichael Lynch	Minneapolis
8.	TBWA/Chiat Day	New York & Los Angeles	21.	CraveroLanis Euro RSCG	Buenos Aires
9.	Agulla & Baccetti	Buenos Aires	22.	Leo Burnett	Prague
10.	BBDO	New York	23.	McCann-Erickson	Madrid
11.	BBDO	Bangkok	24.	DDB	Chicago & Dallas
12.	Forsman & Bodenfors	Gothenburg	25.	Hakuhodo	Tokyo
13.	Saatchi & Saatchi	Hong Kong			

Source: Advertising Age, Gunn Report, 2002 (www.adageglobal.com/cgi-bin/pages.pl?link=543).

[European] corporate structures are smaller. The head of the agency deals with the president of the company. It's the chain of nay-sayers in the United States that gives us such bland advertising." Another agency executive noted that the dominant compensation system in Europe (fees rather than commissions) encourages creativity (Mayer 1991, 213). Regardless of the reason, top creative ideas clearly are born in agencies operating in Europe, Asia, and many other world regions.

Summary

As a strategy, advertising standardization may work well for some products, marketers, and audiences, and in some situations. In other instances, specialization or adaption will prove to be more effective. And sometimes, something in between will be most appropriate (Quelch and Hoff 1986, 59). International marketers must carefully evaluate where along the standardization–specialization continuum a campaign destined for a specific foreign market should fall. Advertisers also must employ appeals suited to each culture and understand how cultural differences impact advertising content. Finally, advertisers must exercise caution in the use of both verbal and nonverbal messages. Translations must be conducted with care, and every aspect of the illustration or visual must be analyzed to ensure a proper cultural fit. And whatever the product, advertisers must select the best media—the subject of Chapter 7.

References

Advertising Age. 1996. Benetton ad banned by European Poster firms. 9 August. <www.adageglobal. com/cgi-bin/daily.pl?daily_id=189&post_date+1996–08–09>

———. 1998. Nokia launches biggest ever campaign in Asia. 8 July. <www.adageglobal.com/cgi-bin/ daily.pl?daily_id=1681&post_date=1998–07–08>

———. 1999. Avon breaks skincare ad in Philippines. 21 October. <www.adageglobal.com/cgi-bin/ daily.pl?daily_id+2661&post_date=1999–10–21>

———. 2000. Coke Turkey launches kids soft drink in Eastern Europe, South Africa. 8 September. <www.adageglobal.com/cgi-bin/daily.pl?daily_id=3645&post_date=2000–09–08>

———. 2001a. Coke hopes Chinese clay dolls will bring it luck. 17 January. <www.adageglobal. com/ cgi-bin/daily.pl?daily_id=4216&post_date=2001–01–17>

———. 2001b. Kylie Minogue to front Pepsi's new global ads. 13 February. <www.adageglobal. com/ cgi-bin/daily.pl?daily_id=4325&post_date=2001–02–12>

Advertising Age. 2002. Gunn Report: 25 most awarded ad agencies in the world. <www.adageglobal. com/cgi-bin/pages.pl?link=543>

Alden, Dana, Wayne Hoyer, and Chol Lee. 1993. Identifying global and culture-specific dimensions of humor. *Journal of Marketing* 57(2) (April): 64.

Al-Olayan, Fahad, and Diran Karande. 2000. A content analysis of magazine advertisements from the United States and the Arab world. *Journal of Advertising* 29(3) (Fall): 69.

Anderson, Michael H. 1984. *Madison Avenue in Asia.* Cranbury, N.J.: Associated University Presses.

Arens, William. 2002. *Contemporary advertising.* Boston: McGraw-Hill Irwin.

Banoo, Sreerema. 1999. TAG Heuer tells what makes its campaigns tick. *Business Times* (Kuala Lampur), 11 August, 15.

Beatson, Ronald. 1989. Europe 1993. Presentation to the Point-of-Purchase Advertising Institute Marketplace 1989, 31 October–2 November, New York. In Rijkens, *European advertising strategies,* 15.

Belch, George E., and Michael A. Belch. 1993. *Introduction to advertising and promotion: An integrated marketing communications perspective,* Homewood, Ill.: Erwin.

Billboard. 2003. Common currency. 18 January, 61.

Biswas, Abhijit, Janeen E. Olsen, and Valerie Carlet. 1992. A comparison of print advertisements from the United States and France. *Journal of Advertising,* 21(4): December, 73–81.

Bowes, Elena. 1992. From cookies to appliances, pan European efforts build. *Advertising Age,* 22 June, 11, I29.

Cateora, Philip. 1990. *International marketing,* Homewood, Ill.: Irwin.

Conti, Samantha. 2000. Stars hawking worldly goods—except in U.S. *San Diego Union-Tribune,* 20 April, E-2.

de Mooij, Marieke. 1994. *Advertising worldwide.* New York: Prentice Hall.

de Mooij, Marieke K., and Warren Keegan. 1991. *Advertising worldwide.* New York: Prentice Hall.

Di Benedetto, C. Anthony, Maiko Tamate, and Rajan Chandran. 1992. Developing creative advertising strategy for the Japanese marketplace. *Journal of Advertising Research* 32(1): January/February, 39–48.

Ellison, Sarah. 2000. About advertising: Agencies find that sexual innuendos don't travel well across cultures. *Wall Street Journal Europe,* 27 March, 36.

Ellison, Sarah, and John Carreyrou. 2003. Face-off: An unlikely rival challenges L'Oreal in beauty market. *Wall Street Journal,* 9 January, A-1.

Fanin, Rebecca. 1984. What agencies really think of global theory. *Marketing and Media Decisions.* December, 74–82.

Frazer, Charles. 1983. Creative strategy: A management perspective. *Journal of Advertising* 12(1): 36–41.

Freemen, Laurie. 1990. Colgate axes global ads, thinks local. *Advertising Age,* 26 November, 1, 51.

Giacomotti, Faboma. 1993. In Europe, there's no place like home. *Adweek,* 7 June, 13.

Green, Robert, William Cunningham, and Isabella Cunningham. 1975. The effectiveness of standardized global advertising. *Journal of Advertising.* 4(3), 25–30.

Harris, Greg. 1984. The globalization of advertising. *International Journal of Advertising* 3: 223–34.

Head, David. 1988. Ad slogans and the made-in concept. *International Journal of Advertising* 7: 237–52.

Hornik, Jacob. 1980. Comparative evaluation of international vs. national advertising strategies. *Columbia Journal of World Business* (Spring): 36–45.

Jaffe, Andrew. 1994. Burnett's Donald Gunn on what wins at Cannes. *Adweek,* 6 June, 46.

Jardine, Alexandra. 2002. Levi's to boost demin with type 1 sub-brand. *Marketing,* 24 October, 1.

Kaplan, Rachel. 1994. Ad agencies take on the world. *International Management* 49(3) (April): 50.

Kaynak, Erdener. 1989. *The management of international advertising: A handbook and guide for professionals.* New York: Quorum Books.

Kilburn, David. 1992. Kao enters Australia, but its detergent is no attack. *Advertising Age,* 22 June, I3.

Koenderman, Tony. 2001. Record punishment: Land Rover forced to advertise apology in South Africa. 6 April. <www.adageglobal.com/cgi-bin/daily.pl?daily_id=4604&post_date=2001–04–06>

Levitt, Theodore. 1983. Globalization of markets. *Harvard Business Review* (May/June): 92–102.

Lin, C. A. 1993. Cultural differences in message strategies: A comparison between American and Japanese TV commercials. *Journal of Advertising Research* (July/August): 40–47.

Lipman, Joanne. 1988. Marketers turn sour on global sales pitch Harvard guru makes, *Wall Street Journal,* 12 May, 1.

Lyman, Eric J. 2001a. Nude beach scenes—yes, it's a Coke ad. 13 July. <www.adageglobal.com/cgi-bin/daily.pl?daily_id=5354&post_date=2001–07–13>

Lyman, EricJ. 2001b. Barilla cooks up first global ads. 5 July. <www.adageglobal.com/cgi-bin/daily.pl?daily_id=5283&post_date=2001–07–05>

Mayer, Martin. 1991. *Whatever happened to Madison Avenue: Advertising in the 90s.* Boston: Little, Brown.

Milner, Laura, and James Collins. 2000. Sex-role portrayals and the gender of nations. *Journal of Advertising* 29(1) (Spring): 67–79.

Miracle, Gordon E. 1988. An empirical study of the usefulness of the back-translation technique for international advertising messages in print media. In *Proceedings of the 1988 Conference of the American Academy of Advertising,* ed. John D. Leckenby, American Academy of Advertising. Austin, Texas, RC51–61.

Mitchell, R., and M. Oneal. 1994. Managing by values. *Business Week,* 12 September, 38–43.

Monjaras, Jorge A. 2003. Uniliver makes dib for Mexican fabric softener market. 19 February. <www.adageglobal.com/cgi bin/daily.pl?daily_id=9160&post_date=2003 02 19>

Mueller, Barbara. 1987. Reflections of culture: An analysis of Japanese and American advertising appeals. *Journal of Advertising Research* 27(3): June/July, 51–59.

Mussey, Dagmar. 2002. Siemens gets friendly in pan-European print ads. 21January. <www.adageglobal.com/cgi-bin/daily.pl?daily_id=6650&post_date=2002–01021>

Neff, Jack. 2002. P & G flexes muscle for global branding. *Advertising Age,* 3 June, 53.

Nelson, Bob. 1994. High tech firms lead the way with global campaigns. *Advertising Age,* 11 August, 22.

Nevett, Terence. 1992. Differences between American and British television advertising: Explanations and implications. *Journal of Advertising* 21(4): December, 61–71.

Norton, Justin. 2002. Leagas Delaney trumpets InterContinental hotels. *Adweek,* 7 October, 5.

O'Dwyer, Gerald. 2003. Swedish ad council says McDonald's spot violates gender law. 25 February. <www.adageglobal.com/cgi-bin/daily.pl?daily_id=9171>

Osborne, Magz. 2002. McDonald's ad mixes burgers and brothels in Singapore. 23 January. <www.adageglobal.com/cgi-bin/daily.pl?daily_id=6665&post_date+2002–01023>

Parmar, Arundhati. 2002. Global youth united. *Marketing News,* 28 October, 1, 49.

Petrecca, Laura. 2000. Twix Bar's global plunge puts Grey work to music. *Advertising Age*, 29 May, 8.

Quelch, John A., and Edward J. Hoff. 1996. Customizing global marketing. *Harvard Business Review* 64(3) (May/June): 59–68.

Radzievsky, Yuri. 1984/1984. The invisible idiot and other monsters of translation. *Viewpoint* (Fall): A Publication "By, For, and About Ogilvy & Mather."

Raffield, Barney T., III. 1987. Marketing across cultures: Learning from U.S. corporate blunders. In *Languages and communication for world business and the professions,* ed. Ann Arbor, Mich.

Recksieck, Charlie. 2003. Fun with automatic translation advertising edition. <www.shtick.org/Translation/translation 48.htm>

Ricks, David. 1983. *Big business blunders: Mistakes in multinational marketing.* Homewood, Ill.: Dow Jones–Irwin.

Rijkens, Rein. 1992. *European advertising strategies.* London: Cassell.

Roth, Robert F. 1982. *International marketing communications.* Chicago: Crain Books.

Rutigliano, Anthony. 1986. The debate goes on: Global vs. local advertising. *Management Review* 75(6),(June): 27–31.

Sivulka, Juliann. 1998. *Soap, sex, and cigarettes: A cultural history of American advertising.* Belmont, Calif.: Wadsworth.

Speer, Lawrence. 2001. Coke urges French youth to "smile through life" in local ads. 7 May. <www.adageglobal.com/cgi-bin/daily.pl?daily_id=4856&post_date=2001-05-07>

Speer, Lawrence. 2002. It's bugs versus bankers in new global ads for BNP Paribas. *Advertising Age,* 11 June. <www.adageglobal.com/cgi-bin/daily.pl?daily_id=7713&post_date=2002-06-11>

Staheli, Paul. 2000. We're the best, but we're not allowed to tell you. *Evening Standard* (London), 26 April, 59.

Terpstra, Vern, and Ravi Sarathy. 1991. *International marketing.* Hinsdale, Ill.: Dryden Press.

Tilles, Danie. 1994. Commercials do win awards and sales. *Adweek,* 11 July, 16.

Tomlinson, Richard. 2002. L'Oreal's global makeover. *Fortune,* 30 September, 141.

Wentz, Laurel. 2003a. Ikea's lamp wins Cannes. *Advertising Age,* 23 June, 1,69.

———. 2003b. Cannes' biggest 2003 winners. *Advertising Age,* 30 June, 1.

Wroughton, Lesley. 2000. Beer ad boosts Canadian pride. *San Diego Union-Tribune,* 29 April, A-17.

Zajc, Lydia. 2000. Cold war idea bears fruit: New software interprets the many languages of global commerce. *South China Morning Post,* 14 November, 12.

CHAPTER SEVEN

Advertising Media in the International Arena

An area that proves to be particularly challenging and often quite frustrating for most international marketers is that of the media function. The basic goals of media planning and purchasing are generally the same whether the planner is operating in New York or New Delhi: to select those media and vehicles that most efficiently and effectively reach the target audience. However, the application of these principles will vary from one market to the next.

The intention of this chapter is not to provide an overview of the media situation in each of the numerous markets around the world. Not only is a complete survey beyond the scope of this text, but such information would soon be outdated. Rather, the goal here is to outline the media options available to international media planners and to highlight the diversity in the various media environments.

National/Local versus International Media

Media planners zeroing in on foreign markets have the option of using national/local media or employing media that cross national borders—better known as international media. Using a combination of the two is clearly an alternative as well. The decision of whether to employ national/local or international media is impacted by a number of factors, including but not limited to: (1) how much centralized control the firm has, (2) what target audience the advertiser is attempting to reach, (3) whether the firm has chosen to employ a localized or globalized campaign, and (4) whether the firm works with national or multinational advertising agencies.

The tendency toward decentralized decision making, the use of campaigns tailored to the local market, and the preference for domestic agencies generally result in more extensive employment of local media than international media. Even where a standardized campaign is employed, media planning and buying usually is conducted on a local basis. Decentraliz-

ing this aspect allows for greater input from local advertising experts, which greatly simplifies the execution of media plans. While the amount of advertising in national media is still vastly greater than that appearing in international media, this may well change significantly in the years to come.

National/Local Media

National or local media offer advertisers a greater variety of vehicles—television, radio, newspapers, magazines, outdoor, direct mail, and transit, as well as many rather unique forms. They also permit use of the local language, which is generally more effective in reaching the local market. However, there are drawbacks to using local media. The practice of media planning and buying at the local level is quite complex because the media environments rarely resemble one another. These differences can take the form of media availability, viability, coverage, cost, quality, and the role of advertising in the media.

Media Availability

Advertisers in the United States are accustomed to the availability of a wide variety of media and vehicles. Yet media that commonly are employed in domestic campaigns may quite simply be unavailable in foreign markets. Until rather recently, for example, Denmark and Sweden did not allow broadcast advertising. And although the United Kingdom does have commercial television networks, the BBC television network—attractive because it is hugely popular among the British—still does not accept advertising. In Saudi Arabia, traditional values do not permit the showing of films to public gatherings; as a result, the cinema medium does not exist in this country. Nor do they permit commercial messages on radio stations. As a result of such limitations, a firm marketing its products in a number of nations may well find it impossible to employ the same media mix in all markets. Even when the same media are available, commercial time may be severely restricted. In Germany, commercial time is limited to 20 minutes a day and is banned on Sundays as well as holidays on each of the government-owned stations. In addition, advertisements are shown in three or four blocks approximately five minutes in length, and, as a result, viewership tends to be rather low. However, Germany's privately owned stations are considerably more liberal—allowing up to 20 percent of airtime to be devoted to television commercials. France controls all its channels—both public and private—with regulations that limit television commercials to about one hour per day (Usunier 1996, 418). In China, no more than 15 percent of the space in newspapers can be allocated for advertising. Such restrictions typically result in high levels of demand, and require that commercial time and space be both booked and paid for well in advance—sometimes up to a year or more. Conversely, where regulation is more limited, the resulting invasion of advertising often translates into clutter. A recent survey (Green 2003) revealed that in 2002 the six U.S. broadcast networks devoted more than a quarter of their prime-time hours to advertising, program promotional messages, and public service

announcements. ABC stood out, having raised nonprogramming minutes per hour to a record 17. The concern is that such clutter may be driving off television viewers.

Table 7.1 highlights the differences existing among countries with regard to how extensively specific media are used, and thereby reveals the relative importance of various media from one market to the next. For example, print's share of advertising dollars ranges from a low of 10.8 percent in Russia to a high of 74.9 percent in Finland. Similarly, TV's share ranges from a low of 13.2 percent in Switzerland to a high of 80.7 percent in Russia. While cinema advertising does not even register for the United States, it ranks comparatively high in Argentina. Such variation necessitates adaptation to the local media environment.

Media Viability

Beyond media availability, Dean Peebles and John Ryans note the importance of media viability. They suggest that the international advertiser look beyond simple media availability and also explore whether the medium is "available in the quality and quantity and at a cost that will permit the international advertiser to successfully employ it." As an example, Peebles and Ryans note that while commercial television is available in Australia to the international advertiser, governmental restrictions require local production of commercials. The added cost of producing a commercial in Australia may well preclude the use of the medium of television if the international advertiser sees a limited market for the product in this country or had planned to use a commercial produced in the domestic market. Also, while a given medium may be available, the cost may be so high in certain markets that the international advertiser's budget prohibits the use of the medium.

Media Coverage

Media coverage also varies from one market to the next. Table 7.2 presents data on numbers of newspapers, television sets, and radio receivers in countries around the world. In the case of broadcast media, both the range of exposure and the ownership of radio and television receivers affect coverage. In the United States there are 854 television sets for every 1,000 Americans, and in Japan there are 725 sets for every 1,000 Japanese. This stands in sharp contrast to the 7 receivers per 1,000 inhabitants in Bangladesh or the 6 receivers per 1,000 in Ethiopia. The pattern is similar for radio receivers. Ownership is again highest in the United States, with 2,118 receivers for every 1,000 inhabitants. In the United Kingdom there are 1,432 receivers for every 1,000 residents. At the other extreme there are fewer than 121 receivers for every 1,000 Indians and only 79 receivers per 1,000 Guatemalans. These figures clearly suggest that the issue of receiver ownership is particularly relevant in developing countries, where a large percentage of the population simply cannot afford individual ownership of radios or television sets.

Coverage of print media is impacted by both national literacy levels and subscription levels to publications, because illiterate consumers generally do not subscribe to magazines and newspapers.

TABLE 7.1 Percent Distribution of Measured Media, 2001

Country	TV	Radio	Print	Cinema	Outddoor/ Transit
Argentina	44.4	8.7	37.1	1.8	8.0
Australia	35.1	9.3	51.8	0.9	2.9
Austria	24.7	8.6	59.5	0.5	6.7
Belgium	44.4	11.3	34.7	1.2	8.4
Brazil	42.8	5.1	47.0		5.1
Canada	39.0	12.4	44.6	0.2	3.9
Chile	43.8	10.9	37.8	0.4	7.1
China	54.9	5.2	39.9		
Columbia	58.2	16.3	25.5		
Denmark	22.5	2.7	70.1	0.5	4.1
Finland	18.1	3.6	74.9	0.2	3.3
France	29.8	7.1	50.9	0.8	11.3
Germany	24.4	3.8	67.1	0.9	3.8
Greece	35.3	3.8	45.6	0.9	14.4
Hong Kong	44.1	3.4	47.9	0.1	4.5
Hungary	59.2	5.2	27.4	0.5	7.7
India	39.6	2.6	48.7	0.5	8.6
Indonesia	58.9	3.1	34.6	0.1	3.3
Ireland	25.9	6.1	57.7	0.9	9.3
Italy	51.9	6.0	37.7	0.6	3.8
Japan	58.4	5.1	36.5		
Malaysia	28.8	3.5	65.8	0.3	1.7
Mexico	56.4	15.6	28.0		
Netherlands	43.8	9.3	42.3	0.4	4.2
New Zealand	32.2	13.2	51.9	0.6	2.2
Norway	33.6	4.5	59.0	0.9	2.0
Pakistan	46.8	2.8	44.2	0.5	5.7
Philippines	66.5	18.5	15.0		
Poland	58.1	6.5	26.0	0.5	8.9
Russia	80.7	4.3	10.8	4.2	
Singapore	36.1	5.3	51.1	1.5	6.0
South Africa	39.7	14.5	41.5	0.7	3.6
South Korea	41.2	3.1	55.6		0.6
Spain	40.9	8.4	44.0	1.0	5.6
Sweden	22.8	3.3	69.2	0.5	4.1
Switzerland	13.2	3.3	68.8	1.0	13.7
Taiwan	52.0	4.3	43.7		
Thailand	55.9	8.4	32.2	0.5	2.9
United Kingdom	30.5	4.5	58.5	1.1	5.4
United States	36.7	13.6	46.1		3.6

Source: International Marketing Data and Statistics, Euromonitor (2003).

TABLE 7.2 Newspapers, Televisions and Radios per 1,000 Inhabitants, 2002

Country	News-papers	Radio Receivers	Television Receivers	Country	News-papers	Radio Receivers	Television Receivers
Algeria	27	244	110	Japan	578	956	725
Argentina	37	681	293	Kenya	10	223	25
Australia	293	1,908	738	Kuwait	374	624	486
Austria	296	753	536	Lebanon	107	687	335
Bangladesh	53	49	7	Libya	15	273	137
Belgium	160	793	541	Malaysia	158	420	168
Bolivia	992	676	119	Mexico	98	330	283
Brazil	43	433	343	Morocco	26	243	166
Bulgaria	257	543	449	Netherlands	306	980	538
Cambodia	2	119	8	New Zealand	207	997	522
Canada	159	1,047	641	Nicaragua	30	270	69
Chile	98	354	242	Nigeria	24	200	68
China	37	339	293	Norway	585	915	669
Columbia	46	544	282	Pakistan	30	105	131
Costa Rica	91	816	231	Paraguay	43	273	218
Cuba	118	353	250	Peru	0	273	148
Czech Republic	254	803	508	Philippines	82	161	144
Denmark	304	1,349	807	Poland	108	523	400
Dominican Republic	156	181	97	Portugal	32	304	630
Ecuador	43	418	218	Puerto Rico	126	742	330
Egypt	35	339	189	Romania	300	334	381
El Salvador	28	478	201	Russia	105	418	421
Ethiopia	0	189	6	Saudi Arabia	326	326	264
Finland	455	1,623	692	Singapore	298	672	304
France	201	950	628	South Africa	32	338	127
Germany	305	948	586	Spain	100	333	591
Ghana	14	710	118	Sri Lanka	29	208	111
Greece	23	478	488	Sudan	26	464	273
Guatemala	33	79	61	Sweden	432	932	574
Honduras	55	412	96	Switzerland	369	1,002	548
Hong Kong	792	684	493	Syria	20	276	67
Hungary	46	690	437	Thailand	64	235	284
India	48	121	78	Tunisia	31	158	198
Indonesia	23	157	149	Turkey	111	573	449
Iran	28	281	163	Ukraine	101	889	456
Iraq	19	222	83	United Kingdom	329	1,432	435
Ireland	150	695	399	United States	213	2,118	854
Israel	290	526	335	Venezuela	206	294	185
Italy	104	878	494	Yugoslavia	107	297	282
Jamaica	62	784	194	Zimbabwe	18	362	30

Source: World Bank, World Development Indicators, 2002.

Levels of illiteracy vary significantly from country to country. As highlighted in Chapter 3, at the high end, 68 percent of Afghanis, nearly half of Indians, and 18 percent of Chinese are functionally illiterate. At the low end, less than 3 percent of Americans, about 2 percent of Russians, and less than 1 percent of Norwegians are illiterate. Differences also exist in the illiteracy levels between males and females. In every instance illiteracy levels are higher among females, and in some instances the illiteracy rate is over 25 percent higher among women. This suggests that in many countries it is still the male who receives formal education and that, as a result, print may be a more appropriate medium for targeting males in many markets. Another factor that comes into play in terms of media coverage is income. In countries with a low per capita income, consumers probably cannot afford to subscribe to print publications. In certain markets a wide variety of media and numerous media vehicles may be required in order to reach the majority of the market. The international advertiser faced with such a situation may no longer find it profitable to attempt to reach the mass market, particularly in many less developed countries.

Media Cost

Advertising rates in all markets tend to be cyclical. During periods of economic prosperity, media tend to inflate their rates. During economic downturns, when many marketers slash their advertising budgets, media rates typically drop significantly. Between 2001 and 2002, ad prices came down at many media outlets worldwide as advertisers pulled back and as the bubble burst for once-hot categories, such as tech and dot-coms. Savvy marketers take advantage of such media recessions. Unilever and the Campbell Soup Company are just two of the firms who reaped the rewards of soft media rates (Unilever is said to have saved some $280 million). In both cases, the monies formerly earmarked to advertising were moved straight to the bottom line or to other corporate priorities. Others as diverse as L'Oreal and Wendy's International took advantage of bargain rates to maximize their media presence. L'Oreal plans to take advantage of reduced rates to buy more media. "We want to gain share of voice so we can gain market share," said Carol Hamilton, president of L'Oreal's North American hair and beauty business. Wendy's said it would boost its ad budget by 30 percent and launch its first national Hispanic push, due in large part to more favorable advertising rates. Smaller advertisers are eyeing the more affordable ad landscape for new opportunities. For example, candy marketer Brach's Confections has traditionally relied primarily on in-store displays to drive sales. As a result of the drop in ad rates, they will begin a television campaign for several new products (Thompson 2002).

In other instances, advertising rates continue to escalate. Often, it is the popularity of the vehicle or program that drives up rates. For example, in 1972, the price of a 30-second Super Bowl commercial, which reached over 56 million U.S. consumers, was $86,000. This translated into a cost per thousand of $1.52. By 2002, a 30-second Super Bowl commercial cost $2.1 million and reached over 88 million Americans. The cost per thousand increased to $23.74, or 16 times as much as the 1972 spot. Even if inflation is figured in, the cost today is 3.7 times as much as the 1972 spot—and a 270 percent increase in three decades is a significant increase indeed (*Business Standard* 2002).

Media Quality

Even if a particular medium is available, the quality may vary from that in the home market. For example, newsprint quality is so poor in many countries—such as India—that it is nearly impossible to obtain adequate halftone reproduction. Many markets still have very limited access to color television, which may play a central role in a visually oriented campaign.

Role of Advertising in the Mass Media

As in the United States, advertising is the principle source of revenue for mass media throughout much of the world. However, the international advertiser should be aware that in numerous markets one or more of the media may be government-owned or -controlled. For example, in many European countries, television is subsidized or owned by the government. In Germany, Italy, and Sweden, as well as a number of other countries, television owners pay annual fees to the government for television viewing, and these fees subsidize programming. With regard to the print media, in many countries readers pay a significantly greater percentage of the cost of subscription rates than do consumers in the United States. As a result, these media are much less dependent on advertising revenues in those countries. In some instances they may choose not to accept commercial messages or to severely restrict the time and space allotted to advertising.

Throughout the world, however, the overall trend is toward privatization and commercialization of both the broadcast and print media. In 1997, Hungary fulfilled its much-delayed plans for media privatization. Hungary was one of the last countries in the former East bloc to liberalize broadcast media, in large part due to fears that the country would be swamped with foreign programming at the expense of local traditions and the Hungarian language. A law was passed to prevent this by requiring 51 percent of programs to be made in Hungary, with a further 30 percent to come from other parts of Europe. Ownership of both radio and television stations must be at least 26 percent Hungarian. In 2001, the Nigerian Bureau of Public Enterprises (BPE) reiterated its commitment to carry out the privatization and commercialization of government media outfits. The government media to be privatized include Nigerian Television Authority (NTA), News Agency of Nigeria (NAN), Federal Radio Corporation of Nigeria (FRCN), and the *New Nigerian* and *Daily Times* newspapers. Privatization Act No. 28 states that NTA, FRCN, and NAN are to be commercialized while the *New Nigerian* and *Daily Times* are to be privatized outright. Since Nigeria's President Olusegun Obasanjo took office in 1999, privatization has been regarded as his administration's core policy.

Media Spillover

There are two kinds of media spillover—incidental and deliberate. *Incidental spillover* refers to those cases in which a local television channel, for example, may be viewed by individuals in other countries as well. Canada provides a prime example of such spillover. Three-quarters of

Canadians are clustered within 100 miles of the U.S. border and more than 95 percent are within 200 miles. Thus, nearly all Canadians are within the broadcast range of U.S. radio and television stations. Similarly, the Netherlands receives broadcasts from Germany, Belgium, and other countries.

Deliberate spillover refers to media created with the specific objective of crossing national borders. An example of deliberate spillover is Rupert Murdoch's British Sky Broadcasting, originally a British satellite service, which has taken its Sky News channel to nearly every continent. A country's broadcasts may spill over into another nation via cable, terrestrial stations, or satellite dishes. However, spillover is not limited to the broadcast media. For example, some German publishers promote significant circulation of their magazines and newspapers in Austria and Switzerland because German is also spoken in these markets.

Certain problems are associated with media spillover as well. If a marketer is running both international and local campaigns for the same product, media spillover can expose consumers to multiple campaigns, resulting in confusion about product positioning, pricing, and promotions. Media spillover may disregard differences in regulations and restrictions. For instance, India's state-run Doordarshan Television bans the advertising of a number of product categories, including liquor, baby food, and foreign banks. However, Hong Kong–based Star TV, the pan-Asian network (now also owned by Rupert Murdoch), reaches millions of households in India and accepts ads for the products banned on Doordarshan TV.

Local Broadcast Media

Television The medium most commonly employed in attempting to reach broad national markets in both developed and many developing countries is television. Television reaches over 90 percent of people in developed countries and over 80 percent even in many developing countries, including China (Balnaves et al. 2001, 46). Household penetration of television is 100 percent in Hungary, Japan, and Singapore, and over 95 percent in Australia, Austria, France, Hong Kong, Italy, New Zealand, Spain, Sweden, Turkey, the United Kingdom, and the United States. However, all consumers do not watch television in the same fashion. In the more industrialized countries, many children and teens have a television set in their own rooms, and each member of the family watches programming individually. For example, in Denmark, 72 percent of youth 12–13 years old have a TV in their own rooms. In the United Kingdom, the figure is 69 percent. In contrast, those with access to television in rural Africa and Asia often watch television in a public venue or as part of a large family or group.

Television is one of the most highly regulated communications media. Even in developed markets, the availability of television advertising time may be quite limited or even nonexistent. This is often true in cases where television is government-owned and -controlled. What can be advertised, and how, is also restricted in most every country. Much as in the United States, many countries prohibit the advertising of cigarettes and alcohol other than beer, while other countries also forbid advertising by financial institutions and baby food producers. Regulation of this medium will be discussed in greater detail in Chapter 9.

Radio Generally perceived as a secondary medium in the United States, in many countries radio plays a much more dominant role. As revealed in Table 7.1, radio as an advertising medium enjoys relative popularity in countries such as Colombia, Mexico, the Philippines, and South Africa. A major plus associated with the medium is its ability to reach illiterate customers; moreover, in many countries it is the only medium capable of delivering to large segments of the population. Radio is also popular because sets are affordable, even among the poor. As Onkvisit and Shaw note, it is a virtually free medium for listeners, and the cost of operating and maintaining a set are negligible (Onkvisit and Shaw 1997, 572). However, the medium's popularity is not limited to developing countries. A study examining media usage in five European countries revealed that the greatest percentage of Europeans listened to radio on the previous day and also spent the most minutes per day listening to radio. In the United States, radio has become a very specialized medium, with stations adopting a particular format: contemporary hit radio, rock, easy listening, news/talk, classical, religious, and so on. In many other markets, stations vary their programming throughout the day, and audience demographics vary accordingly. In addition, radio networks are much less common in developing markets.

Local Print Media

The role that print media will play in the media advertising plan is generally correlated directly with the literacy level of the target audience in each country. The more highly developed the nation, the more heavily newspapers and magazines will be used by consumers in those countries. Overall, the print media tend to receive the lion's share of advertising dollars in almost every country in the world. However, the extent of market saturation that can be obtained via newspapers or magazines will vary from one country to the next.

Newspapers In some countries, such as Britain, Japan, and the United States, one or more newspapers can be said to have a truly national circulation. It wasn't until 1983 that the first general-readership national newspaper began being circulated in the United States. *USA Today* has a circulation of over 1.6 million. The *Wall Street Journal* and the *New York Times* are two additional examples of successful nationally distributed newspapers in the United States; however, both are read by a predominantly business-oriented audience. For instance, an advertisement promoting the *New York Times* to media planners notes that the publication reaches "66% of those in the Executive Branch of the Federal government, and 71% of those in the Congressional Branch. And, the *Times* is read by 66% of opinion leaders in the communications and media industries."

International advertisers must be aware of national newspapers that may be available as an advertising medium in each market. Table 7.3 lists the top 25 newspapers by circulation. Japan, for example, has five national newspapers, the largest of which reaches over 10 million readers. Figure 7.1 shows a message promoting Japan's *Asahi Shimbun* to international advertisers. Advertisers wishing to reach the paper's 8.3 million readers pay upward of $360,000 for a full-page, four-color advertisement, and $306,000 for a full-page, black-and-white advertisement (*Advertising Age* 2002).

TABLE 7.3 Top 25 Global Newspapers by Circulation

Rank	Publication	Country	Circulation
1.	Yomiuri Shimbun	Japan	10,223,923
2.	Asahi Shimbun	Japan	8,321,138
3.	Sichuan Ribao	China	8,000,000
4.	Bild	Germany	5,674,400
5.	Mainichi Shimbun	Japan	3,978,617
6.	Sun	England	3,687,370
7.	Chunichi Shimbun	Japan	3,075,320
8.	Nihon Keizai Shimbun	Japan	2,827,662
9.	Gongren Ribao	China	2,500,000
10.	Daily Mail	England	2,364,315
11.	Daily Mirror	England	2,350,737
12.	Dong-A Ilbo	South Korea	2,150,000
13.	Renmin Ribao	China	2,150,000
14.	Joong-Ang Ilbo	South Korea	2,020,000
15.	Hankook Ilbo	South Korea	2,000,000
16.	Sankei Shimbun	Japan	1,977,122
17.	Chosun Ilbo	South Korea	1,960,000
18.	Eleftherotypia	Greece	1,858,316
19.	Xin Min Wan Bao	China	1,800,000
20.	Wall Street Journal	United States	1,752,693
21.	Kerala Kaumudi	India	1,720,000
22.	Wen Hui Bao	Daily China	1,700,000
23.	USA Today	United States	1,671,539
24.	Rodong Sinmun	North Korea	1,500,000
25.	Kyung-Hyang Daily News	South Korea	1,478,537

Source: Press Release Network 2003 Top 100 Global Newspaper (www.pressreleasenetwork.com/indus22.htm)

A Dutch firm—PEPC Worldwide—is making it easier than ever before for readers to obtain whichever newspaper they desire, no matter where they happen to be. PEPC's digital kiosks have already popped up in about 100 airports, business centers, and hotel lobbies around the world. The kiosks can deliver the latest editions of more than 100 hometown papers. For about $5 a copy, customers can select a paper and, within two minutes, lift out a black-and-white edition complete with photos and advertisements. Newspapers from the *Los Angeles Times* to Reykjavik's *Morgunbladid* have signed up to participate in the service. The papers transmit their latest editions as Adobe PDF files to PEPC, which sends them by satellite to disk drives in each kiosk (Passariello 2002).

In many countries, newspapers tend to be predominantly local or regional rather than national and, as such, serve as the primary medium for local advertisers. Attempting to use a series of local papers to reach a national market is considerably more complex and costly. Unlike in the United States, in many nations there is heavy competition among local newspapers,

Figure 7.1 Advertisement promoting Japan's Asahi Shimbun newspaper to international advertisers.

which tends to benefit advertisers by holding advertising costs down. Indeed, in some markets, up to 200 daily papers may vie for the reader's attention, as is the case in Lebanon. Advertisers must examine several issues when considering the use of local papers. For instance, some publications are sponsored by a particular political party, and the international advertiser must exercise caution in placing advertisements in particularly controversial papers. Content—both editorial and commercial—may very well be limited to what the party in power deems appropriate. Also, many foreign papers have a fixed and much smaller number of pages than typical U.S. papers, thus limiting advertising space. Many foreign national papers run no more than 16–20 pages, often because equipment or paper are limited. Finally, the quality of newspapers may not be consistent from one country to the next. Therefore, for each market, the international advertiser must investigate whether the publication offers high-quality four-color production or low-quality black-and-white.

In the United States most newspapers clearly distinguish between editorial and advertising content. Such is not the case in many other countries, where editorial space is regularly sold for advertising purposes, occasionally making it difficult for readers to distinguish between the two. Advertisements even crop up on the front page of many newspapers around the world. For example, in Mexico, advertising space is sold in the form of news columns—without any indication to readers that the "story" is, in fact, a paid advertisement. Indeed, if a marketer pays for a full-page message in this market, he is likely to find his product advertised on the publication's front page.

Magazines In general, magazines have nowhere near the broad readership of newspapers, although readership levels are considerably higher in many foreign markets than in the United States. Rarely, however, can a single magazine reach a majority of a market. In most countries magazines serve to reach specific segments of the population dependent on their subject matter or area of emphasis. It is this selectivity—or ability to reach narrowly targeted audiences—that is one of the main benefits of this medium in many advertisers' eyes. For example, for fashion and beauty tips, young women in Germany read *Freundin,* in France they read *Marie Claire,* and in the United States they read *Glamour.* International marketers should also note that there is a great deal of variation in terms of the number of magazines available from one market to the next. Table 7.4 provides an overview of the number of consumer and business titles in selected markets.

Other Local Media

Billboards Billboards are an important medium in many markets, both developed and developing. In crowded metropolitan areas, literally millions of consumers may be exposed to a single billboard message, and in countries with high levels of automobile ownership, billboards located along highways also prove an effective medium. Outdoor billboards in the Netherlands are even using interactive techniques to attract attention in a crowded media environment. As Derek Suchard reports, an increasing number of outdoor billboards in this country are

TABLE 7.4 Number of Magazine Titles in Selected Markets

Country	Consumer Titles	Business Titles	Total
Argentina	930	160	1,090
Austria	61	2,800	2,861
Canada	715	443	1,158
Czech Republic	840	1,230	2,070
Finland	329	2,098	2,427
France	1,250	1,667	2,917
Germany	2,012	3,490	5,502
Hungary	138	27	165
Israel	87	296	383
Japan	2,457	1,792	4,249
Jordan	8	3	11
Lebanon	11	26	77
Malaysia	192	47	239
New Zealand	290	390	680
Poland	2,126	967	3,093
Saudi Arabia	26	11	37
South Africa	75	575	1,050
South Korea	756	1,138	1,894
Spain	284	2,413	2,697
Sweden	177	315	492
United Kingdom	3,174	5,713	8,887
United States	9,478	5,229	14,707

Source: FIPP 2003 (www.fipp.com/Data/NoMagTitles.html.)

taking on elements not usually associated with the medium, including live models sitting in board-mounted displays and the use of boards to offer free samples. In one recent example, Westimex, a Belgian potato chip marketer, attached bags of Croky chips on 100 boards along streets across the country, inviting sampling with the headline "Bet these are the best-tasting chips in Holland." Passersby accepted the offer, pulling down individual sized bags that were within reach. (Suchard 1993)

Apparently, both consumers and the trade responded positively to the approach.

Alaris, a Norwegian outdoor advertising company, recently introduced a roadside marketing concept in the United States which captures data from motorists' radio-listening habits to adjust ads or electronic billboards along the highway. Highway electronic billboards (HEBs) are equipped to profile commuters as they whiz by in their cars, using data captured from the radio-listening habits of drivers to instantly personalize freeway messages. For example, if the highway has a large number of drivers listening to country music channels, the billboard would screen ads for casinos. On the other hand, if a large number of drivers using the highway at a particular time of day are tuned to National Public Radio, the billboards would change to ads for a luxury automobile or a gourmet grocery retailer. The Alaris billboards use a consumer

monitoring system to pick up radio waves, which are "leaked" from the antennas of passing cars while pinpointing the stations being played. The system assesses the most popular radio station during a given hour and targets ads to those drivers (O'Dwyer 2003).

In developing markets, where high levels of illiteracy are common, billboards, with their heavy emphasis on visuals and limited use of advertising copy, are a dominant medium. The primary disadvantage related to the use of the billboard medium encountered by international advertisers lies in the different standard sizes offered in different markets. It should be noted that while outdoor advertising is a tightly regulated medium in some markets—such as the United States—in other markets "outdoor" advertising consists of advertisers simply placing posters on any available wall, bus stop, or fence, without cost. The practice encourages one advertiser to replace another advertiser's posters with their own (Onkvisit and Shaw 1997, 580).

Transit Transit advertising is playing an increasingly significant role in many markets. For example, transit advertising is the most effective advertising medium in Romania, according to a survey conducted by the Economic University in Bucharest. Of all consumers surveyed, 91 percent said they remembered the content of transit ads, compared with 82 percent who remembered the content of TV ads and only 44 percent who remembered the content of print ads. Transit ad space there is available on 200 buses, and advertisers have included R. J. Reynolds, Colgate-Palmolive, PepsiCo, Rank Xerox, and Philip Morris. Transit advertising may well rank higher than television because of the few television stations in Romania. In addition, magazines and newspapers are not nearly as sophisticated as Western publications and therefore are less attractive to advertisers (Kelly 1992).

The use of transit media is expanding rapidly in China as well. A small firm in Singapore acquired the worldwide rights to sell ad space on buses, trains, ferries, and airports throughout the vast territory of China. Until rather recently, little transit advertising has been sold in this market. However, observes Ian Stewart, the potential for the development of this medium is enormous: "More than half a million people are carried up and down Changan Avenue in central Beijing every day and in Shanghai more than 160 ferries operate daily" (Stewart 1993). Moscow provides an example of an innovative use of transit media. Mandara—a Swedish firm—signed an agreement with the Moscow Post Office for exclusive 20-year rights to broker advertising on the sides of Moscow's 800 postal vehicles and on the walls of the city's 660 post offices. Under the agreement the Swedish firm also used postal vehicles for client deliveries and outfitted 10,000 Moscow postal carriers in uniforms highlighting a client's logo. The first marketer signed by the company was a Stockholm-based brewery, which bought rights to advertise on 100 postal trucks and one post office wall. Mandara also targeted companies such as Japanese electronics manufacturers and European food companies (Bartal 1993).

Cinema Cinema advertising is commonly overlooked by U.S. marketers because the medium is in its infancy in this country. In many countries, however, where it is common to subsidize the cost of showing movies by running advertising messages, cinema advertising has become an important medium. A common practice is to begin the program by showing slides of advertised

products, followed by commercials. Newsreels and documentaries might also be shown. Then prior to the feature, filmgoers might be exposed to a promotion for coming attractions. For example, India has the highest film audience and the highest level of per capita movie attendance of any country in the world, and as a result, cinema ads play a much greater role in this country than in the United States. Indeed, this medium offers access to market segments that would be impossible to reach via any other medium.

Direct Marketing Direct marketing is a way of doing business that employs a wide spectrum of media, including direct mail, telephone, broadcast, and print media. The usage of direct mail, the most popular form of direct marketing, varies significantly around the world, and depends on the level of acceptance of this approach, literacy rates, and a number of additional variables. In Saudi Arabia, for example, sending consumers a direct mail piece is considered an invasion of privacy. Clearly, direct mail would not be an appropriate medium in markets with high illiteracy rates. Direct mail campaigns are also difficult to implement due to dramatic variations in postal rates and service. In Chile, for example, letter carriers collect additional postage from recipients for every item delivered because senders pay only part of the postage. Clearly, the use of the direct mail medium is quite limited in this country—customers generally do not take kindly to paying for unsolicited advertisements. In addition, various national regulations impact the viability of this medium for many international marketers. For instance, in Germany, if an addressee has a label on their mailbox refusing direct mail, mail carriers are prohibited by law from delivering such advertisements. Finally, the necessary infrastructure may not be available to an international marketer. In the United States, marketers have access to a wide selection of mailing lists, which allow them to target their audience. In comparison, list generation and management are still relatively primitive abroad, both in developed and developing markets. For example, while U.S. marketers may use any combination of demographic criteria to tailor a mailing list, in Germany, only two unique selection criteria per order can be made when renting lists.

Unique Media: Low Tech In developing countries, which tend to lack the media resources of advanced nations, marketers often adopt unusual promotional strategies. For example, Group Africa, a firm based in Johannesburg, developed Roots Television (RTV), an innovative means for reaching South Africa's rural population. Through a network of 550 TV sets and VCRs in country stores, ladies clubs, and traveling shows mixing advertising and entertainment, RTV claims it reaches 3.2 million rural Africans each month—consumers who could not be easily reached via more traditional media. Every four to six weeks, RTV representatives visit rural stores and deliver videotapes featuring six hours of entertainment along with 18 minutes of commercials per hour. The entertainment is tailored to the local village—RTV representatives tape weddings, initiations, coming-of-age ceremonies, gospel music, and sporting events. The raw footage is edited and commercials are inserted in RTV's Durban studios. On the next trip through the village, a premiere of the local tape is held, which remains with the store owners. The ladies clubs are included to help draw customers to participate in a day of fun and games,

songs and contests, and free samples once every three months. Up to several thousand villagers come from far and wide for an opportunity to see themselves on screen. Group Africa's clients include Lipton, Colgate-Palmolive's Stay Soft fabric softener, Nestlé's Nespray baby-milk formula and Gold Cross condensed milk, and Unilever's Van Den Bergh Foods' Rama margarine. Shop owners pay RTV $42 a month for TV and VCR rentals (Barnes 1993).

The best way to see Cairo, according to many, has always been from a felucca—the ancient sailboats that travel up and down the Nile. These days, it is also the best way to see the latest multinational doing business in Egypt. The potential of a market 61 million strong and recent government reforms designed to spur the economy are drawing in major corporations looking for ways to grab the attention of Egyptians. "In Egypt, there's no better place," says Douglas A. Jackson, senior regional manager in Egypt for Coca-Cola Co., the firm that started the felucca-advertising craze. "Except maybe if we put a neon Coke sign on top of the pyramids." At Cairo's advertising agencies, feluccas are considered hot. Feluccas, which had been used to transport goods since the time of the pharaohs, work because they blend a local custom with a great location. Most Egyptians live along the Nile and often rent a felucca for an evening's entertainment. Some feluccas are built to hold 50 people, and, with their triangular-shaped white sails, are also a main draw for tourists. Coke signed a two-year contract with Cairo's most popular felucca operator for around $8,000, plus new sails. Nestlé has also used the sails to promote its brand Perrier. Not everyone is fond of using feluccas to advertise. Some Egyptians criticize the commercialization of the Nile. Others say there is no limit to the craze. Indeed, there is also talk of sponsoring camel races (Dockser Marcus 1997).

Unique low-tech media are not limited to developing countries. Two recent examples illustrate this point. Nytmedie, a Danish media marketing agency, recently introduced the "Push Pram" outdoor marketing concept. Push Pram is based on a simple idea—provide Danish parents of newborn babies with a new baby carriage if parents agree to accept the buggy complete with a corporate sponsor's logo or brand ad. Swedish fashion retailer Hanes & Mauritz and Scandinavian finance group Nordea Bank are among the first multinational brands to have signed on to this new marketing concept. Nyntmedie's goal is to sign up the parents of 10 percent of all babies born in Denmark. A company spokesperson states that ads placed on prams are no less appropriate than on the sides of taxis or athlete's shirts. Under the marketing scheme, parents who enter a contractual agreement with Nytmedie can choose the model of the pram they would like on the company's Web site. The prams may then be used for up to 2.5 years. The company already has a lengthy waiting list for "branded baby buggies" and plans to expand the concept to the rest of Europe and the United States as well (*Advertising Age* 2002). Switzerland is boasting a truly unusual low-tech medium—cows. A Zurich-based "Cow Placard Company" is offering advertiser the chance to have a logo or slogan painted onto a cow's flank using auto paints. One of the first cows to be branded carried the logo of a respected Swiss clothing company. The firm notes that soon thousands of cows will be dotting the Swiss Alps, brightly painted with advertiser's messages. The cost of a cow placard varies depending on the size and duration of the ad, but typically costs around $375. The approach has already been criticized by animal rights groups (Leidig 2002).

Unique Media: High Tech Japanese advertisers are finding dramatic spaces and new techniques for ads, including talking retail shelves, giant outdoor video screens, and train tunnels. Shelf TV, originating from Japan, utilizes a small TV monitor affixed to a shelf providing shoppers with additional product information that normally could not be introduced in conventional TV ads. The sets are strategically placed in store areas where the particular product being promoted is located. While clients can choose to feed their regular commercials into the sets, specially produced infomercials tend to have a greater impact on brand identity. With this new tool, stores can literally become mini-classrooms, where shoppers can instantly learn more details and hands-on tips regarding the advertised product. The sets are equipped with sensors that shut off the infomercials when there is no shopper nearby. Once the scanner detects movement, the set switches on automatically and attracts the attention of the respective shopper. Shelf TV will be introduced to Thailand, Hong Kong, Singapore, and Malaysia (Schmid 2002).

Units of major Japanese agency giants such as Dentsu are at the forefront in developing new media forms. David Kilburn and Julie Skur-Hill report: "Dentsu PROX, for instance, developed a commercial purpose for the sky. With Search Vision, images can be freely suspended by using projectors and aircraft or balloons as screens." Dentsu PROX also developed Tunnel-Vision, using train tunnels as an ad medium. A series of images behind boards placed at 10-meter intervals are lit when the train passes, creating images like those made by flip cards (Kilburn and Skur-Hill 1990).

Interactive television and interactive kiosks are examples of two unusual, high-tech media forms. Interactive Systems, an Oregon-based firm, has been operating TelePick in Spain since early 1993. The service, which allows viewers to play along with game shows, print out coupons, and vote in electronic polls, connects to the viewer's TV and telephone and includes a remote control, a printer, and a small monitor. The company has already sold over 16,000 units to Spanish consumers for about $170 each. Participating advertisers included Gillette, Pizza World, and Chesebrough-Ponds, which ran weekly infomercials that quizzed viewers through the set-top box and rewarded them with beauty-tip booklets and other prizes. When an advertiser offered a coupon, consumers were alerted by a beep and a message on the screen and could then hit a button to print out the coupon from a small printer attached to the set-top box. A similar program was initiated in the Netherlands, where companies such as Coca-Cola, McDonald's, and Procter & Gamble tested various interactive commercials. Interactive Systems plans on introducing the system to the U.S. market (Donaton 1993). Similar technology has been incorporated in the development of the world's first interactive kiosk. *Paris Vogue* and French department store Le Printemps sponsored a multimedia interactive kiosk called Sensaura that helps customers select perfumes. Sixteen fragrances from such companies as Chanel and Estée Lauder participated in the promotion, which ran for two weeks in Le Printemps. Debra Aho describes the process:

> The kiosk used a touch screen to guide customers through a series of questions about what they liked
> to do or wear. After answering the questions, customers got a short analysis of their personality and

the names of two perfumes that might suit them. The customer could then go to the fragrance counter and request a sample of one of the perfumes. (Aho 1993)

Consumers responded favorably to the promotion, waiting in line up to 30 minutes to use Sensaura. In addition, the promotion was a traffic builder for Le Printemps and netted extra ad pages for *Vogue*. Both the publication and the department store are planning to use Sensaura again in the future. The technology uses multimedia computer software that also runs on online services and CD-ROM and that will eventually run on interactive TV. The system currently is being marketed to cosmetics, apparel, and computer companies.

Elevator rides need no longer be dull. Elevators equipped with a 15-inch display panel now entertain consumers with news, weather, and especially advertisements. Elevator ads typically reach an attractive demographic—executives and business professionals who use the elevator an average of six times per day. Research has revealed that the average elevator ride lasts about 60 seconds—long enough for riders to digest several ads. Providers typically install the display screens free of charge and pay the landlord a percentage of its advertising revenue. A typical advertiser's message will be flashed in a building elevator about 10,000 times per month. If one estimates four persons per elevator ride, this translates into 40,000 imprints being viewed each month (Green 2002). See Figure 7.2 for a firm promoting this new medium to advertisers.

Figure 7.2 Elevator ads target attractive demographic group.

Mobile phone ownership is becoming increasingly common in developed and developing markets as well. The ten countries with the highest proportion of mobile phone users are, in order: Finland (with 67.8 mobile phones per 100 inhabitants), Norway (62.7), Sweden (59.0), Italy (52.2), Austria (51.3), Denmark (50.6), South Korea (49.9), Taiwan (49.4), Portugal (47.2) and Switzerland (44.4) (*aneki.com* 2003).

Mobile phones have become a hot advertising medium. Short messaging services (or SMS) allow mobile phone users to transmit text messages quickly and cheaply. Cell phone subscribers sent about 400 billion text messages globally in 2002. Person-to-person texting accounted for most of the traffic—particularly among youth—but marketing applications are becoming more common. SMS is especially popular in Asia, where mobile phone penetration is beginning to outstrip that of fixed lines and even personal computers in some areas. In China, for instance, McCann-Erickson Worldwide, part of Interpublic, partnered with Siemens to create a SMS contest for Coca-Cola. Cell phone users were invited to guess the next day's temperature in Beijing—a correct guess could win a Siemens phone or a one-year supply of Coke. Contestants who didn't win were invited to download Coke's jingle as a free ring-tone. The result: 4 million messages were exchanged during the 40-day promotion, and nearly 50,000 people downloaded the Coke jingle. Coca-Cola has already decided to repeat the contest. Several advertising agencies have set up interactive divisions to handle SMS campaigns, including Ogilvy & Mather (Madden 2002). In the United States, T-Mobile is now offering customers the ability to send 10-second video messages with sound. Undoubtedly, by the time this text is published, this new technology will also be used for advertising purposes.

International Media

While television, via satellites and cable, can send royal weddings, Olympic games, and space shots into the homes of consumers in literally hundreds of countries, no single network controls this global transmission. However, international media that provide nearly global market coverage offer a means for international advertisers to reach consumers across many markets. The number of international media and the expenditures on them are rising rapidly.

International Print Media

International Magazines Print remains the dominant international medium, and magazines rank at the top. A number of U.S.-based magazines have international editions, including *Reader's Digest, National Geographic, Time, Newsweek,* and *Cosmopolitan,* among others. *Reader's Digest,* which produced its first non-U.S. version in 1938 for the U.K. market, is now the world's most widely read magazine, with a circulation of over 28 million in 19 languages and over 170 countries. *National Geographic* has a worldwide circulation of 7.8 million—and a U.S. circulation of just over 6 million. *Time* magazine—with a circulation of over 5 million—offers advertisers 133 different editions, enabling precise targeting of audiences around the globe. *Newsweek* publishes

three English-language international editions (Atlantic, Asia, and Latin America) and now has seven international editions under license, of which six are foreign-language. Most recently, *Newsweek* launched a Chinese language edition (Britt 2002). The magazine's circulation is 3.1 million in the United States and a combined circulation of some 1.3 million for its international and foreign language editions. *Cosmopolitan* has 36 international editions. When the magazine first launched Russian *Cosmo* in 1994, it sold a mere 60,000 copies each month. Today, the magazine sells about 480,000 copies monthly—more than in any country outside the United States. In 1998 *Cosmopolitan* arrived in the Philippines, Indonesia, Hungary, Lithuania, and mainland China, where there are approximately 300 million women between the ages of 18 and 30. Estimates are that *Cosmo* will top out at 50 foreign editions. With a circulation of about 2.7 million in the United States and another 4.5 million abroad, *Cosmo* is already the best-selling women's magazine in the world. Thanks in part to the ads, *Cosmo* looks virtually the same in every market. All editions share the same style, format, and supermodel cover girls—as well as staple articles on career advancement, dieting, and dating. But most foreign editions employ local editors and staff, who tailor each issue to their particular market. Chinese editor Gao Xiaohong, for instance, shuns all stories about sex—because Chinese people are modest and women aren't yet at a point where they can talk about sex (Greenberg 1998). Figure 7.3 shows the cover of the Chinese edition of *Cosmopolitan*.

It is not only U.S. magazines that make their way across foreign borders. *Marie Claire*, a French monthly magazine with 26 editions published worldwide through joint ventures and licensing deals, debuted in the United States in 1993, becoming a member of the Hearst Magazine family. In many markets *Marie Claire* already competes with the international editions of *Cosmopolitan* and *Elle*. *Elle*, another French publication, has a combined global circulation of nearly 5 million, with editions in 30 countries worldwide. *Elle China* was launched in 1988, and today, with a circulation of about 280,000, it is the best-selling foreign magazine on the mainland.

While many of these publications are translated into many different languages and are available in many different markets, their foreign readers are a quite different group in terms of demographics from those who read these publications in their country of origin. In foreign markets these publications appeal predominantly to international travelers and upscale, high-income consumers. However, the publications are generally less effective in reaching mass consumer markets and thus are of less value in promoting mass consumption items.

Business-oriented publications that reach businesspeople on a worldwide basis include *Forbes*, *Business Week*, *Fortune*, and *Harvard Business Review*. A major plus associated with such publications is that they provide verified circulation and audience data. In addition, they tend to lend the magazine's prestige to advertised products. One of the drawbacks of such publications, however, is that they generally offer only English, French, and Spanish editions. *Forbes* has foreign-language editions in Japan, Germany, and Hong Kong, among other markets. In an advertisement promoting *Business Week* to international advertisers, the copy notes: "Every issue delivers an elite international audience: 92% of our subscribers are citizens of their country of residence, 93% are in business, industry or the professions. Of these, 75% are in senior management and 57% are a member of the board of directors of their company."

Figure 7.3 Cover of Chinese edition of *Cosmopolitan* magazine looks much like the U.S. version.

International Newspapers A number of international newspapers exist which provide opportunities for global advertisers. Among the most well-known is the *International Herald Tribune*, a joint venture of the *New York Times* and *Washington Post* companies. Based in Paris, the newspaper is printed simultaneously via satellite at 10 locations worldwide and distributed in more than 181 countries. Figure 7.4 shows an advertisement promoting the *International Herald Tribune.* The *New York Times* is another important international publication, with a weekday circulation of 1.1 million and Sunday circulation of over 1.6 million. A Russian-language edition of the *New York Times* was introduced in Moscow in 1993—the first foreign-language edition of the 141-year-old paper. The *Times* of London and the *Guardian,* also a British newspaper, are also considered global newspapers. Many publishers realize that similar life-styles and interests in many different markets can be catered to using the same or similar publishing formulas. The fact that launching multilocal editions of newspapers spreads costs across several markets is not lost on international publishers.

Many international newspapers are directed toward the business community. For example, the *Wall Street Journal,* a Dow Jones Company publication, boasts that it has more top management circulation than any other global business publication. With the *Wall Street Journal Europe,* published in Brussels, the *Asian Wall Street Journal,* published in Hong Kong, and the *Wall Street Journal Americas,* targeting Latin America, the publication reaches over 1.7 million businesspersons around the globe. The *Financial Times* (London) is another prestigious global business newspaper, though its circulation is significantly smaller than that of the *Wall Street Journal.*

International Broadcast Media

International Television In 1962, AT&T launched Telstar 1—the first communication satellite capable of receiving, amplifying, and returning signals. Telestar was able to process and relay telephone and television signals between the United States and Europe. Today's satellites—orbiting 22,000 miles above earth—have greatly enhanced the ability of global marketers, such as Sony, Coca-Cola, McDonald's, and Gillette—to use television to reach consumers around the globe. Cable has served to bring satellite TV into the homes of consumers and will probably remain the major means of receiving satellite transmissions. Those satellites with stronger transmitters allow households to receive signals directly via their own small dish antenna; however penetration of such satellite dishes in most markets is still rather limited. However, developments in high-powered direct broadcast satellites (DBS) have made reception even easier. DBS is likely to have a significant impact for those regions lagging in cable infrastructure. For example, STAR (Satellite Televisions Asian Region) TV sends both U.S. and BBC programming to millions of Asian households. Figure 7.5 shows an advertisement promoting STAR TV to multinational marketers. STAR TV boasts:

> From a teenager in Taiwan to a housewife in Mumbai, only STAR has the network to help you target anyone, anywhere in Asia. With more than 30 channels in sports, music, movies, news, documentaries and entertainment, over 300 million people watch STAR across 53 countries.

Announcing The New York Times │ International Herald Tribune Global Advertising Bu

If your market is global, we can introduce you to a whole new world of opportunity. With a **New York Times-IHT global advertising buy**, your marketing message will be heard by the world's most influential, affluent and educated consumers, business leaders and decision makers. And you can do it with one easy and efficient buy. **Think Globally. Act Quickly.** If your advertising schedule already runs in The New York Times, you can reach more of the same exceptional audience in Europe and Asia by extending your schedule to the International Herald Tribune. If you are not already advertising in The New York Times or the International Herald Tribune, there's never been a better time. For details on packages, positioning, programs and pricing, please contact you sales representative or **Claire LaRosa, (212) 556-1625, clarosa@nytimes.com.**

Figure 7.4 Advertisement promoting the *International Herald Tribune*.

Figure 7.5 Advertisement promoting STAR TV to multinationals.

The worldwide distribution of cable and satellite infrastructure and services is not simply due to market demand. Terrain, demography, economic uncertainty, politics, and regulations are all factors in national and local decisions to promote these forms of television delivery.

In Iran, the desire to exclude "politically inappropriate" content—especially that which contradicts the religious and moral beliefs of the country's government—informs strong regulatory decisions against satellite TV, although satellite dishes are bought on the black market. In China, the huge growth of cable services is due in part to the vast size of the country—cable is a relatively cheap way to connect people in rural areas to local provincial TV stations. However, the growth of cable is also due to the government's desire to restrict what Chinese citizens are exposed to (Balnaves et al. 2001). Since January 1, 2002, in a bid to tighten control over what residents view on Western media channels, China's government has instructed foreign broadcasters to transmit their channels through a centralized platform, which encrypts them and beams them out over a state-run satellite (Madden 2001).

Foreign broadcasters were warned by the Chinese government that if they did not comply, they would be banned. The new system allows the government to block programming it finds objectionable from Chinese living rooms, as well as hotels, embassies, and expatriate housing compounds.

Satellite technology has made the emergence of global television networks possible. Viacom bills its combined MTV Networks (MTVN) as the largest TV network in the world (O'Guinn et al. 2003, 315). MTV reaches almost 375 million households on its 33 channels worldwide, with eight out of ten MTV viewers outside the United States. MTV is hugely successful. Revenues at MTV Networks International increased 19 percent in 2001 to $600 million, while operating profits grew a hefty 50 percent to $135 million. They are expected to more than double by 2004. The network owes its success to a number of factors. First, demographics: There were 2.7 billion people between the ages of 10 and 34 in 2000. By 2010, there will be 2.8 billion. Increasingly, this age group is acquiring the bucks to buy CDs, jeans, acne cream—whatever brands are hot in each country. This means advertisers increasingly love MTV. Second, music: the claim that music is the universal language is true, and rock is the universal language of the global teen. Third, television: the number of sets in the world's living rooms—especially in places such as China, Brazil, Russia, and India—is exploding. The folks at MTV are shrewd enough to realize that while the world's teens want American music, they really want local music as well. So MTV's producers and veejays scour their local markets for top talent. The result is an endless stream of overnight sensations that keep MTV's global offerings fresh. Viacom is counting on MTV to be one of its biggest growth drivers in the coming decade (Capell et al. 2002, 82).

In 1980, Ted Turner launched Cable News Network (CNN), a 24-hour news channel. Two years later, Turner also launched Headline News. Early on, the two cable services lost nearly $80 million before turning a profit. Gradually the network built up a strong audience and advertiser base. The turning point for CNN came in 1991, with the network's coverage of the Persian Gulf War. Two CNN reporters were able to maintain live phone links from a

Baghdad hotel during the U.S. bombings of the Iraqi capital. Major networks and newspapers around the world quoted CNN, and audiences have since learned to count on CNN for breaking news. During the Gulf War, the network presented a uniform global feed that presented the war largely though U.S. eyes, but since then CNN has increasingly worked to cater its programming to regional audiences and advertisers. Cable News Network International has four major international outlets—the Asian-Pacific region, Europe and the Middle East, Latin America, and South Asia. It tailors these services to their respective markets, with business programs, local anchors, and the like. Expatriate Americans are only 1.5 percent of this audience. "The other 98.5 percent of our audience around the world require us to be relevant to their lives," notes Chris Cramer, president of CNNI (Flint and Goldsmith 2003).

Currently, CNNI reaches more than 170 million households in over 200 countries and territories around the globe. Campbell notes that the success of CNN proved that there is both a need and a lucrative market for 24-hour news. Spawning a host of competition in the United States and worldwide, CNN now battles for viewers with other 24-hour news providers, such as MSNBC, CNBC, Fox News, Euronews, and Sky Broadcasting, among others (Campbell 2000, 188).

Introduced in 1979 as the flagship sports television network, ESPN properties include ESPN2 (the second most popular sports network behind ESPN, featuring MLB, NHL, college football, and basketball), ESPN Classic (a 24-hour all-sports network featuring the greatest games, stories, and heroes in the history of sports), ESPNEWS (the only 24-hour sports news network), ESPN Radio Network, ESPN The Magazine, ESPN.com (the leading sports Web site since its inception), ESPN Zone (a sports-themes dining and entertainment facility), ESPN Enterprises (which develops products and businesses using the ESPN brand and assets), and ESPN International. ESPN began distributing programming internationally in 1983. ESPN International was formed in 1988, helping ESPN establish a global footprint on all seven continents, reaching more than 80 million households. ESPN's 19 international networks reach over 140 countries and territories in nine languages. The network acquires major sporting events for distribution worldwide and local sports for regional distribution, and distributes ESPN domestic programming. Beyond the three networks highlighted above, global consumers can tune into BBC Worldwide, CNBC, the Discovery Channel Network, Turner Network Television, the Cartoon Network, and Animal Planet, among many others.

International Radio International radio broadcasting has been performed primarily by government-run stations. Two such stations have established their credibility as reliable sources of news to listeners worldwide. The BBC World Service broadcasts to an international audience of over 140 million listeners in 44 languages. The Voice of America reaches over 90 million listeners worldwide in 53 languages. Both the BBC World Service and Voice of America are available on the Internet. Other major international broadcasters include Deutsche Welle Radio (German), Radio France International, Radio Nederland, Radio Moscow, Radio Beijing, and All India Radio. Kamalipour explains:

several decades of research on international radio audiences show that listening to BBC, VOA, and the others is highest among people who have few domestic operations, like those in isolated areas. The numbers of such people have been steadily reduced by the increasing advance of domestic AM and FM radio in most countries. International radio is also sometimes sought by those who do not trust the local or national media that are available to them. That is still the case in a number of countries, but the number has been reduced by the fall of authoritarian regimes that exercised tight control over media contents in the former USSR, Eastern Europe, Asia, Africa, and Latin America. (Kamalipour 2002, 135)

"Regional" radio stations are those that are capable of reaching several nations. Regional stations tend to be most common in Europe, where stations have transmitting power up to five times that allowed in the United States, enabling them to cover much of the continent. A prime example of such a regional station is Radio Luxembourg, which broadcasts in five languages, with over 40 million listeners from the British Isles to Germany, Austria, and Switzerland.

The Internet Unlike the media discussed previously, the Internet truly is global in nature. It can provide the marketer with literally instantaneous worldwide communication. As Keegan noted, the Internet defies a narrow marketing classification. It can be used as a market research vehicle, an advertising vehicle, a public relations vehicle, a sales vehicle, and more. Market researchers can conduct database searches and find information about competition on their Web pages. Surveys, given the right demographics, can be conducted via the computer. Advertising and consumer promotions regularly appear on screens. Public relations in the form of Web pages can readily be presented. The computer can even replace retail outlets and sales personnel if so desired by a company. But, while the number of Internet users around the globe is growing exponentially, distribution of the world's online population is still rather uneven. The United States currently has the highest Internet penetration in the world (see Table 7.5), but analysts predict that the Internet's international audience will grow faster in the coming years (Keegan 1999, 487).

Internet advertisers can take advantage of a variety of different formats: Web sites, banner ads, buttons, pop-ups, interstitials/superstitials, and site sponsorships. Literally thousands of corporations have Web sites. Some companies use their Web site like an extended brochure to promote their goods and services; others act as information and entertainment publishers and try to create a place that people will visit often; and still others treat their Web site as an online catalogue store, conducting business right on the Internet (Arens, 2000). The most important difference between Web sites and other forms of online advertising is that consumers actively and voluntarily seek out a company's Web site (to learn more about a company or product, to register for a contest, etc). Another important difference is that much more information about the product or service can be provided on the Web site than via any other form of online advertising. The most valuable Web sites tend to be those that fulfill the consumer's goal-seeking needs by providing useful information rather than attempting to dazzle visitors with excessive graphic cleverness (Shimp 2003, 395).

TABLE 7.5 Internet Users

Rank	Country	Number of Users (million)	Rank	Country	Number of Users (million)
1.	United States	148.0	11.	Brazil	8.6
2.	Japan	27.0	12.	Australia	7.7
3.	China	22.0	13.	Netherlands	6.8
4.	United Kingdom	19.4	14.	Taiwan	6.4
5.	Germany	18.0	15.	Spain	4.6
6.	South Korea	15.3	16.	India	4.5
7.	Canada	13.2	17.	Sweden	4.5
8.	Italy	11.6	18.	Poland	2.8
9.	Russia	9.2	19.	Belgium	2.7
10.	France	9.0	20.	Austria	2.6

Source: Data compiled from: *CIA-World Factbook,* (cia.gov/cia/publications/factbook/index.html).

By far the most common form of Internet advertising is the banner ad—typically a static rectangular message that appears across the top or bottom of a Web page. Users who click their mouse pointer on the banner are transported to the advertiser's site. In 2002, the typical Internet user was exposed to some 700 banner ads daily, and estimates are that the number will increase to 950 banner ads daily by 2005. However, research (Goldhush 2001, 21) reveals that the vast majority of these banner ads are ignored by Internet users—with a "click through" rate of less than one-half percent. Buttons are small versions of the banner that often look like an icon and also provide a link to the advertiser's home page. To be effective, both banner ads and buttons need to be eye-catching, with full motion, animation, or audio to motivate the user to click on the ad.

As a result of the paltry click through rate of banner ads, Internet advertisers have turned to increasingly aggressive means to grab the users attention, such as pop-ups, interstitials, and superstitials. Pop-ups are ads that appear in a separate window that materializes on the screen seemingly out of nowhere while a selected Web page is loading. Interstitials—based on the word "interstitial," which describes the space that intervenes between things—are ads that appear between (rather than within, as is the case with pop-ups) two content Web pages. Users tend to have less control over interstitials because there is no "exit" option to stop or delete an interstitial. In short, they simply have to wait until the entire ad has run. Superstitials are short, animated ads that play over or on top of a Web page. Though all three of these forms of Internet advertising are often a source of irritation to consumers, they are almost twice as effective in catching users' attention than simple banner ads.

Web page sponsorships are a form of Internet advertising that are growing in popularity. An Internet advertiser can be a partial or exclusive sponsor of a particular Web page. In exchange for the sponsorship support, firms are provided with extensive recognition on the Web site. IBM, for example, paid $1 million to be the sole sponsor of the National Football League's Super Bowl

Web page in the mid 1990s. The site generated more than 8 million hits. As a result, IBM has exclusively sponsored the site since 1996 (Shimp, 2003, 399).

Balnaves, Donald, and Donald argue that it is a myth that the Internet is not regulated, cannot be regulated and should not be regulated:

> For the first 15 years of its existence funding from the U.S. government and military made the Internet possible, and they called the shots. Since the early 1990s, an informal regime of commercial regulation has emerged. To gain access to the Internet, we must subscribe to Internet Service Providers (ISPs) such as America Online or Compuserve. Then to track down a specific site, we use search engines such as Excite, Infoseek, Lycos or Yahoo. These service providers and search engine companies play an increasingly powerful role in determining what information is available and the paths by which we can reach it. The regulation of these *de facto* regulators will, primarily, be national governments and national courts—although international bodies such as the UN's World Intellectual Property Organization (WIPO)—are beginning to have some impact too. Net police squads have been formed in Germany, France, Canada, Italy, U.K., U.S., Japan and Russia. Though some of these governments use the pretext of protecting citizens from subversive ideas or defending national security and unity to deny access to the Internet, usually by forcing them to subscribe to a state-run ISP. Nevertheless, there are certain types of conduct that are properly regarded as being unacceptable on the Internet as they are elsewhere. The argument is not really about whether or not the Internet is regulated. It is. The question is, who does the regulating—private, mostly U.S.-owned companies or national governments and international organizations—and where should the limits of acceptable conduct be drawn? (Belnaves et al. 2001, 86)

The information highway is still under construction—and so too are the rules. Currently, advertising and sales promotions laws related to the Internet vary from country to country (Moscardelli, 1999, 10). A recent case provides an excellent example. In 2000, in a potentially precedent-setting ruling with international implications, a French court ordered Yahoo! to block French Internet users from participating in online auctions of Nazi memorabilia conducted in the United States but accessible from France. The court's order was to be carried out within three months, under threat of daily fines topping $13,000, because French law bars the display or sale of racist material. Legal experts said the ruling was important because it challenged the conventional wisdom that activities conducted on the Internet were beyond the scope of national legislation. Yahoo! argued the auctions offering the Nazi memorabilia were accessible from domain names such as www.Yahoo.com or auctions.yahoo.com based in the United States and were targeted at U.S. Web users. Yahoo! added that the English-language sites were protected in the United States under the constitutional right to free speech (*Advertising Age* 2000). Yahoo! subsequently banned the sale of such hate-related items from all sites. After a two-year battle, a Paris court cleared the Internet giant of condoning war crimes and crimes against humanity. The court ruled that justifying war crimes meant "glorifying, praising or at least presenting the crimes in question favourably," and that Yahoo! manifestly did not fit that description (Henley 2003, 17).

Another important issue that remains to be addressed—both within the United States and internationally, is that of privacy. Over the past decade, the Internet has been successfully used in the United States to develop profiles of Web visitors—collecting information such as e-mail addresses, purchase preferences, and more. Such information is obtained through online surveys—for example, an ESPN.com content required users to fill out a survey to be eligible to win sports tickets—or through such sites as Nytimes.com, which requires users to provide demographic information for free access to the newspaper's site (Campbell 2000, 53). Internet firms argue that such tracking is not personal, as it is typically collected anonymously, and assists them in customizing their sites and the content of those sites to better match users' interests. However, a survey conducted in 2000 revealed that most Internet users (54 percent) felt that such tracking was harmful, and a whopping 87 percent believed that the sites should ask permission prior to collecting personal information. Many privacy advocates as well as several lawmakers in Congress have called for legislation to limit the ability of Web sites to collect personal data, to require sites to notify people how the information will be used, and to allow people to disallow the collection of their personal information (Campbell 2000, 54). It should be noted that U.S. laws are currently quite liberal in terms of what data marketers may collect. Differences in privacy laws between the United States and Europe may force U.S. companies to change how they collect and share consumer information collected via the Internet.

Other issues which must be addressed when using the Web for international business include exchange rates and language. International marketers must determine whether to offer prices in their own currency or the local currency. Some advertisers have made different price offers in different markets. Savvy Internet customers who discover such discrepancies may become frustrated with marketers. English is currently the dominant language on the Internet. However, projections are that by 2005, more than 57 percent of Web users will be non-English speakers. As a result, Internet marketers will increasingly need to tailor their Web sites to the language of a specific market. Translating Web pages is no less difficult than translating the copy for any other medium. E-Bay is an example of a Web site that employs the local language. See Figure 7.6 for a print ad promoting E-Bay to German consumers. The headline asks readers what they plan to do with that odd Christmas gift from grandma.

The International Chamber of Commerce recognizes that advertising and marketing in the interactive media is at an early stage of development, and acknowledges that the relevant principles and guidelines may have to change and evolve as we learn more about the new technologies and their specific uses. In light of experiences acquired to date, the ICC has outlined principles for responsible advertising and marketing over the Internet. Interested readers may go to <http://www.iccwbo.org/home/statements_rules/ules 1998/internet_guidelines.asp>

Omis Geschenk im Keller verstecken?

Da verkaufen wir's doch besser bei eBa

Hier machen Sie Überflüssiges zu Geld!

Bei eBay bekommen ungeliebte Weihnachtsgeschenke eine zweite Chance. Denn auf dem

größten Online-Marktplatz der Welt warten mehr als 50 Millionen potentielle Käufer – und

suchen vielleicht genau das, von dem Sie sich gerne trennen möchten. Also: Gabentische

leeren und Portemonnaie füllen! Bei www.ebay.de

www.ebay.de

Besser **kaufen** *und* **verkaufen.**

Figure 7.6 Print advertisement promoting E-Bay to German consumers.

International Media Data

Audience profiles and circulation data are closely monitored in most highly developed nations. Advertisers in these markets have come to expect and rely on data supplied by large, independent, syndicated research services in making virtually all media decisions. One such service is VNU Inc., the top U.S. research firm, which operates in more than 100 countries around the globe. A number of additional services conduct research for specific media and in specific regions, including the Pan-European Television Audience Survey (PETAR), the European Business Readership Survey (EBRS), International Financial Management in Europe Survey (IFME), the Pan-European Survey (PES), the European Media and Marketing Survey (EMS), the European-based Satellite Television Audience Measurement Partnership (STAMP), the Asian Businessman Readership Survey (ABRS), and Asian Profiles 5.

For data in most other countries, comparable services tend simply not to be available, particularly in developing countries. For example, despite the emergence of dozens of commercial broadcasters during the last decade's wave of deregulation and privatization among Africa's 54 nations, regular, credible research is only being conducted in 8 English-speaking and (on a limited scale) 10 Francophone countries (Koenderman 2001). What data is made available in most developing markets are generally supplied by the media themselves, and such unaudited statistics are often viewed by international marketers as rather suspect. Verification of such figures clearly is a difficult task. When data is available, local differences in auditing procedures may make country-by-country comparisons nearly impossible. Data provided is also often outdated and quite simplistic. For example, figures with regard to pass-along circulation are typically not provided, yet such secondary circulation can be quite substantial in many markets. This lack of accurate media information presents one of the primary headaches for media planners operating in foreign markets. Media data will be discussed in greater detail in Chapter 8, which deals with research in the international arena.

International Media-Buying Services

There are a number of ways that the media-planning or -buying function can be handled in the international setting. The traditional model has all planning and buying conducted by the client's domestic or lead agency. Another option is to conduct media planning centrally but to handle media buying on a local basis in each country in which the international advertiser operates. A third option is to turn the function (either all or part) over to an international media agency; such specialists have been cropping up over the past few years. These firms work either directly for international clients or for their advertising agencies. They are generally responsible for finding the local media best suited to the client's needs and the target audience to be reached, providing accurate media data, handling negotiations and obtaining the best rates, making the purchase, and monitoring placement. These media buying agencies are able to obtain significant media discounts by purchasing time and space on behalf of groups of clients instead of on the basis

TABLE 7.6 Top 10 Media Specialists by Worldwide Billings, 2002

Rank	Company	Headquarters	Worldwide Billings (U.S. billion $)
1.	Starcom MediaVest Worldwide	Chicago	$ 18.40
2.	MindShare Worldwide	New York	18.00
3.	OMD Worldwide	New York	17.90
4.	Initiative Media Worldwide	New York	16.85
5.	Carat	London	16.65
6.	Zenith Optimedia Group	London	16.15
7.	Universal McCann	New York	14.95
8.	Mediaedge:cia Worldwide	London	13.55
9.	MediaCom	New York	12.35
10.	MPG New	York	8.55

Source: Agency Report, *Advertising Age,* 21 April 2003, S-12.

of single companies or brands. Such agencies can also afford to hire highly trained personnel, conduct multinational audience research, and establish databases that would be beyond the financial reach of most individual advertising agencies (Russell and Lane 2002, 622). Table 7.6 outlines the world's top 10 media specialists by worldwide billings for 2002.

Summary

In this chapter, by no means were all forms of local and international media available to the international advertiser addressed. A media planner may also turn to autowraps on cars, toilet stall messages, and even advertisements in outer space (Barrington 2001), among a multitude of other media that in many cases may be specific to a particular market. An advertiser planning on entering a specific market must undertake an in-depth analysis of the media situation particular to that country. Basic questions that must be asked relate to the availability and viability of both traditional and unique media; the coverage, costs, and quality of various media; the role of advertising in the media of a specific country; the selection of local or international media or a combination of the two; the availability of reliable media data; and the decision whether the client, agency, or independent media service should be responsible for media planning and buying. It should also be understood that media change in the international arena is rapid and that many of the facts and statistics presented here may well be out of date in just a few years. Therefore, in Chapter 8 we discuss research in the international arena as a means of ensuring the best data possible.

References

Advertising Age. 2002. French court orders Yahoo! to block Nazi items. 21 November. <www. adageglobal.com/cgi-bin/daily.pl?daily_id=3985&post_date=2000–11021>

———. 2002. Read all about it: local newspapers. 11 February. <www.adageglobal.com/cgi-bin/ article.pl?article_id=269>

Advertising Age. 2003. Agency Report. 21 April. S-12.

Aho, Debra. 1993. France says oui to interactive kiosk. *Advertising Age*, 8 November, 25.

Aneki.com. 2002. Countries with highest proportion of mobile phone users. <www.sneki.com/ mobilephone.html.>

Arens, William. 2002. *Contemporary advertising*. New York: McGraw-Hill/Irwin.

Balnaves, Mark, James Donald, and Stephanie Donald. 2001. *The Penguin atlas of media and information*. New York: Penguin Putnam.

Barnes, Kathleen. 1993. Reaching rural S. Africa. *Advertising Age*, 19 April, I3.

Barrington, Stephen. 2001. Look way up: Canada's space agency aims to put ads in orbit. 1 August. <www.adageglobal.com/cgi-bin/daily.pl?daily_id=5488&post_date=2001–08-01>

Bartal, David. 1993. Ads leave stamp on Moscow mail. *Advertising Age*, 3 July, 8.

Britt, Bill. 2002. Newsweek to publish monthly Chinese-language edition. 20 December. <www. adageglobal.com/cgi-bin/daily.pl?daily_id=8987&post_date=2002–12–20>

Business Standard. 2002. Advertising's great fall off the heap. 24 December. <business-standard.com/ strategist/story.asp?Menu=14&story=4648>

Campbell, Richard. 2000. *Media and culture: An introduction to mass communication*. Boston: Bedfort St. Martins.

Capell, Kerry, Catherine Belton, Tom Lowry, Manjeet Kripalani, Brian Bremner, and Dexter Roberts. 2002. MTV's world, *Business Week*, 18 February, 81–84.

CIA World Factbook. 2003. Internet Users. Cia.gov/cia/publications/factbook/index.html.

Dockser Marcus, Amy. 1997. Advertising breezes along the Nile river with signs for sales. *Wall Street Journal*, 18 July, A-1.

Donaton, Scott. 1993. Interactive system tries U.S. market after test in Spain. *Advertising Age*, 8 November, 24.

Euromonitor. 2003. International Marketing Data and Statistics.

FIPP. 2003. Number of magazine titles in selected markets. <www.fipp.com/Data/NoMagTitles. html>

Flint, Joe, and Charles Goldsmith. 2003. CNN International takes a wider view than U.S. programs—with viewers in 200 countries. *The Wall Street Journal Europe*, 11 April, A-5.

Goldhush, Carolyn. 2001. A banner move. *Agency* (Summer): 21–22.

Green, Frank. 2002. Giving their ads a real lift. *San Diego Union-Tribune*, 27 March, C-1.

Green, Andrew. 2003. Clutter crisis countdown. *Advertising Age*, 21 April, 22.

Greenberg, Susan. 1998. Your very own Cosmo; Don't judge a mag by its cover. *Newsweek*, 18 May, 24.

Henley, Jon. 2003. Yahoo! Cleared in Nazi case. *The Guardian* (London), 12 February, 1.

Kamalipour, Yahra R. 2002. *Global communication*. Belmont, Calif.: Wadsworth Publishing.

Keegan, Warren. 1999. *Global marketing management.* Upper Saddle River, N.J.: Prentice Hall.

Kelly, Janice. 1992. Bus ads ride high in Romania. *Advertising Age,* 27 April, I36.

Kilburn, David, and Julie Skur-Hill. 1990. Creativity cracking through ad clutter. *Advertising Age,* 10 December, 41.

Koenderman, Tony. 2001. African marketing industry in need of media research. 4 September. <www.adageglobal.com/cgi-bin/daily.pl?daily_od=5663&post_date=2001-09-04>

Lefton, Terry. 1997. IBMs $1M super buy is Web-topper; Phoenix close on $9M NACAA pact. *Brandweek,* 24 November, 8.

Leidig, Mike. 2002. Branded cows to offer advertisers with new medium in Swiss Alps. 7 October. <www.adageglobal.com/cgi-bin/daily.pl?daily_id=8525&post_date=2002-10-07>

Madden, Normandy. 2001. China could censor foreign channels using screening platform. 5 November. <www.adageglobal.com/cgi-bin/daily.pl?daily_id=6146&post_date=2001-11-05>

————. 2002. Text messaging ads on fast track in Asia. *Advertising Age,* 2 December, 12.

Moscardelli, Deborah. 1999. *Advertising on the Internet.* Upper Saddle River, N.J.: Prentice Hall.

O' Dwyer, Gerald. 2002. Danish company sells advertising space on prams. 9 August. <www.adageglobal.com/cgi-bin/daily.pl?daily_id=8163&post_date=2002-08-09>

————. 2003. Norway's Alaris launches interactive billboards along U.S. highways. 9 January. <www.adageglobal.com/cgi-bin/daily.pl?daily_id=9078&post_date=2003-01-09>

O' Guinn, Thomas, Chris Allen, and Richard Semenik. 2003. *Advertising and integrated brand promotion.* Mason, Ohio: Thompson Learning.

Onkvisit, Sak, and John Shaw. 1997. *International marketing: Analysis and strategy.* Upper Saddle River, N.J.: Prentice Hall.

Passariello, Christina. 2002. The Podunk post on sale at the Eiffel Tower. *Business Week,* 16 December, 125.

Peebles, Dean M., and John K. Ryans. 1984. *Management of international advertising: A marketing approach.* Boston: Allyn & Bacon.

Press Release Network. 2003. Top 100 Global Newspapers. <www.pressreleasenetwork.com/indus22.htm>

Russell, J. Thomas, and W. Ronald Lane. 2002. *Kleppner's advertising procedure.* Upper Saddle River, N.J.: Prentice Hall.

Schmid, Thomas. 2002. Thai supermarkets shelves sprout TV screens carrying ad messages. 24 July. <www.adageglobal.com/cgi-bin/daily.pl?daily_id=8031&post_date=2002-07-24>

Shimp, Terence. 2003. *Advertising, promotion, & supplemental aspects of integrated marketing communications.* Mason, Ohio: Thompson Learning.

Stewart, Ian. 1993. Chinese ad space open to new world. *Advertising Age,* 8 November, 114.

Suchard, Derek. 1993. Netherlands boards get added dimensions. *Advertising Age,* 17 May, I19.

Thompson, Stephanie. 2002. Buyer's market. *Advertising Age,* 18 February, 1.

Usunier, Jean-Claude. 1996. *Marketing across cultures.* Upper Saddle River, N.J.: Prentice Hall.

World Bank. 2002. World Development Indicators.

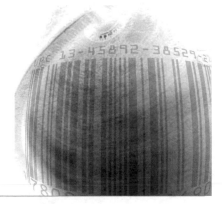

CHAPTER EIGHT

Research in the International Arena

The role of research is equally important in domestic and international marketing and advertising. Its basic purpose is to assist advertising and marketing managers in making more informed, and therefore better, decisions. When planning to sell goods to foreign consumers, each element of the marketing mix must be investigated. As noted in Chapter 2, the product must be appropriate for a given market. In some cases the same product can be marketed around the globe; in others modifications may be required. The marketer must determine the most appropriate price, which may be influenced by the firm's short- and long-term objectives, the competitive environment, and a variety of other factors. The marketer must establish the availability of various channels and select the most efficient means of distribution. Marketing research can address each of these areas. Finally, the international marketer must consider promotion of the product: personal selling, sales promotion, direct response, public relations efforts, and, of course, advertising. Advertising research may involve life-style studies, concept testing, message pre- and posttesting to determine reactions to different types of advertising appeals and executions, and, determination of appropriate media vehicles. Each of the marketing-mix decisions will be influenced by the international marketing environment, outlined in Chapter 3. The marketer must familiarize him- or herself with demographic factors such as market size and population growth; economic factors, including degree of urbanization and income distribution; geographic characteristics such as topography and climate; and the political-legal climate in terms of potential political risk and regulatory restrictions. In addition, the marketer must understand the cultural environment—verbal and nonverbal language, values and attitudes, and religion and ethical standards, as well as customs and consumption patterns, as explored in Chapter 4. "The complexity of the international marketplace, the extreme differences from country to country, and the frequent lack of familiarity with foreign markets accentuate the importance of international market research" (Jeannet and Hennessey 1988, 203). Research can help prevent a multitude of marketing blunders.

Despite the importance of undertaking such research, it is not as frequently employed internationally as it is domestically. Indeed, for many reasons, a significant number of both consumer- and industrial-goods firms conduct little or no research in most of the foreign markets in which their products are sold. The dominant reason is the high cost associated with conducting research, particularly if primary research is deemed essential. Many companies for which foreign markets represent a relatively low profit potential find it difficult to justify such an investment. In addition, conducting international research is no easy task. Coordinating research and data collection across a number of countries can prove quite challenging, and there is the associated difficulty of establishing comparability and equivalence (Douglas and Craig 1983, 18). Finally, all too many marketers have a rather limited appreciation for the significantly different character of foreign marketing environments. As a result, management relies on little more than casual observations or generalizations drawn from other markets rather than basing their marketing and advertising decisions on solid research. In this chapter we outline the basic steps in international marketing and advertising research.

Currently, the vast majority of research related to marketing and advertising—both commercial and academic—is conducted within the nations of the Industrial Triad (North America, Europe, and Japan). In 1995, the world market for commercial research was estimated at over $10 billion. Of this, approximately 45 percent was conducted in Europe (42 percent within the EU), 34 percent in the United States, and 10 percent in Japan. These three geographic areas accounted for all but 11 percent of total spending on marketing and advertising research (ESOMAR 1996). This reflects the current size and attractiveness of these markets. However, this imbalance is likely to change in the future. The countries with the highest growth potential are the emerging market economies in Asia, Latin America, Africa, and Eastern Europe. Firms that wish to succeed in the global markets of the 21st century will need to pay greater attention to examining markets in these regions of the world and developing or acquiring the capabilities to conduct research in these markets. As businesses continue to expand in international markets, the role of timely and accurate marketing and advertising research to guide decision making becomes increasingly critical (Craig and Douglas 2001, 80).

Steps in Research Design

The procedures and methods related to conducting marketing and advertising research in the international arena are conceptually and methodologically similar to conducting such research in domestic markets. Most research studies involve a common series of tasks: (1) define the research problem, (2) identify information sources, (3) design the research, (4) collect data, and (5) analyze and report the research data.

Problem Definition

Subhash Jain defines marketing research as the process of:

> gathering, analyzing and presenting information related to a well-defined problem. The focus of the research is a specific problem or project with a beginning and an end. Marketing research differs from marketing intelligence, which is information gathered and analyzed on a continual basis. (Jain 1984, 550)

Defining the problem is the most important task in international research because at this stage the researcher determines precisely what information is required. Problems may even vary from one market to another. This may reflect differences in socioeconomic conditions, levels of economic development, cultural forces, or the competitive market structure (Douglas and Craig 1983, 39).

Determination of Information Sources

Next, the researcher must determine where necessary information can be found. In some instances research may be limited to the collection of *secondary data*. Secondary data refers to information that has previously been collected and is available from another source—for example, governmental bodies, trade associations, or syndicated research suppliers. The collection of secondary data is generally considered the appropriate starting point for all international investigations, as it is most easily accessible and least expensive to obtain. Secondary data can assist in identifying areas of interest not adequately addressed and therefore deserving of additional attention. Marketers may then collect *primary data*. Presumably, primary data provides more relevant information because it has been collected for the sole purpose of addressing the researcher's stated problem. Both qualitative and quantitative methods can be employed in the collection of primary data. The advantages and disadvantages of both secondary and primary data will be discussed in detail later in the chapter.

Research Design

As Brian Toyne and Peter Walters explain:

> A research design is simply a framework or plan adopted to study a particular research problem. It is the blueprint followed when collecting and analyzing data. Its dual purpose is to ensure that the study is relevant to the problem and that it employs economic, effective procedures. (Toyne and Walters 1989)

The research design typically entails determination of research techniques and instruments to be employed as well as the sampling plan. Each of these areas will be discussed in greater detail later in this chapter. The researcher may choose among several research techniques: observation, focus-group interviews, experimental techniques, and surveys. The most commonly employed instrument for gathering primary data is the survey questionnaire. Issues critical to the design of survey questionnaires include functional equivalence, instrumental equivalence, measurement, scaling, and wording. For surveys, the investigator must know how to draw a sample from the population to be studied that is both representative and comparable.

Data Collection

Tracking down secondary data sources can be both time consuming and labor intensive. Further, the marketer must realize from the outset that secondary data is unlikely to be available for all variables or in all markets. With regard to secondary data, the issues of accuracy, comparability, and timeliness will be of concern. In the case of primary data collection, the sample must be drawn and the survey instrument must be administered, generally via telephone, mail, or in-person interviews. Here, the researcher must watch for and guard against nonresponse bias, topic bias, and social bias, as well as researcher and respondent bias. Again, each of these issues will be discussed in greater detail in a later section.

Data Analysis and Reporting

Because secondary data was originally collected to serve other purposes, analyzing it requires combining and cross-tabulating various data sets in order for the information to be of use to the researcher. In the case of primary data, the information collected must first be edited and coded. Care must be taken in applying those analytical tools appropriate to the quality of the data collected. Only then can interpretation take place. Finally, the researcher compiles a report that highlights how the research results relate to the originally stated research problem. This report is generally presented to headquarters management as well as local subsidiaries.

Secondary Data

Secondary data, or pre-existing statistics or information gathered for a purpose other than that of the immediate study, offers some real advantages to the international marketer (Toyne and Walters 1989). Collection and analysis of secondary data is typically the first step in market research for most firms, because a tremendous amount of information can be obtained in this fashion. In addition, secondary data generally can be collected fairly quickly and easily, and, most important, relatively inexpensively—most secondary sources provide the information free or for only a minimal fee. The primary cost, then, for accessing this information can be viewed in terms of the time and energy spent by the research staff. Secondary data is particularly valuable for firms planning on entering smaller markets, because their more limited profit potential may permit only modest research expenditures.

 Problems with Secondary Data

A major problem international marketers face with regard to secondary research is data availability. While the United States is unmatched in terms of the abundance of demographic and economic information available to marketers, this is certainly not the case in every country. In developing markets in particular, secondary data is relatively scarce. Indeed, a direct relationship seems to exist between the availability of secondary data in a country and its level of economic development. Further, while much demographic or economic information may be accessible, more specific types of data, such as information regarding consumer needs or lifestyles, are nearly impossible to obtain from secondary sources. Available data must be evaluated in terms of accuracy, comparability, and timeliness.

Secondary data often is less accurate than the international marketer would prefer. The data available in developing markets in particular tends to be a good deal less accurate than information from developed nations. Industrially advanced countries typically tend to be quite skilled in market research and to possess well-developed data collection mechanisms. In less sophisticated markets, data collection is generally rather rudimentary and experienced research personnel are not abundant. This directly impacts the quality of the data. For example, if a sample has not been randomly drawn, the results cannot be assumed to be representative of the total population. Data collection methods should always be examined to determine whether proper research methods were employed. More often than not, statistics available in third world nations represent little more than estimates or even, in some cases, wishful thinking. International marketers should be wary of who collected the data and for what reason. In many countries the primary data-gathering organization is the government, which may have reason to under- or overrepresent certain statistics. For instance, a specific country may wish to downplay statistics that might be associated with a negative image, such as high levels of illiteracy or disease; or politicians may overemphasize favorable items, such as industrial production levels, in an attempt to attract foreign investment. Such manipulation of the data is often associated with a country's attempt to obtain assistance from various donor organizations, nations, or agencies.

Even when secondary data is available and accurate, it may not be comparable. If the international marketer is to evaluate foreign countries, the data collected must be comparable. Items of interest to the international marketer may be defined differently from one country to the next. For instance, Susan P. Douglas and C. Samuel Craig explain how the definition of the term "urban" varies from market to market:

> In Japan, for example, urban population is defined as a shi (city) with 50,000 inhabitants or more, or shis (population usually 30,000 inhabitants) with urban facilities. In India it includes all places with 5,000 inhabitants or more. In Nigeria, it includes the forty largest towns; and in Kenya and Zaire, agglomerations with at least 2,000 inhabitants. Similarly, in France and West Germany, it includes communities with 2,000 or more inhabitants, while in Norway and Sweden it goes down to localities or built-up areas with as few as 200 inhabitants. (Douglas and Craig 1983, 80)

Likewise, one researcher attempted to collect international data on the number of women in the work force in different countries. She obtained wildly conflicting estimates, depending on the source. In Brazil, the percentage of women in the work force ranged from a low of 20 percent to a high of 39 percent—a 19-point difference. In Canada, percentages ranged from 46 to 62 percent. Even within the United States, depending on the source, percentages ranged from 54 to 63 percent. Explanations for the diversity in figures are myriad. For instance, some figures are based on different age parameters. Some are gathered by survey rather than census, and censuses and surveys do not always collect the same information. Some figures represent estimates, while others represent hard data. Finally, different definitions of what constitutes the "work force" impact the ultimate number (Bartos 1989, 205). Regarding such differences in definitions, ESOMAR (The European Society for Opinion and Marketing Research) has produced a working paper on the harmonization of demographics within the European Union. ESOMAR notes that with the Common Market now firmly in place, it should be possible to conduct marketwide research, rather than having to do separate and different studies in each country. To that end, it recommends that a common set of definitions of demographic terms be employed by all member countries.

There is also the question of the *timeliness* of the data. In some countries data may be collected annually, while in others, literally decades pass before a survey is again undertaken. For example, Bolivia hasn't had a census since 1950 and Congo since 1958. In 1980, when China was opening up to dealings with Western firms, some of the first figures on the Chinese economy were made publicly available. Officials admitted that some of the figures were drawn from CIA studies. China's first official census was conducted in 1986 (Terpstra and Russo 2000). There is often a very good reason for this lag in data collection activity. Information gathering is an expensive endeavor, so that in a country with limited resources, data collection may simply not be a priority. Few countries—developed or not—can match the frequency of U.S. data collection efforts.

Data from secondary sources from any country (including the United States) must be checked and interpreted carefully. As a practical matter, the following questions should be asked in order to judge the reliability of the data sources:

- Who collected the data? Would there be any reason for purposely misrepresenting the facts?
- For what purposes was the data collected?
- How was it collected (methodology)?
- Is the data internally consistent and logical in light of known data sources or market factors? (Cateora and Hess 1979, 262)
- International marketers may turn to both domestic and foreign sources of secondary data.

Domestic Sources of Secondary Data

The U.S. Government More information is collected by the U.S. government than any other source in the world. The data, which is characterized by its timeliness and accuracy, is generally available to the public either at no cost or for a minimal fee. The Department of Commerce is

heavily involved in promoting the expansion of U.S. business in the international arena through its International Trade Division. The International Trade Division regularly publishes a variety of materials of interest to the international marketer, and this data can be accessed at field offices in every major city in the country. Much of this data is also available on CD-ROM. One publication, *Overseas Business Reports,* offers basic marketing background information for almost every market throughout the world. In addition to marketing and economic data, the reports include information on taxation and trade regulations, copyright and trademark law, and channels of distribution. *Business America,* a weekly newsletter, is an excellent source of trade leads and lists of foreign governments interested in doing business with U.S. firms. Another series of documents focusing on foreign market opportunities, *Global Market Surveys,* provides in-depth reports on products and industries with export growth opportunities in foreign markets. *Foreign Economic Trend Reports* reviews current business conditions country by country, including statistics on GNP, wage and price indices, foreign trade levels, unemployment rates, and construction starts. Also, the Department of Commerce keeps firms abreast of developments in Washington that might impact international business undertakings. Many other governmental agencies and departments—including the State Department, the Federal Trade Commission, the Department of Labor, the Bureau of the Census, the Department of the Treasury, and the Department of Agriculture—also publish information pertaining to international trade.

Foreign Embassies and Consulates As Subhash Jain notes, virtually all foreign nations have embassies in Washington, D.C., as well as United Nations mission offices in New York City. In addition, foreign governments may have one or more consulate offices in the United States. Jain writes:

> For example, the government of Brazil maintains consulate offices in New York, Chicago, Dallas, San Francisco, and Los Angeles in addition to their embassy in Washington, D.C. Usually an embassy has a commercial attaché who may be a good source of secondary information on a country. The consulate and U.N. mission usually have basic information on their country to offer the researcher. (Jain 1984, 562)

Foreign Trade Offices A number of foreign governments also maintain foreign trade offices (FTOs) in the United States—mostly in Washington, D.C., and New York. The function of these FTOs is to assist U.S. exporters and importers, the end goal being the stimulation of trade. These offices can provide the international marketer with brochures, booklets, and newsletters outlining various aspects of doing business in their countries. One example of such an FTO is the Japan External Trade Organization, which has available over 100 complimentary publications and films on doing business in Japan (Ferraro 1990, 132).

Industry and Trade Associations Industry associations are generally formed to represent entire industry segments. For example, the industry associations for the automotive and pharmaceutical industries gather both national and international data from their members and publish them in

aggregate form. A variety of business groups, such as chambers of commerce, the Conference Board, and the National Foreign Trade Council, also can provide marketers with counsel and information on local markets.

Banks and Other Service Institutions Major U.S. banks that operate multinationally (such as BankAmerica Corp. and CitiCorp—now known as CitiGroup), foreign banks with branches in the United States (such as Sanwa), and national banks located abroad (such as the Bank of England) provide assistance to their client companies engaging in marketing efforts around the globe. Marketers may find these banks' annual reports or yearbooks to be useful sources of information. In addition, many of these banks maintain libraries accessible to both current and potential customers. These banks may also provide a variety of services, including suggesting overseas markets for goods and services, locating potential foreign investors, contacting distributors, and obtaining information on foreign exchange regulations. In addition to banks, the international marketer can turn to accounting firms and transportation companies (such as major airlines and freight services) for information on business practices in foreign markets as well as basic trade data.

Universities Universities in general and schools of business administration in particular, both in the United States and abroad, are excellent sources of information. For example, Harvard has an abundance of case studies on almost every country worldwide. The University of Texas has published close to 100 case studies on foreign markets. Similarly, libraries at the University of Washington, Pennsylvania State University, and the University of Southern California all house relevant bodies of information.

Research Firms Marketing research firms can provide relevant secondary data—however, at a cost to users. While they are a more expensive source of secondary data than published (e.g., government) information, such services are still much less expensive for a company than if it were to gather its own primary data. Some market research firms simply retrieve previously printed materials requested by clients, while others also conduct primary data. Not unlike U.S. advertising agencies, U.S. research firms have followed in the footsteps of their clients and turned to foreign soil for growth. These organizations are devoted to the gathering and selling of marketplace information, specializing in data related to consumer behavior so difficult to obtain from other sources. Table 8.1 lists the top 10 U.S. research companies, presenting U.S. revenues along with non-U.S. revenues. In 2001, AC Nielsen became part of VNU, pushing it into the number one position. With headquarters in both the United States and the Netherlands, operations in more than 100 countries across six continents, and nearly 40,000 employees, VNU is the world leader in marketing information, media measurement and information, business media, and directories. Among just a few of the services VNU provides to its clients are retail measurement (including data on product movement, market share, distribution, and price), consumer panels (used to explore consumer behavior and identify new markets), customized research (to support decision making at each state of product marketing—from the identification of market

TABLE 8.1 Top 10 U.S. Research Firms, 2001 (U.S. million $)

Rank	Organization	U.S. Revenues	Worldwide Revenues	Non-U.S. Revenues
1.	VNU Inc.	1,300.0	2,400.0	1,100.0
2.	IMS Health Inc.	469.0	1,171.0	702.0
3.	Information Resources Inc.	420.3	555.9	135.6
4.	The Kantar Group	299.1	962.3	663.2
5.	Westat Inc.	285.8	285.8	—
6.	Arbitron Inc.	219.6	227.5	7.9
7.	NOP World US	206.6	224.1	17.5
8.	NFO WorldGroup	163.0	452.9	289.9
9.	Market Facts Inc.	156.2	189.7	35.5
10.	Taylor Nelson Sofres USA	150.5	166.9	16.4

Source: American Marketing Assoc., 2003 *(www.data.ama.org/publications/honomichl/display2.php)*

opportunities, the development of product concepts, and product positioning to sales forecasting, advertising testing, and tracking), and test marketing (including live/in-store test marketing of new and existing products as well as simulated test marketing).

A complete list of international market research firms can be found in the U.S. Department of Commerce's *Trade List;* the Market Research Organization's *World Book;* the American Marketing Association's *International Directory of Marketing Research Houses and Services* (also known as the Green Book), and *Bradford's Directory of Marketing Research Agencies and Management Consultants in the United States and the World.*

Consulting Firms, International Advertising Agencies, and Other Sources A number of consulting firms gather, organize, and make available information of value to international marketers. For example, Business International (BI), headquartered in New York City, is an excellent source of information on GNP, population, foreign trade, and production for over 130 countries. Weekly newsletters also highlight the experiences and challenges firms face in various international markets. In addition, BI conducts regular and ad hoc studies dealing with international marketing issues. Another service that can prove useful in evaluating international market environments is the Economist Intelligence Unit (EIU), which is based in London and associated with *The Economist* magazine. EIU reports on economic and political trends for over 150 countries around the globe, publishes a large number of special reports, and also conducts customized market studies for international firms.

Major international advertising agencies, through their overseas offices, can provide clients with guidance in marketing goods in foreign countries. International advertising agencies may be affiliated with local research firms or may offer clients the services of their in-house research departments. Backer Spielvogel Bates Worldwide invested more than $2 million in Global Scan, a program that sponsors annual surveys of consumers in 17 different countries. Via a scale that measures 250 attitudes, including 130 that are specific to an individual country and 120 that

cross-cultural boundaries, Global Scan identified five global psychographic types: strivers, achievers, pressureds, adapters, and traditionals. Such research can often reveal cultural differences that can either make or break an advertising campaign (Purto 1990). In a nod to globalization and the purchasing power of kids, DDB Worldwide expanded its U.S.-based youth-market-research consultancy into 16 countries. Kid Think provides counsel on product packaging, strategic planning, new product development, and licensing for youth-oriented clients. Other agencies which have youth-related market research consultancies are Grey Advertising's G Whiz, WWP Group's Geppetto Group, Leo Burnett Co.'s Kid Leo, and Saatchi & Saatchi's Kid Connection. The race to establish youth units is a reaction to clients' needs. Marketers have begun to flood shelves with kid-friendly versions of products—everything from soap to shampoo to soup (Petrecca 1999). Even advertisers are investing in the market research business. Unilever, the Anglo-Dutch marketer, has taken a 40 percent stake in BrainJuicer, a U.K.-based automated market research business. Unilever will provide funding plus expertise to help grow the firm, and create a large global consumer research panel. BrainJuicer claims to combine the deep insight of focus groups with the quantitative breadth of traditional surveys, but in shorter times and at less cost than most other conventional methods. Current clients include Nike, Renault, Allied Domecq, and Publicis Group (Bidlake 2003).

Finally, the international marketer should also investigate a number of trade journals and other periodicals as potential sources of secondary information. For example, *Business Week, Business International, The Economist,* the *New York Times,* and *Advertising Age* often publish special reports on specific countries or regions as well as data reflecting global marketing trends.

International Sources of Secondary Data

Simply because secondary data is not available domestically does not mean it may not be available abroad. Various international organizations as well as regional bodies (such as the European Union) and even the governments of individual countries can be tapped for international marketing data.

International Organizations International organizations such as the United Nations, the World Bank, the International Monetary Fund (IMF), and the Organization for Economic Cooperation and Development (OECD) all provide extensive data of value to the international marketer.

The UN—and its affiliated organizations—is the official source of many international statistics. UN data is carefully compiled and generally acknowledged to be quite accurate. It should be noted, though, that UN statistics are not always completely reliable because the UN must occasionally depend on unsubstantiated statistics provided by member countries. The UN publishes the *Statistical Yearbook of the United Nations* (which provides demographic and economic development data plus political, geographic, and cultural information on over 250 countries). A monthly statistical supplement to the *Yearbook* is available as well. The UN also publishes a variety of regional reviews, including the *Economic Survey of Europe* and the *Economic Survey of Asia*

and the Far East (which cover developments on topics such as trade and balance of payments). The *World Trade Annual* provides data from the principle trading nations by commodity and country. The UN Industrial Development Organization's (UNIDO) primary objectives are the advancement of developing nations and the fostering of industrial cooperation between regions and countries of the world. As part of these efforts, UNIDO publishes a variety of documents useful to the international marketer. UNIDO's annual report, *Industry and Development: Global Report*, presents forecasts of industry output for most countries and regions of the world.

The World Bank's *World Tables* summarizes for international marketers valuable data on living patterns for 124 countries, including such indicators as radio, television, telephone, and auto ownership per thousand households. The *World Bank Atlas*, published annually, presents information on population size, growth trends, GNP, life expectancy, infant mortality, and education levels for various countries. The World Bank is also an excellent source for information on production, industrialization, trade, energy usage, and social and military spending.

The IMF publishes *International Financial Statistics* on a monthly basis to provide information on the financial status of over 100 countries. In addition, the IMF makes available data on a variety of national economic indicators, such as GNP, industrial production, inflation rate, and money supply.

The OECD conducts studies on the economic performance of its member countries, publishing both quarterly and annual data. Two publications in particular will be of interest to those conducting business internationally: The *OECD Economic Outlook*, which provides statistics from a semiannual survey of trends in member nations, and The *OECD Economic Surveys*, which contains information on the economic standing of each member country.

International Marketing and Market Research Organizations A number of international organizations, including the International Advertising Association (IAA), the World Federation of Advertisers (WFA), the American Marketing Association (AMA), the American Academy of Advertising (AAA), and the European Society for Opinion and Marketing Research (ESOMAR), publish a wealth of marketing- and advertising-related information. Some also regularly undertake surveys—for example, the International Advertising Association conducts an annual survey of all international advertising agencies. Such organizations also organize conferences where delegates from around the globe present papers and exchange experiences (de Mooij and Keegan 1991). Conference proceedings also serve as valuable resources.

Regional Organizations The European Union is an excellent resource for statistics specific to European countries. Eurostat, the statistical office of the EU, publishes *Demographic Statistics*, which provides, as the name implies, basic demographic information on member countries. Euromonitor, headquartered in London, publishes two volumes on European markets as well as an additional volume on all other markets. An incredible amount of detailed information is available in these publications, from population, employment, production, trade, and economic data to statistics on consumption, housing, health, education, communications, and standard of living. With regard to standard-of-living data, Euromonitor provides information on comparative wages and earnings, consumer prices, comparative costs, consumer durables, household expenditures, and ownership of radios, TVs, and autos.

Foreign Governments The governments of the countries that the international marketer is planning to enter can be an important source of secondary information, although both the quantity and the quality of the data is likely to vary from one market to the next. Even if the requested information is not available on hand, governmental employees are generally able to direct the international marketer to the appropriate source. Unfortunately, much of the data available in foreign markets may be published only in the native language. Another drawback is that political bias may potentially skew the data.

The preceding provides just a brief overview of major sources of secondary data. Clearly, it is impractical to include a complete listing of all secondary sources available for all international markets. However, for an expanded discussion of the topic, see C. Samuel Craig and Susan P. Douglas's discussion of secondary data sources (Craig and Douglas 2000).

 Primary Data

Although secondary data is likely to reveal most basic demographic and economic information needed by international marketers in order to conduct business in a specific country, many marketing and advertising decisions require more specific kinds of information. As Philip Cateora and Susan Keaverney point out:

> Consumer buying behavior, attitudes about products or promotional messages, relevance of product attributes, product positioning and other manifestations of cultural and societal norms are usually product- or industry-specific and must be gathered by primary research. This information may be critical to sound tactical decisions and usually warrants the time, energy, creativity and expense required to collect it. (Cateora and Keaverney 1987, 47)

This statement highlights the major advantage of conducting primary research—the fact that the data collected is specific to the firm's needs.

The greatest disadvantage associated with primary data collection is that it can be quite expensive. The international researcher's golden rule should be to exhaust all secondary sources before doing primary research, and then to obtain only the data that is absolutely necessary (Peebles and Ryans 1984, 156). Research conducted abroad is generally a good deal more costly than comparable research conducted in the domestic market. For example, the cost of conducting a usage-and-attitude study with similar specifications was compared for a number of European countries. If the index average base equals 100, then Italy, for instance, would have a cost index of 136, France an index of 149, and Switzerland an index of 155 (Honomichl 1986, S.1). Even in developing markets, research tends to be expensive. This increased cost stems from a number

of factors, including limited availability of marketing research firms abroad and differences in the level of sophistication of such firms. For this reason the use of primary research in the international arena is a good deal less widespread than it should be, particularly in less industrialized markets. Yet it is precisely in these countries that management is likely to be less familiar with market conditions and more prone to making marketing errors. Dean Peebles and John Ryans provide the following advice:

> We recommend one particular criterion when considering the value of a research project: will the benefits obtained from the information be greater than the cost of conducting the research. In answering the question, the advertising manager must recognize both the short-term and long-term value of the information and its potential use across markets. (Peebles and Ryans 1984, 145)

As might be expected, larger companies are more likely to conduct primary research in foreign markets than smaller or even medium-sized firms.

Primary Research Methods

The manner in which primary data is collected is strongly influenced by culture. U.S. managers tend to prefer methods allowing them to collect large quantities of data that can then be manipulated statistically. Quantitative methods are generally the tool of choice. In fact, suggests Joseph T. Plummer, "American marketers are number crazy and need numbers or scores to make decisions" (Plummer 1986, 11). This is not to say qualitative techniques do not have a place in Western research. Focus-group and in-depth interviews are commonly employed in advertising investigations. The preoccupation with numbers is not nearly so prevalent in other countries. For example, Japanese-style market research depends to a greater extent on nonquantitative approaches, including both soft data (obtained from visits to dealers and other distribution channels members) and hard data (dealing with shipments, inventory levels, and retail sales). Indeed, many Japanese managers express disdain for large-scale consumer surveys and other scientific research tools so commonly employed in the West. Johny K. Johansson and Ikujiro Nonaka write: "As the head of Matsushita's videocassette recorder division once said: Why do Americans do so much marketing research? You can find out what you need by traveling around and visiting the retailers who carry your product" (Johansson and Nonaka 1987, 16).

Qualitative and quantitative research methods include observation, focus-group and in-depth interviews, experimental techniques, and surveys. Because each method has certain strengths and weaknesses when used in foreign markets, international marketers and advertisers are increasingly relying on triangulation studies. Here, two or more entirely different methods are employed to study the same research question. If similar results are obtained by the various techniques, the researcher can feel relatively confident that the findings are both valid and reliable.

Observation

Observational or ethnographic research can take a number of forms. Typically, an anthropologist or other trained observer is sent into the field to chart the hidden recesses of consumer behavior, or behaviors may be videotaped. Subjects may be either aware or unaware that they are being observed. The traditional view of observation as a data-collecting technique was that it was simply too cumbersome and snail-like in its pace to be of any real value. However, over the past decade, an increasing number of international marketers and advertisers have adopted this approach. For example, in the early 1990s, Nissan Motor Co. redesigned its Infiniti car after anthropologists helped it see that Japanese notions of luxury-as-simplicity were very different from Americans' yen for visible opulence. A few years later, Volkswagen's ad agency, Arnold Communications, used the approach to reposition the brand toward active users with its "Drivers wanted" campaign. These days, plenty of other companies are hiring anthropologists who are trained to observe without changing the outcome. Though often more expensive than traditional focus groups, such ethnographic research is quickly becoming a standard agency offering. As products mature and differences diminish, marketers are anxious to hook into subtle emotional dimensions that might give them an edge. The approach enables the marketer to know the individual consumer on an intimate basis. It is also useful in helping marketers figure out how different demographic and ethnic groups react to their products. Recently, for example, Best Western International paid 25 over-55 couples to tape themselves on cross-country journeys. Their goal was to learn how seniors decide when and where to stop for the night. The video tapes of the older couples on three-to-seven-day-long drives revealed that the hotel chain didn't need to boost its standard 10 percent senior discount. The tapes showed that seniors who talked the hotel clerk into a better deal didn't need the lower price to afford the room; they were after the thrill of the deal. Instead of attracting new customers, bigger discounts would simply allow the old customer to trade up to a fancier dinner down the street, doing absolutely nothing for Best Western. Indeed, Best Western captured such a wealth of customer behavior on tape that it delayed its marketing plan in order to weave the insights into its core strategy. "The process definitely opened out eyes," said Tom Dougherty, manager of programs, promotions, and partnerships for the Phoenix-based chain. "Unfortunately for seniors, that means the rooms won't be getting any cheaper" (Khermouch 2001).

Focus-Group Interviews and In-Depth Interviews

In focus-group interviews, some seven to ten members of the target audience are invited to discuss a specific topic related to the marketer's or advertiser's research question, typically in a home or laboratory setting. A focus-group moderator guides the discussion, which can last from two to four hours. Participants may be more willing to discuss certain issues in such a group setting than they would be in a one-on-one interview. While focus-group interviews

do not provide statistically significant data due to the small sample size, they help provide insights into underlying consumer motives and attitudes. Focus-group interviews are effective in studying everything from product development to advertising strategy and execution. For example, Unilever recently launched Persil Aloe Vera for sensitive skin in the United Kingdom. The spin-off of the $336 million Persil U.K. brand is positioned as a breakthrough in cleaning and skin care. The company is convinced the product is a winner, and this confidence is largely build on painstaking research and development. Initially, consumer focus groups identified "skin reassurance" as a key feature they wanted from laundry detergents. The sap of the aloe vera plant is well known for its soothing properties. Then dermatologists were employed, not just to test the product, but to design it. Part of the analysis involved patching together fragments of the top layer of skin taken from willing volunteers and testing its reaction to various ingredients commonly found in detergents. Investigations even included taking brain scans of test participants to analyze the effect on the brain when an itch was felt on the skin. The fruits of all this research hit the U.K. supermarket shelves in the fall of 2002. The J. Walter Thompson ad campaign featured an animated world in which a drop of aloe vera falls to earth and bursts to create a world in which plants grow clothes. Little naked people explore the world and the clothes, admiring the softness. Focus groups will again be employed to ascertain the new brand's chances for success in other European countries (Bidlake and Mussey, 2002).

In-depth interviews are basically unstructured means of collecting information from either individuals or small groups. They can be applied across a very wide range of areas and types of study including exploratory, broad market studies; diagnostic studies; creative development (advertising, packaging); and tactical research studies (Birn 2000). Both focus-group interviews and in-depth interviews, while still huge in the research arsenal, have a number of limitations. They tend to be time consuming and costly. Stronger personalities can wield undue influence and participants often won't admit in public—or may not even recognize—their behavior patterns and motivations. Also, there are significant cultural differences in the willingness of respondents to discuss their feelings openly. Because of this, a highly skilled interviewer or moderator capable of stimulating discussion is essential. Note, too, that neither focus-group sessions nor in-depth interviews are amenable to statistical analysis.

Experimental Techniques

On the topic of experimental techniques, Susan P. Douglas and C. Samuel Craig state:

> Experimental techniques are, at least in theory, potentially applicable to all cultural and socio-economic backgrounds. In practice, however, it is often difficult to design an experiment that is comparable or equivalent in all respects in every country or socio-cultural context. Experiments, particularly field experiments, typically incorporate certain elements of the specific socio-cultural context in which they are conducted. (Douglas and Craig 1983, 40)

Surveys

Surveys are employed where quantitative data are desired. Collection of primary data in foreign markets via survey methods presents a variety of challenges generally not encountered when conducting research in the domestic market. These include, but are not limited to, problems relating to data comparability, instrument design, sampling, data collection, and infrastructure limitations. Note Brian Toyne and Peter Walters: "At best, failure to recognize these problems results in findings that are of no value to the decision maker. At worst, it results in decisions that may prove extremely costly for the firm" (Toyne and Walters 1989).

Challenges Relating to Data Comparability The issue of comparability was discussed previously with regard to secondary data. However, it also plays a significant role in the collection of primary data. A researcher may examine a particular phenomenon in just a single market or undertake an investigation in a number of countries. For example, the research objective may be to explore the potential effectiveness of a specific advertising theme in Germany or to determine the feasibility of employing the same theme across the European Union. If cross-cultural research is being conducted, every effort must be made to ensure that the findings from different test markets can indeed be compared. The challenge of comparability increases with the number of markets under investigation. Even when the research program initially focuses only on a single country, similar research may be required for markets that the firm subsequently enters—again reinforcing the importance of comparability.

In order to achieve comparability, researchers engaging in cross-cultural investigations must deal with the external environmental factors of *functional equivalence* and *conceptual equivalence*. In addition, researchers must concern themselves with the internal measurement issue of *instrument equivalence* (which will be addressed in the next section). The researcher must be sensitive to functional equivalence, which refers to whether a concept, behavior, or product serves the same or a different function in the markets under consideration. For example, while refrigerators are used to store frozen foods in some countries and to chill water and soft drinks in others, in certain markets they serve as status symbols and are prominently displayed in the home—often in the living room rather than the kitchen. If similar products have different functions in different societies, their parameters cannot be used for comparative purposes (Choudhrey 1977, 18). Consider the example of hot milk-based chocolate drinks. While in the United States and United Kingdom, they are primarily considered an evening drink, best before going to sleep, in much of Latin America, a "chocolate caliente" is a morning drink. Functional equivalence is realized neither in the consumption time period nor in the purpose for use (waking/energizer versus sleep/relaxer) (Usunier 1996, 144).

A second consideration in cross-cultural research is conceptual equivalence. Explains Yusuf A. Choudhrey:

Sometimes concepts have totally different meanings in different cultures and are thus inappropriate for use on an international scale. This means that proper care has to be exercised to ensure that

the words used to elicit response carry similar meanings to individuals in different cultures. (Choudhrey 1977, 20)

For example, the word "family" has very different connotations in different parts of the world. In the United States it generally refers to the nuclear family consisting of mother, father, and children, whereas in other countries it could also include grandparents, aunts, uncles, cousins, and so on.

Instrument Design Challenges For purposes of comparative evaluation, the international researcher also must strive for instrument equivalence, which Choudhrey defines as "the necessity of an instrument that measures a phenomenon uniformly in different cultures. . . . Unfortunately, the most popular instrument for collecting consumer data, the survey questionnaire, is susceptible to considerable bias in cross cultural applications" (Choudhrey 1977, 21). Fortunately, however, instrument design is one element over which the researcher does have some control.

The issues of measurement, scaling, and wording are central to the design of the research instrument. Asking the right question—in the right way—is always a challenge in marketing research, whether conducted in domestic or foreign markets. In designing the survey instrument, the researcher must ensure that the questions are measuring the same thing in each market. Susan P. Douglas and C. Samuel Craig note that the "most significant problems in drawing up questions in multicountry research are likely to occur in relation to attitudinal, psychographic, and lifestyle data. Constructs such as aggressiveness, respect for authority or honor may not be relevant in all countries and cultures" (Douglas and Craig 1983, 176). W. Fred Van Raaij provides an excellent example of a totally inappropriate questionnaire statement designed to measure social responsibility in a foreign market: "'A good citizen is responsible for shoveling the sidewalk in front of his home.' This statement assumes private ownership of houses, one-family housing, and a climate with snow in winter, and is clearly not applicable in an African country" (Van Raaij 1977, 693). Here, social responsibility would need to be measured with a completely different statement or perhaps even a series of statements.

The appropriateness as well as the effectiveness of various scales and response categories is dependent on the market in which the research is to be conducted. The semantic differential is one type of scale that is widely believed to be pan-cultural. However, even here the international researcher must exercise caution. While the 5- or 7-point semantic differential scale is commonly employed in the United States to rate objects and other items, in some countries consumers are much more familiar with 10- or even 20-point scales, while in still others respondents are most comfortable with a 3-point scale. When confronted with a verbal 7-point scale ranging from "excellent" to "terrible," Westerners tend to start from the extreme positions and then work inward, whereas Japanese tend to take a neutral position and move outward, seldom reaching the extremes (Fields 1980, 52). Thus, the range of Japanese scores is generally much more limited than that of Westerners, making the use of such scales problematic. This seems to be a cultural phenomenon—Japanese tend to arrive slowly at a fixed position, carefully weighing all known facts and consequences before responding.

Response categories may need to be expanded or collapsed depending on the specific market. For instance, in a study that required the determination of marital classification in Gabon, the standard categories of "married," "single," "divorced," and "widowed" were used. The category of "concubine" was not included even though about 20 percent of the female respondents fell into this category. This is a typical case of applying Western classifications and assuming that they will be inclusive in other cultures (Mueller 1990, 194). On the other hand, some categories may need to be dropped. When asking third world customers where they purchase an item, it may be advisable to delete "supermarkets" as a possible response if a particular area is not blessed with this institution.

In an interesting situation, a category that was dropped from market research in South Africa was later reinstated. The South African Advertising Research Foundation (SAARF), an organization that is responsible for managing surveys covering newspapers, magazines, television, radio, and the Internet, reversed a decision to remove all reference to the race of the market research respondents. The original decision, which was made in an attempt to defuse accusations that market and media research was racist, led to a heated debate. Previously, race was included in survey questionnaires because it was seen as a fact of life, which surveys needed to reflect. However, explained Paul Haupt, SAARF chief executive:

> race is not essential for media planning or target marketing, so its presence is not only unnecessary but harmful. The basis of racial segmentation is inherently unsound as it accepts that all people in a specific population group are similar and that they differ from those in other groups, which is patently untrue.

The foundation argued that other demographics, such as age, gender, language, and education were adequate to achieve target marketing and media selection. But many people in the research industry were appalled by SAARF's decision. Erik du Plessis, managing director of Millward Brown Impact, noted the decision was a

> big step backward for market research. We will have no means to measure the progress of the black community. We will be reliant on anecdotal information about our largest community, which is the one growing in terms of wealth and consumer spending power.

Mr. Haupt concedes that the "removal of race might lead people to believe all problems have been resolved and inhibit the debate." He said, "We will return to the practice of asking respondents for the racial group to which they belong" (Koenderman 2002).

With regard to wording, the translation of a survey instrument into a foreign language can pose significant problems for the international researcher. While some questions are relatively easy to translate (for instance, those dealing with such demographic information as age, sex, or education), if the goal is to collect data regarding motivations and attitudes, the researcher must ensure that questions are understood by foreign respondents. Some questions simply cannot be translated into another language because the words do not exist to express precisely the same

thought (Cundiff and Hilger 1988, 245). The problem of survey instrument translation is compounded in multilingual societies—for example, 14 different languages are spoken in India. Here, the researcher may be tempted to use the official language (say, English or French), only to find that just a fraction of the population speaks that language (Terpstra 1988).

In order to minimize translation errors, many experts suggest that researchers employ the back-translation technique. Back-translation, as noted in Chapter 6, involves independent translators translating the questionnaire into the foreign language and then back into the original language and comparing the two versions for equivalence. Even when using the same language, care must be taken in transporting the survey from one country to the next. Translation difficulties were experienced in a questionnaire designed for the United Kingdom. A question aimed at business executives was to have read: "Should advertising practitioners be certified?" but instead was understood as: "Should advertising practitioners be confined to an insane asylum?" The British word "certificated" should have been employed because it is the equivalent of the American "certified" (Mueller 1990). It is generally advisable to pilot-test all survey instruments prior to undertaking the investigation, ideally with a subset of the population under investigation.

Problems with equivalence can be encountered in other areas of international research as well, including sampling, data collection procedures, and the analysis and interpretation of results.

Sampling Challenges After designing the survey instrument and translating it into the foreign language(s), the researcher must determine the appropriate respondents and the procedures best suited to selecting a sample from the population. Respondents selected for a survey may, in fact, vary significantly from one market to the next. For example, in examining purchase behavior of major household durables, researchers in the United States are likely to focus on women in their survey. In some foreign markets, however, men may be the primary decision makers. And in still others, several family members might be involved in the decision; thus, the focus would most appropriately be on the group rather than on an individual.

Sampling refers to the selection of a subset or group from a population that is representative of the entire population (Keegan 1984, 233). Most commonly employed sampling methods were developed for use in economically advanced markets, such as the United States, and as a result, these methods are not always transferable to other nations (Cundiff and Hilger 1988, 183). For example, in most Western countries researchers prefer to employ a *probability sample* because it allows an accurate prediction of the margin of error. Since the size of the population in a probability sample is known, data collected from the sample (if it is of adequate size) can be projected to the entire population. In a *random probability sample* each unit selected has an equal chance of being included in the sample. In a *nonrandom probability sample* each unit has a known probability of being selected.

In any probability sampling the researcher must have access to reliable information that can be used as sampling frames—such as census data, census maps, electoral lists, telephone listings, and mailing lists. While such data are readily available in industrialized countries, they may simply not exist in many poorer markets—or if available, they may be sorely out of date.

For example, as Philip Cateora and Susan Keaverney point out, "Neither Cairo nor Tehran have telephone books. Saudi Arabia has neither street names nor house numbers. Street maps are frequently unavailable in parts of South America" (Cateora and Keaverney 1987, 47). A lack of infrastructure may further complicate sampling procedures. In many third world countries only a small percentage of the population may own telephones, and it may be nearly impossible to access rural areas if adequate transportation is not available. In short, it is often extremely difficult to obtain a proper random sample in less developed markets. The researcher's only viable alternative may be to employ nonprobability sampling procedures, such as convenience sampling or judgment sampling. A convenience sample involves selecting any respondent who happens to be readily available. A judgment sample involves selecting respondents based on the assumption that certain individuals are likely to be better informed than others or possess expert knowledge in a given area. For example, the researcher may focus on village elders or local authority figures (Douglas and Craig 1983, 212). Such nonprobability samples generally do not lend themselves to inferential statistical analysis, and as a result, the data collected cannot be assumed to be representative of the entire population.

The researcher must also consider whether the same sampling procedures should be employed across markets. Sampling procedures may vary in their reliability from one country to the next; thus, employing identical procedures is no guarantee of comparability. Instead, it may be preferable to utilize different methods that have equivalent levels of accuracy or reliability.

Data Collection Challenges A variety of data collection methods can be employed, including mail, telephone, and in-person surveys. Each has its advantages and disadvantages, and the method ultimately employed depends largely on individual market conditions. The international marketing researcher must also consider the various forms of respondent bias, which may be related to the specific survey method selected, the country under investigation, the topic being explored—or a combination of these variables. One form is *nonresponse bias,* which refers to the fact that in some cultures individuals are more reluctant to answer questions posed by a stranger. While Americans are quite familiar with market surveys and generally willing to answer even the most personal questions, this is not the case in every country. In some markets respondents may be unwilling to share information because they suspect that the interviewers might, in fact, be government agents or perhaps tax auditors. Tax evasion is a way of life in some countries, and respondents are hesitant to answer any questions related to income or expenditures. The international researcher must also recognize that it may be extremely difficult to obtain responses from some segments of the population. For example, in Muslim countries women aren't allowed to speak with male interviewers, and the number of female interviewers is still quite limited because this is not considered an appropriate career choice for women.

Willingness to respond to questions dealing with certain topics is likely to vary from country to country as well. Some topics in certain cultures are simply perceived as more sensitive than others. For example, the subject of sex is considered taboo in India. Even in the United States many individuals are wary of responding to questions about their income. Therefore, potential areas of *topic bias* must be identified during the design of the research instrument. The interna-

tional researcher is also likely to face some form of *social bias*. For instance, social acquiescence bias refers to the increased tendency for respondents in some markets—particularly in Asian countries where courtesy is highly valued—to provide the response they believe will most please the interviewer, rather than stating their true beliefs. In societies with a collective orientation, respondents are not used to making individual decisions; therefore, questions demanding individual answers may be problematic. Likewise, respondents may attempt to give an answer they think reflects popular opinion so as not to appear to deviate from the norm. This social desirability bias is a particular danger in group interviews, where a participant might look to others for the "appropriate" response.

When researchers from one country conduct an investigation in another country, they also must deal with what is termed *researcher bias*—the tendency to observe phenomena or behavior in the host country and define it in home-country terms (Cateora and Keaverney 1987, 47). One way to counter researcher bias is to incorporate the perspectives of researchers from a variety of different cultural backgrounds.

Finally, there is the danger of *researcher–respondent bias,* which refers to the interaction that may take place between the interviewer and respondent, thus tainting the survey results. For example, sexual bias may result in a reluctance to grant interviews. In many traditional countries, housewives may be reluctant to provide information to male interviewers. Ethnic bias may also exist. A Chinese person, for instance, may refuse to be interviewed by a Malay. Often, ethnic membership between interviewer and interviewee must be shared for the interview to take place. If the interviewer is perceived to be a foreigner, there may be an increased level of mistrust, further contaminating the data collected.

Mail surveys are quite popular in industrialized markets for a number of reasons. First, the cost of administering mail surveys tends to be relatively low on a per-questionnaire basis. Respondents may also be more willing to respond to sensitive questions via a mail survey, and there is no potential for researcher–respondent bias. On the downside, nonresponse may be higher than with other survey methods, which can bias the results of the investigation. Also, all control over responses to the survey instrument is lost in mail surveys. For instance, the respondent may fail to answer some questions and respond incorrectly to others. The use of a mail survey may be inappropriate in many developing markets due to a lack of available mailing lists or poor mail service. Surprisingly, even some developed markets—such as Italy—are notorious for their unreliable mail delivery. In addition, many developing countries are characterized by high levels of illiteracy (up to 50 percent in some Asian and African markets); clearly, where illiteracy prevails, written questionnaires are of little use.

Much like mail surveys, costs per respondent are relatively low for telephone surveys—at least in developed markets. Telephone surveys are an extremely fast means of obtaining necessary data, and nonresponse rates tend to be low. A major disadvantage associated with telephone surveys is that the interview itself cannot take too long, and questions cannot be overly complicated. In addition, respondents may be rather reluctant to answer certain types of questions over the telephone. Researcher–respondent bias can also come into play with telephone surveys. Even in economically advanced markets, the researcher must exercise caution when attempting

to employ telephone surveys. For instance, Germany's laws are such that, if followed to the letter, telephone interviews would not be permitted unless the interviewee had previously agreed to be interviewed. This would, in effect, require two interview attempts—one to gain permission and one to conduct the interview. In addition, telephone numbers are not a fixed length, making random-digit dialing almost impossible. Developing countries pose a number of additional challenges. If levels of telephone ownership are low, as they are in many less developed markets, other survey methods may be more appropriate, unless the researcher is limiting data collection to urban areas. Telephone numbers may be difficult to access given that telephone books are nonexistent in some third world markets, which is the case, for example, in Cairo and Tehran. Further, telephone costs tend to be higher in many developing countries, making this a rather expensive means of obtaining data.

With in-person interviews, nonresponse rates are particularly low. Given data and infrastructure limitations, this approach may be the most viable means of data collection in poorer markets. Yet even this method is not without its disadvantages. With a largely rural population in many developing countries, reaching potential respondents becomes a major challenge. Roads are likely to be poor, and reliable public transportation may simply not be available. In addition, in-person interviews are the most expensive method of administering a questionnaire to a sample population in any market. Finally, interviewer bias is a very real problem.

In much the same way that sampling procedures vary from one country to the next in terms of comparability, so, too, do data collection procedures. For example, in one country, telephone surveys may be known to offer a certain level of reliability, while in another market, mail surveys offer the equivalent level of reliability. In collecting data, international researchers must be sensitive to such cross-cultural variations because they directly impact the comparability of the research results.

Infrastructure Limitations Skilled marketing and advertising researchers can be found in primary overseas markets as well as a number of developing markets (Peebles and Ryans 1984, 144). However, the researcher should be aware that obtaining facilities, field staff, and other resources will probably be a significantly greater challenge in third world countries. Not only must these individuals be well trained in the area of marketing research, they should be familiar with the local culture and conversant in the local language(s). In addition, they should recognize that infrastructure limitations pose a major stumbling block in many international investigations. As noted above, mail surveys are not feasible without reliable postal service. Similarly, telephone surveys are not possible if ownership of telephones is limited. Finally, undertaking research abroad becomes a good deal more difficult without adequate roads and transportation systems.

Research Relating to Message Design and Placement

Message research can help marketers to avoid promotional blunders in the international arena. For example, research allows the marketer to determine whether creative strategies

should vary by country or whether a single strategy can be adopted for all markets in which the firm plans to operate (the issue of standardization versus specialization was addressed in detail in Chapters 5 and 6). Message research must be conducted in each market, as findings do not necessarily cross borders. Just because a particular advertisement tests well in Austria does not ensure that it will be equally successful in Germany or Switzerland.

Some of the same tools employed in domestic markets are also used in international advertising research. Life-style data is of particular value to marketers, yet it can be exceptionally difficult to access, especially in developing markets. The researcher should begin by exploring secondary data—the anthropological literature is ripe with detailed studies of life-style patterns and cultural values in a large number of countries. In order to select concepts and position brands, international marketers may find it necessary to conduct life-style research to determine which patterns are similar across markets. For example, Turner Broadcasting's Cartoon Network launched a major children's life-style survey in Asia called New GenerAsians. The Cartoon Network commission AC Nielsen to survey 7,500 children aged 7–18 in 29 cities across 14 countries (*Advertising Age* 2000). The survey was conducted via face-to-face interviews. According to the data collected, kids in the region have significant influence on their parents when it comes to buying home computers (40 percent), toothpaste (30 percent), breakfast cereals (43 percent), fruit juice (60 percent), and cookies (48 percent). Other results show that Cola-Cola is the favorite drink and McDonald's is the favorite restaurant. Gameboy is the favorite game, followed by Nintendo. The "latest things" are body piercing (Australia), computing (China), electronic games (Hong Kong), jeans (India), stretch shorts (Indonesia), and electronic games and yo-yos (Japan). Regarding media, television ranked as a particularly popular pastime, with 64 percent of Asian kids listing it as one of their three favorite activities, above playing sports or playing with friends in most countries. Such insights allow advertisers to tailor to their Asian youth.

If advertisers wish to know whether foreign consumers understand the basic selling idea or product benefit highlighted and whether the message elicits the desired response, they may employ concept testing. The use of concept testing in international advertising research is growing rapidly because, although it employs qualitative methods such as focus group discussions or in-depth interviews, it can provide considerable insights quickly and relatively cheaply (Peebles and Ryans 1984, 144). For example, a U.S. manufacturer of dishwashers introduced its product to the Swiss market using the same product benefit employed in the United States: convenience. The firm did not research the effectiveness of the convenience appeal and assumed (incorrectly) that the Swiss consumer would respond much as U.S. consumers had. What the firm did not realize was that Swiss homemakers are much more involved in their role than their U.S. counterparts. Swiss homemakers rejected the idea of being replaced with a machine, and consequently, sales were dismal. Later, in-depth interviews revealed the source of the problem, and the product was successfully repositioned in terms of hygiene. The Swiss apparently place great value on cleanliness, and responded favorably to a "kills bacteria and germs" appeal (Douglas and Craig 1983, 13). Ideally, concept testing should take place in the early stages of creative development. The logic behind this approach, explains Joseph Plummer, is that

"if the basic selling idea has little relevance or appeal in a significant number of the markets, there is no value . . . to proceeding further by testing executions" (Plummer 1986, 15).

Once there is agreement on the strategy, the international marketer must determine whether the message execution will be appropriate. Pretest research focuses on the potential effectiveness of an advertising execution prior to its full-scale use in a market or markets. For example, a number of years ago, Colgate-Palmolive wanted to relaunch Alert shampoo throughout Latin America. The antidandruff shampoo had been reformulated to deliver a better fragrance with a creamier, thicker lather. Initial research revealed a dichotomy in the target audience's attitudes toward dandruff. While the prospects—younger men and women—were quite interested in impressing the opposite sex, they perceived dandruff as little more than a minor annoyance that could be easily treated. Therefore, the agency team developed a strategy that emphasized how "new Alert helps you look and feel your best because your hair is healthy, shiny *and* dandruff free." The execution of this strategy was problematic: how to deliver the message without making the dandruff problem too serious and how to handle the sex appeal angle so as not to offend specific cultural mores. The pretest research design used a test-and-control methodology—the test cell being the newly designed spot for Alert ("Rapunzel") and the control cell being the former commercial. The test employed both open-ended and closed questions, along with a series of questions that asked respondents for their impression of what type of person might use Alert. These questions were included to help determine whether the spot was portraying users as more fashionable, younger, and stylish. Reports Joseph Plummer: "The research study was conducted in both Mexico and Venezuela and results from the two countries were remarkably similar. Rapunzel performed well in each test, delivering the key strategic message in a relevant, meaningful and refreshing way" (Plummer 1986, 11).

It should be noted that many creatives are critical of pretesting, suggesting that it serves merely to kill creativity. General Motors is studying whether to revamp its ad-pretesting process. Creatives at two of GMC's agencies said the process hamstrings their executions. Defending pretesting, John Middlebrook, vice president and general manager of GM's vehicle brand marketing and advertising, said that the first custom-designed system is "just one gate we go through in advertising development." Consumers are shown storyboards, which he said "keeps you from doing bad stuff. You have to be very careful how you use it. It's more of a disaster check." Apparently pretesting is a mixed bag among other automakers. Ford does some pretesting of ads to ensure commercials meet objectives, but Volkswagen of America doesn't pretest ads. "If we want to say who we are, we need to be risky," said Frank Maguire, vice president of sales and marketing at VW. He admitted sometimes the executions don't work, but on the other hand, the marketer wouldn't have produced some popular well-recalled ads. Clearly, pretesting isn't always the answer (Halliday 2001, 41).

Focus groups and in-depth interviews are commonly employed techniques in pretest research. Posttest research, on the other hand, is employed to determine whether the advertisement or campaign has achieved its objective—whether that be to build awareness, convey knowledge, generate liking, or create preference for the brand in each market. Not only is such

research necessary in determining the success or failure of a campaign, but insights garnered through posttesting can suggest how the message might be modified or adapted in the future. While focus-group interviews may be employed here as well, telephone and mail surveys are more commonly conducted to measure recognition and recall as well as changes in attitude ascribed to the advertising.

International advertisers are increasingly employing ad-tracking studies—the continual monitoring of brand awareness, image, trials, and usage trends. Not long ago, 7 UP introduced a new campaign sporting the tagline "Make 7 UP Yours." The primary objective of the campaign included differentiating 7 UP from other beverages, especially lemon-lime carbonated soft drinks, and re-establishing consumer equity in 7 UP as a refreshing, fun, desirable brand to motivate people to buy more. The campaign featured actor/comedian Orlando Jones as a well-meaning, yet hapless new marketer of the venerable brand. Soon after the Make 7 UP Yours advertising began, it was obvious the campaign was a "home run." The marketer began receiving thousands of phone calls and e-mails from teenagers and young adults, all wanting to know where they could buy the T-shirt Orlando Jones wore in the popular 30-second commercial. As the new 7 UP marketer, Jones has great ideas, but invariably each one misfires when he tries to implement them. In the T-shirt commercial, Jones walks down a busy city street smugly touting the new 7 UP tagline, which he has split to read "Make 7" on the front and "UP Yours" on the back. Research International provided ongoing quantitative research results on brand awareness, advertising awareness, and brand usage, utilizing its 7 UP tracking study. To illustrate the power of the Make 7 UP Yours campaign, survey results revealed a 40 percent increase in 7 UP awareness and a 142 percent increase in unaided brand awareness with 12–24-year-olds—the primary target audience. For the year, 7 UP volume was up twice the carbonated soft drink category and outpaced its lemon-lime competitors in volume and market share gains (*PR Newswire* 2000). It should be noted that different conditions in different markets make comparison of tracking study results difficult. These conditions include: (1) the size of advertising expenditures, (2) the nature of the brands, (3) the differences in advertising styles and cultures, (4) media differences in advertising practice, and (5) differences in legal restrictions (De Mooij and Keegan 1991).

With regard to message placement, marketers will require information relating to the availability of media for commercial purposes as well as data relating to advertising readership, listenership, and viewership and audience characteristics. The individual media in established markets are capable of providing such information to the marketer. This is increasingly true of the media in developing markets as well. In addition, media-generated research—such as audience profiles, product perception surveys, and brand preference or awareness studies—may be available without cost from various foreign print and broadcast media. A number of general resources are likely to be of value to the international marketer, including the *World Radio and Television Handbook*, the *Media Guide International for Business and Professional Publications and Newspapers*, and Euromonitor's *European and International Marketing Data*. The number of quality international media placement services is also on the increase.

Technological Advances and Research

C. Samuel Craig and Susan Douglas (2001) note that as the Internet evolves, it offers the potential to dramatically change the way in which much international marketing research is conducted, both in providing ready access to secondary data, and in providing a new means of collecting primary data. Rather than visiting a traditional library, marketers have virtually instant access to data from both traditional sources as well as sources that are only available on the Internet. Primary data can also be collected via the Internet, either by tracking visitors to a Web site, or through administering electronic questionnaires over the Net. To the extent that Web sites are increasingly likely to be accessed by users worldwide, information on an international sample can be gathered. Behavior at the site can be tracked, revealing interest relating to the products and services or information offered, as well as response to promotional materials or offers.

The Internet can also be used to collect primary date in a more systematic fashion. Subject to the availability of suitable Internet sampling frames, questionnaires can be administered directly over the Internet. Questionnaires can be sent via e-mail to respondents and responses are returned via e-mail. Birn (2000) highlights both the advantages and disadvantages of using the Internet to conduct research. On the plus side, responses tend to be objective as respondents are typing in their own feedback; the use of the Internet is unintrusive, because respondents typically complete surveys at their own pace; responses tend to be speedy; there are no international boundaries and so questionnaires can be completed as easily on the opposite site of the world as at a more local address; and, because data is collected in a predefined electronic format, there is no need to re-enter responses manually, making for considerable cost savings. Indeed, it is estimated that data can be gathered online at a cost of 25–50 cents per completed survey, compared to $2–$5 for mail and $6–$10 by telephone (Agrawal 1999). On the downside, currently the target audience is still rather narrow—the vast majority of users are based in the United States, and the system is biased toward males aged 25–35 and largely the more affluent individuals within this group, although the balance is changing and there are an increasing number of female users (over 30 percent, according to some estimates). Other problems include identifying Internet users (e-mail addresses alone give little indication as to the type of person using e-mail) and technical restrictions (some users may be using high-speed modems over a digital telephone network while others may have something far more basic).

As Craig and Douglas (2001) note, as the use of the Internet becomes more commonplace, e-mail surveys will begin to replace mail and phone surveys. For example, Havas, owned by Euro RSCG Worldwide, recently conducted a series of e-surveys among youth aged 18–29 throughout the world. The survey revealed a heightened sense of insecurity worldwide, sparked off by the economic crisis, war in the Middle East, and the general fall-out after September 11. Top global trends identified by the agency's STAR (Strategic Trendspotting and Research) team include: anxiety avoidance (anxious to ignore the harsh realities of job insecurity and an increasingly tense international scenario, consumers will focus on the here and now),

pursuit of safety (with consumers willing to spend money to feel safe, there will be a greater emphasis on defensive and preventative products), family focus (with the backlash against artificial, high-tech environments, consumers think companies owned and managed by families are more likely to make products they can trust), and emphasis on the home (home has gained new meaning, whether it is interest in household comfort, home schooling, cooking, or creating personal spaces) (Qassim 2002).

Control of International Research

There are three major approaches to organizing international marketing and advertising research: (1) centralized control, (2) decentralized control, and (3) coordinated control. Each has its advantages as well as disadvantages. The approach ultimately adopted is largely influenced by the overall manner in which the marketer's organization is structured, as well as by the size of the firm's international operations in general and specific markets.

Where a centralized mode of control is employed, headquarters is responsible for all aspects of the investigation to be conducted in each market. This includes determining data sources, outlining the research design and sampling procedures, and specifying the data analysis to be performed. Fieldwork may be undertaken by either headquarters staff or an outside organization. One of the major benefits of the centralized approach is that it ensures maximum comparability of studies conducted across a number of markets. It is also a good deal less expensive to coordinate research design and data processing and analysis in the home office, particularly if the firm is doing research on a regular basis. In addition, it is an excellent way for a firm to gain familiarity with a particular market. The primary drawback of this approach is that local conditions may not be taken into consideration. Too often, headquarters will prefer a uniform research design that may not be sensitive to host country differences. Also, headquarters staff may be too limited in size or lack the necessary skills in the areas of marketing and advertising research to conduct multicountry investigations.

Where research efforts are decentralized, headquarters establishes the research objectives but assigns supervision of the research program to local personnel. Local units may then opt to hire domestic research firms to assist in the design and implementation of the investigation. Data collection and analysis are handled in the host market, and upon completion of the study, a representative from the research firm or local management presents a report to corporate headquarters. This is often the mode of choice when a firm is completely unfamiliar with a particular country or is undertaking a specialized or one-time-only investigation. It may also be employed in cases where the volume of business in a particular market is limited and does not warrant headquarters' full attention. The major advantage of this approach is that researchers can adapt to differences in the local culture and infrastructure. In addition, local management may be more likely to implement changes based on research in which they were involved. The use of an outside research firm may also provide an added degree of objectivity, which is often

of great importance to management. The potential danger associated with a decentralized approach is that the research design and data collection techniques may not be comparable with efforts undertaken in other markets, thus limiting the usefulness of the findings.

With a coordinated approach headquarters maintains its involvement in defining the research objectives but turns over the coordination of the research efforts in different countries to either an international research agency or the corporation's regional headquarters. The research agency or regional headquarters generally involves, to varying degrees, both headquarters and staff in the local operating units in the research endeavor. As a result, local operating units may be less likely to object to plans based on such research. The coordinated approach increases, but does not guarantee, the comparability of research results between markets, particularly if modifications are incorporated based on local input.

Summary

As companies increase their involvement in foreign markets, they recognize the importance of conducting international marketing and advertising research. This process involves defining the research problem, identifying information sources, collecting data, and analyzing and reporting the data. The two means of obtaining marketing information are collecting secondary data and conducting primary research. Secondary data is quick and inexpensive to obtain, so almost all international research begins with the collection of previously compiled data. However, as the extent of a firm's international involvement increases, so does its recognition of the importance of primary research. While secondary data can provide the marketer with a wealth of information, only primary data can truly address the marketer's more specific questions. Data collection methods include observation, focus-group interviews, in-depth interviews, and surveys—telephone, mail, and in-person. Firms must also recognize that conducting research in the international setting differs from that in domestic settings, and must decide on a centralized, decentralized, or coordinated approach to research efforts. A sincere commitment by management to conduct both secondary and primary research in each of the foreign markets in which their firm operates is sure to reduce the potential for marketing blunders. We now turn our attention to regulatory considerations in the international arena.

References

Advertising Age. 2000. Cartoon network to launch largest Asian kids survey: taps AC Nielsen. 5 January. <www.adageglobal.com/cgi-bin/daily.pl?daily_id=2808&post_date=2002 –01–05>

Agrawal, D. 1999. Strategy and market research on the Internet/Web. Microsoft Corporation, Redmond, Washington. Mimeo.

American Marketing Association. 2003. Top 10 U.S. research firms. Data.ama.org/publications/honomichl/display2.php.

Bartos, Rena. 1989. November. International demographic data? Incomparable! *Marketing and Research Today* 17: 205–12.

Bidlake, Suzanne. 2003. Unilever buys into research agency. 3 February. <www.adageglobal.com/cgi-bin/daily.pl?daily_id=9130&post_date=2003–02–03>

Bidlake, Suzanne and Dagmar Mussey. 2002. Unilever claims innovation with aloe vera sensitive detergent. 6 May. <www.adageglobal.com/cgi-bin/daily.pl?daily_id=7502&post_date=2002–05–06>

Birn, Robin. 2000. *The handbook of international market research techniques.* London: Kogan Page.

Cateora, Philip R., and John M. Hess. 1979. *International marketing.* Homewood, Ill.: Irwin.

Cateora, Philip R., and Susan M. Keaverney. 1987. *Marketing: An international perspective.* Homewood, Ill.: Irwin.

Choudhrey, Yusuf A. 1977. Pitfalls in international marketing research: Are you speaking French like a Spanish cow? *Akron Business and Economic Review* 17(4) (Winter): 18–28.

Craig, C. Samuel, and Susan P. Douglas. 2000. *International marketing research.* Chichester, Eng.: John Wiley & Sons.

———. 2001. Conducting international marketing research in the twenty-first century. *International Marketing Review* 18: 80–90.

Cundiff, Edward, and Marye Tharpe Hilger. 1988. *Marketing in the international environment.* Englewood Cliffs, N.J.: Prentice Hall.

De Mooij, Marieke, and Warren Keegan. 1991. *Advertising worldwide.* New York: Prentice Hall.

Douglas, Susan P., and C. Samuel Craig. 1983. *International marketing research.* Englewood Cliffs, N.J.: Prentice Hall.

ESOMAR. 1996. ESOMAR 1995 Pricing study. Amsterdam.

Ferraro, Gary P. 1990. *The cultural dimension of international business* Englewood Cliffs, N.J.: Prentice Hall.

Fields, George. 1980. Advertising strategy in Japan. *Dentsu's Japan Marketing/Advertising* (Fall/Winter): 52–56.

Halliday, Jean. 2001. GM rethinks the merits of ad pre-testing. *Advertising Age,* 23 April, 41.

Honomichl, Jack J. 1986. Marketing/advertising research: Ranking top players in growing global arena. *Advertising Age,* 24 November, S1.

Jain, Subhash. 1984. *International marketing management.* Boston: PWS-Kent.

Jeannet, Jean-Pierre, and Hubert Hennessey. 1988. *International marketing management: Strategies and cases.* Boston: Houghton Mifflin.

Johansson, Johny K., and Ikujiro Nonaka. 1987. Market research the Japanese way. *Harvard Business Review* 65 (May/June): 16–22.

Keegan, Warren J. 1984. *Multinational marketing management.* Englewood Cliffs, N.J.: Prentice Hall.

Khermouch, Gerry. 2001. Consumers in the mist. *Business Week,* 26 February, 92.

Koenderman, Tony. 2002. Unilever claims innovation with aloe vera sensitive detergent. 6 May. <www.adageglobal.com/cgi-bin/daily.pl?daily_id=7502&post_date=2002–05–06>

Mueller, Barbara. 1990. Cultural pitfalls in international advertising research. In *Proceedings of the 1990 Conference of the American Academy of Advertising*, ed. Patricia Stout, American Academy of Advertising, Austin Texas. RST 194–96.

Peebles, Dean M., and John K. Ryans. 1984. *Management of international advertising: A marketing approach.* Newton, Mass.: Allyn & Bacon.

Petrecca, Laura. 1999. DDB exports Kid Think unit across network. *Advertising Age*, 6 December, 10.

Plummer, Joseph T. 1986. The role of copy research in multinational advertising. *Journal of Advertising Research* 26(5) (October/November): 11–15.

PR Newswire. 2000. Make 7 UP yours campaign scores big with consumers. 2 October, 1.

Purto, Rebecca. 1990. Global psychographics. *American Demographics* 12 (December): 8.

Qassim, Ali. 2002. Havas survey shows consumers seek control in uncertain world. 17 December. <www.adageglobal.co,/cgi-bin/daily.pl?daily_id=8964&post_date=2002–12–17>

Terpstra, Vern. 1988. *International dimensions of marketing.* Boston: PWS-Kent, 73.

Terpstra, Vern, and Lloyd Russow. 2000. *International dimensions of marketing.* Cincinnati, Ohio: Southwestern College Publishing.

Toyne, Brian, and Peter Walters. 1989. *Global marketing management: A strategic perspective.* Boston: Allyn & Bacon.

Usunier, Jean-Claude. 1996. *Marketing across cultures.* London: Prentice Hall.

Van Raaij, W. Fred. 1977. Cross-cultural research methodology: A case of construct validity. *Advances in Consumer Research* 5: 693–710.

CHAPTER NINE

Advertising Regulatory Considerations in the International Arena

Much as the media scene of a particular country changes rapidly, so, too, does the regulatory situation. In fact, the two are often related. As new media forms evolve, such as satellite broadcasting and the Internet, new regulations also develop regarding advertising messages that may appear in those media. Currently, advertising regulations differ significantly among nations. A message considered perfectly acceptable in one market might well be deemed inappropriate in another. Product categories that can be advertised freely in one country may be banned altogether elsewhere. In this chapter we will highlight the various types of advertising regulations and regulatory agencies the international advertiser may encounter when promoting goods and services in foreign countries. We will also discuss the role of self-regulation in both national and international markets and the implications of advertising regulation for the international marketer. Each of these points is relevant, regardless of whether the international marketer plans to undertake a standardized campaign or anticipates localizing promotional efforts for each country. Because it is beyond the scope of this text to provide a complete overview of the regulatory environment of each and every market, examples will be provided instead to reinforce the variety of advertising regulations worldwide.

Influences on National Regulations

Much in the same way international marketers must familiarize themselves with the foreign marketing environment, as discussed in Chapter 3, so, too, must they investigate the regulatory environment. Indeed, demographic, economic, geographic, political-legal, and cultural factors may all directly influence the regulatory situation. In particular, the degree to which advertising is regulated, as well as the forms that regulations take, is inextricably intertwined with the political system and the dominant religion of a country. The political environment in a nation shapes the prevalent attitudes toward business. Edward Cundiff and Marye Tharp

Hilger explain: "Differences in attitudes may be due to different political structures or to party philosophies, history and tradition, the roles of interest groups or the political elite, an unstable political environment and forces of nationalism" (Cundiff and Hilger 1988, 196). Just a decade ago, for instance, foreign investment was forbidden by law and foreign investors were considered agents of treason in Albania. The Stalinist totalitarian regime that had ruled Albania since 1944 fell apart with the collapse of communism in Eastern Europe. Coca-Cola became the first major foreign investor in 1994, opening a $10-million bottling plant just outside the capital (Tagliabue 1994).

Legal restrictions often are based on religious foundations, and particular religions may frown on certain business practices. For example, writes Katherine Toland Frith:

> Islam is the national religion in Malaysia and there have been cases where commercials have been withdrawn from the media because of complaints from religious authorities. The Seiko watch company had been running a worldwide campaign using the theme: "Man Invented Time, Seiko Perfected It." A series of commercials with this theme ran on RTM networks . . . until RTM received a complaint from the Head of Islamic Studies at University Malaya charging that this commercial should be withdrawn because God, not man, invented time. RTM complied. The agency was told that if they wanted to advertise in Malaysia they must change their slogan. After lengthy consultations with the client, a new slogan was developed: "Man Invented Timekeeping, Seiko Perfected It." The agency had to change all TV commercials, as well as outdoor and press ads. (Frith 1987)

In some countries, regulation may be quite limited, and the laws that reinforce such regulation quite lax, particularly in the developing markets. In others, advertising regulation may be perceived as quite extensive and often may be stringently enforced. As Barbara Sundberg Baudot points out, "International law accords the host country sovereignty over all peoples, resources and activities within their territorial limits. The capacity, willingness and effectiveness of the host countries to perform such roles vary considerably" (Baudot 1989, 31). In a study conducted by the International Advertising Association, international executives identified fourteen countries as being highly restrictive: Germany, the United Kingdom, the United States, France, Canada, Australia, Sweden, Austria, Belgium, Argentina, Mexico, Italy, Finland, and Denmark (Ryans et al. 1974, 37).

At the national level, deceptive advertising practices are considered a crime in every country. The U.S. criteria for defining deception include determining whether the claim is false, whether the information presented is partially true and partially false, whether the message lacks sufficient information, whether the claim is true but the proof is false, and whether the message creates a false implication. Similar standards hold in other countries and have been adopted by international regulatory bodies as well. Clearly, such deceptive practices should be avoided because they are harmful not only to the consumer but also to honest advertisers and the public image of advertising in general.

Beyond deception, advertising regulation also focuses on the type of products that may be advertised, the audience the advertiser may address, the content or creative approach that may be employed in advertising, the media that all advertisers (or different classes of product/service advertisers) are permitted to employ, the amount of advertising that a single advertiser may employ in total or in a specific medium, the use of advertising materials prepared outside the country, and the use of local versus international advertising agencies. Each of these areas will be addressed in turn.

Types of Products That May Be Advertised

Alcohol In the United States, alcoholic beverage ads are restricted in terms of where the messages can appear, as well as what they can say. In 1936 the makers of distilled spirits agreed collectively not to air ads on radio, and a decade later followed suit for television. However in the mid 1990s, the Distilled Spirits Council—the industry trade group—announced that it would reverse the decades-old voluntary ban and would being purchasing commercial time on radio and television stations willing to accept the messages. These actions prompted many opposed to hard liquor ads in the broadcast media to push for congressional action to impose an official ban on the industry. Such action proved unnecessary, as the U.S. airwaves were never flooded with liquor ads. This is due in part to broadcasters' massive resistance to the ads (the major networks still will not air them), but also to an unwillingness on the part of distillers to make a serious financial commitment to radio and television ads. These factors, together with widespread public opposition, have served to preserve the status quo (Hacker 1998, 139). It should be noted that beer and wine ads are allowed on U.S. television as long as they do not appear in programs appealing to minors.

Some countries have more lenient guidelines on the marketing of alcoholic beverages than does the United States, while others have restrictions that are significantly more stringent. In Japan, advertising for wine, spirits, and beer is allowed in all major media vehicles. In fact, practices that would not be deemed acceptable in the United States are common practices in Japan. For example, Anheuser-Busch recently introduced Buddy's, a beer created for the Japanese market that contains less malt but more alcohol than most other beers. This allows Anheuser-Busch to advertise both the product's lower price and to promote it as "extra strong," a claim backed up by its alcohol content, which is 20 percent higher than Budweiser's. The use of celebrities to advertise hard liquor in television is also common. At the other extreme is Nepal. In 1999, all alcohol advertising was banned from Nepal's radio and television station. The ban of wine, beer, and hard liquor is a culmination of a government's public service campaign questioning some of the themes—"glamorous," "brave," "modern," and "Western"—used in the industry's advertising (Bhattarai 1999).

Tobacco In the United States, broadcast ads for cigarettes were officially outlawed under the Federal Cigarette Labelling and Advertising Act in 1971. Two decades later, the heads of seven top U.S. tobacco firms swore before Congress that nicotine was not addictive. The blatant lie ushered in a wave of litigation on the addictive nature of tobacco products. In 1998, tobacco producers and 46 states came to a $246 billion settlement to resolve state claims for health costs

related to smoking. As part of the settlement, stricter guidelines related to the marketing of cigarettes were imposed. Gone, or soon to be gone, were outdoor billboard messages; ads on the sides of buses, in subways, and on the tops of taxis; stadium advertising; branded merchandise such as caps and T-shirts; and point-of-sale advertising excessive in size. During the Clinton administration, even stricter regulations on the promotion of tobacco were imposed, including a ban on magazine ads that have a 15 percent or greater readership among those under 18, a ban on the sponsorship or sporting or entertainment events, and a ban on cigarette vending machines in stores or restaurants. The Bush administration is proposing a ban on terms such as "low tar" and "light," as well as requiring that health warnings cover 50 percent of cigarette packs and advertisements and eliminating cigarette vending machines altogether (Zuckerbrod 2002, 3A).

While U.S. tobacco firms are lamenting long and loud about the federal government's restrictions on their promotional activities, in the realm of tobacco advertising, the U.S. government is comparatively lenient. Consider Malaysia, where virtually all forms of tobacco advertising have been banned for over a decade—though cigarette manufacturers were able to sponsor sporting events and advertise their brand name at the point of sale, as long as no product images were used. But new regulations in 2002 even put a stop to that. In addition, the new restrictions prohibit scenes in movies and television shows that depict people smoking. Further, such scenes will be edited out of existing movies and television programs (Vance 2002, 1). Of course, there are markets with significantly fewer restrictions. Until recently, Japan was among the least restrictive industrialized nations with respect to cigarette advertising. Indeed, it has been dubbed a "smoker's paradise," where over 60 percent of males smoke. Even today, smoking is common in restaurants, vending machines abound, and free samples are frequently given out. Despite the high consumption rate of tobacco, Japan is just beginning to address the public health issues related to smoking. The Tobacco Institute of Japan announced a voluntary ban on all television, radio, cinema, and Internet advertising as of April 1998. While the Tobacco Institute's new policies are much more restrictive than was the case in the past, it is worth noting that self-regulation is the dominant force behind the restrictions—cigarette ads are not formally banned in any medium—and that advertising in magazines and newspapers and on billboards remains legal (Taylor and Raymond 2000, 289).

Pharmaceuticals In 1997, the U.S. Food and Drug Administration relaxed the rules regarding the advertising of pharmaceutical products. Under the new guidelines, companies need only mention the significant side effects in television commercials, referring viewers to magazine ads, toll-free phone numbers, Internet sites, or to medical professionals. Over the past five years, U.S. consumers have been bombarded with advertisements for everything from asthma medications to remedies for impotence. In 2002, well over $2 billion was spent on direct-to-consumer advertising (Shields 2003).

Both New Zealand and China also allow drug manufacturers to communicate directly with consumers via the mass media. In the past, however, the policing of pharmaceutical advertising in China was clearly insufficient. Chinese consumers were annually inundated with

hundreds of messages for medicines and medical devices purported to diagnose, cure, or prevent illness or regulate body functions (many of them variations on traditional Chinese herbs and methods of treatment). While some of the ads for these products were harmless, others were outrageous, such as a TV spot for an antiaging tea that showed older people becoming young and virile. Other messages were potentially dangerous. Love Solution, a "sterilizing spray," claimed it could protect the user from contracting AIDS; print ads claimed the product was approved by the Virus Institute of the Chinese Academy of Preventative Medicine. The Chinese government has since clamped down on the promotion of pharmaceutical products. According to new guidelines, all pharmaceutical messages are now subject to review. The advertisements must be true, accurate, and scientific. When advertising pharmaceuticals, manufacturers must back up any statistical claims with recognized research. Pharmaceutical ads may not make extravagant claims or feature names or images of medical or research units, academic institutions, medical experts, or testimony from doctors or patients (Taylor and Raymond 2000, 292).

In other countries the promotion of pharmaceutical products is banned. Under current U.K. law, pharmaceutical companies cannot provide any additional information about their prescription products. The patient receives only the leaflet that accompanies the medication. British regulatory officials argue that pharmaceutical companies cannot be trusted to provide impartial advice, and so any information on new drugs should come only through an independent source. British consumers concur. The Consumer Association released an opinion survey which revealed that almost 60 percent of the British believe that if advertising were allowed, pharmaceutical companies would try and convince people they had illnesses they did not have (Timmins 2002). Clearly, the British public prefers to maintain the ban on advertising and prescription drugs.

Other Products Although most international marketers are accustomed to some form of restrictions on the products noted above, there are numerous unanticipated restrictions as well. While South Africa has allowed the advertising of condoms for over a decade now, after years of hesitation, China lifted its ban in 2002. The ban was based on a regulation passed in 1989, which outlawed the advertising of "sex products." China's Industrial and Commercial Bureau (IBC), the government department which rules on advertising, said this included condoms. It argued that the public was not ready for such ads. A campaign by one condom maker on buses in Guangzhou brought a flood of complaints from the public that it was poisoning the minds of young people. But the spread of AIDS finally changed the government's mind. According to official figures, there are more than 1 million people infected with the virus in China. By 2010, there will be more than 10 million. An Baohan, who works at the Yi Dian Health Center, hailed the decision: "As a doctor, I strongly support this. It will help us in controlling the population, is a symbol of modern thinking, and will help to prevent sexual diseases, especially AIDS" (*South China Morning Post* 2002).

In Vietnam, municipal authorities announced restrictions on feminine hygiene products and even lingerie, noting that depictions of these products are inappropriate for the public arena.

An official from Ho Chi Minh City's Culture and Information Department explained that the restrictions were the result of complaints that some advertisements did not respect Vietnamese culture and traditions. State-owned Vietnam television (VTV) has informed advertisers that manufacturers of feminine hygiene products and underwear would not be allowed to sponsor films or programs on television. Nor would these ads be allowed on billboards or buses (Timms 2001).

Among restricted product categories around the world, undoubtedly the most unusual is Thailand's restriction on the promotion of energy drinks containing caffeine. New rules prohibit athletes and blue-collar workers from being featured in the ads in order to avoid associating the drinks with increased energy—the main promise of the energy drinks. In addition, warnings must be printed clearly on both ads for the products and on product packaging. The warnings cite that not more than two bottles of the energy drinks should be consumed in a day, and that pregnant women and children should avoid the caffeine-laden beverages altogether (Schmid 2002).

The Audiences That Advertisers May Address

In the United States, children are seen as a lucrative market, and an ever-increasing number of advertisers targets this group. U.S. marketers are guided in the development of child-directed messages by the Children's Advertising Review Unit (CARU), a self-regulatory body established by the Council of Better Business Bureaus. The basic activity of the CARU is to review and evaluate child-directed advertising in all media. If an ad is found misleading or inaccurate, the CARU seeks change through the voluntary cooperation of advertisers. It should be noted that the United States is one of the most lenient countries in the developed world when it comes to marketing to children.

In Sweden, the law forbids all television ads aimed at children under 12. In Norway, Austria, and the Flemish part of Belgium, no advertising is allowed around children's programs. Germany and Holland prohibit the sponsorship of children's shows. Toy ads are banned on Greek television, and Italy, Poland, Denmark, and Latvia are studying plans for tighter regulations. Currently, there are no continent-wide rules regarding marketing to children; however, Sweden is pushing for its ban on children's advertising to be extended across Europe. Axel Edling, Sweden's Consumer Ombudsman, says:

> Young children do not understand what advertising is all about. Our research has shown that a child
> can't distinguish between commercials and programs until they are five or six, and they don't really
> understand the commercial purpose behind advertising until they are 10 or 12. (Ford 1999)

In addition, studies have shown that children pay much more attention to ads than grown-ups and that they are three times more likely than parents to remember a brand name from an ad. The European Commission, the EU's ruling body, has launched a continent-wide study of marketing to kids that will ultimately form the basis of any revision of EU rules related to advertising to children.

Halfway around the world, New Zealand's government is proposing a ban on junk food ads aimed at children. The Health Ministry's proposal focuses on controls for marketing potentially health-endangering goods. Spokesperson Robyn Toomath, a hospital specialist, notes that action is needed to regulate "intensive food marketing to children. Billions of dollars are being spent getting children into inappropriate food and drinks," she said. "Children are getting fatter faster than any other group." The proposed law would ban "calorie-dense" foods such as pies, fries, and soft drinks around children's television programs—as well as from school lunches (*Financial News* 2002). Australia allows no advertising at all on programs aimed at preschool children.

 The Content or Creative Approach That May Be Employed

Many countries have restrictions on the types of claims advertisers can make, the manner in which products can be presented, and the appeals that may be employed in advertisements.

Comparative Claims In the United States, the Federal Trade Commission encourages advertisers to employ comparative claims, as they are seen as providing consumers with relevant product information. Indeed, it is estimated that nearly one-third of commercial messages incorporates a comparative claim. As noted previously, until recently, some European nations allowed comparative ads, while others did not. An EU directive was passed allowing strictly regulated comparative claims—both implicit and explicit. South Africa's Advertising Standards Authority, the industry's self-regulatory body, is also considering loosening its strict policy against comparative ads. Marketers currently are prohibited from naming competitors, showing rival brands, and making any comparisons that would identify a specific brand. Advertisers in the country favor relaxation of the policy and have made their opinions known to the Authority (*Advertising Age* 1993).

In Japan, comparative ads remain a rarity, not because of specific regulations, but rather because in Japanese culture direct confrontation and actions that cause another to lose face are considered taboo. Unaccustomed to comparative claims, Japanese consumers were astonished by a newspaper ad for the Ford Motor Co. that criticized Volkswagen's Golf by questioning why the model was so expensive in Japan. Some thought the provocation would spark an ad war or force foreign automakers into cutting prices, but, unlike in the United States, such aggressive campaigns do not easily take root. Comparative ads in Japan are mainly the domain of foreign firms. But even so, to go so far as mentioning the names of rivals or their product, as Ford did, is extremely rare (*Daily Yomiuri* 1996). Direct-comparison advertising is not allowed in the Philippines. Indirect-comparison ads may be permitted provided they do not use symbols, slogans, titles, or statements that are clearly identified or directly associated with competitive brands.

Health and Nutrition Claims The European Commission is currently preparing a proposal for the regulation of nutrition and health claims made on food. The draft documents suggests prohibiting vague terms such as "low fat," "fat-free," "high fiber," and "light." Products that do not have a positive nutritional value, such as cookies, cakes, and confectionary, would not be allowed to carry reduced-fat or reduced-sugar labels. The Commission also wants to ban food giants such as Nestlé and Kellogg from using vague slogans promising their product can "boost your immune system" or "help your body resist stress," because it believes such claims can lure consumers into buying products that frequently fail to deliver on their promises. Companies will also be banned from claiming the product can assist in weight control. References to seeking the advice of doctors or health professionals will also be restricted. The Commission's proposal seeks to harmonize rules on claims and boost the free movement of goods within the EU (Cozens 2003). It should be noted that the United States is also becoming increasingly critical of claims being made on behalf of weight-loss products as well as weight-loss programs.

Price Comparisons Price comparisons are another area of concern—some countries allow them while others do not. Wal-Mart has officially left Mexico's National Retailer's Association (AN-STAD), enraged by a new code that would prohibit price comparisons in advertising among its members. One paragraph of the code explicitly prohibits price comparisons in advertising campaigns. The main theme of Wal-Mart's advertising in Mexico is "everyday low prices." AN-STAD stated the code was introduced because price comparisons created confusion among customers (Monjaras 2002).

Other Limitations Multinational marketers must be aware of more obscure restrictions on advertising content. In Mongolia, a new law prohibits advertisers from defaming and slandering the state emblem and symbols, historical personalities, the national currency banknote, religion and faith, and any tradition that needs to be revered by every Mongolian (BBC Monitoring 2002). In Greece, ads also prevented from making humorous references to national monuments. In Britain, ads referring to death or religion, and those containing bad language, are considered a "no-no" (*Dominion* 1998).

The Media That Advertisers Are Permitted to Employ

Media availability is severely limited in many markets. With regard to outdoor advertising, while Italian marketers know that billboard ads are banned on highways, they must now comply with a code that also bans the outdoor messages from panoramic roads, inside parks, and within 50 meters of bus shelters. The code also imposes strong limits on the colors that billboards can employ—only 20 percent of a poster's surface can be red (the only exception is for registered trademarks). City planning officials have segmented China's capital into areas where outdoor advertising is permitted—including commercial zones where only well-known Chinese and foreign ads can be displayed—and where it is not. Areas such as Tiananmen Square, Zhongnanhai, Changan Street, the Palace Museum, and Diaoyutai State Guest House are officially off limits to marketers. The guidelines also forbid outdoor advertising within 200 meters of historical and cultural sites, government offices, foreign embassies and consulates, and offices for international trade organizations. However, limited advertising will be allowed in scenic areas, the city's airport, and Zhonggauncun Science and Technology Park, the planned site of the 2008 Olympics (Madden 2001). Some media are banned outright. In Saudi Arabia, direct mail is considered an invasion or privacy, and is thus not used.

Media bans may also be related to specific product categories—in particular, tobacco and alcohol. In China, there is regulation banning the television advertising of spirits with over 40 percent alcohol content. In Taiwan, the government only allows companies to advertise alcohol on network television from 9:30 P.M. until 6:00 A.M. In South Korea, alcoholic beverages may be advertised on television after 10:00 P.M. and on radio after 1:00 P.M. Interestingly, ads for undergarments in this country are only allowed on broadcast media on weekdays between 8:30 A.M. and 4:00 P.M., or after 10:00 P.M.

How the media are used for advertising purposes also differs from market to market. U.S. television viewers are accustomed to having their programming interrupted at regular intervals with commercial messages. The EU's Television Without Frontiers Directive, which aims to harmonize regulation of television across Europe, is significantly more strict. Implementation of the directive, set for the end of 2004, includes strict rules on commercial-break frequency. Commercial breaks must occur not more than every 20 minutes for dramas and documentaries and every 45 minutes for movies (Bowes 2002). A new Russian law prohibits the interruption of children's, religious, or educational programs by advertisers. All other programs must not be interrupted more frequently than every 15 minutes. Programs shorter than 15 minutes in length are not to be interrupted with commercial messages. During transmission of the ads, the volume must not be louder than the volume of the program that has been interrupted. Finally, laws also stipulate that ads of similar content for one and the same product must not be transmitted more than twice per hour and their overall duration must not exceed two minutes (*BBC Monitoring* 2001).

The Use of Advertising Materials Prepared Outside the Country

A study conducted by the International Advertising Association revealed that of the 46 countries surveyed, 22 percent restricted foreign-produced ads and foreign talent and another 38 percent had partial restrictions (Boddewyn and Mohr 1987, 20). The Malaysian Ministry of Information, for example, requires that all footage for and music in television commercials be produced locally and use local talent. Reports Katherine Toland Frith: "This means that all people involved in the production must be Malaysian—including actors and actresses, technical people, voice, etc. The government requires a 'made in Malaysia' (MIM) form to be submitted with the final checkprint (the finished, edited footage)" (Frith 1987). No imported commercials may be used in Australia or the United Kingdom unless a local crew performs or attends the shooting, and in commercials intended for U.S. audiences, a union agreement is required to film outside the United States if U.S. personnel are not used (Boddewyn 1988). Peru bans foreign-inspired models and materials in advertisements appearing in

that country in an effort to protect and enhance its national identity. Beyond nationalistic and cultural objectives, restrictions on foreign-prepared materials often are motivated by economic considerations—such as the desire to provide jobs for the local print production and film industry (Boddewyn and Mohr 1987, 21). There is also the fear that multinational ad agencies will hamper the development of the local advertising businesses.

As discussed earlier in the text, some countries are quite sensitive about the use of foreign words in advertising messages as well. The International Advertising Association survey mentioned earlier also found that of the countries surveyed, while 90 percent permitted the use of foreign languages in print ads and direct mail, only 72 percent allowed foreign-language commercials on TV, on radio, or in the cinema. Over 25 percent of the countries restricted foreign-language ads to media targeted to foreigners in their country. France, Korea, and Russia are examples of countries that resist the foreignization or anglicization of the local language in advertising messages. French law specifically forbids the use of foreign words and expressions when French equivalents can be found in the official dictionary. The French government has published a *Dictionary of Official Terms of the French Language* as a reference guide for enforcing culturally correct speech. "If someone uses foreign words in publicity or consumer information on products, they will be fined," notes Brigitte Peyrou, an official with the General Delegation for the French Language. "Repeat offenders will pay double" (Waxman 1994). Article 22 of Korea's regulations on broadcast advertising stipulate that:

> commercial advertisements shall not unnecessarily use foreign languages except for the brand names, corporate names or corporate slogans of foreign companies. Any brand names, corporate names or corporate slogans, etc in a foreign language shown shall also be expressed in Korean letters. Furthermore, commercial advertisements shall not use foreign language commercial jingles. (*Korea Herald* 2001)

The rationale behind such restrictive use of foreign languages in aired advertisements lies in the desire to protect the Korean language as a cultural asset. But this reasoning is perplexing, given that many other foreign broadcast programs, including movies, sitcoms, and documentaries are fully aired in the original languages (with subtitles), and recent technological advances in television sets now allow viewers to switch off the Korean language voice-overs. A recent law in Russia attempts to purge advertising and media of Westernized words. Under the law, anyone caught employing Westernisms such as "biznes," "menedgment," or "merchendaizing" faces up to two months of "corrective work"—the Russian term for community service. Variations of English words have become common since the country was flooded with Western culture after the break-up of the Soviet Union (Walsh 2003).

The Use of Local versus International Advertising Agencies

An increasing number of advertising agencies are positioning themselves as "global," or capable of providing services to clients worldwide. J. J. Boddewyn notes that "such a reach requires that they be allowed to establish themselves, or to merge with and acquire others, rather

freely around the world" (Boddewyn 1988). The previously mentioned IAA survey reveals that such maneuvers are generally allowed to enable advertisers to coordinate their international campaigns through a single or limited number of agencies. Of the 46 countries surveyed, 34 (74 percent) allow full ownership of an ad agency, particularly in the developed countries. Even partial or total exclusion of foreigners does not prevent foreign agencies from entering into joint ventures as well as technical and managerial agreements with local agencies, and some locally owned agencies simply serve as shells for multinational ones in developing countries. For example, Hakuhodo, Japan's second largest advertising agency, was recently granted permission by the Vietnam Ministry of Planning and Investment to enter into a joint venture relationship with state-run agency Saigon Advertising Co. Japanese companies have been increasing their advertising activities in line with their advance into the booming Vietnamese market. Their home-based agencies have naturally followed. In addition to Hakuhodo, the other two of Japan's "big three," Dentsu and Asatsu-DK, have a presence in Vietnam as well. Hakuhodo and Saigon Advertising petitioned the Vietnamese government to allow the venture, because Saigon Advertising was under the control of the Culture and Information Service of Ho Chi Minh City. This is the first time a foreign agency has entered into a joint venture with a state-run agency where the foreign entity holds the majority equity ownership (65 percent/35 percent). In addition, the newly named Hakuhodo & Saigon Advertising Co. is the first Japanese-affiliated business permitted to conduct media buying in Vietnam, thus being able to offer a full slate of services to its clients (Gray 2001).

International and Regional Regulation

International and regional regulations consist of those rules and guidelines that states and nations consider to be binding upon themselves. Among the major bodies or organizations that have developed or are developing international or regional regulations related to marketing and advertising are the various United Nations agencies, the World Trade Organization (WTO), and the Organization for Economic Cooperation and Development (OECD), as well as a number of regional bodies, including the European Union and the Gulf Cooperation Council.

The United Nations

The United Nations and its various agencies influence advertising regulation in member countries. The most important of these agencies are the World Health Organization (WHO); the Commission on Transnational Corporations; the United Nation's Educational, Scientific and Cultural Organization (UNESCO); and the UN Conference on Trade and Development (Dunn 1982, 29). Barbara Sundberg Baudot explains their functions:

> These organizations lack the attribute of sovereignty, or the legislative authority of a world government to legislate enforceable regulation. Thus their roles are restricted to the development of vol-

untary codes and guidelines whose effectiveness depends on moral suasion and public acceptance. However, these codes may be translated through national legislation into laws. By consensus, members also may decide to adopt regulations by treaty, which becomes enforceable law in ratifying countries. Alternately, countries may decide to adopt conventions or resolutions binding members in accordance with voting rules in organizational charters. (Baudot 1989, 31)

Several issues appear to have top priority at the various UN agencies. First, the UN is beginning to perceive market data as a type of national resource. In a report on transborder data flow that highlighted the significant expansion in this area as well as the great value of such data to international marketers, the UN expressed concern over whether such data flow helps or hinders developing countries. The report implies that developing countries should limit the flow of information from their country to the headquarters of international firms, and that they should use their data to negotiate advantageous contracts and agreements. Second, the various UN agencies have all targeted pharmaceutical advertising for special attention. The UN is particularly concerned with international firms that may be dumping substandard or hazardous pharmaceutical products on unsuspecting developing markets as well as with the costly, high-pressure marketing and promotional methods employed by many international pharmaceutical firms. Third, the UN agencies acknowledge that media depend on advertising for much of their financial support and are concerned that media dollars may not always support those media of greatest importance to developing countries. Unfortunately, the developing nation's most critical media forms may not provide the proper target audience coverage for the international marketer. Finally, several of the UN agencies probably will develop rules and regulations that cover advertising in the international arena.

World Trade Organization

The World Trade Organization is the regulatory body with the broadest impact on international business activities. First mentioned in Chapter 3, the WTO is the international body concerned with fair trade and open markets, as well as intellectual property protection. Apart from trade liberalization, the WTO addresses a number of subjects relevant to consumers. In its most recent round of trade negotiations, WTO discussions covered labeling, product safety, and deceptive practices. The WTO serves as a permanent, comprehensive forum to address new or evolving issues in the global market.

The Organization for Economic Cooperation and Development

The Organization for Economic Cooperation and Development is the international organization or the industrialized, market-economy countries—including those of Europe and North America, and Australia, New Zealand, and Japan. The OECD regularly gathers statistical information on foreign trade and makes the statistics internationally comparable by converting the information into uniform units (Onkvisit and Shaw 1997, 174). In addition, the OECD addresses a wide range of issues relevant to international business, in particular through its Committee on Consumer Policy. A primary focus of this committee is on cross-border consumer transaction issues. As such, it has established guidelines in the following areas: consumer protection in the online marketplace, disputes arising out of business-to-consumer electronic commerce, and the use of credit and debit cards online.

 The European Union

One of the major issues confronting the European Union is that of regulations and restrictions related to promotional activities. As evidenced by the numerous examples throughout this text, EU states have greatly differing legislation regarding marketing and advertising. There is a good deal of controversy over whether to impose harmonized laws across the 15 member states. Some favor harmonizing national legislation and encourage the European Commission, the EU's highest executive body, to draw up a black list of types of misleading and unfair advertising that would be forbidden across the continent. Indeed, supporters of this view argue that the divergent legislation is, in fact, a hindrance to the adoption by consumers of cross-border trade and service. Others fear that this would give too much regulatory power to Brussels, and prefer allowing member states to retain national responsibility for advertising regulation. This camp suggests that Euro-consumers continue to buy locally because of cultural reasons, trusted brands, distribution channels, language issues, price advantages, and so on—but not because of differing regulations.

The European Commission is currently developing a new framework directive, which is expected to be completed sometime in 2003. In addition to taking a stance on the harmonization debate, the new directive will include provisions to tackle misleading advertising, aggressive marketing methods, and failure to provide after-sales assistance and the effective handling of complaints. David Byrne, EU Commissioner on Consumer Affairs, has noted that further progress depends on the fundamental principles of consumer protection being adopted at the European level. Additional issues facing the EU include new media, privacy, and protection of children. Finally, the impending enlargement of the EU is also an area of concern. An important Commission aim is to ensure that candidate countries apply the same high levels of consumer protection and safety that currently exist in the EU.

The Gulf Cooperation Council

Saudi Arabia, Qatar, Kuwait, Oman, the United Arab Emirates, and Bahrain have forged a common consumer and trade policy to ensure economic integration. The Gulf Cooperation Council (GCC) presents significant marketing opportunities for multinational firms. An understanding of the advertising regulatory environment of these member states is essential for marketers interested in this region. Because Saudi Arabia is the largest and economically strongest member of the GCC, it plays a dominant role in shaping the regulations that will govern all commercial activity (including advertising) among member states.

With regard to the marketing environment, religion takes precedence over all other cultural considerations in Saudi Arabia. Mushtaq Luqmani and colleagues explain:

> The Saudi legal system is unique in that it identifies law with the personal command of the "one and only one God, the Almighty." The Islamic laws known as Sharia are the master framework to which all legislation is referred and with which it must be compatible. The Sharia is a comprehensive code governing the duties, morals and behavior of all Muslims in all areas of life, including commerce. Sharia is derived from two basic sources, the Quran or Holy Book and the Hadith, based on the life, sayings and practices of the Prophet Muhammad. The implications of religion on advertising regulation in this country are far-reaching. (Luqmani et al. 1989, 59)

Several sets of quranic messages have special significance for advertisers and advertising regulation. The most important have to do with strict taboos dealing with alcohol, gambling, and immodest exposure. For example, at no time may alcoholic beverages be consumed, and games of chance are illegal. Religious norms require women to be covered, both in public and in advertising messages. Advertising messages may also be considered deceptive by religious standards. For example, according to Islam, fraud may occur if the seller fails to deliver everything promised, and advertisers may need to use factual appeals based on real rather than perceived product benefits.

No specific governmental agency is responsible for controlling advertising behavior in Saudi Arabia. There is no self-regulatory industry group and no evidence of any plans to develop one. Companies are, however, involved in self-compliance, which may eventually lead to self-regulation. As Luqmani and colleagues state:

> Possible violations are monitored in two ways. The government is involved through the Ministry of Commerce which ensures that ads remain within legal bounds, and the Ministry of Information which approves television commercials. Less formal oversight is provided by a voluntary religious group, the Organization for the Prevention of Sins and Order of Good Deeds. Members observe public and commercial behavior (including promotions) for any violations of Islamic law. (Luqmani et al. 1989, 59)

Obviously, advertisers must take great care to ensure that advertising content is compatible with the Islamic religion and its laws.

In addition to the European Union and the Gulf Cooperation Council, as well as the North American Free Trade Agreement (NAFTA) mentioned previously in this book, there are a number of additional major regional economic organizations:

- Asia-Pacific Economic Cooperation (AEPC);
- Central American Common Market (CAMC);
- Andean Group;
- Southern Cone Common Market (Mercosur);

- Caribbean Community and Common Market (CARICOM);
- Association of Southeast Asian Nations (ASEAN);
- Central European Free Trade Association (CEFTA);
- Economic Community of West African States (ECOWAS);
- South African Development Coordination Conference (SADCC).

International and regional codes and guidelines contribute to the harmonization of national laws and, in doing so, pave the way for global advertising campaigns. International marketers planning on promoting their products or services in a particular region may be faced with a multitude of advertising regulations—many of which may conflict with one another—and therefore have little choice but to employ a localized campaign for each country. However, with standardized advertising regulation in the European Union or the Persian Gulf region, marketers have the option of employing the same or similar message strategy.

Self-Regulation

The Trend toward Self-Regulation

De Mooij notes:

> Self regulation started in the USA at the beginning of the 20th century with the foundation of local clubs consisting of agents, advertisers, and media representatives. The American Advertising Federation (AAF), the American Association of Advertising Agencies), and the Association of National Advertisers (ANA) jointed to form the central organization for the regulation of advertising. This is the National Advertising Review Board (NARB). The NARB, together with the Federal Trade Commission (FTC) has helped in setting standards for developing the regulation of advertising in other parts of the world. (De Mooij 1994, 498)

During the past several decades, both consumer groups and governments around the globe have increasingly turned their attention toward the control of advertising, and advertising, trade, and industry associations, as well as the media in many countries, have realized the importance of voluntary self-regulation. In addition to avoiding government-mandated regulation, self-regulation in advertising generally has three objectives:

1. to protect consumers against false or misleading advertising and against advertising that intrudes on their privacy through its unwanted presence or offensive content;
2. to protect legitimate advertisers against false or misleading advertising by competitors;
3. to promote the public acceptance of advertising so that it can continue as an effective institution in the marketplace. (Rijkens and Miracle 1986, 40)

Consumer protection laws in the United Kingdom are among the strongest in the world. The United Kingdom's Advertising Code is a comprehensive set of rules for advertising and sales promotion. The basic principles of the code are that advertising should be: (1) legal, decent, honest and truthful, (2) prepared with a sense of responsibility to consumers and to society, and (3) in line with the principles of fair competition generally acceptable in business. The Advertising Standards Authority (ASA) is responsible for supervising the system and for applying the code to make sure the public is not misled or offended by commercial messages. The ASA is independent of both government and the advertising industry. Television ads in Britain are regulated by the Independent Television Commission, and radio ads by the Radio Authority. The Committee on Advertising Practice (CAP) enforces the code for all nonbroadcast advertising in the United Kingdom.

Advertising Standards Canada (ASC) is the national, not-for-profit industry body committed to creating and maintaining community confidence in advertising. ASC membership includes Canada's leading advertisers, advertising agencies, and media organizations. The ASC administers the Canadian Code of Advertising Standards, the industry's principal self-regulatory code. The ASC accepts written complaints from consumers who have a concern about an advertisement they see or hear. In 2002, the ASC received 1,828 complaints about 870 advertisements. Of these, 206 complaints regarding 51 advertisements were upheld. Out-of-home advertising attracted the highest number of complaints, followed by television ads. Accuracy and clarity was the primary problem with most of the commercial messages consumers complained about. Common concerns involved pricing errors and omission of details. Upheld complaints and statistics are included in the ASC's Ad Complaints Report (*Canada NewsWire* 2003).

Also hoping to combat government restrictions and censorship, industry groups from 13 Latin American countries have formed the Inter-American Society for the Freedom of Commercial Speech. Members have signed the Caracas Pact, an agreement to create a self-regulatory code. Included in the group are agencies, media, and advertiser associations from Brazil, Colombia, Costa Rica, Chile, El Salvador, Guatemala, Honduras, Mexico, Nicaragua, Panama, Paraguay, Puerto Rico, and Venezuela; Argentina has also signaled its support but has not yet signed the pact. The new group will gather information about each country's current industry and government regulations before developing a pan–Latin American code. After the code is in place, the group proposes to foster a wider understanding of advertising's objectives and to sponsor campaigns in favor of freedom of commercial speech (Kirby 1992).

National media are also involved in the monitoring of advertising content. Both media associations and individual media are concerned about advertising messages that may be deceptive, offensive, or even contrary to public standards. In addition to advertising-association, industry, and media codes, individual firms, including Procter & Gamble, General Foods, and Revlon, have begun to develop their own guidelines. Developments in this area, however, have not been particularly well studied and deserve further attention.

The International Chamber of Commerce

The International Chamber of Commerce (ICC) was established in 1919 to promote the interests of international business. The ICC, which today is represented in over 130 countries, is the most important international body influencing self-regulation of marketing and advertising. The ICC provides business input to the United Nations, the World Trade Organization, and many other intergovernmental bodies, both regional and international. With the support of advertisers, agencies, and the media, the ICC has developed a number of important codes (see the ICC's Web site at www.iccwbo.org/home/statements_rules/rules_1997/advercod.asp), including the following:

- International Code of Advertising Practice;
- International Code of Sales Promotion;
- International Code of Direct Selling;
- International Code of Direct Marketing;
- Compendium of Rules for Users of the Telephone in Sales Marketing and Research;
- International Code on Sponsorship;
- ICC/ESOMAR International Code of Market Research and Social Science.

The ICC Code of Advertising Practice states that all advertisers have an overall duty to be "decent, honest, legal and truthful." The code goes on to state that advertisements "should be prepared with a due sense of social responsibility . . . and not be such as to impair public confidence in advertising." With these words, the code moved away from addressing only "hard" matters that center on the deceptive character of advertisements and on proper substantiation of advertising claims. It also encompassed "soft" issues, which include matters of sex and decency in advertising. Jean J. Boddewyn notes that: "reflecting these ICC principles, various clauses on decency, taste, public opinion and social responsibility are usually found in advertising self-regulatory codes and guidelines around the world" (Boddewyn 1991, 25). Sex and decency can be broken into five major subcategories:

1. tasteless/indecent ads, which do not conform to recognized standards of propriety, good taste and modesty;
2. sexy ads, which use sexual imagery or suggestiveness;
3. sexist ads, which diminish or demean one sex in comparison with the other—particularly through the use of sex-role stereotypes;
4. objectification-of-women ads, which use women primarily as decorative or attention-getting objects with little or no relevance to the product advertised;
5. violence-against-women ads. (Boddewyn, 1991, 25)

An IAA survey inquired about the salience of these five advertising issues. Table 9.1 reveals that a larger number of developing countries (15) than of developed ones (11) rated one or more

TABLE 9.1 Countries Rating Advertising Taste/Decency Issues as "Major"

Tasteless/ Indecent	Sexy	Sexist	Objectification of Women	Violence Against Women
Bahrain*	Austria	India*	Argentina*	Chile*
Canada	Bahrain*	Ireland	Austria	Lebanon*
Chile*	Indonesia*	Lebanon*	Brazil*	New Zealand
Indonesia*	Ireland	Peru*	Lebanon*	Spain
Kenya*	Italy	Sweden	Portugal	Trinidad & Tobago*
Lebanon*	Kenya*	Switzerland	Singapore*	United States
Malaysia*	Lebanon*	United States	Spain	
Philippines*	Norway		Sweden	
Taiwan*	Philippines*		Switzerland	
Trinidad & Tobago*				
United States				

* = countries that are usually classified as "developing" or "less developed."

Source: J. J. Boddewyn, *Sexism and decency in advertising: Government regulation and industry self-regulation in 47 countries* (New York: International Advertising Association, 1989).

of these issues as "major." Lebanon and the United States appeared to be most concerned with these issues, and these countries are the only ones represented in at least three columns. The subcategory of tasteless/indecent ads generated the most mentions, particularly in developing countries.

Some self-regulatory bodies refuse to handle soft issues, limiting themselves to the hard issues of truth and accuracy. This is true of the United States's National Advertising Review Board. Other bodies, including those in Germany and Canada, readily deal with "taste and opinion" complaints. For example, the German Advertising Council recently dealt with a case of indecent advertising developed by a national retailer, Media Markt (*Sudkurier* 2002). Media Markt sells a wide variety of goods, including audio and video equipment, computers, vacuum cleaners, blenders, and even batteries. To convey the variety of products sold, Media Markt developed a campaign with the slogan "There's more in there than you might think." The visual associated with the campaign caused a good deal of public outcry, particularly among German women (see Figure 9.1). The German Advertising Council required Media Markt to remove all 15,000 outdoor posters it had distributed throughout Germany.

Most bodies, however, stand in-between, occasionally agreeing to handle soft cases on the basis of the general principles they apply—particularly when gross breaches of social standards occur, as in matters of obscenity, racism, and denigration (Boddewyn 1991, 25).

The primary problem with indecency is that what is considered improper in one country is deemed perfectly acceptable in another. For example, the mere use of the word "erection" is enough to get consumers up in arms in some markets. Dozens of consumers in South Africa lodged complaints with the Advertising Standards Authority (ASA) for the liberal use of that word in a Pfizer campaign for its impotence pill, Viagra, charging the campaign would lead

Figure 9.1 The German Advertising Council required Media Markt to remove these offending posters.

to the destruction of South Africa's moral fiber (Koenderman 2002). Britain's regulatory bodies have also become notorious for their Victorian mind-set when it comes to issues of decency in advertising. Recently, a campaign for Yves St. Laurent's Opium perfume was banned by British regulators. The outdoor poster campaign featured a model posing naked on a fur rug. Christopher Graham, ASA's Director General, said: "This was the most complained about ad in the last five years." He said it was visually suggestive and likely to cause serious or widespread offence, thereby breaking British codes of advertising and sales promotion. Britain's ASA received over 1,000 complaints about the ad from members of the public (Allison 2000, 1). It should be noted that regulatory officials can ban an ad that receives as little as one complaint (Kapner 2002).

To demonstrate the variety of definitions of "decent" even within the European Union, consider the case of France, which has developed a reputation for bare-all ads. The ads in this nation have become so risqué that they have been dubbed "porno-chic." But apparently a number of campaigns during 2001 crossed the invisible barrier that had previously prevailed against the use of sadomasochistic and zoophilic images in advertising (Speer 2001). The campaign for La City, a French clothing retailer, provides a good example of one that overstepped the bounds of what even French consumers were willing to accept. Consumers found it degrading to depict a nearly naked woman in a sexually suggestive position next to a sheep with the tagline "I need a sweater." As a result of the offensive campaigns, France introduced a new self-regulatory code that replaces the outdated standards on the image of women in advertising first drafted in 1975. Authorities emphasized that nudity in and of itself is not under attack—because bare breasts are used to promote everything from pullovers to Parmesan cheese. Rather, the new standards insist ads must respect human dignity and refuse any "degrading" or "humiliating" portrayals of human beings (Galloni 2001).

In developing self-regulatory guidelines, many countries have turned to the ICC codes. Because latecomers often borrow from the ICC codes as well as from codes outlined by U.S., U.K., and Canadian associations, voluntary codes often appear to resemble one another. In addition to a code of advertising practices, the ICC also outlines codes of practice in marketing, market research practice, and sales promotion practice.

Industry, trade, and advertising associations have developed codes of ethics and guidelines in more than 50 nations, and the number is increasing each year. This is particularly true of developed markets and countries where advertising expenditures are relatively large. Increasingly, we will also see movement toward self-regulation in developing markets.

Implications for International Advertisers

Although it is nearly impossible for international advertisers to be familiar with the regulation of advertising worldwide, they are still responsible for making every effort to inform themselves of the regulatory environment of markets they plan to enter. Because of the chang-

ing regulatory environment, advertisers must develop a system for keeping abreast of new developments. Often, advertisers will retain the services of an attorney familiar with the local laws of the market or markets they are planning to enter.

Beyond the impact of the regulatory environment on a single campaign, the global regulatory climate will influence how successfully international advertisers can conduct their business in the years to come. In the meantime, international advertisers should do the following:

1. Have their in-house and external legal counsels check and double-check the true nature of advertising restrictions in relevant foreign markets.
2. Monitor and oppose the spread of regulations, taxes, and other obstacles that hamper international advertising. In particular, advertisers should support U.S. and other governments' efforts to liberalize trade and investment in services through GATT and other bilateral agreements. Defending the freedom of commercial expression and communication at home and abroad is part of this agenda.
3. Support and assist the development of advertising self-regulation around the world. Advertising self-regulation exists in only 55 countries and is well developed in only 20. It is largely nonexistent or ineffective in most of the developing countries where the spread of regulation is imminent. (Boddewyn 1991, 29)

Local and national resources should be tapped for current information on legislative or self-regulatory efforts. National advertising associations can provide invaluable assistance. In the United States the American Advertising Association (AAA), the American Association of Advertising Agencies (AAAA), and the American Advertising Federation (AAF) are all excellent resources. Most developed countries have similar associations. For example, in Europe the international advertiser may contact the European Association of Advertising Agencies (EAAA), the Institute of Practitioners in Advertising (IPA), or the European Advertising Tripartite (EAT). Likewise, the Asian Federation of Advertising Agencies (AFAA) provides current data to advertisers entering Asian markets.

Finally, the International Advertising Association (IAA) conducts numerous surveys that deal with governmental regulations as well as specific industry guidelines. In addition, the IAA publishes a report on government regulation and industry self-regulation in more than 50 countries entitled *Barriers to Trade and Investment in Advertising*.

Summary

Some experts propose that the extent and severity of advertising regulation worldwide is likely to increase; others predict it will decline. However, many governments currently are developing tougher regulations with regard to advertising in general as well as stricter restrictions relating to specific product categories such as cigarettes, alcohol, and pharmaceuticals.

On the other hand, many governments—particularly those in developed markets—are moving toward deregulation. Especially in markets facing slow- or no-growth economies, politicians are questioning the wisdom of further increasing the costs associated with doing business.

Regardless of the regulatory environment in which international marketers find themselves, every effort should be made to comply with both national and international rules and guidelines. In addition, international marketers should strive to operate abroad in a socially responsible fashion. Such efforts can assist in avoiding legal entanglements and stemming any erosion of consumer confidence in advertising worldwide. The issue of social responsibility and ethical standards in the international arena will be addressed in the next chapter.

References

Advertising Age. 1993. *Advertising Age* legal briefs: Comparative advertising mulled. 15 March, 16.

Allison, Rebecca. 2000. Offensive opium posters to be removed. *The Guardian.* 19 December, 1.

Baudot, Barbara Sundberg. 1989. *International advertising handbook: A user's guide to rules and regulations.* Lexington, Mass.: Lexington Books.

BBC Monitoring. 2001. Russia: Duma bids to curb advertising on TV, radio. 15 November, 1.

———. 2002. Mongolian parliament passes advertising law. 31 March, 1.

Bhattarai, Binod. 1999. Nepal clamps down on alcohol and tobacco ads. *Financial Times* (London), 4.

Boddewyn, J. J. 1981. Advertising regulation, self-regulation and self-discipline around the world: Some facts, trends and observations. *International Marketing* 1(1): 52.

———. 1988. The one and many worlds of advertising: Regulatory obstacles and opportunities. *International Journal of Advertising* 7(1): 13.

Boddewyn, Jean J. 1989. Sexism and decency in advertising: Government regulation and industry self-regulation in 47 countries. New York: International Advertising Association.

———. 1991. Controlling sex and decency in advertising around the world. *Journal of Advertising* 20(4): December, 25–35.

Boddewyn, Jean J., and Iris Mohr. 1987. International advertisers face government hurdles. *Marketing News,* 8 May, 20–22.

Bowes, Elena. 2002. No change to EU TV directive until 2004 after all. 31 May. <www.adageglobal.com/cgi-bin/daily.pl?daily_id=7668&post_date=2002–05031>

Canada NewsWire. 2003. Advertising Standards Canada releases 2002 ad complaints report. 18 February, 1.

Cozens, Claire. 2003. EU plans crackdown on food health slogans. *MediaGuardian,* 3 February. <media.guardian.co.uk/advertising/story/0,7492,886565,00.html>

Cundiff, Edward, and Marye Tharp Hilger. 1988. *Marketing in the international environment.* Englewood Cliffs, N.J.: Prentice Hall.

Daily Yomiuri. 1996. (Tokyo). Comparative advertising fails to take off in Japan. 22 March, 1.

de Mooij, Marieke. 1994. *Advertising worldwide.* Hemel, Hempstead, Eng.: Prentice Hall International.

Dominion. 1998. (Wellington, New Zealand). Forum told of overseas taboos in advertising. 5 May, 7.

Dunn, S. Watson. 1982. United Nations as a regulator of international advertising. In *Proceedings of the 1982 Conference of the American Academy of Advertising,* ed. Alan Fletcher, Lincoln, Neb.: American Academy of Advertising, 29–32.

Financial News. 2002. (Wellington, New Zealand). Ban on fast food adverts which target children proposed. 3 December, 1.

Ford, Peter. 1999. Europe puts mute on kid ads: The EU is launching a study of children's TV ads. *Christian Science Monitor,* 16 December, 1.

Frith, Katherine Toland. 1987. The social and legal constraints on advertising in Malaysia. *Media Asia* 14(2): 103.

Galloni, Alessandra. 2001. Clampdown on "porno-chic" ads is pushed by French authorities. *Wall Street Journal,* 25 October, B-4.

Gray, Campbell. 2001. Hakuhodo allowed to place ads in Vietnamese media. 28 September. <www.adageglobal.com/cgi-bin/daily.pl?daily_id=5877&post_date=2001–09–28>

Hacker, George. 1998. Liquor advertisements on television: Just say no. *Journal of Public Policy and Marketing* 17 (Spring): 139–42.

Kapner, Suzanne. 2002. Agencies say British regulators are too quick to ban ads. *New York Times,* 4 January, C-4.

Kirby, Catherine. 1992. American group to push self-regulation. *Advertising Age,* 26 September, 16.

Koenderman, Tony. 2002. Viagra ad causes offence in South Africa. 2 April. <www.adageglobal.com/cgi-bin/daily.pl?daily_id-7282&post_date=2002–04–02>

Korea Herald. 2001. Irrational regulations hindering global branding strategies. 19 December, 1.

Luqmani, Mushtaq, Ugur Yavas, and Zahir Quraeshi. 1989. Advertising in Saudi Arabia: Content and regulation. *International Marketing Review* 6(1): 59–72.

Madden, Normandy. 2001. Beijing reinforces out-of-home ad restrictions. 29 August. <www.adageglobal.com/cgi-bin/daily.pl?daily_id=5623&post_date=2001–08–29>

Monjaras, Jorge. 2002. Wal-Mart quits Mexican retail body to protest ban on comparing prices. 17 October. <www.adageglobal.com/cgi-bin/daily.pl?daily_id=8586&post_date=2002–10–17>

Onkvisit, Sak, and John J.Shaw. 1997. *International marketing: Analysis and strategy.* Upper Saddle River, N.J.: Prentice Hall.

Rijkens, Rein, and Gordon E. Miracle. 1986. *European regulation of advertising.* New York: North-Holland.

Ryans, John K., Jr., James R. Wills, Jr., and Henry Bell. 1979. International advertising regulation: A transnational view. In *Midwest Marketing Association Conference Proceedings,* ed., 37. Carbondale: Southern Illinois University.

Schmid, Thomas. 2002. Thailand to limit advertising of energy drink. 26 November. <www.adageglobal.com/cgi-bin/daily.pl?daily_id=8844&post_date=2002–11–26>

Shields, Todd. 2003. Drug-ad fight looms in congress. *Adweek,* 27 January, 2.

South China Morning Post. 2002. Beijing Mark O'Neill Advertising Condoms. 2 December, 16.

Speer, Lawrence. 2001. France sets code on portrayal of women in advertising. 17 October. <www.adageglobal.com/cgi-bin/daily.pl?daily_id=6018&post_date=2001–10–17>

Sudkurier. 2002. Posters removed after protests. 1 April, 1.

Tagliabue, John. 1994. Albania, Europe's poorest state, gets big Coca-Cola bottling plant. *San Diego Union-Tribune,* 20 May, A24.

Taylor, Charles, and Mary Anne Raymond. 2000. An analysis of product category restrictions in advertising in four major East Asian markets. *International Marketing Review* 17: 287–304.

Timmins, Nicholas. 2002. Public says ban on drug adverts should remain. *Financial Times* (London), 3 June, 2.

Timms, Jonathan. 2001. Ho Chi Minh officials restrict ads for lingerie, sanitary towels. 18 December. <www.adageglobal.com/cgi-bin/daily.pl?daily_id=6651&post_date=2001–12–18>

Vance, Deborah. 2002. Match game. *Marketing News,* 11 November, 1.

Walsh, Nick Paton. 2003. "Biznesmen" face fine for lapses into English. *Guardian* (Manchester), 7 February, 1.

Waxman, Sharon. 1994. French tell English users: Just say "Non." *Chicago Tribune,* 14 June, 1.

Zuckerbrod, Nancy. 2002. Bush seeks tough, new rules on nation's tobacco industry. *Charleston Gazette,* 12 March, 3A.

CHAPTER TEN

Social Responsibility and Ethics in the Global Marketplace

Advertisers and agencies should take note of a number of trends that may well impact how business is conducted in the global marketplace of the future. First, there appears to be a growing concern with regard to the social responsibility and ethical standards of international advertisers, probably in large part because of a number of well-publicized incidents, from the infant-formula scandal (discussed later in this chapter) to the marketing of drugs in third world countries and, most recently, the use of child labor by multinationals (Kole 1997). Second, the consumer movement is expanding in both developed and developing markets. As Dean M. Peebles and John K. Ryans point out:

> Consumer protection groups . . . are focusing sharply on advertising that misleads, misrepresents, takes advantage of consumer's lack of knowledge, degrades local competition, or that is in poor taste according to local standards—and they are looking even more closely at multinationals that invade their markets. (Peebles and Ryans 1984, 273)

Finally, during the past several years, both developed and developing nations have sharply increased their regulation of promotional activities. In a growing number of countries, the advertising agency shares liability with the advertiser for any violation of advertising practices, so that both parties are fined or otherwise penalized equally. Further, to encourage agencies to take greater responsibility for the content of the messages they produce, a number of European nations have removed the blanket of anonymity by requiring that the agency name appear on its client's advertising. Other countries are considering similar measures. If international marketers and advertisers are to avoid the wrath of increasingly powerful consumer associations as well as the limitations imposed by the associated increase in regulation, they must engage in socially responsible behavior when operating in both industrialized and industrializing countries. The adoption of codes of ethics may well serve as a means to this end. These issues will be discussed in this chapter.

The Growth of the Consumer Movement

Consumerism has been defined in a variety of ways. Stephen A. Greyser and Steven L. Diamond provide a classic definition: consumerism is "the organized movement to increase the rights and powers of buyers in relation to sellers in an imperfect market" (Greyser and Diamond 1974, 38). William T. Kelley defines it as an "effort to put the buyer on equal footing with the seller. Consumers want to know what they're buying. What they're eating. How long a product will last. What it will and will not do. Whether it will be safe for them and/or the environment" (Kelley 1973, vi). Organized consumer groups are especially influential in the United States, the United Kingdom, Sweden, and Australia, and their success in these countries has spurred the development of similar groups in other nations. For example, the consumer movement in Malaysia has become quite strong, and the Consumer Association of Penang (CAP) is one of the harshest critics of advertising in that nation (Frith 1987). The consumer movement in general has made demands in three main areas:

1. *Consumer information:* Data about products and services offered for sale and information to assist specific buying decisions, especially comparative data;
2. *Consumer education:* The development of the knowledge base necessary to be an intelligent consumer, to know how the economy operates, how buyers and sellers interact, and how to deal with the people and institutions one encounters;
3. *Consumer protection:* The call for governments and regulatory bodies to safeguard consumer rights, protect against deceptive practices, and set health and safety standards. (De Mooij and Keegan 1991, 399)

In general, consumer organizations have not been overly impressed with industry attempts to produce an effective self-disciplinary system. They claim that the advertising industry in particular lacks the authority to be a viable alternative to state or national regulatory systems. Consumerists argue that regulation by governmental agencies is necessary to ensure that advertisers take responsibility for informing, educating, and protecting consumers. Given such views, the conflict between consumer organizations and advertisers is likely to continue, particularly in third world countries.

Social Responsibility and the Marketing Mix

Because of growing concern on the part of consumers, consumer organizations, and governments with the practices of international advertisers and marketers, the highest standards of marketing behavior must be applied to each of the marketing-mix elements—product, price, distribution, and promotion. With regard to product responsibility, firms should strive to produce high-quality goods that are safe for both consumers and the environment, as well as being

culturally sensitive. The right product targeted at the right audience can benefit both marketer and consumer. Micronutrient deficiencies—or the lack of vitamins and minerals such as Vitamin A, iron, and zinc—are believed to affect about 2 billion children around the world, and research suggests they have a huge impact on learning difficulties, health problems (from anemia to blindness) and even mortality. With vitamin pills costly to distribute and pill-taking regimens hard to enforce, fortified goods offer the most promising prospect for combating such deficiencies. In 2001, Procter & Gamble launched Nutristar in Venezuela after literally years of research and development. The powdered drink mix contains eight vitamins and five minerals and is sold in flavors like mango and passion fruit. The product boldly promises "taller, stronger and smarter kids." Sold in stores, the product is also available at McDonald's, where it is the chosen beverage in about half of the Happy Meals the restaurant sells. Clinical tests of such fortified drinks have revealed increased levels of nutrients in children's blood in just eight weeks (McKay 2001).

Advertising agencies must question whether they will represent clients whose products do not live up to such standards. For instance, a number of chemical and pharmaceutical products that had been banned in developed markets because they were deemed unsafe were subsequently exported to less developed countries where such controls were lacking. In another example some German companies have been accused of using Poland as a dumping ground for packaged goods (such as condiments) with expiration dates that had already passed (McKay 1993). Such practices have led Poles to embrace domestically manufactured goods and eye foreign marketers with great suspicion.

Pricing responsibility refers to charging only what the market will bear. The Commonwealth of Independent States provides excellent examples of marketers engaging in pricing practices who are sensitive to the local economic situation as well as those who are completely oblivious to it. Coca-Cola has moved into the Volgograd region—listed as among the poorest in Russia. Average per capita monthly income reached $28 in 1999, compared to the $200 per month that Muscovites earned. Rather than attempting to sell 2-liter bottles of Coke for $1 as it does in the rest of Russia, Coca-Cola launched a 200-milliliter bottle costing just 12 cents. The small bottle is affordable to nearly every category of Russian consumer (*Advertising Age* 1999). This stands in stark contrast to the international manufacturer of dog food that introduced its product to the newly formed Commonwealth. One must question whether it is socially responsible to sell a 40-pound bag of dog food at a price equivalent to a month's salary in such a market. The international marketer also must evaluate whether the price charged offers grounds for foreign governments or competitors to claim that goods are being dumped.

Place responsibility relates both to export and manufacture abroad. Regarding exporting, marketers must assess whether bribes or payoffs will be required in order to enter foreign markets and to distribute products. In terms of manufacturing abroad, a number of international marketers have run into difficulties when hiring labor—particularly child labor. The United Nations enacted a convention calling on nations to set 15 as the basic minimum work age, with 13 the minimum for light work and 18 the minimum for hazardous work. Most countries have

ratified at least some aspect of the agreement, but reforms haven't taken hold in some developing nations where low living standards force many children to help their families make ends meet. As many as 250 million children between the ages of 5 and 14 work in jobs that pay little or nothing according to the International Labor Organization. Asia has the greatest number of underage workers, with 44.6 million children aged 10–14 on the job. Africa has 23.6 million workers in this age group, and Latin America 5.1 million (Kole 1997).

In 1997, Nike was accused of using underage workers in Vietnam. Fearful of bad publicity and boycotts, Nike chairman Philip Knight agreed to a demand that the company had long resisted: pledging to allow outsiders from labor and human rights groups to join independent auditors who inspect factories in Asia, interviewing workers and assessing working conditions. Nike also said it would raise the minimum age for hiring new workers in shoe factories to 18, and the minimum age of new workers in its other factories to 16. Footwear factories have heavier machinery and more dangerous raw materials, including solvents that cause toxic air pollution. The company also promised to tighten air-quality controls to ensure that the air breathed by workers meets the same standards enforced by the Occupational Safety and Health Administration in the United States However, Knight's pledge did not include increased wages, a major demand of critics who say Nike and other companies pay workers in China and Vietnam less than $2 per day, and less than $1 per day for workers in Indonesia. Even though the cost of living is lower in these countries, critics say workers need to make at least $3 a day to achieve an adequate standard of living (Cushman 1998).

Additionally, goods must be distributed in a socially responsible fashion, and international marketers must ensure that products are made available to consumers where they require them. For over a decade, Hindustan-Lever—the Indian subsidiary of Unilever—has been selling products geared to low-income Indians in rural areas. Research revealed that these consumers tend to shop at small, decentralized outlets. So, rather than ship truckloads of Lever products to supermarkets primarily concentrated in the urban areas, which would have proven prohibitively expensive as well as ineffective, the company employed locals to deliver small quantities of their products to kiosks in the village markets (James 2001). The approach has served Hindustan-Lever well—it anticipates that by 2010, half of all sales will come from the developing world. Similarly, appliance retailers are not common in rural India. This hasn't stopped Whirlpool from reaching every nook and cranny of the vast nation. The company uses local contractors conversant in India's 18 languages to collect payments in cash and deliver appliances by truck, bicycle, or even oxcart. Since 1996, Whirlpool's sales in India have jumped 80 percent and the company is now the leading brand of India's fast growing market for fully automatic washing machines (Engardio et al. 2001).

Promotion responsibility refers not just to advertising message content, but to all promotional activities. Advertising's high visibility, however, makes it particularly vulnerable to criticism. Key questions facing advertising practitioners on a day-to-day basis include the following:

- Who should and who should not be advertised to?
- What should and should not be advertised?

- What should and should not be the content of the advertising message?
- What should and should not be the symbolic tone or actual character of the advertising message?
- What should and should not be the relationship among clients, agencies, and the mass media?
- What should and should not be advertising's business obligations versus its societal obligations? (Rotzoll et al. 1986, 147)

Environmental Concerns in the Global Marketplace

It has been suggested that the 1990s was the decade of the environment. Consumers around the world became increasingly concerned with issues such as toxic waste, pollution, depletion of the ozone layer, nuclear waste, and energy conservation. See Table 10.1 for a ranking of the most serious environmental concerns of global consumers. As Jacquelyn Ottman reports:

TABLE 10.1 Seriousness of Environmental Concerns

Environmental Concerns	Percent describing as "very serious" problems
Industrial water pollution	55%
Destruction of ozone	53
Destruction of rain forests	53
Industrial accidents	53
Hazardous waste	52
Oil spills	52
Industrial air pollution	52
Radiation from nuclear powerplant accidents	52
Drinking-water contamination	51
Ocean contamination	50
Auto air pollution	50
Endangered species	47
Pesticides on food	44
Greenhouse effect	43
Solid waste	42
Destruction of wetlands	42
Acid rain	34
Biotechnology	34
indoor air pollution from household cleaners, tobacco smoke, asbestos, etc.	33
indoor air pollution from radon	30

Source: Green Guage, *Roper Starch Worldwide,* 1996

Pessimism over the state of the environment reigns in virtually every corner of the world. A Roper/International Research Association Poll of more than 35,000 adults in 40 countries on 5 continents—one of the most comprehensive surveys conducted to date—found that three times as many people now think their country's environmental situation is close to—or is—the worst possible, as opposed to the best possible (25 percent versus 8 percent). At 17 percent, North America has its share of adults who believe the environmental situation will be worse—or near the worst possible state—in five years. However, and most likely due to North America's relatively cleaner environment, these figures pale in comparison to the acute pessimism that prevails in the former USSR, Latin America and the Middle East. (Ottman 1998, 2)

See Table 10.2 for a summary of this survey.

A growing number of CEO's now appreciate the link between environmental responsibility and more effective and profitable business practices. And more and more business communicators know how to use green marketing strategies to boost their corporate environmental images and thereby appeal to environmentally sensitive consumers. It appears, however, that international firms have an advantage over U.S. firms here. Some investigations have examined which marketers are substantively changing their environmental activities as evidenced by their increased use of substantive environmental advertising claims, rather than simply jumping on the "green" bandwagon. Researcher Michael Polonsky and colleagues (1997) undertook a content analysis of environmental ads in four English-speaking countries: Australia, Canada, the United Kingdom, and the United States The researchers proposed that the types of claims being made in environmental ads fell into one of two broad categories:

1. *Product Orientation and Process Orientation:* Product-oriented claims focus on the environmentally friendly attributes of the product. The advertisement for the Toyota Prius—a hybrid automobile—in Figure 10.1 is a good example of a product-oriented claim, as it specifically states the benefits to the consumer. The copy notes that the hybrid combines a superefficient gas engine with an advanced electric motor that never needs to be plugged

TABLE 10.2 Global Optimism and Pessimism

Percent who believe their country's environment will be the best or near best possible within five years.		Percent who believe their country's environment will be the worst or near worst possible within five years.	
Middle East	27%	Ex-USSR*	65%
North America	26	Latin America	44
Asia	25	Middle East	42
Latin America	24	Central Europe	35
Western Europe	19	Asia	30
Central Europe	11	Western Europe	26
Ex-USSR*	4	North America	17

* In this study, Russia and the Ukraine.

Source: Roper/International Research Associates Global Study, Business Letter, September 1995.

The gasoline/electric hybrid Prius. It drives efficiently even when you don't. It combines a super-efficient gas engine with an advanced electric motor that never needs to be plugged in. It idles less, so it wastes less energy. It even comes with available GPS navigation. All of which makes Prius a more intelligent way to drive. So you can concentrate on other things.

52/45 MPG'   PRIUS | genius

Figure 10.1 Product-oriented environmental claim employed in ad for Toyota's Prius.

in; and because it idles less, it wastes less energy. Process orientation refers to claims that deal with an organization's internal technology, product technology or disposal methods that yield environmental benefits. (For example, Toyota claims in another campaign that they annually recycle 376 million pounds of steel and that their other recycling programs keep another 18 million pounds of scrap materials from landfills).

2. *Image or Environmental-Fact Orientation:* In image-oriented ads, claims associate the organization with an environmental cause or activity for which there is broad-based support (for example, an advertiser might claim that they are committed to preserving our forests). An environmental-fact orientation refers to claims involving an independent statement that is factual in nature about the environment at large (for example, the world's rain forests are being destroyed at a rate of two acres per second).

In the case of product- or process-oriented claims, firms must in fact improve their environmental performance. Image- and environment-fact–based claims do not require any modification of the firm's environmental performance—thus they are considered posturing rather than substantive. In the cross-cultural analysis, the United States was found to make the most posturing claims and the least substantive claims. Australian ads employed the most substantive claims and the least posturing. The researchers propose that posturing claims may not be effective in targeting green consumers, as these consumers will realize the firm is not promoting real change in their environmental behavior. As such, differing levels of consumers' involvement with the environmental issue may require changes in behavior by U.S. firms going international. U.S. firms involved in image and environmental-fact types of claims in their ads will most likely be less successful with more environmentally knowledgeable and aware consumers. Environmental performance may be a short- and long-term competitive advantage. If this is true, countries and firms that produce less environmentally harmful products will also have a competitive advantage. International U.S. firms may lose out to others, because their poorer environmental performance puts them at a competitive disadvantage compared with firms of other countries (Polonsky et al. 1997, 219).

Because of the growing importance of environmental issues and the complexity of judging and verifying environmental claims, the International Chamber of Commerce (ICC) published an Environmental Advertising Code to help businesses make responsible use of environmental advertising. Much like their more general Code of Advertising Practice (addressed in Chapter 9), the code is intended to complement the existing frameworks of national and international law (see the ICC's Web site at www.iccwbo.org/home/statements_rules/ rules/ 2001/ code_of_ environmental_advertising.asp). The code applies to all ads containing environmental claims. This covers any form of advertising in which, explicitly or implicitly, references are made to environmental aspects relating to production, packaging, distribution, use/consumption, or disposal of goods and services. The code recognizes that environmental claims can be made in any medium, including labelling, package inserts, promotional and point-of-sale materials, product literature, telephone, and digital or electronic media such as e-mail and the Internet. The code is a practical tool to be used by all concerned with environmental advertising.

Advertising in Developing Markets

Engaging in socially responsible marketing and advertising means doing what's best for consumers in general or for specific groups of consumers. The manner in which marketers and advertisers have operated in third world countries has generated a particularly high level of controversy. Clearly, international marketers will continue to look to developed markets to sell their goods and services. A well of opportunities has been created by the formation of the European Union. Yet despite the fact that the newly expanded EU market is over 450 million consumers strong, it is not growing. The same is true of both the U.S. market (with its 282 million consumers) and the Japanese market (half the size of the U.S. market). Reports Bill Saporito: "As a well-known packaged goods CEO tells his new product staff about the developed world: Just remember, nobody needs anything anymore" (Saporito 1993, 63). However, this is definitely not the case for the vast majority of consumers worldwide. According to World Bank estimates, over three-quarters of the world's population live in developing areas. And while many advanced markets are mired in recession or, at the very least, face slow or no growth, the economy in the developing world is expanding at a rate of about twice that of developed markets. In 2001, for example, developing countries grew approximately 2.8 percent compared with only .9 percent for high-income countries. Projections for the coming years are that economic growth is expected to pick up in the third world to between 3.5 percent and 3.8 percent, while it will be nearly stagnant in developing countries (James 2001). Only in the past few decades have manufacturers and distributors begun to aggressively target consumers in developing markets. As a result, while a good deal is known about the role of marketing and advertising in markets with economic systems based on plenty, relatively little is known about how advertising operates in a situation of comparative scarcity and poverty.

Economic and Social Conditions in Developing Countries

Terms such as "developing markets," "low-income countries," "third world economies," and even "less-developed countries" often are used interchangeably to refer to specific markets that share some common characteristics. The main criterion used to classify economies and broadly distinguish stages of development is gross national income per capita. The world's economies are classified into three groupings: low-income (with an average of a mere $410 per capita annually), middle-income (encompassing both lower-middle, where the annual per capita average is $1,130, and upper-middle—$4,640 per capita), and high-income, where the annual per capita income average is $27,680 (World Bank 2002, 16).

Contrary to what is often repeated, globalization, according to the International Chamber of Commerce (2003, 1), has contributed to unprecedented advances in increasing the living conditions of many of the world's poorest people. As reported in Chapter 3, new research shows that absolute poverty and poverty rates have substantially declined over the last 30 years. On a global

scale, the proportion of people living on less than $2 a day is now below 20 percent, less than half of what it was in the 1970s. Measures of income equality show that many developing countries (with Africa as a serious exception) are actually converging toward the richest countries' living standards. Both education and health are improving in the developing countries. The Australian Department of Foreign Affairs and Trade reports that the number of undernourished people in the world has been reduced from 920 million in 1970 to 810 million today. A study for the Brookings Institution Inequality Group shows that mortality rates have declined, and life expectancy has been rising almost everywhere in the world (Burtless 2002). This trend can be attributed to progress in sanitary conditions and public health practices.

Despite their relatively limited resources, even the lowest-income groups become appealing to international marketers. In examining gross national income per capita in developing countries, marketers need to consider purchasing power parity (PPP) exchange rates, which estimate the value of a currency in terms of the basket of goods that it buys (compared with the cost of a similar basket in a reference country and currency) rather than in terms of the existing market exchange rates. By this measure, most currencies in emerging markets are severely undervalued relative to Western currencies—meaning they can buy more than one might expect from the exchange rate (Allott 2002, 28). For example, Unilever's Rexona brand minisize deodorant sticks sell for just 16 cents, and are a huge hit in India, the Philippines, Bolivia, and Peru. A nickel-size Vaseline package and a tube containing enough Close-up toothpaste for 20 brushings sell for about 8 cents each. For a growing number of firms, an ever-increasing share of their profits is coming from developing markets (see Table 10.3).

In less developed countries, for the most part, local production is generally confined to meeting the limited needs of consumers. Generally, whatever is produced will find a buyer. Local manufacturers typically refrain from promotional efforts because of (1) financial restraints, (2) unfamiliarity with the concept of promotional strategy, and (3) an inability to perceive its effectiveness. The prevailing conditions of such "sellers' markets" typically do not stimulate the need for advertising (Kaynak 1989, 26). Under such conditions marketers often are tempted to let their products sell themselves—to rely on word of mouth and perhaps personal selling rather than advertising. Of course, the larger the firm in such developing markets, the greater the likelihood that advertising will be employed. These trends are reflected

TABLE 10.3 Estimated Sales Distribution by Region for Major Multinationals/Products

Company	North America	Latin America	Western Europe	Eastern Europe	Asia/ Africa
Avon	38%	32%	11%	5%	14%
Colgate	33	26	21	3	17
Clorox	88	10	0	0	2
Gillette	43	11	30	4	12
Kimberly-Clark	59	11	19	1	10
P & G	51	8	22	5	14

Source: Jack Neff, Submerged. *Advertising Age,* 4 March 2002, 14.

in the relatively low levels of advertising expenditures in developing countries. Whereas in developed markets advertising expenditures usually account for approximately 3 percent of the GNP, in less developed countries they generally account for about 1 percent or even less. Similarly, per capita advertising expenditures are lower in less developed markets than in more economically advanced countries. For example, advertising expenditures per person in the United States are as much as 40–50 times greater than in most less developed countries.

The debate regarding advertising's effects on developing nations is a heated one. On the positive side, advertising serves to educate consumers by informing them of what goods are available and where they may be obtained; it enables consumers to compare goods, which often results in lower prices and improved product quality; it stimulates the local economy by encouraging consumption; and it has the potential to improve living standards. Agencies often offer employment to locals as well as provide career training. In addition, many of the messages aired in developing countries serve to promote desirable social aims, such as increased savings, reduced illiteracy, lower birth rates, and improved nutrition and hygiene. Advertising has even been successfully employed in the fight against AIDS. Modern marketing techniques have substantially increased condom usage in Turkey, Ecuador, the Caribbean, and south-central Africa. Notes Dr. Jeff Harris, director of the AIDS program for the United States Agency for International Development: "Successful programs have borrowed sales techniques from consumer products. We market condoms like we would Coca-Cola" (*New York Times* 1991). Indeed, many of the television spots employed have featured songs by well-known entertainers.

A good deal more attention has been paid to the negatives associated with the efforts of international advertisers in developing countries. Charles Frazer points out that:

> the idea that marketing, and particularly advertising, activities come to have disruptive, perverse and subversive effects in other cultures, especially the third world, travels under a variety of labels, including cultural dependence, social mobilization . . . and cultural imperialism. (Frazer 1990, 75)

The dependency approach, claims Michael H. Anderson, suggests that "imported western institutions and values intentionally or unintentionally generate dependency and function as a hindrance to the development of genuinely independent nations" (Anderson 1984, 42). According to social mobilization theory, writes John McGinnis, "It is not economic development or modernization that leads to political instability, but the rate of rising expectations and the failure to satisfy those expectations" (McGinnis 1988, 14). With regard to cultural imperialism, Herbert I. Schiller notes:

> No part of the globe . . . avoids the penetration of the internationally active American advertising agency. These transnational advertising agencies have made deep inroads into most of the already industrialized states, and many of the third world nations are experiencing the same loss of national control of the image-making apparatus and internal communications systems. Advertising, and the mass media that it eventually transduces, are, therefore, the leading agents in the business of culture, and the culture of business. (Schiller 1973, 29)

Regardless of the label, at the heart of the matter is the charge that international marketers attempt to re-create Western-style consumer cultures in countries outside the United States and Western Europe. Critics claim that consumers in these countries are particularly vulnerable to the efforts of international advertisers because they probably are poor and illiterate, lack experience with consumer goods, and have not been exposed to decades of media messages common in more developed markets. In addition, developing countries tend to lack legal systems for consumer protection. While there is much speculation on the possible impact of both multinational corporations and advertising agencies on developing countries, there exists little empirical evidence of these effects (Del Toro 1986). Specific charges as well as counterclaims will be discussed in greater detail in the next section.

▊ Charges against and Arguments for Advertising in Developing Markets

Advertising's Influence on Competition Critics claim that firms which advertise heavily make it impossible for competitors in developing countries to enter the marketplace because of the enormous sums spent on advertising. Supporters claim that by encouraging competition among producers, advertising actually stimulates the economy. Not surprisingly, because there is little consensus as to the impact of advertising on competition in developed markets, there is also a good deal of debate over its role in evolving economies. Although no significant studies document advertising's effect on competition, some interesting statistics suggest there may be some validity to this criticism. For example, multinational corporations outspend local firms by six to one in advertising. With so much exposure, international brands generally have substantially higher recall levels among consumers than do local brands. In some places, the international brand even serves as the generic name. "Kellogg's," for example, has come to mean "breakfast cereal" in many developing markets. In addition, significant status is associated with foreign brands of consumer goods.

Advertising's Influence on the Domestic Media Scene A major criticism of international advertising is that it promotes commercialism of the media, as well as introducing Western media content. Wherever international corporations operate, the local mass media have been summoned to promote sales of consumer goods. As a result, the structure of national communications systems, as well as the programming offered, has been transformed according to the specifications of international marketers. In terms of media structure, many developing countries shifted away from public- or state-financing models to the U.S. model whereby the media are supported by advertising. The broadcast media appear to be particularly susceptible to the lure of advertising dollars. Today, the overwhelming number of radio and television stations in developing markets, both government-owned and private, are financed through advertising revenue. This model typically favors amassing profits over serving public needs. In Latin America, for example, 30–50 percent of newspaper content, over 33 percent of magazine content, and as much as 18 percent of television content is advertising. Not surprisingly, advertising clutter in many developing markets is even worse than in the United States.

With regard to media vehicles, multinational corporations generally prefer Western programming in which to air their messages. Because such reliance on imported foreign programming reduces opportunities for locals, governments increasingly are taking steps to ensure that a certain percentage of programming remains domestically produced. However, foreign styles and production standards are often copied while traditional styles are abandoned. For example, South African Education Minister Kadar Asmal recently slammed the local version of the TV reality program *Big Brother* as "imbecilic and pornographic." Said Mr. Asmal: "It's appalling. I watched the program for a few minutes and saw a woman painting a man's testicles. It was vulgarity of the worst possible kind." He slammed the pay-TV station M-Net for importing the concept, which he said "debased human values, portrayed violence and is vulgar and gratuitous." But the show has continued to attract large audiences. M-Net viewing has almost doubled in the time slot it occupies on Sunday evenings (*Advertising Age* 2001a). Fortunately, Argentina's broadcasters have done a better job of adapting the format. Currently, Argentina is suffering one of its worst crises in decades. The peso has lost about 65 percent of its value against the U.S. dollar, salaries have fallen at least 10 percent, and unemployment is at 22 percent and rising, as is poverty. In light of this, Telefe, the country's No. 1 broadcaster, feared it could lose audiences and possibly stir up bad press if it went with the traditional version of *Big Brother*. So instead, the dozen contestants on the program did community service, making food and clothes for the poor (*Advertising Age* 2002a). When the multinationals do utilize local programs, they prefer entertainment-oriented programming over more culturally oriented offerings. Further, they tend to prefer broadcast media over print, so that advertising revenues flow to the broadcast media rather than to print. The end result may well be ever-increasing costs for print media and ever-decreasing levels of readership, which does not bode particularly well for literacy levels. Finally, multinational corporations have been accused of attempting to influence media content by threatening withdrawal—thus exerting powerful pressure on local media.

Some researchers have emphasized the beneficial effects of advertising on the local media scene. Supporters claim that, given the limited governmental funding available in many developing countries, advertising support is indeed essential to the health of local media. For instance, international advertising revenues may help to make the media autonomous from politics (Pollay 1986, 18).

International Advertising Agencies' Influence on Local Advertising Institutions Critics claim that international advertising agencies have the ability to dominate advertising in ways that small, local advertising agencies in weak, poor nations cannot. They suggest that powerful global agencies have a direct impact on a nation's efforts to build autonomous advertising institutions. It should be noted that this claim was a good deal more valid a decade ago than it is today. In the 1960s many agencies opened shop in the third world—generally by setting up subsidiaries or purchasing local advertising firms. These agencies typically were staffed with Westerners who brought along not only their marketing skills but also their personal and professional values. Separating skills from values is difficult if not impossible, and tensions developed when host countries wanted some of the skills but not the full package of foreign professional values and styles

(Anderson 1984, 42). Because of their high level of creative sophistication and innovation, multinational agencies more or less set the criteria by which all advertising was measured. Local agencies were forced to provide similar services (such as audience research) and were also expected to reproduce the quality and style of multinational advertising in order to remain competitive. Fred Fejes notes that:

> another very important way in which multinational agencies affect national advertising practices is through their dominance of national and regional advertising associations. Often multinational agencies are the driving force behind the creation of such associations and set the criteria for agency accreditation. (Fejes 1990)

Many developing nations, which at one time welcomed foreign agencies with open arms, have increasingly passed regulations limiting ownership and investment in domestic agencies. The advertising agency is seen in many developing nations as a national communications system that should not be handed over to foreigners. For example, in Latin America, foreign investment is limited to 19 percent, and in India 40 percent. In addition to ensuring that the majority of an agency's ownership rests in the hands of locals, many nations are taking steps to ensure that agency personnel are also nationals and, therefore, will have a greater familiarity with the indigenous culture of the country. In China, for instance, because international agencies are still required to have a local joint-venture partner before they can directly purchase media, locally hired people now make up 80–90 percent of the staff at international agencies (Kloss 2002, 36). All too often, despite such efforts, foreigners are hired in decision-making roles while locals are employed for the more routine tasks.

In order to support local advertising institutions, many countries have passed a variety of laws. Among the strictest are those in Malaysia, in which all commercials require the Made-in Malaysia (MIM) certificate. The certification is proof that a particular commercial fulfils policy requirements, which state that all or a majority of the production crew are to consist of Malaysians, the location shoot shall be in Malaysia, negative or print processing is to be done in Malaysia, the music and voice-over must be done in Malaysia, and at least 80 percent of production costs is to be spent locally. If foreign footage is to be used, approval from the Ministry of Information must be obtained. The country's guidelines have contributed tremendously to developing local production activities. Local practitioners in Malaysia are now noted for their high level of technical competency and discipline (Bani 1999).

Advertising's Influence on Consumerism Critics claim that international marketers promote consumerism in developing markets. For example, Malaysia's Consumer Association of Penang describes the situation as follows:

> A worrying trend is the growing influence of negative aspects of Western fashion and culture on the people of the third world countries, including Malaysia. The advertising industry has created the consumer culture which has in fact become our national culture. Within this cultural system

people measure their worth by the size of their house, the make of their car and the possession of the latest household equipment, clothes and gadgets. (Frith and Frith 1989b, 4)

Indeed, concern over the consumer orientation is so great in some developing markets that governments are banning ads that encourage profligate spending. South Korea's Ministry of Consumers Affairs is contemplating a ban on ads that encourage excessive spending—and violations will carry a penalty of $23,000 (*Advertising Age* 2001b).

International advertising messages are said to stimulate artificial wants and needs and to encourage consumers to demand goods inappropriate for their level of development. Such charges are difficult to answer empirically. Distinguishing between a real and an artificial want or need is no easy task. Even in markets where there are no active selling and promotional efforts, demand for Western-style products appears to be widespread. For example, despite the nineteen-year trade embargo imposed on Vietnam (which was finally lifted in 1994), Coca-Cola is extremely popular in this country, one of the poorest in the world today. Apparently, brand-conscious and America-loving Vietnamese consumers have been purchasing Coca-Cola on the black market for years (Saporito 1993, 63). Conceivably, a variety of underlying social and environmental factors (such as church and school) play a more significant role in stimulating wants and needs than does advertising.

While consumerism is generally attacked as a negative consequence of advertising, it may also benefit a host society. Advertisements may, for example, convey messages about higher standards of living to a society and, as such, be viewed as a force contributing to the betterment and advancement of people's lives (Kaynak 1989, 26). For example, every society has a need for clean laundry. In many developing nations clothing typically was laundered in a stream of running water or on a rock. To meet the needs of such consumers, a small, plastic, hand-powered washing machine was developed, marketed, and widely accepted (Keegan 1984, 169). Brazilians (like most Latin Americans) typically do not eat a morning meal. Kellogg's and its advertising agency, J. Walter Thompson, introduced the nutrition concept, highlighting the importance of eating breakfast, within telenovelas, Brazil's most popular form of television programming. The increased demand for this product category attests to their success in this "altruistic endeavor"(Del Toro 1986). Multinationals note that even the poorest of the poor can be choosy about brands. If brands exist as a store of value—a promise about the products distinctive qualities and features—then offering poor consumers a real choice of brands means offering them a slightly better quality of life. Marketing well-made products to the poor is not just a business opportunity, it is a sign of commercial respect for people whose needs are usually overlooked (Balu 2001, 120).

Advertising and the Allocation of Precious Resources The criticism here is that scarce national resources are squandered for the production, promotion, and consumption of products that simply are not needed by consumers in developing markets. International businesses are accused of engaging in advertising to shift consumer behavior from rational consumption of locally produced goods to conspicuous consumption of foreign-made goods (Del Toro 1986). To

compete with foreign advertisers, local firms increasingly must also employ promotional techniques. These monies, it is argued, could be better spent assisting the local population via health and welfare programs. For example, in Kenya, one study has documented that expenditures for soap advertising are higher than government expenditures for rural health care. Not only do businesses spend unnecessarily, but so do consumers in these countries, because the cost of many international products is significantly higher than that of local goods. U.S. products, in particular, carry a premium price. For instance, in India, Camay soap costs 27 cents while local soaps are priced at 19 cents; Head & Shoulders shampoo sells for $4.77 while local shampoos are priced at $2.00 (Khan 1994). Clearly, the poor can ill afford such items, because the majority of their income is spent on sustenance. The counterargument here is that while multinational corporations and their advertising agencies may change the patterns of consumption, they do not impact levels of consumption (Tansey and Hyman 1994, 27). Regardless of perspective, the question remains, who is to decide which expenditures are wasteful and which are not? From the viewpoint of many international marketers, this is a decision best left to consumers themselves. Critics argue, however, that local governments in developing countries must consciously decide where valuable resources are to be spent.

Advertising's Influence on Rising Frustrations In a related criticism, it is claimed that advertising creates demand for goods consumers cannot possibly afford. The concern here is that the associated dissatisfaction and frustration might possibly lead to social unrest or even political destabilization. In selling goods in developing countries, advertisers may communicate with three major markets: (1) the urban-center dwellers, consisting of foreign expatriates as well as sizable pockets of both high- and middle-income locals who often are as sophisticated in their tastes as their counterparts in developed markets; (2) suburbanites living in outlying areas some 10–15 miles from the urban centers; and (3) the rural population, whose life-styles remain provincial and whose incomes are meager (Hill 1984, 39). Note that nearly 80 percent of the population in most less-developed countries lives outside the cities, and that the cultural and economic gap between the urban centers on the one hand and the villages or rural areas on the other is quite substantial (Hill and Hill 1984, 40). The problem lies in targeting promotional messages only to the most appropriate market segment. For example, international marketers may decide to offer a product to those consumers who are relatively well off with sufficient disposable income—primarily those in urban centers. This creates a taste for Western life-styles and values that often trickles down to the lower classes. Inevitably, consumers in rural areas will seek ways to expend their limited resources to obtain these very same items. Ultimately, the lower sectors are perceived not simply as passive bystanders but as potential consumers of these very same products (Del Toro 1986). Philippine author Renato Constantino voiced his concern:

> In the Philippines for example, where recent estimates place fully 70 percent of families below the
> poverty line, money sorely needed for food, shelter and basic health is often squandered on tobacco,

cosmetics, soft drinks and the latest fashion jeans. Although the targets of transnational corporation sales are the elite and middle classes, their advertising is "democratically" heard via transistor
radios, seen on billboards and to a lesser extent on television. (Frith and Frith 1989b, 4)

Further, in many third world countries upward mobility is virtually nonexistent. Generally,
less than 10 percent of the population owns 60 percent or more of a nation's wealth. Many consumers in these countries do develop a desire—whether through advertising or other stimuli—
for goods they can ill afford. In Mexico, for example, U.S. soft drinks control over 75 percent
of the market, and schoolchildren will save money to purchase Pepsi, which costs three to five
times what a local soft drink would cost. However, little evidence indicates that consumer frustrations have resulted in demands for radical change. Nonetheless, governmental bodies in
some developing markets have undertaken steps to avoid the potential social or political unrest.
For example, in 1981, the Indonesian government exerted a ban on commercial television in order
to reduce the negative impact of advertising in remote villages where purchasing power is quite
limited (Napis and Roth 1982, 12).

Advertising's Influence on Indigenous Culture Advertising was heavily criticized in UNESCO's 1980
report *Many Voices, One World: Communication & Society Today and Tomorrow,* in which the McBride
Commission took advertising to task for its uninvited cultural intervention in third world countries. Paulo Freire, a philosopher from Brazil, argues:

> The invaders penetrate the cultural context of another group, in disrespect of the latter's poten-
> tialities; they impose their own view of the world upon those they invade and inhibit the creativ-
> ity of the invaded by curbing their expression. (Freire 1970)

Note Katherine and Michael Frith:

> While multinational marketers and advertisers might consider a western-style global marketing cam-
> paign to be an efficient way to reach new audiences in the developing countries, critics like Freire
> would characterize this as an act of violence against the persons of the invaded culture. (Frith and
> Frith 1989a, 179)

Much of the criticism of foreign messages asserts that the advertisements project nonindige-
nous values and beliefs. For example, in the mid 1990s Tony Koenderman pointed out that
although over 85 percent of South Africa's population is black,

> advertising continues to focus on the white minority and advertising is largely fashioned by whites,
> for whites. Creative concepts tend to be Western with little relevance for local lifestyles and values,
> according to the head of the country's only black-owned advertising agency. They use white mod-
> els even when the main market for a product is black. Until recently, advertisers could justify this
> Euro-centric approach on the grounds that whites accounted for most of the buying power in the

South African market, which spends $1.2 billion annually on advertising. But official statistics show that the white share of total household expenditures fell from 57 percent in 1978 to 49.5 percent in 1988. Today it is closer to 40 percent. (Koenderman 1994)

Nearly a decade has passed, and little has changed. The South African government recently held its first round of hearings on racism in marketing and advertising. Although white people represent only 12 percent of the population, resentment is increasing that most of the people in ad agencies today are white and media ownership is dominated by and targeted to whites because the generally more affluent white community tends to be favored by advertisers. Critics argue that the advertising business in South Africa commands huge budgets that determine who creates, develops, packages, and distributes content on TV, radio, and print. As a result of this first meeting, a task force was established to eliminate racism in South African advertising. Only 31 percent of agency employees are black, and it is estimated that only 16 percent of ad expenditures went to black media. Critics argue that an ideal model is one in which the racial mix of consumers is exactly mirrored by the placement of ads (*Advertising Age* 2002b).

Western advertising clearly presents Western values, particularly when standardized campaigns are employed. What it means to be successful or attractive and what roles men, women, and children should play are all outlined for consumers in developing markets in 30-second messages, radio jingles, and outdoor billboards. Sales messages are overlaid with cultural messages glamorizing Western lifestyles. To counter this, many countries have taken protective steps. The governments of some developing countries demand messages that are created exclusively for their local consumers—messages designed to preserve and strengthen their own culture rather than reflect imported values. In Peru, for example, advertising must be locally produced in order to ensure that local values are projected. The Malaysian advertising code stipulates that advertisements must project Malaysian culture and identity, as well as reflect the multiracial character of the population. Advertisements that highlight Western values are forbidden. Further, scenes of an amorous, intimate, or suggestive nature are forbidden on Malaysian television. In addition, provocative scenes that show naked or scantily clad models are also not allowed to be shown (Kloss 2002, 74). Real or imagined fears of cultural imperialism have spurred numerous governments to take preventive action.

Advertising's Potential to Exaggerate Claims and Deceive Consumers That advertising often exaggerates claims and deceives consumers is widely accepted as a valid concern by both consumers and the advertising industry. This problem has always been associated with advertising, but in developed countries regulatory bodies sprang up alongside the advertising industry, offering consumers some degree of protection. In contrast, more than half of developing nations have no regulatory agencies to speak of. This leaves consumers in developing nations open to misleading advertising. In addition, there is little self-regulation of advertising in third world markets, resulting in numerous instances of less than scrupulous advertising. The classic example of de-

ceptive advertising—the infant-formula scandal—will be addressed in detail later in this chapter. In another example, flame-retardant sleepwear that had been shown to cause cancer and was therefore banned in the United States was sold freely in third world countries. Increased public awareness of the health risks of smoking, along with increasing regulation, have taken their toll on cigarette smoking in the United States, where sales volume has dropped by almost 10 percent since 1999. And smoking rates in other industrialized countries are decreasing at a rate of 1–2 percent annually. In contrast, thanks to aggressive marketing tactics, smoking in developing countries is increasing at a rate of about 3 percent a year. While multinational tobacco companies market high-tar and -nicotine cigarettes worldwide, in developing countries, they advertise their products with techniques that are banned in their home markets (Bettcher and Subramaniam 2001, 2737). For example, a Public Citizen's Health Research Group study shows that cigarettes sold in Asia, Africa, South America, and Eastern Europe give consumers less warning about the risks of smoking. The study suggests that non-Americans are being denied vital information available in the United States. Further, it appears the providers of such information—the media—are also being manipulated. British-American Tobacco, which is owned by B.A.T. Industries, held seminars at luxury resorts worldwide at which it offered foreign journalists data that plays down the health risks of smoking. And advertising agencies, such as Leo Burnett Inc., the creator of the legendary Marlboro Man campaign, have used their talents on behalf of tobacco producers to thwart antismoking campaigns outside the United States (Meier 1998). Of the 8.4 million deaths that tobacco is expected to cause by 2020, 70 percent will occur in developing countries. Clearly, it is imperative that global legislation hold tobacco companies to the same standards of safety in developing markets as in their industrialized home markets.

Problems in Assessing Advertising's Effects in Developing Markets The most striking factor in the preceding discussion is the lack of empirical evidence regarding the effects of marketing and advertising in developing countries. The claims made are complex—and not easily substantiated or refuted. More often than not, arguments are based on anecdotal or scanty evidence, and conclusions clash depending on whose perspective is embraced (Del Torro 1986).

Several problems are associated with assessing the influence of promotional efforts. First, in the debate regarding advertising's effects, the type of advertising often is not clearly defined. Criticisms are levied against advertising in general, yet advertising for specific product categories tends to generate more objections than others. For example, retail advertising, which brings together buyers and sellers and provides consumers with information about the local market, is generally not the target of criticism. Similarly, industrial advertising, directed not at the consumer population but rather at businesses, has received little criticism. This type of advertising also tends to be high in information content. On the other hand, advertising for brand-name products, such as soft drinks, sweets, alcoholic beverages, and, in particular, cigarettes, has received the greatest amount of criticism. Cigarette manufacturers, for example, have been targeted for aggressively marketing cigarettes in developing countries in order to replace lagging sales in the West.

Second, in assessing advertising's effects, oversimplified models of buying behavior often are employed. Critics of advertising in developing countries ascribe great power to advertising, assuming advertising directly causes purchase behavior. Clearly, many additional factors come into play in stimulating buyer behavior.

Finally, advertising is a process in which a great many intervening variables—some of which are not all that clearly defined—play a role. For example, research regarding the impact of international advertising on indigenous culture is complicated by the methodological problems associated with identifying exactly what indigenous culture is. A multitude of factors may impact the culture of a society, and each must be taken into consideration when analyzing both positive and negative claims against advertising. Charles Frazer notes that, unfortunately, advertising effects are not separable from those of other social forces: "How advertising effects might be disentangled from marketing, mass media, social, political, cultural and individual impetus is indeed a staggeringly complex undertaking" (Frazer 1990, 76).

Promotional Strategies in Developing Markets

The promotional strategies destined for developing countries often require significant changes from those used in more advanced or industrialized countries, for several reasons:

- The illiteracy rate in many developing countries is often very high, so written communication is of limited value.
- The media infrastructure is often underdeveloped, so that the media frequently used elsewhere, such as television, may have limited uses for advertising purposes.
- Some countries may be multilingual, making translation quite costly.
- The company's products, brands, and so on may be unknown.
- The markets may be narrow because of wide variations in income and extremes in income distribution.
- The markets may be geographically diverse and dispersed and therefore difficult and expensive to reach. (Toyne and Walters 1989, 549)

Yet despite such differences, campaign adaptation is more common for developed markets than for developing markets. Hill and James (1990) compared both sales-platform decisions and creative-context decisions for products sold in relatively poor markets (per capita GNP less than $6,000) versus relatively affluent markets (per capita GNP greater than $6,000). "Sales platform" refers to the product feature emphasized while "creative context" is defined as the way the message is expressed. Their research revealed that changes in sales platforms and creative contexts were more likely to occur in more affluent markets than in less affluent markets. This may well be a primary reason that international advertising messages targeted to consumers in developing markets are so heavily criticized. International marketers wishing to avoid further regulation and vicious social criticism should create advertisements that do the following:

1. express local social values and needs (an admittedly difficult task because local values are complex and often in conflict with one another);
2. encourage the economic austerity and personal savings needed to create domestic investment capital;
3. foster greater awareness of the effect of personal consumption on the local environment. (Tansey and Hyman 1994, 28)

As Vern Terpstra notes:

> Transferring promotional messages between markets is not difficult. Ensuring that they are at least appropriate for their market audiences is not so easy, especially in developing country circumstances where there is greater cultural diversity. (Terpstra 1978, 16)

The Future of Advertising in Developing Markets

As previously discussed, advertising in the third world can have both positive and negative effects. It is, in many ways, a sword that cuts both ways. On the one hand, host nations obviously realize that international marketers and their agencies do make contributions to host societies, which is why they allow them to operate within their borders in the first place. Indeed, in numerous instances corporations and agencies are invited to enter these markets and are even offered concessions, incentives for foreign investment, and tax exemptions (Del Toro 1986). A good many products have proven to be both of value to third world consumers and profitable for international marketers. And, as noted, advertising has been employed in combating social ills in many third world markets. Promotional efforts have also assisted in improving both health and hygiene in numerous less developed countries.

On the other hand, there are real dangers associated with the use of marketing and advertising in developing countries. Overcommercialization of the media may well result in the decline of local programming unless protective steps are taken. Deceptive campaigns and the promotion of undesirable or dangerous products pose potential health and other risks for third world consumers. Additional regulatory bodies are needed to fulfill a watchdog function. It is indeed possible to limit the negative effects with planning and regulation. Scholars and researchers must continue to attempt to understand the effects of advertising in developing markets. Michael H. Anderson summarizes:

> Generalizations about the precise costs and benefits that the transnational advertising agencies bring to their host nations are difficult to make. This is because nations and their development policies and patterns, problems and pressures are in a constant state of flux and are products of various interwoven factors operating within and between nations. What can be said with some certainty, however, is that the presence of the transnational advertising agencies in any third world society *does* generate some tensions and conflict. (Anderson 1984, 42)

IIIII Ethics in the International Arena

A survey of U.S. marketing managers revealed that one-quarter agreed with the statement that "managers in international business often engage in behaviors I consider unethical," while fully 56 percent agreed with the statement that "there are many opportunities for U.S. managers in international business to engage in unethical behaviors (Armstrong et al. 1990, 5).

Corporations and their advertising agencies are required to make many difficult decisions when operating both in domestic markets and abroad. Granted, numerous laws govern what can and cannot be done. However, not every issue is covered by a written rule, and even where laws exist, there is a good deal of room for interpretation. With regard to business behavior, most marketers would agree that it is important to maintain high ethical standards, whether operating in domestic or international markets. Determining what is meant by "high ethical standards" is a good deal more complex. While interest in the ethical issues pertaining to international business has grown enormously in the past two decades, research on the ethical dimensions of international business and marketing has been relatively limited and nonempirical (Taylor et al. 1989).

IIIII Determining What's Ethical

Ethical standards are often perceived as difficult to define. However, taking or offering bribes, cheating, stealing, lying, and spying are generally considered unacceptable behaviors. For example, a U.S. pharmaceutical company and two U.S. advertising agencies (Young & Rubicam and Foote, Cone & Belding) were accused of ethical violations in relation to alleged involvement in a kickback scandal in Italy. Prosecutors claimed that advertising managers bribed ministry officials in order to obtain portions of an AIDS awareness campaign (Klein 1993, A7). More recently, in Peru, the names of several agency and media executives surfaced in an ongoing investigation of alleged kickbacks and influence peddling during former President Alberto Fujimori's administration. Over 1,700 videos have surfaced showing Vladimiro Montesinos, Fujimori's national security advisor, meeting with media and advertising executives as well as other business people. Media executives allegedly received vast sums of government advertising in exchange for slandering Fujimori's opponent. In addition, the Peruvian government was the country's largest advertiser and the former president himself decided which agencies and media outlets would be included in the state's largess. Arrest warrants have been issued for more than 50 people in the widening corruption scandal (*Advertising Age* 2001c).

Researchers surveyed U.S. international business managers to determine the aspects of international marketing that pose the most difficult ethical or moral problems. The most frequent ethical problem faced was, in fact, bribery; the next most salient related to governmental interference, customs clearance, transfer of funds, and cultural differences (Mayo et al. 1991, 61). Apparently, other marketers around the globe find bribery to be similarly challenging. In a study comparing Australian and Canadian manager's perceptions of international marketing ethics problems, Chan and Armstrong found that "gifts/favors/entertainment" and "traditional small-scale bribery" to be among the top challenges. The researchers define "gifts/favors/en-

tertainment" as including items such as lavish gifts, opportunities for travel at the company's expense, and gifts received after the completion of a transaction, as well as extravagant entertainment. "Traditional small-scale bribery" was defined as payment of somewhat small sums of money typically to a foreign official in exchange for the violation of some official duty or responsibility to speed routine government actions.

Interestingly, both Australian and Canadian managers also noted "cultural differences" to be a critical problem. Here the managers expressed concern about cultural misunderstandings related to the traditional requirement of the exchange process—in other words, transactions regarded in one culture as bribery may be perceived as acceptable business practices in another (Chan and Armstrong 199, 3). For example, report Gene Laczniak and Patrick Murphy, "Gift giving is part of the Korean business ethic although lavish gift giving is reserved for special occasions such as weddings and funerals. Gift giving has become the norm and those who choose not to follow the custom are socially ostracized. In contrast, the former Soviet Union "stipulated a penalty of death for bribery. Even dinners and small souvenirs are scrupulously accounted for" (Laczniak and Murphy 1990).

Even within the category of bribery, a distinction is often made between "lubrication" and "subornation." Philip R. Cateora and Susan M. Keaverney explain:

> When a relatively small payment or gift is made to a low level official to facilitate or expiate otherwise legal transactions, this is referred to as lubrication. It is fairly common throughout the world and is not strictly considered a bribe and often not considered illegal. Subornation involves a fairly substantial payment, frequently not properly accounted for, designed to entice officials to turn their heads or to perform an illegal act. Subornation is a bribe and is usually considered illegal. (Cateora and Keaverney 1987)

Indeed, the issue of bribery often is more than merely an ethical question, because the offering or taking of bribes is illegal in some countries. The U.S. Congress passed the Foreign Corrupt Practices Act (FCPA) in 1977, making it illegal for U.S. firms to bribe foreign officials, candidates, or political parties. The act provides for fines of up to $1 million for offending firms, and company executives, directors, and employees may be fined up to $10,000 and face five years in prison (Mayo et al. 1991). Other countries, however, may not have laws against bribery. It is estimated that foreign companies use bribes to eliminate U.S. competitors on approximately $45 billion in international business each year (*Globe and Mail* 1997). Because of the great concern regarding bribery in the global business community, the International Chamber of Commerce (ICC) published Rules of Conduct to Combat Extortion and Bribery. As with their codes related to marketing and advertising, the ICC's rules on extortion and bribery are intended to complement existing international and national laws. For more information on these rules, see the ICC's Web site at www.iccwbo.org/home/statements_rules/rules/1999/briberydoc99.asp.

Many firms engage is what is euphemistically called "competitive analysis," but which is, in reality, nothing more than corporate spying. Indeed, corporate security experts say gathering information on competitors is both commonplace and necessary. "All companies keep their eyes

on their competitors," said Stephen Miller, spokesman for the Society of Competitive Intelligence Professionals, which is, in fact, an association for corporate spies (Stammen, 2001).

Competitive intelligence, the process of legally gathering information on competitors, has grown into a $2 billion annual industry. Practiced by America's largest companies since the 1960s, competitive intelligence is now increasingly being used by small and mid-sized businesses as they try to find ways to survive and grow in their industries. "What you don't know can hurt you," noted Alden Taylor, of Kroll Inc., a New York-based security consulting company. "If you're foolish enough not to be alert about your competitors, you are giving your competitors an advantage. It allows them to move deftly without being concerned about you because you're not paying attention" (Stammen 2001).

Procter & Gamble is one of the major marketers that employs competitive intelligence—however it gathered the information that ultimately got it into trouble. The consumer-goods giant said that while it did nothing illegal, the methods it used, which included going through Unilever's trash, violated even P&G's own internal policies. Fierce rivals in the hair-care business, P&G's goal was to glean competitive data on Unilever's product line, which includes Salon Selectives, Finesse, Thermasilk, and Helene Curtis, in order to bolster P&G's own brands, which include Pantene, Head & Shoulders, and Pert. P&G said it fired three employees involved in the operation and informed Uniliver as soon as it discovered what was going on. The two companies, fierce rivals in the hair-care–products business, reached a settlement in the amount of $10 million over the incident. In addition, an independent, third-party auditor would be appointed to review P&G's entire business plan in the hair-care area and report back to Unilever to ensure that any trade secrets stolen from Unilever would not be used (Barnes 2001). Undoubtedly, any attempt to conceal the truth would have done even greater damage to P&G in the long-term. Experts agree that the vast majority of information collected in competitive intelligence is public information, and the rest is typically gained through interviews. Competitive intelligence experts give P&G high marks for promptly going to Unilever to admit what it had done. Notes Professor Rajan Kamath, who teaches competitive analysis at the University of Cincinnati:

> Being responsible and behaving responsibly is, in fact, good business. In the long run, you are going to get more hurt by doing things which could be represented in the public eye as unethical, irresponsible, or not in the best interests of the consumer. I'm pretty sure that even before P&G went to Unilever and said "We fess up to what we did," they put a dollar value on what would happen if this got out there. (Stammen 2001)

Experts say that increased global competition has ratcheted up pressure on companies to find ways to gather information on their competitors. Companies now need to know what's going on with competitors half way around the globe. The espionage case involving P&G is apparently only the tip of the iceberg. For example, China has thousands of technology intelligence analysts, and France has even developed master's-degree programs to train intelligence specialists. The question, then, is not whether a company will gather competitive research, but how. Apparently, there are plenty of gray areas concerning acceptable methods of such information gathering.

Research has revealed that there is a wide divergence in the level of importance attached to ethics and social responsibility in different countries (Czinkota and Ronkainen 1998). A survey of over 1,000 top business executives of corporations whose annual sales exceed $500 million revealed that 95 percent of the respondents perceived that differences exist in business ethical standards even between developed countries (Touche-Ross 1989). Differences in the level of economic development among markets appear to play an influential role. A full 65 percent of U.S. marketing managers agreed that they encounter more ethical problems when dealing with less developed countries than when dealing with developed countries (Armstrong et al. 1990, 6). Other variables that influence differences between markets include cultural standards and legal/political systems. In addition, there is great divergence in the enforcement of policies (Mittelstaedt and Mittelstaedt 1997, 14).

There appears to be little agreement as to what principles should be used to guide business behavior in the international arena. For example, should the international marketer or advertiser adhere to the ethical mores of the home country, the host country, or the international marketplace? Advertisers probably will operate in markets that reflect a wide spectrum of ethical standards that may well be in conflict with one another. For example, a U.S. marketer may adhere to the U.S.'s Foreign Corrupt Practices Act and refrain from engaging in bribery in markets where such behavior is considered perfectly acceptable. However, many businesspeople believe such strict adherence to the laws of the home country places U.S. companies at a distinct disadvantage in foreign markets.

Another perspective is that the legal and political system of the host country should set the parameters for ethical behavior—that is, "When in Rome, do as the Romans do." The fundamental idea here is that as long as the international marketer and advertiser operate within the confines of these parameters, they need not be concerned with ethical issues. Yet just because a specific foreign country deems a particular business behavior acceptable does not necessarily make it ethical. Indeed, a number of U.S. firms have been criticized for engaging in business practices abroad that are quite legal in the host country but that are frowned on or even illegal in the United States. Moreover, this philosophy does not address the fact that in many developing countries the legal system may not sufficiently protect consumers.

There are numerous examples of multinational marketers who behaved highly irresponsibly in foreign markets but broke no laws. Swiss-based Nestlé, the world's largest food company, provides a classic example. The firm has been selling milk formula for infants to developing countries for over 50 years. In the late 1970s the firm was heavily criticized for its aggressive marketing tactics. In selling the formula to consumers in third world markets, Nestlé failed to address a number of environmental factors that resulted in an international scandal. First, illiteracy rates in many developing markets were quite high, and a large percentage of consumers in the target audience were unable to understand the instructions on the product packaging. As a result, many consumers diluted the formula improperly, and many third world children suffered from malnutrition. Many consumers also did not know to sterilize the bottles, often mixing the formula with impure water, and thus fed their babies contaminated milk. Studies revealed that the overall death rate of formula-fed babies was three times higher

than among breast-fed babies. Another problem was related to price. To purchase just one-week's supply of the formula, the typical Nigerian family spent up to 67 percent of its household income. In the late 1970s consumer outrage around the globe led to a boycott of Nestlé products. During the same period a Swiss court ruled that Nestlé had to undertake fundamental reconsideration of its promotional efforts if it wished to avoid charges of immoral and unethical behavior. The boycott ended after seven years when Nestlé finally complied with the infant-formula marketing codes established by the World Health Organization (WHO). The code banned all promotional efforts, including advertising, sampling, and any direct contact with consumers. Nestlé was required to limit its activities simply to taking orders for the product from distributors (Post 1985, 113). The marketing code has been used as a basis for advertising regulation in numerous countries. Unfortunately, still today infant-formula manufacturers are aggressively marketing their wares in developing markets. In response to ads claiming that breast-milk substitutes are equal to or better than breast milk in Vietnam, officials there have drafted legislation forbidding the advertising of all breast-milk substitutes for infants younger than six months. Vietnam says it is banning the ads to promote breast feeding among young mothers and to reduce infant malnutrition (*Advertising Age* 2000). Even more recently, makers of breast-milk substitutes have been accused of violating international marketing codes in poor African countries. In a report in the *British Medical Journal*, researchers said that firms are still advertising directly to the public, often suggesting that their products would improve an infant's health. Further, they failed to provide sufficient information about the health hazards of such substitutes. Nestlé was named in the report, along with French firm Danone and U.S.-based Wyeth. It is clear that better monitoring mechanisms to curb violations of the code are needed (*Irish Times* 2003).

The third perspective holds that the responsibility for ethical behavior rests squarely in the hands of international advertising managers and practitioners. Companies and agencies should apply high standards of ethical behavior regardless of what a particular system might allow. Universal standards should be outlined to be followed in each and every market. The primary criticism of this philosophy is that cultures differ so greatly that the creation of a viable set of worldwide ethical standards becomes nearly impossible. Despite cultural differences, a number of firms operating in the international arena have developed worldwide codes of ethics and expect the rules outlined therein to be followed in all areas of operation and in all markets. For example, Citicorp's (now known as CitiGroup) code states:

> We must never lose sight of the fact that we are guests in foreign countries. We must conduct ourselves accordingly. We recognize the right of governments to pass local legislation and our obligation to conform. Under these circumstances, we also recognize that we can survive only if we are successful in demonstrating to the local authorities that our presence is beneficial. We believe that every country must find its own way politically and economically. Sometimes we believe that local policies are wise; sometimes we do not. However, irrespective of our views, we try to function as best we can under prevailing conditions. We have also felt free to discuss with local governments matters directly affecting our interests, but we recognize that they have final regulatory authority. (Naor 1982, 219)

Constructing Codes of Ethics

Increasingly, progressive firms such as IBM, Caterpillar, S. C. Johnson, and Citicorp have developed codes that outline their objectives, duties, and obligations in the international markets in which they operate. Many advertising agencies and professional organizations also have adopted codes of ethics. The goal of a code of ethics is to give expression to the actual core values of an organization and then to use these to guide management and marketing decisions. Core values are beliefs that are so fundamental to the organizational structure that they will not be compromised. Codes may also embody peripheral values, which may be adjusted according to the local customs of various markets (Laczniak and Murphy 1990, 155).

The most effective codes of ethics recognize the importance of all individuals, agencies, and institutions relevant to the operation of the firm or agency, including customers, employees, the host community, relevant governmental agencies, the population at large, and so forth. A company must consider the impact of each of its decisions on these various publics. Such guides to ethical behavior may well assist international marketers and advertisers in avoiding some of the costly ethical mistakes of the past. Even the most detailed code, however, cannot cover each and every morally difficult situation. While most marketers and advertisers typically have little difficulty in making the "correct" decision with regard to health and safety issues, many other situations have no easy solutions and must be handled on a case-by-case basis. In some instances, when the gap between the values of the multinational corporation or advertising agency and the host country is too wide, voluntary suspension of all marketing and promotion activities must be considered.

Summary

International marketers need to behave in a socially responsible manner in terms of product development, pricing, distribution, and promotion. With the growth of consumerism worldwide, especially in developing countries, the need for ethical and socially responsible practices by international marketers and advertisers has become a crucial issue. Unfortunately, it is difficult to assess advertising's effects in a given market. Moreover, what is considered ethical business behavior in one country is not necessarily acceptable in another. A key consideration is whether the international marketer or advertiser should adhere to the ethical mores of the home country, the host country, or the international marketplace. To address these issues, international marketers as well as individual countries have stepped up the debate over what is ethical and have begun constructing codes of ethics for the international arena.

References

Advertising Age. 1999. Coke tests selling small bottles to low income Russians. 24 June. <www.adageglobal.com/cgi-bin/daily.pl?daily_id=2404&post_date=1999–06–24>

———. 2000. Vietnam to ban ads for breast milk substitutes. 13 June. <www.adageglobal.com/cgi-bin/daily.pl?daily_id=3198&post_date=2000–06–13>

———. 2001a. South African official slams *Big Brother* program. 29 October. <www.adageglobal.com/cgi-bin/daily.pl?daily_id=6101&post_date=2001–10–29>

———. 2001b. South Korea to curb ads that encourage excessive spending. 25 July. <www.adageglobal.com/cgi-bin/daily.pl?daily_id=5441&post_date=2001–07–25>

———. 2001c. Corruption probe of former Peruvian president puts spotlight on ad execs. 23 January. <www.adageglobal.com/cgi-bin/daily.pl?daily_id+4232&post_date=2001–01–23>

———. 2002a. *Big Brother* gets a conscience in crisis-ridden Argentina. 15 April. <www.adageglobal.com/cgi-bin/daily.pl?daily_id=7351&post_date=2002–04–15>

———. 2002b. Hearings on racism in South African advertising show little progress. 18 November. <www.adageglobal.com/cgi-bin-/daily.pl?daily_id=8784&post_date=2002–11–18>

Allott, Anita. 2002. Caveat vendor. *Financial Management.* October: 28–29.

Anderson, Michael H. 1984. *Madison Avenue in Asia.* Cranbury, N.J.: Associated University Press.

Armstrong, Robert, Bruce Stening, John Ryans, Lary Marks, and Michael Mayo. 1990. International marketing ethics: Problems encountered by Australian firms. *European Journal of Marketing.* 24(10), 5–18.

Balu, Rekha. 2001. Strategic innovation: Hindustan Lever. *Fast Company,* June, 120–36.

Bani, Eirmalasare. 1999. Ad guidelines helping local productions gain expertise. *Business Times* (Kuala Lumpur), 15 September, 15.

Barnes, Julian. 2001. P&G said to agree to pay Unilever $10 million in spying case. *New York Times,* 7 September, C-7.

Bettcher, Douglas, and Chitra Subramaniam. 2001. The necessity of global tobacco regulations. *Journal of the American Medical Association* 286(21) (December): 27–37.

Burtless, Gary. 2002. June. Is the global gap between rich and poor getting wider? The Brookings Institution.

Cateora, Philip R., and Susan M. Keaverney. 1987. *Marketing: An international perspective.* Homewood, Ill.: Irwin.

Chan, Robert, and Robert Armstrong.1999. Comparative ethical report card: A study of Australian and Canadian manager's perceptions of international marketing ethics problems. *Journal of Business Ethics* 18(1) (January): 3–15.

Cushman, John. 1998. Nike to step forward on plant conditions. *San Diego Union-Tribune,* 13 May, A-1.

Czinkota, M. R., and I. A. Ronkainen. 1998. *International marketing.* Orlando, Fla.: Dryden Press.

De Mooij, Marieke, and Warren Keegan. 1991. *Advertising worldwide.* New York: Prentice Hall International.

Del Toro, Wanda. 1986. Cultural penetration in Latin America through multinational advertising agencies. Paper presented at the annual meeting of the International Communication Association, 22–26 May, Chicago.

Engardio, Pete, Manjeet Kripalani, and Alysha Webb. 2001. Smart globalization. *Business Week*, 20–27 August, 132.

Fejes, Fred. 1990. Multinational advertising agencies in Latin America. Paper presented at the annual meeting of the Association for Education in Journalism and Mass Communication, 9–13 August, Boston.

Frazer, Charles. 1990. Issues and evidence in international advertising. *Current Issues and Research in Advertising* 12(1,2): 75–90.

Freire, Paulo. 1970. *Pedagogy of the oppressed.* New York: Continuum.

Frith, Katherine Toland. 1987. The social and legal constraints on advertising in Malaysia. *Media Asia* 14(2): 103.

Frith, Katherine Toland, and Michael Frith. 1989a. Advertising as cultural invasion. *Media Asia* 179–84.

———. 1989b. The stranger at the gate: Western advertising and eastern cultural communications values. Paper presented at the International Communication Association Conference, San Francisco.

Globe and Mail. 1997. (Toronto). OECD nations agree to ban bribery, 24 May, B-3.

Greyser, Stephen A., and Steven L. Diamond. 1974. Business is adapting to consumerism. *Harvard Business Review* (September/October): 38.

Hill, John S. 1984. Targeting promotions in lesser-developed countries: A study of multinational corporation strategies. *Journal of Advertising* 13(4): 39–48.

Hill, John S., and Richard R. Hill. 1984. Effects of urbanization on multinational product planning: Markets in lesser-developed countries. *Columbia Journal of World Business* 19 (Summer): 62–67.

International Chamber of Commerce. 2003. New facts on globalization, poverty and income distribution. Issues paper.

Irish Times. 2003. Breaches of baby formula code denied, 18 January, 12.

James, Dana. 2001. B2–4B spells profits. *Marketing News*, 5 November, 1.

Kaynak, Erdener. 1989. *The management of international advertising: A handbook and guide for professionals.* New York: Quorum Books.

Keegan, Warren J. 1984. *Multinational marketing management.* Englewood Cliffs, N.J.: Prentice Hall.

Kelley, William T. 1973. *New consumerism: Selected readings.* Columbus, Ohio: Grid.

Khan, Alam, and Mir Maqbool. 1994. Another day in Bombay. *Advertising Age*, 18 April, I11.

Klein, Maureen. 1993. Three U.S. companies dragged into Italian investigation. *Wall Street Journal*, 25 June, A7.

Kloss, Ingomar. 2002. More advertising worldwide. Berlin: Springer.

Koenderman, Tony. 1994. S. African marketers take new direction. *Adweek*, 3 January, 16.

Kole, William. 1997. International conference hears from child laborers. *Greensboro News Record*, 27 February, B-6.

Laczniak, Gene, and Patrick Murphy. 1990. International marketing ethics. *Bridges: An Interdisciplinary Journal of Theology, Philosophy, History and Science* 2(3/4) (Fall/Winter): 155–77.

McGinnis, John. 1988. Advertising and social mobilization. Paper presented at the Association for Education in Journalism and Mass Communication, Portland, Oregon.

McKay, Betsy. 2001. November 28. The sweet taste of good health: Coca-Cola and P&G compete for fortified-drink market. *Wall Street Journal Europe*, 28 November, 8.

Marsh, Ann. 1993. Polish-made goods come into their own. *Advertising Age*, 19 July, I10.

Mayo, Michael, Lawrence Marks, and John K. Ryans. 1991. Perceptions of ethical problems in international marketing. *International Marketing Review* 8(3): 61–75.

Meier, Barry. 1998. Tobacco industry, conciliatory in U.S., goes on the attack in the Third World. *New York Times*, 18 January, 14.

Mittelstaedt, J. D., and R. A. Mittelstaedt. 1997. The protection of intellectual property: Issues of origination and ownership. *Journal of Public Policy and Marketing* 16(1): Spring, 14–25.

Naor, Jacob. 1982. A new approach to multinational social responsibility. *Journal of Business Ethics* 1: August, 219–25.

Napis, M., and F. R. Roth. 1982. Advertising in Indonesia. *International Advertiser* 3(3): 12.

Neff, Jack. 2002. Submerged. *Advertising Age*. 4 March, 14.

New York Times. 1991. A Lesson on AIDS fight from developing nations, 28 November, B15.

Ottmann, Jacquelyn A. 1998. *Green marketing*. Lincolnwood, Ill.: NTC Press.

Peebles, Dean M., and John K. Ryans. 1984. *Management of international advertising: A marketing approach*. Boston: Allyn & Bacon.

Pollay, Richard W. 1986. The distorted mirror: Reflections on the unintended consequences of advertising. *Journal of Marketing* 50 (April): 18–36.

Polonsky, Michael, Les Farlson, Stephen Grove, and Norman Kangun. 1997. International environmental marketing claims: Real changes or simple posturing. *International Marketing Review* 14(4): 218–32.

Post, James E. 1985. Assessing the Nestlé boycott. *California Management Review* 27 (Winter): 113–31.

Roper/International Research Associates. 1995. Global Study. Green Business Letter. September.

Roper Starch Worldwide. 1996. Green gauge: Very serious environmental concerns.

Rotzoll, Kim B., James E. Haefner, and Charles H. Sandage. 1986. *Advertising in contemporary society*. Cincinnati, Ohio: South-Western.

Saporito, Bill. 1993/1994. Where the global action is. *Fortune*, Special Issue: 128(13), Autumn/Winter, 63–65.

Schiller, Herbert I. 1973. *The mind managers*. Boston: Beacon Press.

Stammen, Ken. 2001. Corporate spying common. *Cincinnati Post*, 7 September, 1-A.

Tansey, Richard, and Michael R. Hyman. 1994. Dependency theory and the effects of advertising by foreign-based multinational corporations in Latin America. *Journal of Advertising* 23 (March): 27–42.

Taylor, R. E., D. Edwards, and J. R. Darling. 1989. The ethical dimensions of trade barriers: An exploratory study. *Columbia Journal of World Business*.

Terpstra, Vern. 1978. *The cultural environment of international business.* Cincinnati, Ohio: South-Western.

Touche-Ross. 1989. Ethics in American business. *American Business* 6 (January).

Toyne, Brian, and Peter G. P. Walters. 1989. *Global marketing management: A strategic perspective.* Boston: Allyn & Bacon.

World Bank. 2002. World Development Indicators.

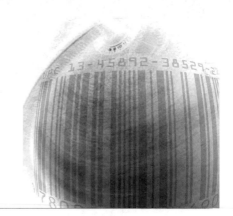

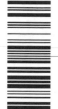

Index